650

A MUSICIAN LOOKS AT THE PSALMS

A Musician Looks at the Psalms
Copyright 1988 by Donald J. Wyrtzen

Panorama Photos © by Gary Irving

Daybreak Books are published by the Zondervan Publishing House
1415 Lake Drive, S.E., Grand Rapids, Michigan 49506

Library of Congress Cataloging in Publication Data

Wyrtzen, Don.
    A Musician Looks at the Psalms
    1. Bible. O.T. Psalms—Meditations.   2. Music in the Bible—Meditations.   3. Devotional calendars.   I. Title
BS1430.4.W97 1988   242.5—dc19   88-15276
ISBN 0-310-36360-8

Edited by Julie Ackerman Link, Nia Jones, and Anne Severance.
Printed in the United States of America.

Designed by Roy Irving Associates.

88 89 90 91   5 4 3 2 1

A Musician Looks at the Psalms

BY DON WYRTZEN

Daybreak Books

Zondervan Publishing House
Grand Rapids, Michigan

NOTES FROM THE COMPOSER

*On the inception of the work
and the key players*

On my way to a concert at Grace Youth Camp in Western Michigan in the summer of 1984, I was stressed out. Playing the piano and sharing with an audience was the last thing I wanted to do. Earlier in the year I had lost two of the dearest people in the world to me—my mom and my pastor, and my spirits were at an all-time low. How could I be expected to bring hope to others when I couldn't even help myself?

I did then what I've done many times before and since. I turned it all over to the Lord. Later, sharing intimately about the death of my mom with the group of campers, we mutually experienced some exciting new insights from Psalm 40:1–3: "I waited patiently for the LORD; he turned to me and heard my cry. He lifted me out of the slimy pit, out of the mud and mire; he set my feet on a rock and gave me a firm place to stand. He put a new song in my mouth, a hymn of praise to our God. Many will see and fear and put their trust in the LORD."

Listening attentively that night were Roy and Sandy Irving. Roy is editor of the renowned Sunday school magazine, *Power for Living.* After the concert, he told me that he had been deeply touched and requested an interview. A wonderful germ idea was born in his mind that night, but it was almost a year later before he suggested to me that I consider writing a very personal devotional journal based on the Psalms. He felt that a composer trained in theology could make a unique contribution.

The idea grew on me. I had studied the Psalms with the brilliant Hebrew scholar, Dr. Bruce Waltke, had taught them to a large Sunday school class at Calvary Church in Grand Rapids, Michigan, and had read them voraciously for years. Not only that, but much of the praise music I was writing was inspired by the Psalms. I decided to accept the challenge.

The process became biblical therapy for me. As I jotted down notes on planes, in motels, at home on the weekends, I found that I was writing in order to better grapple with reality, to find emotional equilibrium, and to cope with midlife concerns. Gradually I realized that I was experiencing more consistency, stability, and security in life—that there was real in-depth change taking place.

If I'm the composer of this magnum opus, Roy Irving is the orchestrator. As the project art director, Roy's sensitive visual ideas have brought to life the musical structure I superimposed on the Psalms. Without him, this score would never have been heard. I am also honored to feature the exquisite nature photography of Roy's son, Gary Irving, a superb young talent.

Making my words really sing is senior editor Anne Severance. She is truly a verbal virtuoso, a semantic Paganini. She helped me rewrite the manuscript and pulled out of me a lot of deeply personal material. What a beautiful, sensitive Christian she is and what an encouragement she has been to me.

My family has been extremely supportive and caring during this project. My wife Karen, God's special gift to me, helped enormously with the selection of pictures and offered invaluable feed-back on the manuscript itself. I thank my terrific kids, D.J. and Kathy, for letting me make this large time investment. They grew up, bumping their heads underneath the piano while

Daddy wrote his music. Standing by while I hammered out a book has been a new experience for them.

My publisher, Zondervan Publishing House, believed in the concept from the beginning. Bob DeVries and Cheryl Forbes caught the vision and accepted the manuscript for publication. Julie Link helped me get off the ground with her editorial expertise. Bruce Ryskamp, Joe Allison, and Phil Bandy committed their administrative and marketing skills to spreading the word. Nia Jones has been my faithful contact with the publishing house, serving as confidante, comrade, and cheerleader! Jim Buick, president of The Zondervan Corporation, has become a dear friend and encourager, along with other premiere musicians, artists, and Christian leaders who have supported me in this venture. And how can I thank Chuck Swindoll for launching this project on such a high note?

May all the glory, honor, and praise go to our Lord and Savior, Jesus Christ.

Don Wyrtzen
Brentwood, Tennessee

Contents

DEDICATION

Dedicated to my parents, Jack and Marge Wyrtzen,
whose precious gifts to me are reflected in this book.

From my dad comes the gift of his love for the Scriptures.
From my mom came her emotional sensitivity.
Thanks, Dad, and my loving tribute to you, Mom, for
all of life's melodies you have shared with me.

FOREWORD

Most people know Don Wyrtzen only as a musician — a gifted composer and master of the keyboard. It has been my privilege to know him as a personal friend. For over two decades, I have appreciated the man's life, which has depths and dimensions he is much too modest to promote.

Hidden within the heart of this artist is a wellspring of fresh creativity that seems bottomless. From it flows imagination, spontaneity, insight, vulnerability, humor, realism, tenderness, and a dozen other qualities seldom found within the same individual. The combination of these traits has resulted in what I call "that Wyrtzen touch." Whatever he puts himself into results in a work that pulsates with such an inimitable style, it makes me smile with amazement. I find him exceedingly refreshing in our day of predictable duplications and same-song, second-verse compositions. To put it plain and simply, Don Wyrtzen is rare.

Unknown to most, he has been pondering the ancient hymnbook of the Psalms for years. With persistent faithfulness he has invested untold hours not only reading the psalmist's words, but feeling the ebb and flow of his emotions. As only a musician of Don's caliber could do, he has slipped silently into the studio and listened to the varied strains of thought as he studied the harmonious chords and changing rhythms of the original masterwork as they flowed from the psalmist's fingers. Unhurried, he allowed these observations to linger until they emerged into a natural transition that led into the issues of life we face today. The result is now in your hands: *A Musician Looks at the Psalms.*

This is not "just another daily devotional" to be thumbed through and tossed aside. It is a well-arranged composition from the hands of an artist, who decided to write his lyrics on the pages of a book instead of a musical score. It will soon become your close companion.

For each day of the calendar year, you will find a brief exposition of a psalm, a relevant development of the theme with today's world in mind, and a sensitive prayer that will give you a boost into the real world . . . just enough to make you wish for more. Woven through the fabric of this literary tapestry are several lovely photographs that provide additional delight. Living in a world where speed and efficiency are fast replacing quietness and beauty, you will find these serene scenes a solace.

I commend my long-time friend, Don Wyrtzen, for providing this volume for all of us to enjoy. I commend you for choosing it from among thousands of others you could have selected. Believe me, you will not be disappointed! It will be a source of much encouragement and comfort. Furthermore, it is the only book available with "that Wyrtzen touch."

Chuck Swindoll
Pastor, Author, Radio Bible Teacher

PRELUDE *by Don Wyrtzen*

The Psalter, the ancient hymnal of Israel, gives a magnificent picture of reality. These lyricists and composers wrestled with the nitty gritty of life in the ancient world. They wrote incredibly honest and beautiful songs about their struggles and triumphs. Some of what they wrote seems messy to a purely rationalistic mind, but it all rings true to a full view of reality.

I believe the Lord wants us to relate to Him with our whole beings, with the totality of our personalities. But many of us intellectualize Christianity. We approach it much as we would a crossword puzzle in *The New York Times.* We are quite satisfied if all the little squares are filled in properly, both horizontally and vertically. If everything fits, matches, goes together, we feel content. However, a vital relationship with the Lord is based on more than head knowledge! He wants to get inside our hearts too—our psyches, our *personas.*

I also believe that intellectualized Christianity is too brittle and rigid for life. Brittle things tend to snap! Modern life is unpredictable, constantly changing, and complex. Both our external and internal worlds keep shifting and moving. Life seems to have a rhythm—work to rest, tension to resolution, and dissonance to consonance. We even tend to think in terms of black versus white and of relative versus absolute.

What do we need? What will give us comfort and direction in our complex modern society? We need an adequate view of reality! Intellectual precision, sound doctrine, and impeccable theology are essential, but they are not enough. They are basic blocks in the structure of reality, but they are not the whole building. Those of us who have bought into that system, to the neglect of other crucial areas of our personality, have often found our lives bankrupt sooner or later.

The Lord isn't interested in a half-hearted,

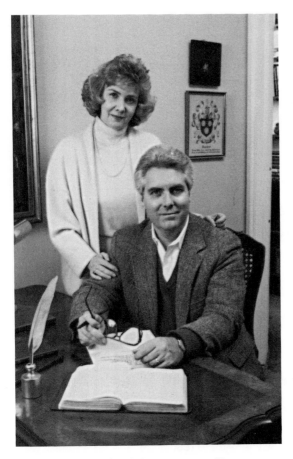

commandments—loving God with our whole beings, and loving our neighbors as ourselves (Matthew 22:37–40).

The love of God was displayed, not only in the Law, but also on a grand and glorious scale through His "one and only Son" (John 3:16). The thrill of the gospel is that it enables us, as never before, to live on the basis of these two great commandments. As we do, we come to know the Lord with our whole beings.

As I've written this journal, I have identified with these ancient songwriters. Their sharing with me, under the power and inspiration of the Holy Spirit, has taken me to new heights and depths of reality. They have pulled, stretched, challenged, and comforted me.

The motifs and musings that follow are personal. These are not an exegetical and theological treatise. They are written from an artistic, musical, and emotional perspective. All 150 psalms are included, with a few key thoughts for each day of the year.

I believe that art must be perceived in terms of both form and content. Form refers to how something is said; content relates to what is said. Form relates to style; content relates to substance. There should be congruity between the form and the content (i.e., you don't depict a thunderstorm with a piccolo solo!). Form is very important, though often neglected. I don't think it was an accident that Psalm 51, David's magnificent poem of confession, was written in poetic form. Poetry is much more passionate and multi-layered than prose. So both form and content are highly significant in this journal.

A sonata or symphony (a sonata for orchestra) generally has three parts: exposition of the theme, development of the theme, and recapitulation of the theme. I have loosely followed that format in my journal.

The book itself is a three-part form—prelude,

casual relationship. Hear His compelling command: "Love the LORD your God with all your heart and with all your soul, and with all your strength" (Deuteronomy 6:5). He demands that we love Him with our hearts, the seat of our love and emotions; with our souls (*nephesh*), the center of our personalities and self-consciousness; and with our strength, our physical bodies.

This is at the fountainhead of living on the basis of the Law. It was in love that the Israelites were to obey the Law, because of an awesome respect (fear) and reverence for the Lord Christ. The Messiah taught us that the whole Law and the Prophets hang on two great body, postlude. For each day there are three sections:

Theme—usually several key verses from each psalm.
Development—some personal thoughts on those verses, and
Personal prayer—an attempt to apply by faith a biblical concept for each day.

I've also included some traditional hymns and contemporary lyrics along the way.

Where possible, I have tried to tie in a musical perspective, because I believe that music can be seen as a metaphor for life. What's wrong with many of us is that the song has gone out of our lives!

I have given each psalm its own title, using modern musical forms—sonatas, fugues, variations, rhapsodies, dirges, marches, hymns, etc.—to enhance the meaning of the text. I have also tied in some of the literary forms of the psalms—descriptive praise, individual and national lament, imprecatory, enthronement, etc.—which have only recently been discovered. The stunningly beautiful artwork and layout highlight this artistic structure.

But this is a personal, devotional journal. If taken to heart a little at a time, I hope that you will be enabled to take a giant step toward authenticity and harmony in your life.

King David, the chief musician, says, "The Law of the LORD is perfect, reviving the soul. The statutes of the LORD are trustworthy, making wise the simple. The precepts of the LORD are radiant, giving light to the eyes. The fear of the LORD is pure, enduring forever. The ordinances of the LORD are sure and altogether righteous. They are more precious than gold, than much pure gold; they are sweeter than honey, than honey from the comb. By them is your servant warned; in keeping them there is great reward" (Psalm 19:7–11).

A CONTEMPORARY LYRIC

Adoration

May I love You, Lord, with all my heart,
    With my whole life, not just in part;
May I love You, Lord, with all my soul,
    Make loving You my highest goal.

May I love You, Lord, with all my might,
    Fill my being with radiant light;
May I worship You more than anything,
    Filled with glorious praise I'll sing.

May I bow before You, Lord, on high,
    As Your holy name I glorify;
May I worship You on bended knee,
    King of Kings who reigns in majesty.

May I learn to know You more each day,
    With my family walking by the way;
May I worship You more than anything,
    Filled with glorious praise I'll sing.

Words and music by Don Wyrtzen
Based on Deuteronomy 6:5-7 © 1984 Singspiration

January *PSALMS 1–23*

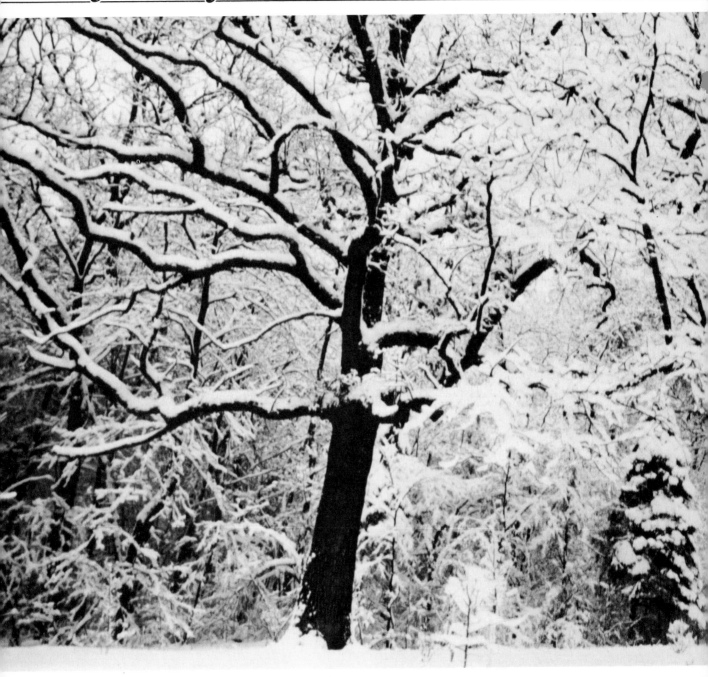

I will praise you, O Lord, with all my heart, I will tell of all your wonders. PSALM 9:1

PANORAMA PHOTO BY GARY IRVING

Ode to Joy

First Movement—in minor

Exposition of theme

PSALM 1

Blessed is the man who does not walk in the counsel of the wicked or stand in the way of sinners or sit in the seat of mockers (v. 1).

Development of theme

Deep inside, I long to be happy. At the core of my being I crave fulfillment, meaning, and significance. The mindset I choose and the lifestyle I live can only partly satisfy these longings.

> **"Taking advice from the ungodly, hanging around with sinners, and socializing with scoffers will sap my life of meaning and joy."**

To get a clear picture of happiness, I need to come to grips with what sort of behavior brings unhappiness. Taking advice from the ungodly, hanging around with sinners, and socializing with scoffers will sap my life of meaning and joy.

The people close to me—arrangers, composers, vocalists, and instrumentalists—strongly influence me. They have a subtle yet pervasive effect on my life. How easy it would be for me to impress them with my gifts and abilities in an attempt to "make it big" in records, films, or television. I don't want to compromise my commitment to Christian music, but if I'm not careful, I will walk, then stand, and ultimately sit with people who couldn't care less about God.

A CONTEMPORARY PSALM

Appreciation for Music
by Joseph T. Bayly

Thank You for music
Lord
Handel and Haydn Society
and Boston Symphony
present Handel's Messiah
He shall feed His flock
like a shepherd
shall gather the lambs with His arm
and carry them in His bosom.
Students on Fairview Island
singing
Who is on the Lord's side
who will serve the King?
Mother holding little boy
rocking
humming
All through the night
my Savior will be watching
and Like a river glorious
is God's perfect peace.
Little group of people
before an open grave
singing
Jesus I love Thee
and up from the grave He arose.

From *Psalms of My Life* © 1987. Used by permission of David C. Cook Pub. Co.

If I choose friends from a secular environment, my personal values will gradually change, the song of my life will shift to a minor key, and I'll lose a deep sense of personal joy. I need to keep my motives pure in my professional dealings; I don't want to become a clone of someone I admire.

Personal prayer

Lord, help me not to be brainwashed by materialistic society, but give me a deep sense of personal joy in knowing You.

Ode to Joy

Second Movement — in major

Exposition of theme

PSALM 1 CONTINUED

But his delight is in the law of the LORD, and on his law he meditates day and night (v. 2).

Development of theme

My mind is the key to my happiness, joy, and personal meaning. I am "transformed by the renewing of my mind" (Romans 12:2). I must delight in the magnificence of the Law. I must revel in the glory of biblical truth so that it shapes my thinking and changes my life.

I must meditate on it, fantasize about it, and be imaginative with it. I often struggle with low self-esteem and feel inadequate. But I know that when I'm weak, the Lord gives me strength. My source of strength and adequacy is the Lord, not I. As I learn to pray more honestly, I will apply the Word more personally. Inspired by the Word, my life will burst forth with song.

What made the ancient Jews distinctive from the surrounding nations? The magnificence and glory of the Mosaic Law. What will make my life ring true today in the modern world? God's truth, the Holy Scripture! I must move beyond a cognitive perception of it and relate it to my total personality. I must delight in it!

Personal prayer

Heavenly Father, I'm moved by the lyric poetry of Your Word. May my life become a motif of praise as I learn to love Your truth.

17

Psalm of My Life

Like worthless chaff the wind blows
    away,
Scorched by the bright desert sun
    through the day,
No root below, no fruit borne above,
My life was thirsting for rains of His
    love.

While roaming far away on my own,
I stood with sinners with hearts cold
    like stone,
I sat with scoffing cynics at play,
Until my life changed direction one
    day.

While meditating day and night,
His Word brought pleasure and highest
    delight,
It quenched my thirst and nurtured my
    soul,
It satisfied me and made my life whole.

Then, like a lovely well-watered tree,
Nourished by rivers that flow endlessly,
Weighed down with luscious fruit from
    His hand,
My full life prospered for Him in the
    land.

Words and music by Don Wyrtzen © 1975 Singspiration

Ode to Joy

Third Movement
Righteousness in Three Parts:
Planted, Productive, Prosperous

Exposition of theme

PSALM 1 CONTINUED

He is like a tree planted by streams of water, which yields its fruit in season and whose leaf does not wither. Whatever he does prospers (v. 3).

Development of theme

When water flows through a pipe, the pipe remains unchanged; but when it flows through a tree, the tree receives nourishment and is changed. For a tree is a living organism.

In this passage we learn three things about this tree: it is planted; it is productive; and it is prosperous. This beautiful, flourishing tree is a stunning simile for the righteous person. The chaff of verse 4 is an apt word picture for the person who throws his life away.

When I read this passage, I think of my friend, D. J. DePree, founder of the Herman Miller furniture firm. His love for the Word enlightens his life. He is the only man I know who is equally competent in biblical studies, in business, and in the arts. He has walked with the Lord for over seventy years. Perhaps his greatest contribution is his Sunday school teaching, which he's still doing in his nineties.

I want to be like D. J. Depree:
- Planted—firmly rooted and stable.
- Productive—marked by effectiveness.
- Prosperous—showcasing God's blessing.

Personal prayer

Lord, make my life a well-watered tree rather than chaff that the wind blows away.

THE LANGUAGE OF MUSIC

Ode

A poem of variable metric and verse structure which is usually festive in nature and addressed to a deity.

The last movement of Beethoven's *Ninth Symphony* (the Choral Symphony) is called "Ode to Joy." The magnificent hymn, "Joyful, Joyful, We Adore Thee" is based on this glorious theme.

Ode to Joy

Recapitulation

Exposition of theme

PSALM 1 CONTINUED

For the Lord watches over the way of the righteous, but the way of the wicked will perish (v. 6).

Development of theme

This psalm presupposes two destinies: the destiny of the righteous and the destiny of the unrighteous. The godly person, living on the basis of the law of the Lord ends up holy and happy. The ungodly person, living on the basis of a secular environment, ends up condemned and doomed. And the Lord deeply cares about both. We will hear a lot more from this righteous person. He is the man of prayer who speaks most often in the Psalms.

Personal prayer

Lord, remind me of life's destinies. Help me choose righteousness over unrighteousness.

King of Kings and Lord of Lords

Exposition of theme

PSALM 2

"I have installed my King on Zion, my holy hill." I will proclaim the decree of the LORD: He said to me, "You are my Son; today I have become your Father" (vv. 6-7).

Development of theme

"King of Kings and Lord of Lords . . . and He shall reign forever and ever." My ear keeps playing Handel's *Messiah* as I approach Psalm 2, and I am overwhelmed by its majesty

---

"He was so overcome with the beauty and intricacy of the music and the message, that tears flowed down his cheeks and he was unable to sing."

---

and glory. My friend Larry McGill had a similar experience when he sang Handel's *Messiah* with four thousand others. During the "Hallelujah Chorus," he was so overcome with the beauty and intricacy of the music as well as the message that tears flowed down his cheeks and he was unable to sing.

God chose King David, the chief musician, to be the greatest king in Israel's history. But God also chose David's great Son to be King of kings. His kingdom will be established and His reign will be forever. Verses 6 and 7, the centerpiece of this psalm, speak of the coronation of the King and the pledge of adoption given to David's heir. As Christ, the Messiah, fulfills this, He becomes the basis for mis-

sionary ventures throughout the world.

As I enter the throneroom of God through this psalm, the nations of the world come into focus and perspective. But in a more compelling manner, I am overwhelmed by the dignity, solemnity, and majesty of this King of all the universe. May I learn to give Him my full allegiance and loyalty today. May I learn to worship Him, adore Him, glorify Him, and enjoy Him! But may the awesomeness of His majesty not rob me of personal intimacy with Him.

Personal prayer

Thank You, Lord, that I can approach Your throne of grace with confidence and can receive Your grace and help as I need them.

Elegy in the Night
First Movement

Exposition of theme

PSALM 3

I lie down and sleep; I wake again, because the Lord sustains me. I will not fear the tens of thousands drawn up against me on every side (vv. 5-6).

Development of theme

Anxiety is deep and profound. Fear controls and dominates. Long nights become threatening. Children cause distress and personal grief. Big questions start to press upon me, and I start to feel that God has withdrawn from me. Sometimes in the middle of the night, I awake disturbed over the changes and uncertainties in the music business; other times I feel uncertain if I don't have my wife's approval on a major issue. How vulnerable and needy I am.

> *"I want to learn to share my total personality with Him: the mood swings, the ups and downs, the consonance as well as the dissonance of my life. There is no resolution without tension. This is true whether in symphonic form or in the structure of my own life."*

At times like this I'm learning to pour out my soul to my heavenly Father. I'm learning that spirituality begins with honesty. I'm learning to express myself emotionally to God. I don't want to have just a cognitive relationship to Him. I want to learn to share my total personal-

THE LANGUAGE OF MUSIC
Elegy
A mournful, plaintive, sorrowful poem or song.

The Scripture is full of lamentation (The Psalms, Jeremiah, Lamentations). In Romans 8:26 we learn that the Holy Spirit "intercedes for us with groans that words cannot express."

ity with Him: the mood swings, the ups and downs, the consonance as well as the dissonance of my life, the harmony as well as the disharmony. There is no resolution without tension. And this is true whether in symphonic form or in the structure of my own life.

King David experienced all of these textures in his full but turbulent life. He even had to cope with a son, who though so full of promise and potential, out of rebellion was trying to kill him. Yet somehow David was able to roll all of this trauma over on the Lord. He entrusted his troubles to the Lord—overwhelming as they were—and turned over and got a good night's sleep. He learned that faith could flourish in the soil of fear and that anxiety could be transformed into tranquility.

Personal prayer

Teach me, Lord, how to honestly lament. Then when You miraculously deliver me, I can really praise You.

Elegy in the Night
Second Movement

Exposition of theme

PSALM 4

Answer me when I call to you, O my righteous God. Give me relief from my distress; be merciful to me and hear my prayer. Let the light of your face shine upon us, O LORD. You have filled my heart with greater joy than when their grain and new wine abound. I will lie down and sleep in peace, for you alone, O LORD, make me dwell in safety (vv. 1, 6-8).

Development of theme

King David had a melancholic cast to his psyche. Artistic, sensitive, and creative by nature, he also tended to be a perfectionist. But unlike many creative people, who often feel inadequate because they can't do everything perfectly, he didn't allow his perfectionism to add to his guilt. Instead he allowed the nightmares of his life to motivate him to express himself intuitively as well as intellectually. Recently, I wrote a theme which I called "Elegy In the Night." I was hurting so much when I wrote it, I expressed my emotions musically but not lyrically. I don't know if I'll ever be able to find the words for that melody.

When humiliated, exasperated, surrounded by lies, and filled with doom and gloom, David took all of this to God in prayer. He also wrote songs about all of it — songs that reveal the innermost working of his soul and lead other believers into profound, personal worship.

In distress, David learned to pray more meaningfully, to trust God more implicitly, and, as a result, to compose more freely and

> *"I was hurting so much when I wrote it, I don't know if I'll ever be able to find the words for that melody."*

imaginatively. As David learned to bring his experiences into harmony with his artistic temperament, God led him to a deep wellspring of peace and contentment. The New Testament insight on this is 1 Peter 5:7: "Cast all your anxiety on him because he cares for you."

Personal prayer

Just as the dominant seventh pulls toward a deeply satisfying resolution in the tonic chord, may the tensions of my personal life be resolved in You, O Lord, my Deliverer.

JANUARY 8

Morning Song

Exposition of theme
PSALM 5

*In the morning, O LORD, you hear my voice;
in the morning I lay my requests before you
and wait in expectation. . . . But let all
who take refuge in you be glad; let them ever
sing for joy. Spread your protection over them,
that those who love your name may rejoice
in you (vv. 3, 11).*

Development of theme

Living in the complexity of the modern world
puts me under a lot of stress. My mind continually mulls over unresolved personal conflicts, domestic hassles, competitiveness at
work, and the pressure to perform. All of this
rises to the surface very early in the morning.
At my first moments of consciousness, I
often feel despair. For me, many days are
blue Mondays.

Often beneath creativity lies a fragile psyche. When I immaturely demand the respect
and admiration of my colleagues, an honest,
too-objective criticism deeply hurts me. I have
experienced undue depression because I
have placed too much value in myself instead of
in the Lord.

Sensitive, artistic, and high-strung, King
David also experienced severe depression
early in the morning. Yet he didn't wallow in
despair nor nurture his black moods. Instead,
he started his day with God by offering daily
sacrifice at God's threshold. He met God there,
spoke with him, and committed all of his troubles to the Lord.

David approached God with great expectation. He didn't deny his many problems, but
he broke free of his loneliness. He realized
he was not alone in the world but part of a company of believers who could join him in
praise. God responded by covering him, encir-
cling him, and caring for him. And the sun
came up, and the black clouds were blown
away.

Personal prayer

*Dear Lord, I praise You and thank You that I
am not alone in the universe. Because of the
presence of Christ in my life, I can live today
with deep peace and joy.*

> *"At my first moments of
> consciousness, I often feel
> despair. Sensitive, artistic,
> and high-strung, King David
> also experienced severe
> depression early in the
> morning. Yet he didn't wallow
> in despair nor nurture his
> black moods. Instead, he start-
> ed his day with God and com-
> mitted all of his troubles to the
> Lord. And the sun came up,
> and the black clouds were
> blown away."*

Kyrie — "Lord Have Mercy!"

Exposition of theme
PSALM 6

O Lord, do not rebuke me in your anger or discipline me in your wrath. Be merciful to me, Lord, for I am faint; O Lord, heal me, for my bones are in agony. My soul is in anguish. How long, O Lord, how long? . . . The Lord has heard my cry for mercy; the Lord accepts my prayer (vv. 1-3, 9).

Development of theme

The painful, heart-wrenching discipline of the Lord caused David to cry out for mercy. But the heavenly Father, an example to all fathers, had to discipline His son. Hebrews 12:5-6, the classic New Testament commentary on discipline, says, "My son, do not make light of the Lord's discipline, and do not lose heart when he rebukes you, because the Lord disciplines those he loves, and punishes everyone he accepts as a son."

Deeply troubled and alarmed, David almost lost heart. His conscience was uneasy, and he was exhausted and depressed. Even his prayer had died away. He could only weep.

THE LANGUAGE OF MUSIC
Kyrie
A Greek term for "O Lord."

The complete phrase is *Kyrie eleison,* "Lord, have mercy." David said, "I am in deep distress. Let me fall into the hands of the Lord, for his mercy is very great" (1 Chronicles 21:13).

> "I sometimes find it hard to be vulnerable enough to face my predicament, to come to grips with my life, and to share my hurt and pain with brothers or sisters in Christ who are close to me."

Unlike David, I sometimes deny such feelings, or at least compound my problems with rationalization. I find it hard to be vulnerable enough to face my predicament, to come to grips with my life, and to share my hurt and pain with brothers or sisters in Christ who are close to me.

David faced squarely the reality of his messed-up life. He cried out to his heavenly Father for mercy and discovered that his walk with the Lord must begin with reality. He moved from petition to praise and found answered prayer. Then he wrote this moving psalm for those of us who have a hard time admitting, much less expressing, the deep hurt and pain of our lives. When we do as David did, God goes to work in our lives, giving us authentic reasons to praise Him.

Personal prayer
Lord, make the tough things of my life a black velvet backdrop against which You showcase the diamond of Your grace.

Song of the Slandered Saint

Suggested by Spurgeon

Exposition of theme

PSALM 7

O Lord, my God, I take refuge in you; save and deliver me from all who pursue me, or they will tear me like a lion and rip me to pieces with no one to rescue me. . . . O righteous God, who searches minds and hearts, bring to an end the violence of the wicked and make the righteous secure. . . . I will give thanks to the Lord because of his righteousness and will sing praise to the name of the Lord Most High (vv. 1-2, 9, 17).

Development of theme

Betrayed, hounded, and unjustly accused as a result of Saul's jealousy and rivalry, David broke forth with the plea, "Lord, it isn't fair!" I can remember a producer who accused me of too much self-confidence and arrogance when actually I had many self-doubts. I felt I had been judged unfairly.

David didn't just complain. He moved on to honest prayer and finally to praise. He came down on the side of God instead of on the side of despair. Deep in his soul, David knew that the "Judge of all the earth will do right" (Genesis 18:25). He found security in God's

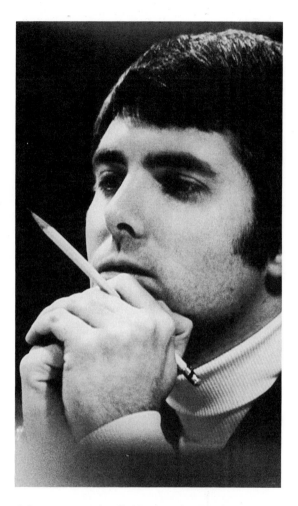

righteousness (v. 9). He practiced in the ancient world what the Apostle Paul later taught: "Do not be anxious about anything, but in everything, by prayer and petition, with thanksgiving, present your requests to God. And the peace of God, which transcends all understanding, will guard your hearts and your minds in Christ Jesus" (Philippians 4:6-7).

Personal prayer

O Lord Most High, may I not wallow in despair today, but may I completely trust Your righteousness and fairness.

> **"I can remember a producer who accused me of too much self-confidence and arrogance when actually I had many self-doubts. I felt I had been judged unfairly."**

JANUARY 11

How Majestic Is Your Name in All the Earth

Exposition of theme
PSALM 8

O LORD, our LORD, how majestic is your name in all the earth! You have set your glory above the heavens. From the lips of children and infants you have ordained praise . . . (vv. 1-2).

Development of theme

Psalm 8, a consummate example of what a hymn should be, celebrates the glory and the grace of God. Its major thesis, "How excellent is your name," shows that God's glory is more than a theological concept; it is also linked to an emotional component—joy. C. S. Lewis, in *Reflections on the Psalms*, reminds us that "to glorify God is to enjoy Him."

Majesty combined with intimacy characterizes our relationship with God. On one hand, we can relate to Isaiah, who witnessed the holiness of God: "Woe to me!" he cried. "I am ruined! For I am a man of unclean lips, and I live among a people of unclean lips, and my eyes have seen the King, the Lord Almighty" (Isaiah 6:5). On the other hand, God wants us to approach His throne with confidence so that we may receive mercy and find grace (Hebrews 4:16).

> *"That the Sovereign of the Universe desires a close, personal relationship with me is almost beyond comprehension."*

That the Sovereign of the Universe desires a close, personal relationship with me is almost beyond comprehension. He is my heavenly Father, and I am His child.

Personal prayer

Lord, may I move from sterile, inattentive worship to an intimate relationship with You. May I learn to enjoy Your presence!

The Majesty of Man

Exposition of theme

PSALM 8 CONTINUED

You made him a little lower than the heavenly beings and crowned him with glory and honor (v. 5).

Development of theme

When compared to the vastness of the universe, I am infinitesimal. Yet even though I am dwarfed by the magnitude of God's creation, I have profound meaning and significance because I am made in God's image (Genesis

> *"I can pray directly to the Lord of Hosts. Because I'm part of God's family, the universe isn't meaningless and empty; it is my home."*

1:26-27). Because His glory is revealed not only in nature but also in me, I possess majesty. Even though I may not like certain things about myself (my height, my weight, my age), I need to remember that I am a reflection of the image of God.

Humanism has deified man and attempted to make him the "measure of all things." I sometimes overreact to this and think that I am nothing. But I am only a little lower than the angels in God's hierarchy. I am crowned with glory and honor. I reflect God's glory just as much as the starry heavens do.

Unlike the animals, which also reflect God's incredible imagination, I have a sense of my own existence and I can communicate.

But even more significant, I can pray directly to the Lord of Hosts. Because I'm part of God's family, the universe isn't meaningless and empty; it is my home.

In size, I may be infinitesimal, but in worth I am infinitely valuable because I reflect God's glory.

Personal prayer

Lord, help me to think soberly and objectively about myself. May I not get so wrapped up in my weaknesses that I forget that Your glory and majesty is revealed in me.

JANUARY 13

Triumphal March

Exposition of theme
PSALM 9

I will praise you, O Lord, with all your heart; I will tell of all your wonders. I will be glad and rejoice in you; I will sing praise to your name, O Most High. My enemies turn back; they stumble and perish before you. For you have upheld my right and my cause; you have sat on your throne, judging righteously (vv. 1-4).

Development of theme

This psalm, a stirring lyric to a triumphal march, celebrates a glorious victory in battle. Although flushed with the new wine of success, David didn't use the occasion to boast; instead he broke forth in praise, celebrating God's actions and his Person.

David was happy about his victory, but he also saw the bigger picture. As God worked in David's personal life and daily experiences, he also works in history through great redemp-

tive acts. David knew that the Lord would ultimately triumph and usher in a worldwide reign of justice.

This psalm assures me that I can live in confidence, knowing that God has a firm hold on history. Things are not careening out of control! He holds the momentous events of the future as well as the ordinary events of my daily life in His hands. I recall when I really tasted success for the first time. A top-notch London symphony played my scores for a recording session. I had to fight to retain my composure as I conducted the orchestra. That experience boosted my sagging self-image.

As I taste the sweet elixir of success from time to time, may I not become drunk with personal pride. May I be reminded that God is the One who has composed the score and has personally orchestrated my life.

Personal prayer

O Lord, Most High, I praise You for being in control of history, including the details of my life today.

28

A Mournful Lament

Exposition of theme
PSALM 10

Why, O Lord, do you stand far off? Why do you hide yourself in times of trouble? In his pride the wicked does not seek him; in all his thoughts there is no room for God. His victims are crushed, they collapse; they fall under his strength. You hear, O Lord, the desire of the afflicted; you encourage them, and you listen to their cry, defending the fatherless and the oppressed, in order that man, who is of the earth, may terrify no more (vv. 1, 4, 10, 17-18).

Development of theme

When I desperately need God, where is He? I feel the terror of being abandoned. God seems far away, as if He is in hiding. How must I react when I'm in this kind of corner?

First, *I can lament.* As David did, I can pour out my soul to God and let my raw emotions flow out to my Creator.

Second, *I can face reality.* In verses 2-11, the psalmist described a wicked tyrant who is

> "David's response is an excellent model for me to follow when I face problems. God is much greater than any problem."

boastful, greedy, blasphemous, and atheistic. Yet he appeared to be prosperous, stable, and happy. This harmony between evil and success seems grossly unfair! But the psalmist faced squarely the tyranny of this wicked ruler and confronted God with His responsibility.

THE LANGUAGE OF MUSIC
Lament

A mournful song portraying the downfall of Israel.

To lament means to sorrow, grieve, or bemoan. Lamentation is the opposite of celebration and rejoicing. For example, see David's moving lament for Saul and Jonathan in 2 Samuel 1.

Third, *I can pray.* The psalmist prayed for God to remember the helpless, to see their trouble and grief, and to break the power of this evil man. This response is an excellent model for me to follow when I face problems. God is much greater than any problem, so I need not fear that I'm asking too much.

Fourth, *I can praise.* David expressed faith that the Lord hears, listens, encourages, and defends. As he worshiped the Lord of eternity, his terror diminished.

I too must learn to lament, to face reality, to pray, and to praise. I must free myself of empty cliches and repetitive, time-worn phrases. When I'm honest with my heavenly Father, I will begin to praise Him with my whole being.

Personal prayer

Instead of internalizing anxiety and anger, may I learn to lament to You, O Lord, my King forever.

Finding Refuge

Exposition of theme

PSALM 11

In the Lord I take refuge. How then can you say to me: "Flee like a bird to your mountain." The Lord is in his holy temple; the Lord is on his heavenly throne. He observes the sons of men; his eyes examine them. For the Lord is righteous, he loves justice; upright men will see his face (vv. 1, 4, 7).

Development of theme

David's friends advised him to flee to a mountain cave for safety. He was being pursued—perhaps by Saul or by Absalom. But instead of giving in to panic, he placed his faith in the Lord as his refuge.

I'm a peacemaker. I'll go to any lengths to avoid conflict and as a result experience much distress in interpersonal relationships. Not

---

A GOSPEL SONG LYRIC

A Shelter in the Time of Storm

The Lord's our Rock, in Him we hide,
A Shelter in the time of storm;
Secure whatever ill betide,
A Shelter in the time of storm.

O Jesus is a Rock in a weary land,
A weary land, a weary land;
O Jesus is a Rock in a weary land,
A Shelter in the time of storm.

O Rock divine, O Refuge dear,
A Shelter in the time of storm;
Be Thou our helper ever near,
A Shelter in the time of storm.

Words by Vernon J. Charlesworth. Music by Ira D. Sankey.

"I'm a peacemaker. I'll go to any lengths to avoid conflict and as a result experience much distress in interpersonal relationships."

---

only I—people today flee pain and stress through the misuse of work (even the Lord's work), sex, drugs, and alcohol.

The Lord is in residence, not in flight. He is always there as a refuge and shelter for His people. His city has foundations; His temple is secure. Instead of wallowing in fear, David exercised faith and found a complete and satisfying security in the righteousness and justice of God.

When I feel trapped, I must trust God and believe in the freedom that comes from His truth (John 8:31-32). Because of His just rule, the wicked will go down in judgment and ruin, but I will behold Him face to face. The child of God always has a happy ending to look forward to.

Personal prayer

O Lord, as I live in the middle of the rootlessness and complexity of modern life, may I find my refuge and shelter in You.

Double-Tonguing

Exposition of theme

PSALM 12

Help, LORD, for the godly are no more; the faithful have vanished from among men. Everyone lies to his neighbor; their flattering lips speak with deception. The words of the LORD are flawless, like silver refined in a furnace of clay, purified seven times (vv. 1-2, 6).

Development of theme

In music, the effect of double-tonguing is delightful. In life, it is devastating and cruel. James tells us that "no man can tame the tongue. It is a restless evil, full of deadly poison" (3:8). The music industry is notorious for its hype and its manipulation of people. Since the art form of music is so subjective and since aesthetic taste is so personal, relationships between people are very important. Unfortunately, positive, healthy relationships can easily degenerate into negative, unhealthy "politics."

The untamed tongue of Psalm 12 lies, flatters, deceives, and boasts. Empty talk, smooth talk, and double talk take the place of satisfying communication, and deceit and manipulation rule. I'm amazed at how deceitful my own heart is. As I read Crabb's *The Marriage Builder*, I see how often I use manipulation for my own ends in our marriage. Often I don't even realize it! By nature I am unaware of my own deceitfulness.

In stark contrast stand the flawless and pure words of the Lord, a wealth of silver refined in God's crucible.

I want my life to be permeated with God's words, not marked by an uncontrollable tongue. If I'm controlled by the Spirit, I won't manipulate people. I will minister to them. And I will ex-

A CONTEMPORARY LYRIC

The Refiner's Fire

The words of the Lord are flawless
Like silver refined in a furnace of clay,
Purified in the refiner's fire,
They will stand sure on the Judgment Day!

Words by Don Wyrtzen © 1988

perience fullness in place of emptiness, wholeness in place of fragmentation, and fellowship in place of loneliness.

Personal prayer

Help me, Lord, to minister to people rather than manipulate them.

Dirge of Depression to Descant of Delight

Exposition of theme

PSALM 13

How long, O Lord? Will you forget me forever? How long will you hide your face from me? How long must I wrestle with my thoughts and every day have sorrow in my heart? How long will my enemy triumph over me? But I trust in your unfailing love; my heart rejoices in your salvation. I will sing to the Lord, for he has been good to me (vv. 1-2, 5-6).

Development of theme

How long? Repeated four times, this question indicates that David was distressed with God, with himself, and with his enemy. Much good can come from tension. For example, the music from stringed instruments is a result of tension. For me there is nothing quite like the glorious resolution of the rising tension produced in a Beethoven symphony.

David was restless. His mind was in turmoil, and he felt dejected. His enemy seemed

to be ascending, threatening his kingship and causing personal humiliation. God seemed distant. The friendship between David and his Lord has clouded over.

But things are not always as they seem. Part of David's genius was his ability to tran-

THE LANGUAGE OF MUSIC

Descant

A soaring counter melody, usually sung by several sopranos.

Used as a decorative addition to a hymn, the descant is a very effective musical device which can leave listeners feeling exhilerated.

scend such difficulties. Without tension there can be no resolution. The tension in David's life came from his difficulties with the enemy and his devotion to God. This conflict led to personal maturity, which he attained because he maintained intimacy with God.

His dirge of depression became a descant of delight. Like an eagle, David soared to new heights. His life took flight when he pledged himself to God's unfailing love, when he chose to praise and thank God, when he realized that God had a higher purpose. "His ways are not our ways, and his thoughts are not our thoughts" (Isaiah 55:8-9). A spiritual metamorphosis took place when David wrapped himself in God's love instead of in his besetting circumstances. He reached the loftiest height of all when he started to sing of God's goodness.

THE LANGUAGE OF MUSIC

Dirge

A song or hymn of grief or lamentation.

Dirges are especially intended to accompany funeral or memorial rites. They are slow, solemn, and mournful. The "teacher" tells us in Ecclesiastes 3:4 that there is "a time to weep and a time to laugh, a time to mourn and a time to dance."

Personal prayer

Lord, I want to trust in Your unfailing love, rejoice in Your salvation, and sing of Your goodness today.

Discord of Depravity

Exposition of theme

PSALM 14

The fool says in his heart, "There is no God." They are corrupt, their deeds are vile; there is no one who does good. All have turned aside, they have together become corrupt; there is no one who does good, not even one (vv. 1, 3; also Romans 1).

Development of theme

The mood of this piece is arrogant. The theme is total depravity—leaving God out of life. The motifs are materialism, secularism, exploitation, and corruption. The essence of living in the flesh is to live as if God doesn't exist. I know of a prominent evangelist who arrogantly decided no longer to call God his Father.

What happens when we leave God out of our lives? Psalm 14 graphically and poetically answers the question.

Denying God begins a downward progression. Suppressing the truth leads to idolatry, self-destructiveness, and gross immorality. Error replaces truth, behavior becomes totally depraved, and people are oppressed.

THE LANGUAGE OF MUSIC

Discord

A musical dynamic characterized by dissonance and unpleasantness.

The opposite of discord is "concord" which emphasizes consonance and pleasantness. Our Lord encourages harmony and unity (John 17:23). Like light and darkness, however, discord and concord would lack definition without their opposites.

Apostates think they are wise, but they are fools. When we choose the foolish route of denying God, we end up in rebellion against God, in alienation from others, and in personal corruption because we have killed off the source of all love and meaning for our lives.

This psalm is discordant and dissonant until the last verse, when David returns to the theme of salvation. The Lord will restore the fortunes of His people and make them glad. We don't need to be mannequins—lifeless and stripped of all love and meaning.

Personal prayer

Heavenly Father, make me fully aware that it is Your existence alone that fills my life with love and gives it meaning.

Rhapsody of Righteousness

Exposition of theme
PSALM 15

Lord, who may dwell in your sanctuary? Who may live on your holy hill? He whose walk is blameless and who does what is righteous (vv. 1-2).

Development of theme

Psalm 15 portrays a man of integrity who stands in bold contrast to the depraved man of Psalm 14.

Because he is a man of worship and sacrifice, his sins are covered by the blood. Therefore he has nothing to hide and he deceives

no one. He is marked by five sterling characteristics:

1. *Integrity* (v. 2)
2. *Truth* (v. 3)
3. *Allegiance* (v.4)
4. *Honor* (vv. 4-5)
5. *Stability* (v. 5)

One of the most authentic people I know is my friend, Bill Rigg. He is filled with quiet, steadfast conviction. When he spoke at the funeral service for his fifteen-year-old son, Jim, I saw unbelievable pain, but I also saw the reality of Jesus Christ.

I want God to create these personality strengths in me. They will be God's gift to me when I place complete trust in Him.

Personal prayer

Lord, I pray that You will produce transparency, authenticity, and integrity in my life.

A CONTEMPORARY LYRIC

Make Me Real, Lord

Make me real, Lord,
Marked by integrity;
May what I say be one with what I am!

Make me true, Lord,
Living reality;
And make my life ring true — not a sham.

May my instrument give forth a pure,
wholehearted sound,
May the choices of my life in truth
abound.

Make me real, Lord,
Create transparency;
And may I glorify the Great I Am,
And may I magnify the Spotless Lamb!

Don Wyrtzen © 1988

Song of Security
In Life and in Death

Exposition of theme
PSALM 16

Keep me safe, O God, for in you I take refuge. I said to the LORD, "You are my LORD; apart from you I have no good thing." Therefore my heart is glad and my tongue rejoices; my body will also rest secure, because you will not abandon me to the grave, nor will you let your Holy One see decay. You have made known to me the path of life; you will fill me with joy in your presence, with eternal pleasures at your right hand (vv. 1-2, 9-11).

Development of theme

How can I be secure in life when I know I will someday die and when I feel at times that I am only an animal, a machine, or a combination of molecules? Death fascinates me, yet I was shocked by my mother's sudden death. Death seems to be an assault on humanity, impossible to grasp and comprehend.

Though very aware of my mortality and fallenness, I know that I bear God's image. As Augustine reminds me, my heart has a God-shaped vacuum that will never be satisfied apart from the Lord. In short, my security must be in Him. My profound need to be loved and accepted must be met by God.

How will He meet my deep longing for security?

1. He assigns me my portion and makes my lot secure (v. 5).
2. He gives me a delightful inheritance (v. 6).
3. He helps me face hard facts at night (v. 7).
4. His presence is at my right hand (v. 8).
5. He gives me a glad heart and a joyous tongue (v. 9).
6. He watches over my body—even after death (v. 9, also Acts 2:22-37).
7. He makes known to me the path of life, fills me with joy in his presence, and gives eternal pleasures at his right hand (v. 11).

Therefore, I will place my faith in these promises and let the Lord be my reference point. I will let Him integrate, authenticate, and inform my life. As He brings wholeness, my insecurities will be transformed into peace and rest. My fears will begin to disappear, and I will be able to face life and even death with confidence.

Personal prayer

Lord, I praise You because I am one of Your loved ones. Help me to count on the fact that because I am in You, no one could be more secure.

A CONTEMPORARY LYRIC

My Everything

Lord, You are my everything, My highest
    joy and prize;
You meet my needs in every way with
    grace that satisfies.
Lord, You are my everything, My food and
    drink today;
You lead to brooks and meadows green and
    guide in a special way.

Since I am your own precious sheep,
    You watch me even when I sleep;
You have become my All-in-all, You always
    lift me when I fall.
Lord, You are my everything, My highest
    joy and prize;
You meet my needs in every way with
    grace that satisfies.

Lord, You are my everything, My highest
    joy and prize;
You meet my needs in every way with
    grace that satisfies.
Lord, You are my everything, My Shelter,
    Refuge, Friend;
You are my great Inheritance, Whose blessings never end.

You give me wisdom in the night, You fill
    me with complete delight;
Your presence fills my heart with joy,
    Which nothing ever can destroy.
Lord, You are my everything, My highest
    joy and prize;
You meet my needs in every way with
    grace that satisfies.

Words and music by Don Wyrtzen © 1981

Prayer for Justice

Exposition of theme

PSALM 17

Hear, O LORD, my righteous plea; listen to my cry. Give ear to my prayer—it does not rise from deceitful lips. May my vindication come from you; may your eyes see what is right. I call on you, O God, for you will answer me; give ear to me and hear my prayer. Show me the wonder of your great love, you who save by your right hand those who take refuge in you from their foes. Keep me as the apple of your eye; hide me in the shadow of your wings (vv. 1-2, 6-8).

Development of theme

I want to pray with the same warmth, intimacy, and immediacy with which King David prayed. He unveiled his inner self, crying out to God and pleading for refuge. The old Gospel song says it so well:

Under His wings I am safely abiding,
Tho' the night deepens and tempests are
   wild;
Still I can trust Him, I know He will keep me,
He has redeemed me and I am His child.

Under His wings, under His wings,
Who from His love can sever?
Under His wings my soul shall abide,
Safely abide forever.

Under His wings, O what precious
   enjoyment!
There will I hide till life's trials are o'er;
Sheltered, protected, no evil can harm me,
Resting in Jesus I'm safe evermore.

Words by William O. Cushing. Music by Ira D. Sankey.

Once again, David confronted his problem head-on and talked honestly to God about his callous, arrogant, and murderous enemies who were frustrating him on every side.

He ends with an exquisitely beautiful verse: "And I—in righteousness I will see your face; when I awake, I will be satisfied with seeing your likeness" (v. 15).

Personal prayer

Help me, Lord, to give up my quest to find satisfaction in anyone but You. Make me intensely aware that only You can totally satisfy.

JANUARY 22

Doxology

Exposition of theme
PSALM 18

I love you, O LORD, my strength. The LORD is my rock, my fortress and my deliverer; my God is my rock, in whom I take refuge. He is my shield and the horn of my salvation, my stronghold. I call to the Lord, who is worthy of praise, and I am saved from my enemies (vv. 1-3).

Development of theme

The psalms contain more lament than praise. Uninhibited praise is usually preceded by authentic lament. Perhaps today our praise and worship are shallow and superficial because we have not learned to lament. Unlike David, we have little or no concept of how profound our personal need is.

Miraculously delivered from his enemies and from Saul (see 2 Samuel 8, 22), David broke forth in this moving song with intense feeling. Because of his artistic discipline, he was able to hone this experience into a care-

THE LANGUAGE OF MUSIC
Doxology
An expression of praise to God, this term is based on the Greek word, Doxa which means "glory."

Louis Bourgeois's "Doxology" from the *Genevan Psalter* is an excellent example:

Praise God, from whom all blessings flow;
Praise Him, all creatures here below;
Praise Him above, ye heavenly host;
Praise Father, Son, and Holy Ghost. Amen!

fully crafted psalm of beautiful structure and symmetry:

Doxology (vv. 1-3)
Metaphors of deliverance (vv. 4-6)
Theophany (vv. 7-15)
Personal application (vv. 16-45)
Doxology (vv. 46-50)

This song deals with David's dramatic deliverance from Saul and from his enemies, but it also deals with the quintessential Deliverer to come, the Messiah. In Romans 15:9, Paul applies Psalm 18:49 directly to Christ, our Messiah.

Psalm 18 comforts and encourages me. Like David, I can be set free—physically and emotionally. The liberation of my personality will occur as I place more and more trust in Christ, my Deliverer, rather than in human effort unempowered by God.

Personal prayer

I praise You, Yahweh, for being my Rock, my Savior, and my Deliverer. May You be exalted in my life today, and may I sing praises to Your Name.

Glorious Proclamation

Exposition of theme
PSALM 19

The heavens declare the glory of God; the skies proclaim the work of his hands. The law of the LORD is perfect, reviving the soul. The statutes of the LORD are trustworthy, making wise the simple. May the words of my mouth and the meditation of my heart be pleasing in your sight, O LORD, my rock and my redeemer (vv. 1, 7, 14).

Development of theme

No nobler, more majestic psalm has ever been written about God's revelation than Psalm 19. It tells us how God took the initiative to reveal Himself to us—a concept beyond my comprehension. He did not leave us in

> *"Our heavenly Father, a creative virtuoso, dazzles us with his power and might. Yet because he wants to be close to us, he bridged the distance between us with his Word, making possible an intimate relationship."*

darkness; He communicated through the sky and the Scripture.

Creation reveals Gods' invisible qualities. His power and divine nature can be seen clearly in what He has made (Romans 1). He holds each of us accountable for our response to this revelation. If we respond favorably, He sends more revelation (Acts 10). If we suppress this truth, we have no excuse!

Our heavenly Father, a creative virtuoso, dazzles us with His power and might. Yet because He wants to be close to us, He bridged the distance between us with His Word, making possible an intimate relationship. His Word is perfect, restorative, and trustworthy (v. 7). It brings wisdom, joy, radiance, and light (vv. 7-8). His ordinances are pure, eternal, sure, and righteous (v. 9). They are more precious than gold and sweeter than honey (v. 10). Living on the basis of the Law has its own great reward (v. 11).

A CONTEMPORARY LYRIC

But Greater Still

God speaks to me in creation and my
    heart sings His praise,
He paints His revelation in a thousand
    different ways;
His handiwork reveals His glory in its
    intricate design,
His infinite creativity is a miracle divine.

The skies tell me of His glory—what a
    dazzling display!
They give a silent witness of His
    presence every day;
The skies tell me a moving story by their
    interplay of light,
Their message reaches everywhere on a
    starry summer night.

But greater still is His perfect Word so
    rich with wealth untold,
It's sweeter than a honeycomb,
    worth more to me than gold,
So may my life always please my Lord in
    every simple way,
And may I praise His precious name in
    thoughts and words today.

Words and music by Don Wyrtzen © 1981

The compelling message of the contemporary lyric, *But Greater Still,* convinces me that the value of God's Word defies description. Its worth to me is intensely personal. It nourishes my soul and its truth sets me free.

Personal prayer

O Lord, my rock and my Redeemer, may the words of my mouth and the meditation of my heart be pleasing in Your sight.

JANUARY 24

Invocation

Prayer Before Battle

Exposition of theme

PSALM 20

May the LORD answer you when you are in distress; may the name of the God of Jacob protect you. May he give you the desire of your heart and make all your plans succeed. We will shout for joy when you are victorious and will lift up our banners in the name of our God. May the LORD grant all your requests. Some trust in chariots and some in horses, but we trust in the name of the LORD our God (vv. 1, 4-5, 7).

Development of theme

Knowing he faced a life-or-death struggle, David prepared for battle by offering prayers and sacrifices. The congregation prayed for

"I too face confrontation — in the big and the small hassles of daily living. I don't want to rely on modern insights or popular solutions. They are sterile and useless."

him, and David voiced his certainty of God's answer (vv. 6-8).

The focus of David's cry for help was the Name of the Lord, which he knew had power. Any hope for conquest, and all protection, support, and help, come only from that Name. The most formidable weapons of the ancient world were impotent against the Name of the Lord.

I too face confrontation — in the big hassles of life and the small hassles of daily living. I don't want to rely on modern insights or popular solutions. They are sterile and useless. Only the Name of the Lord can give me relief and support. I don't want it to be the last place I go for help. I don't have the resources to make it on my own. I'm a dependent person. When I am weak, then I am strong. As Sandi Patti sings so gloriously, "There is power in the Name of the Lord."

Personal prayer

Lord, keep me from placing my trust in the might of men; remind me that Your Name is the only reliable source of strength.

Victory March

Exposition of theme

PSALM 21

*O LORD, the King rejoices in your strength.
How great is his joy in the victories you
give! You have granted him the desire of his
heart and have not withheld the request of
his lips. For the king trusts in the LORD;
through the unfailing love of the Most High he
will not be shaken. Be exalted, O LORD, in
your strength; we will sing and praise your
might (vv. 1-2, 7, 13).*

Development of theme

After pouring out my soul in lament and
prayer, I need to wait patiently for the Lord to
answer. As He answered David, He will also
answer me. In Psalm 21, a glorious royal hymn,
David celebrated the Lord's answer to his petition in Psalm 20. The Lord brought victory
rather than defeat, gave life instead of death,
and blessed him by granting him his heart's
desire.

Even under pressure, David modeled stability and security. I too need to grasp that my
safety, steadiness, and confidence are
based on God's loyal love (Romans 8:35–39).
David's faith, centered squarely on the rock-
solid, permanent, eternal love of the Lord, stabi-
lized and strengthened him.

David didn't win the battle with his own

> *"Even under pressure, David
> modeled stability and security.
> I too need to grasp that my
> safety, steadiness, and confi-
> dence are based on God's
> loyal love."*

THE LANGUAGE OF MUSIC

March

*Music for soldiers, usually involving strongly
accented beats in groups of four.*

Marches are usually dignified, ceremonial,
and military. A good example is Arthur
Sullivan's stirring hymn, "Onward Christian Soldiers."

strength, expertise, or military genius. But that
didn't diminish his exhilaration. To celebrate
God's victory, David wrote glorious music. Like
David, I too will sing praise when I lift up my
life to the Lord, and He will bring music back
into my life.

Personal prayer

*Lord, may I learn to "throw a party" to cele-
brate Your glory, majesty, and unfailing love.*

Song of the Suffering Servant

First Movement
The Eloquence of Darkness—Part 1

Exposition of theme

PSALM 22

My God, my God, why have you forsaken me? Why are you so far from saving me, so far from the words of my groaning (v. 1)?

Development of theme

When I face an obstacle that I can't go over, under, or around, I need to acknowledge my pain and helplessness. Denial and fantasy only compound my problem with dishonesty. I need to look squarely at my situation and admit my inability to resolve it.

The parallels between this psalm and Christ's crucifixion are astounding. This exquisite lyric poetry portrays deep personal shame and intense suffering. Reading it makes me feel vicariously what Christ went through to win my redemption on the darkest day in history. Since Christ lived the experiences described here and quotes it in the New Testament, I believe this lament applies to Him.

Throbbing with urgency and immediacy,

the first movement of this psalm (vv. 1-21) eloquently portrays darkness in several related themes:

First, *David cried out to God* (vv. 1-2). "My God, my God, why have you forsaken me?" According to Gospel accounts, Christ said these exact words at the height of His agony on the cross (Matthew 27:46; Mark 15:34). As death closed in, Christ felt that His Father had turned His back on Him and had withdrawn protection. He felt helpless, disoriented, and betrayed.

Second, *David remembered history* (vv. 3-5). He praised the Lord and affirmed His holiness by citing the experiences of his fathers who trusted God through adversity and were delivered.

Third, *David described Christ's experience of shame* (vv. 6-8). Scorned and despised, He was mocked by a blood-thirsty crowd that was cynical and cruel.

Fourth, *David reflected on God's care* (vv. 9-11). The Hebrew word for trust means "to lie prone—completely helpless." David trusted God from the beginning—even from birth. He pleaded for God to be close because there was no one else to help.

> *"This exquisite lyric poetry portrays deep personal shame and intense suffering. Reading it makes me feel vicariously what Christ went through to win my redemption on the darkest day in history."*

Personal prayer

Help me, Father, to identify my suffering and need with the Savior. Help me, by faith, to become aware that when I participate in His sufferings, I also share in His glory.

Song of the Suffering Servant

First Movement
The Eloquence of Darkness—Part 2

Exposition of theme

PSALM 22 CONTINUED

Many bulls surround me; strong bulls of Bashan encircle me. Roaring lions tearing their prey open their mouths wide against me (vv. 12-13).

Development of theme

Continuing the theme of suffering, David portrayed a fifth scene of darkness: Christ's intense suffering on the cross. He pictured the mocking crowd as a menagerie of wild animals. They were like ravenous wolves closing in on their prey. Murder, sin, and hate filled their wild eyes.

Verses 16-18 describe in uncanny detail the Roman execution—piercing the hands and feet, counting the bones, people staring and gloating, soldiers dividing the garments and casting lots for them.

Sixth, David pleads for immediate help (vv. 19-21). He prays intensely for God to come close and deliver him from these wild, murderous, unclean predators.

What a model for me to follow when I am called to suffer. Romans 8:17-18 says it all, "Now if we are children, then we are heirs—heirs of God and co-heirs with Christ, if indeed we share in his sufferings in order that we may also share in his glory. I consider that our present sufferings are not worth comparing with the glory that will be revealed in us."

It is easy to live under the mistaken notion that if I do the will of God, my life will be a paragon of perfection, free from anxiety and trauma. But I need to recognize that I may suffer *because* I am doing the will of God. This happened to David, and it happened to Christ in Gethsemane and on the Cross.

> **"My goal in life should be holiness, not happiness."**

My goal in life should be holiness, not happiness. But grabbing hold of this concept in our affluent society is difficult at best. The fullest, most richly textured life is the holy life. Only the refiner's fire produces pure gold. The holy life yields the richest, most enduring rewards.

Personal prayer

Lord, though I live in a pagan, materialistic culture, may I commit my life to the higher value of holiness over happiness. Let me experience a deep wellspring of joy, no matter what happens.

A GOSPEL CHORUS LYRIC

Eternity's Values in View

With eternity's values in view, Lord,
With eternity's values in view;
May I do each day's work for Jesus,
With eternity's values in view.

Words and music by Alfred B. Smith © 1941. Renewed 1941.

Song

The act or art of singing.

The word *song* can also designate a poetical composition or a short, musical composition of words and music. It also refers to a melody for a lyric, ballad, or poem. The psalmist says, "Your decrees are the theme of my song wherever I lodge" (Psalm 119:54).

Song of the Suffering Servant

Second Movement — The Joyful Feast

Exposition of theme

PSALM 22 *CONTINUED*

I will declare your name to my brothers; in the congregation I will praise you (v. 22).

Development of theme

After the powerful lament of verses 1-21, the Lord miraculously hears and delivers. Heartwrenching, soul-searching lament is the basis for the true praise of God.

In the Old Testament economy, this praise and worship was accomplished through prayer, sacrifice, a commemorative feast, and vows of service to God (Leviticus 7:16). Joy and happiness were not to be kept private. Servants, poor people, and especially Levites were to be invited to the feast (Deuteronomy 12:17-19). The whole congregation was to celebrate what God had done for them.

David threw a party in the Lord's honor. He got carried away with expressions of thanksgiving and praise (vv. 27-31). He sang a stirring canticle of blessing, and his worship found its ultimate focus in God's eternal kingdom — where the poor will be fed, where nations will bow down before the Lord, and where His righteousness will be proclaimed to people yet unborn.

The secular mind looks at life and says, "Is this all there is?" The believer looks at life and sees something to look forward to.

Personal prayer

Lord, may I move today from lament to praise, from darkness to light, and from ordinary business to celestial celebration.

Satisfaction

Exposition of theme
PSALM 23

The LORD *is my shepherd, I shall not be in want (v. 1).*

Development of theme

Perhaps the most creative and artistic person in the Bible, David, was a virtuoso harpist, a military genius, a capable administrator, and a cultural innovator. He led a sweeping renaissance of Jewish culture. Perhaps his most enduring literary achievement was to write and/or compile this psalm, the most-loved and well-known of all. It comforts, satisfies, and meets the deepest longings of the human heart.

It starts straightforwardly with the simple words, "The Lord is my shepherd." "Lord" is emphatic here. It is the *Lord* who makes our faith distinctive. No other person fits: not Mohammed, not Buddha, not Gandi. "My" personalizes the relationship, revealing intimacy and closeness.

"Shepherd" is the most comprehensive and intimate metaphor in the Psalms. The shepherd lives with his flock and is everything to it—guide, physician, and protector.

The last phrase, "I shall not be in want," means that God will fulfill my deepest personal needs and that I will find meaning and true identity in Him. In short, I don't need God plus anything or anyone. All my emotional and psychological longings for significance and security will find fulfillment in the Lord.

Personal prayer

Thank You, Lord, that You meet all my needs and that You are the key to my wholeness and fulfillment.

45

JANUARY 30

Rest

Exposition of theme

PSALM 23 CONTINUED

He makes me lie down in green pastures, he leads me beside quiet waters, he restores my soul (v. 2).

Development of theme

Just as the ark of the covenant went ahead of Israel to find places of rest, so the Lord guides us to refreshment and relaxation. He provides green pastures and quiet waters. He doesn't want us to work nonstop.

I need to be intellectually "driven" in my work. I used to work on a fairly regular basis with the London Symphony musicians doing recording projects. On many occasions I would

fly all night to London, write music the first day, record the following day, write all that night, and record the next day. By that time, I was more like a zombie than an arranger–composer badly in need of rest.

A shepherd thinks in terms of the needs of

A SHEPHERD'S PERSPECTIVE

My Creator — Shepherd
by Phillip Keller

"It is a staggering fact that Christ, the Creator of an enormous universe of overwhelming magnitude deigns to call Himself my Shepherd and invites me to consider myself His sheep — His special object of affection and attention. Who better could care for me?"

A Shepherd Looks at Psalm 23 © 1970. Zondervan Publishing House his flock just as a father thinks in terms of the needs of his family. God has taken on a flock, a family. He is involved with us, bound up with us, and deeply concerned about meeting our innermost personal needs. Modern psychology has pointed out how essential it is for normal, emotional development that we have an adequate father. Ultimately, only our heavenly Father is adequate.

I want the Lord to balance my life today, to define my lifestyle and my priorities, to deliver me from neurotic activity and workaholism, and to keep me from trying to meet my own needs through work and achievement instead of through Him.

Personal prayer

Lord, help me to turn over to You the pressure and stress that I feel. Teach me to relax in Your Spirit.

Guidance

Exposition of theme
PSALM 23 CONTINUED

He guides me in paths of righteousness for his name's sake (v. 3).

Development of theme

The Lord not only renews my life physically and emotionally, but He also guides me in paths of righteousness. I need to trust the authority of Scripture as my rule of faith and behavior. I need to commit myself to doing God's will, whatever it is. And I need to walk closely with God so I know Him intimately. If I trust Him and nurture and cultivate intimacy with Him, He makes my paths smooth and straight (Proverbs 3:5-6). Living righteously and blamelessly has its own reward. If we place God's authority and our commitment to and intimacy with Him in proper perspective, He leads us by the hand through life and manages our affairs. What a comfort to know that the Lord is right in front of me, removing obstacles!

Why does the Lord do this for me? "For his name's sake." The Lord takes His Name very seriously. We are to uphold His holy Name. When we do, God makes us new. In Ezekiel 36:22, 26 the Lord says, "It is not for your sake, O house of Israel, that I am going to do these things, but for the sake of my holy name. . . . I will give you a new heart and put a new spirit in you; I will remove from you your heart of stone and give you a heart of flesh."

Personal prayer

Sovereign Lord, I lift up Your holy Name today. Renew my spirit and give me a new heart.

February PSALMS 23–30

PANORAMA PHOTO BY GARY IRVING

Comfort

Exposition of theme
PSALM 23 CONTINUED

Even though I walk through the valley of the shadow of death, I will fear no evil, for you are with me; your rod and your staff, they comfort me (v. 4).

Development of theme

The greatest insult to humanity is the spector of death. At certain moments the fear of it grips and mystifies us. When it does, we need to come to the soothing, timeless truth of Psalm 23:4.

I will never forget the night my mom died. We had just experienced a joyous reunion with my parents over the Christmas holidays. Because of a business trip, I had left my family in northern Michigan for a skiing vacation and returned home. When I arrived, I heard the phone ringing. My close friend Bob Steed told me my mom had gone to be with the Lord. I was shocked! That

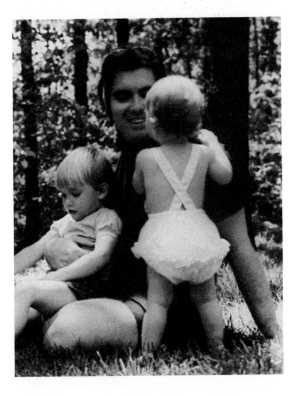

> *"My mom had gone to be with the Lord. I was shocked! That long night became a melange of crying, reminiscing, praying, and fitful sleep. But I didn't feel alone; I felt the Lord walking with me through my grief."*

long night became a melange of crying, reminiscing, praying, and fitful sleeping. But I didn't feel alone; I felt the Lord walking with me through my grief.

The valley of the shadow is a dark ravine. Yet, like the green pastures (v. 3), it too is a right path. People today fear death, so they don't talk about it very often. But the Bible discusses it in very comforting terms as part of the nature of reality.

In verse 4, the lyric switches from "he" (vv. 2-3) to "you," a much more personal pronoun. I am to fear no evil for "you are with me." Instead of walking ahead of me, the Lord now walks alongside me, as an escort. He is not distant and impersonal. He is my companion — even in death. His presence overcomes the worst thing that remains: fear.

Armed as He walks beside us, our Shepherd and Companion protects us with His rod and staff. The rod — a cudgel or short, heavy club — symbolized defense. The staff, which the shepherd used to help him walk or to round up the flock, symbolized control. The Lord defends us even in death and gives us His security.

Personal prayer

Lord, I thank You that You walk beside me as my Friend and Companion. I thank You that You are at my side even at the moment of death.

Interlude

Exposition of theme

1 Corinthians 15

Where, O Death, is your victory? Where, O death, is your sting? The sting of death is sin, and the power of sin is the law. But thanks be to God! He gives us the victory through our Lord Jesus Christ (vv. 55-57).

Development of theme

The Apostle Paul gave us the New Testament picture of death in 1 Corinthians 15:55-57 and in 2 Corinthians 5:7-9. The more we see death from the biblical perspective, the more our fear will melt away. The events described in Psalm 23:4 happen instantaneously. In the light of eternity, death is just a walk through the gates of glory to a forever of eternal joy.

Originally written for Dr. W.A. Criswell, pastor of First Baptist Church in Dallas, Texas, the song, "Finally Home," has brought peace and comfort to hundreds of people. Dr. Criswell's daughter, Anne, first sang the chorus coupled with a chorus of "The Glory Song" because we didn't have any verses yet. John W. Peterson, one of my mentors and a noted songwriter, en-couraged me to write verses that would describe a human's fear of death and provide the background for this glorious chorus. I wrote the lyrics and music; the Lord gave the song His special touch.

Personal prayer

Lord, I thank You and praise You that someday I will wake up in glory and discover that I've finally arrived Home.

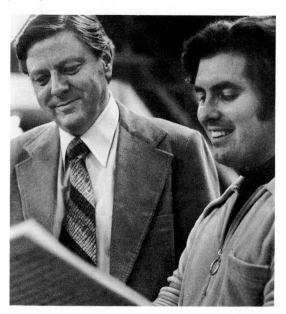

A CONTEMPORARY LYRIC

Finally Home

When alarmed by the fury of the restless sea,
Towering waves before you roll;
At the end of doubt and peril is eternity,
Though fear and conflict seize your soul:

When surrounded by the blackness of the darkest night,
O how lonely death can be;
At the end of this long tunnel is a shining light,
For death is swallowed up in victory!

But just think of stepping on shore and finding it heaven!
Of touching a hand and finding it God's!
Of breathing new air and finding it celestial!
Of waking up in glory and finding it home!

Words © by L.E. Singer and Don Wyrtzen. Music © by Don Wyrtzen.

to do with sheep? The answer is — nothing. The songwriter simply changed his imagery from that of the shepherd to one of even greater intimacy and closeness: the friend.

The threat of verse 4 becomes the triumph of verse 5. We transcend the depths of the valley to the heights of a victory celebration. The Lord not only leads through the dark valley, but He provides a feast for us as well. Our enemies are present, but they are captives.

I felt a genuine sense of injustice when another musician was chosen to do a project that had been promised to me. When I realized my vulnerability to jealousy, I committed the entire mat-

---

"The Lord, our Host, provides abundantly. He sets a beautiful table, anoints us with costly perfume, and fills our cups to the brim. In other words, He more than meets our needs."

---

ter to the Lord in prayer. Later I became involved in two other projects, which were so well received that my musical ministry was given an enormous boost.

The Lord, our Host, provides abundantly. He sets a beautiful table, anoints us with costly perfume, and fills our cups to the brim. In other words, He more than meets our needs.

How limited is our faith! The Lord, our Friend and Host, wants to supply us *abundantly*. Believers, of all people, should not be running scared. As the old Sunday school song says, "My cup is full and running over."

Personal prayer

Lord, thank You for bringing truth and beauty into my life. Thank You that I don't have to live in poverty but can be satiated by Your glorious riches.

Celebration

Exposition of theme
PSALM 23 CONTINUED

You prepare a table before me in the presence of my enemies. You anoint my head with oil; my cup overflows (v. 5).

Development of theme

As great art so frequently does, verse 5 throws us a curve. What do a table, oil, and a cup have

Prosperity

Exposition of theme

PSALM 23 CONTINUED

Surely goodness and love will follow me all the days of my life, and I will dwell in the house of the LORD forever (v. 6).

Development of theme

The modern perspective on success and prosperity is often very narrow, defined only in materialistic terms. But David defined true prosperity in Psalm 23:6. Rather than being pursued by enemies, the believer is pursued by the Lord's prosperity. The Lord's goodness and love define that prosperity.

The most richly textured Hebrew word for love, *hesed*, is used here. It's also used to describe Hosea's miraculous love for his prostitute wife and to describe God's love for Israel even when she worshipped idols. Similar to *agape*, the Greek word for love used in the New Testament, *hesed* describes God's loyal, unfailing, unconditional love. This love is hard for us to comprehend because human love so frequently has mixed motives.

Even though He knows everything there is to know about us (Psalm 139), God loves us. Even though we stand naked before Him, He fully accepts us. The Lord's love for us is also the core of the gospel message. That I can be fully exposed and yet totally accepted is the thrill of the gospel.

When we learn to accept this love, we will be able to love ourselves, which is the foundation for self-worth. Then we'll also be free to love other people, which is the basis for friendships, marriage, and a fulfilled family life. In the arms of our heavenly Father, we are vulnerable—yet fully safe.

I am beginning to be aware of God's love for me. I see wonder in ordinary things and I accept

> *"Rather than being pursued by enemies, the believer is pursued by the Lord's prosperity."*

them as gifts of God's grace. God's love is so vast, it is impossible for me to fully comprehend.

What a promise the last phrase is! "I will dwell in the house of the Lord forever!" Death is not a threat to me. I don't go into oblivion, buried beneath the sod. I have no cause for despair. "I will dwell in the house of the Lord, forever!" I wonder what resplendent music the chief musician wrote for that!

Personal prayer

I praise You, Lord, that I don't have to live in fear—even of death—because You have promised I can dwell in Your house forever.

The King of Glory Processional

First movement — The Lord's Creativity

Exposition of theme

PSALM 24

The earth is the LORD's, and everything in it, the world, and all who live in it; for he founded it upon the seas and established it upon the waters (vv. 1-2).

Development of theme

The creative power of God inspires awe. I'm filled with reverent wonder as I contemplate it. To think that He spoke and worlds came into being! In contrast to God, I work with raw materials that He created. My creativity is derived from His. I put the wrapping paper and ribbon on His packages.

Several years ago, Karen and I traveled to Brazil. Along with lecturing and ministering to missionaries, we scheduled some sightseeing. I will never forget the awesome Iguacu Falls. There in the majestic grandeur of cascading water, I saw the omnipotence of the almighty God. I shouted spontaneously, "How great Thou art!"

Because the Lord made the earth and everything on it, He owns it. He founded the earth (Genesis 1) and established it upon the waters. The heathen nations feared the restless, perilous, foaming seas. But even the violent waters belong to God and reflect the variety and depth of His creative imagination.

The Lord didn't create the earth and then abandon it. He is intimately involved with sustaining it. He watches over what belongs to Him. My Lord doesn't like loose ends! He not only sus-

> *"In contrast to God, I work with raw materials that He created. My creativity is derived from His. I put the wrapping paper and ribbon on His packages."*

tains His creation; He watches over me too and allows me to reflect His creativity!

Personal prayer

I praise You, Lord, for Your incredible imagination and creativity. I thank You that I can, in a very small way, imitate it.

THE LANGUAGE OF MUSIC

Processional

A musical composition, such as a hymn, designed for a procession — a group of individuals moving along in an orderly, often ceremonial, fashion.

The psalmist declares, "The Lord is Good, and he has made his light shine upon us. With boughs in hand, join in the festal procession up to the horns of the altar" (Psalm 118:27).

The King of Glory Processional

Second Movement — The Lord's Holiness

Exposition of theme

PSALM 24 *CONTINUED*

Who may ascend the hill of the LORD? Who may stand in His holy place? He who has clean hands and a pure heart, who does not lift up his soul to an idol or swear by what is false. He will receive blessing from the LORD and vindication from God his Savior (vv. 3-5).

Development of theme

David speaks eloquently about God's holiness and our need for purity which, in today's language, we would call integrity. He concludes that only a person marked by integrity can stand before God's absolute holiness.

Isaiah understood that purity is the prerequisite for knowing God. When exposed to the stunning radiance of God, he said, "I am a man of unclean lips, and I live among a people of unclean lips, and my eyes have seen the King, the Lord Almighty" (Isaiah 6:5). Jesus Himself taught that only the pure in heart would see God (Matthew 5:8). And the Apostle Paul drove home the same point when he said, "I want you to be wise about what is good, and innocent about what is evil" (Romans 16:19). We cannot begin to know the holiness of God until we cultivate purity in our personal lives.

The quest for purity and integrity challenges believers today. Modern technology provides easy and private access to seductive entertainment. Nuances of temptation common today were unknown in the ancient world. Yet even so, David's words remain true today. Integrity is the prerequisite for knowing God and being able to stand before His holiness.

Personal prayer

Heavenly Father, my desire is to have clean hands and a pure heart today. By Your Spirit, change me into a person of integrity and purity.

The King of Glory Processional

Third Movement — The Lord's Might

Exposition of theme

PSALM 24 CONTINUED

Lift up your heads, O you gates; lift them up, you ancient doors, that the king of glory may come in. Who is he, this King of glory? The LORD Almighty — he is the King of glory (vv. 9-10).

Development of theme

The dramatic scene at the end of Psalm 24 may have been enacted as the processional arrived at the city gates. Begun in Egypt, this stately march ascended to Zion and broke forth into a dazzling festival of praise.

"What pageantry and excitement they had in their worship! Not lifeless, boring, predictable rituals. They exulted in praise to the King of glory. They celebrated His creativity, His holiness, and His might."

There have been a number of times in my life when a musical experience has also become a spiritual experience. During the World's Fair in New York, I directed a mass choir of a thousand Christian women. As I fought to keep my composure, my heart overflowed with praises for God.

As the ancient doors swung open, the spotlight focused on the King of glory riding through the gates. He was a King of towering stature, strong and mighty in battle, the Warrior of War-

riors! No doubt the marching band started to sing and play the song of Miriam and Moses: "The Lord is a warrior; the Lord is his name" (Exodus 15:4).

What pageantry and excitement they had in their worship! Not lifeless, boring, predictable rituals. They exulted in praise to the King of glory. They celebrated His creativity (24:1-2), His holiness (24:3-6), and His might (24:7-10). What a battle cry for us today as we look forward to seeing the King of Glory face-to-face!

Personal prayer

Lord, teach me to worship You with genuine fervor and vitality. May I be excited by Your presence rather than embalmed by lifeless liturgy.

A Personal Hymn for the Congregation
First Motif—Protection

Exposition of theme
PSALM 25

To you, O LORD, I lift up my soul; in you I trust, O my God. Do not let me be put to shame, nor let my enemies triumph over me. . . . Guard my life and rescue me; let me not be put to shame, for I take refuge in you. May integrity and uprightness protect me, because my hope is in you (vv. 1–2, 20–21).

Development of theme

Although written as a hymn for the whole congregation, Psalm 25 is very personal. And, like many of David's artistic creations, it is highly structured. Crafted around the Hebrew alphabet, it is difficult to outline. But David seems to have focused on four basic motifs: protection from his enemies, guidance for his life, forgiveness from sin, and hope for deliverance.

Knowing that only integrity and uprightness could protect him from his enemies, David asked for forgiveness from past sins. And knowing that only those whose hope is in the Lord could walk in integrity, he asked for guidance and placed his hope in God.

Like David and my dad, I want the kind of personal integrity and uprightness that I can depend on for protection. Integrity is a word that beautifully encompasses honor, sincerity, and wholeness. My dad, who lives consistently on the basis of his convictions, personifies integrity. He advances his evangelism on the basis of biblical principles and is not easily distracted from reaching his goals. By daily example, he teaches me that if my hope is truly in the Lord, not in secu-

"Like David and my dad, I want the kind of personal integrity and uprightness that I can depend on for protection. By daily example, my dad teaches me that if my hope is truly in the Lord, not in secular thinking and methods, I will be able to cultivate personal integrity and be protected."

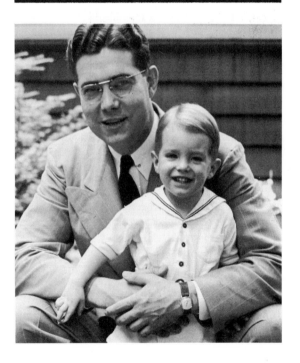

lar thinking and methods, I will be able to cultivate personal integrity and be protected.

Personal prayer

Lord, may I be preoccupied with You rather than with the enemies who surround me. Mark my life with integrity and uprightness.

A Personal Hymn for the Congregation

Second Motif—Guidance

Exposition of theme

PSALM 25 CONTINUED

Show me your ways, O LORD, teach me your paths; guide me in your truth and teach me, for you are God my Savior, and my hope is in you all day long. . . . Good and upright is the Lord; therefore he instructs sinners in his ways. He guides the humble in what is right and teaches them his way (vv. 4-5, 8-9).

Development of theme

Pagans had an irrational approach to guidance. They trusted magical pointers and omens. David, in stark contrast, had an intimate walk with his Lord. Walking with the Lord may seem irrational to modern minds; however, when in severe trauma or stress, I believe we naturally cry out to our heavenly Father for help, as Christ cried out to Him on the cross. When David cried out to God, he received guidance and direction within a loving father-child relationship.

In this psalm, David listed four characteristics necessary for knowing God's will: discernment, persistence, obedience, and reverence.

Discernment is the ability to distinguish good from evil (Hebrews 5:14). Because God's will is always true and good, those who have poor discernment—who cannot distinguish between truth and falsehood, good and evil, right and wrong—cannot know God's will.

Knowing right from wrong doesn't come naturally, however; it takes a lifetime of learning. Consequently, without a persistent search for truth, we will never know God's will. David dem-

onstrated persistence by keeping his eyes "ever on the Lord" (v. 15). His hope was not a fly-by-night thing; it was in the Lord "all day long" (v. 5).

Doing what is right doesn't come naturally, either. We need lots of practice. Obedience, therefore, is another prerequisite for knowing God's will. David modeled obedience by being good, upright, humble, and teachable (vv. 8-9).

Obeying God's will is to obey His Word. As the prophet told King Saul, "Does the Lord delight in burnt offerings and sacrifices as much as in obeying the voice of the Lord? To obey is better than sacrifice, and to heed is better than the fat of rams" (1 Samual 15:22). Therefore, persis-

> *"Knowing what isn't God's will is perhaps easier than knowing what is, but God promises guidance to those who walk intimately with Him."*

tence in studying Scripture is essential.

Because "the Lord confides in those who fear him" (v. 14), those who want to know God's will need to learn reverence. David viewed the Lord with awe and respect, and the Lord became his friend. The Hebrew words for friendship and counsel are closely related.

Knowing what isn't God's will is perhaps easier than knowing what is, but God promises guidance to those who walk intimately with Him. The only way to know the will of God is through discernment, persistence, obedience, and reverence.

Personal prayer

Lord, may I walk closely and intimately with You so that I will experience Your guidance and direction in my life.

A Personal Hymn for the Congregation

Third Motif—Forgiveness

Exposition of theme

PSALM 25 CONTINUED

Remember not the sins of my youth and my rebellious ways; according to your love remember me, for you are good, O LORD. Good and upright is the LORD; therefore, he instructs sinners in his ways. . . . Turn to me and be gracious to me, for I am lonely and afflicted. The troubles of my heart have multiplied; free me from my anguish. Look upon my affliction and my distress and take away all my sins (vv. 7-8, 16-18).

Development of theme

David readily admitted his sins; he didn't hide behind rationalization. His honesty reflected a clear-cut, ethical value system that today's world seriously lacks. It is rare to hear someone say, "I lied!" We often hide behind highfalutin phrases and euphemisms; Charles Van Doren vividly illustrates this. Instead of saying, "I lied," he said,

"I've been involved in an incredible delusion." This was his statement after he was found to be cheating in television quiz scandals.

Guilt had been eating away at David, and his troubles had multiplied. He knew that only the Lord could relieve him of his affliction and so he cried out for the Lord to "take away all my sins" (v. 18). Confession is still the only way out of anxiety caused by sin and guilt. A clear conscience leads to good health. A solid theology is the best psychology.

As New Testament Christians, we need never surrender to the erosion of unresolved guilt. We can claim the Apostle John's promise: "If we confess our sins, he is faithful and just and will forgive us our sins and purify us from all unrighteousness" (1 John 1:9).

Personal prayer

To You, O Lord, I lift up my soul. Deliver me from trouble today and take away all my sins.

THE LANGUAGE OF MUSIC

Hymn

A song of praise to God that involves adoration, worship, and reverence.

Paul admonishes us, "Let the word of Christ dwell in you richly as you teach and admonish one another with all wisdom, and as you sing psalms, hymns and spiritual songs with gratitude in your hearts to God" (Colossians 3:16).

A Personal Hymn for the Congregation

Fourth Motif—Hope

Exposition of theme

PSALM 25 CONTINUED

To you, O LORD, I lift up my soul; in you I trust, O my God (vv. 1-2).

Development of theme

Instead of feeling anxious because of the stress of his life, David had a sense of well-being and security. Because his confidence was in the Lord, he had no fear. He did not base his hope on his own righteousness; he based it on the loyal love (*hesed*) of the Lord. He didn't trust sacred formulas and structures; he trusted the faithfulness of God. David was fully aware of the graciousness and dependability of his Lord. For him to place his confidence in anything or anyone else would be groundless.

Only the Lord can provide the deep inner

> *"Only the Lord can provide the deep inner sense of security, which we all long to feel. God doesn't promise insulation from all harm. Nor does He guarantee that ungodly people will not prosper or succeed."*

sense of security, which, I believe, we all long to feel. God doesn't promise insulation from all harm. Nor does He guarantee that ungodly people will not prosper or succeed. But He does

promise to take us through the storms of life if we place our trust in Him, not ourselves. We must risk the life of faith to become truly secure.

David was high-strung, sensitive, and fragile, yet he exhibited unusual strength and authority. What really informed his leadership was bed-rock security that came from his trust in the Lord.

Personal prayer

Lord, I thank You that You are fully aware of all my insecurities. I turn them all over to You today, because I choose to place my complete trust in You.

FEBRUARY 12

Devotional Leitmotifs

First Leitmotif—Personal Integrity

Exposition of theme
PSALM 26

Vindicate me, O LORD, for I have led a blameless life; I have trusted in the LORD without wavering. Test me, O LORD, and try me, examine my heart and my mind (vv. 1-2).

Development of theme

Psalm 26 is all about personal integrity. Integrity signifies soundness, completeness, and honesty. People with these characteristics identity with Yahweh and keep themselves separate from sinners.

The psalmist petitioned the Lord for two things: vindication and examination. On the basis of his integrity, he asked to be delivered and avenged. He also asked to be critically examined. He wanted his heart and his mind tested because he was confident of his integrity. His life had not been dominated by ulterior motives, nor had he played political games. He had been sin-

---

> *"Transparency is the prelude to genuine spiritual intimacy. Because David experienced this, he was a man after God's own heart."*

---

gular in his purpose to trust the Lord.

How I need to cultivate total openness before the Lord! Transparency is the prelude to genuine spiritual intimacy. Because David experienced this, he was a man after God's own heart (Acts 13:22). No higher compliment could ever be paid!

Personal prayer
Lord, may my life be an open book before You!

THE LANGUAGE OF MUSIC
Leitmotif
A German term meaning "leading motif."

Refers to a short theme or musical idea linked with a character, object, place, situation, or recurring idea. It is like a mini-theme, consistently repeated, to give a musical piece unity and cohesion.

Devotional Leitmotifs

Second Leitmotif—Separation from Sinners

Exposition of theme

PSALM 26 *CONTINUED*

For your love is ever before me, and I walk continually in your truth. I do not sit with deceitful men, nor do I consort with hypocrites; I abhor the assembly of evildoers and refuse to sit with the wicked (vv. 3-5).

Development of theme

David demonstrated his integrity in two specific ways: his separation from sinners and his identification with Yahweh. The structure of David's life rested on two pillars: God's love and God's truth.

David kept God's unconditional love before him. Knowing that God would love him no matter what he thought of himself or what behavior he

---

> *"Because he knew that friends and associates would play a major role in shaping his attitudes and values, David chose them carefully."*

---

engaged in, David walked confidently through life.

He also walked continually in God's truth. Because he knew that friends and associates would play a major role in shaping his attitudes and values, he chose them carefully. Deceivers, hypocrites, evildoers, and other wicked people were not part of his group. It wasn't that he disapproved of them socially, but rather that he would not align himself with them spiritually. For as Sol-

omon warned his young son, "Do not go along with them, do not set foot on their paths" (Proverbs 1:15). Their way of life leads to spiritual death.

I need to model David in his careful choice of personal friends and confidants because they do influence my value system. In this David showed great wisdom because his friends affirmed him and kept him on track.

Personal prayer

O Lord, lead me to friends who will encourage me and lead me closer to You.

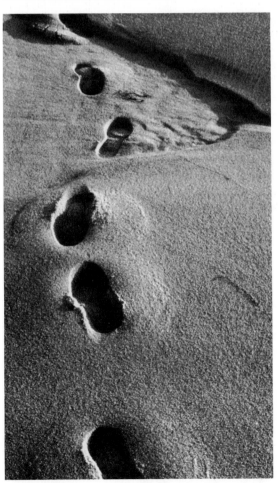

Devotional Leitmotifs

Third Leitmotif—Identification with Yahweh

Exposition of theme

PSALM 26 CONTINUED

I wash my hands in innocence, and go about your altar, O LORD, proclaiming aloud your praise and telling of all your wonderful deeds. I love the house where you live, O LORD, the place where your glory dwells (vv. 6-8).

Development of theme

Picture in your mind an open court with singers marching around the altar. Before the priests approached this altar, they stopped at the laver for cleansing. David put himself in this picture and used it to personalize his praise.

David loved to "let go" in praise of the Lord. He told of God's wonderful deeds, and he did it loudly in songs of thanksgiving. He loved the Lord's

> **"I want to avoid boredom in God's house. With words and music, I want to bring excitement about the Lord to His dwelling place."**

house because the glory of the Lord dwelt there.

Recently I attended The Praise Gathering, where Ronn Huff led ten thousand of us in singing Michael W. Smith's "Great Is the Lord." The voices of the mass choir—accompanied by brass, percussion, and organ—lifted us right out of our seats. Then, without accompaniment, we sang "Great Is Thy Faithfulness." What a sense of the Lord's presence!

In praising the Lord and expressing love for His house, David clearly identified himself with Yahweh. He proved this by his actions: He offered acknowledgment to his Lord.

Like David, I want to continually praise the Lord with my imagination, animation, and with everything I've got. Above all, I want to avoid boredom in God's house. With words and music, I want to bring excitement about the Lord to His dwelling place.

Personal prayer

Lord, as I identify with You and with Your house, help me find my own personal identity.

63

Devotional Leitmotifs

Fourth Leitmotif — Petition for Redemption

Exposition of theme

PSALM 26 CONTINUED

Do not take away my soul along with sinners, my life with bloodthirsty men, in whose hands are wicked schemes, whose right hands are full of bribes. But I lead a blameless life; redeem me and be merciful to me. My feet stand on level ground; in the great assembly I will praise the Lord (vv. 9-12).

Development of theme

David prayed for deliverance from the fate of sinners and petitioned the Lord to redeem him. He

> *"Making music is part of the fellowship that binds believers together. Ultimately, personal involvement is the key to the joy of music."*

trusted Yahweh to spare him from the fate inevitably coming to the wicked.

David's beautiful prayer unveiled his true character. In it we see his authenticity, integrity, and deep humility. Wholehearted in his commitment, David would continue to walk along the path he had chosen. His life was characterized by loyalty and righteousness.

Assured of God's deliverance, he ended the psalm by praising and blessing the Lord. He added his voice to a choir of believers whose lives rang true to reality because they trusted the Lord.

Making music is part of the fellowship that binds believers together. The enjoyment of music is enhanced when we listen with another person. If we participate in a vocal or instrumental ensemble, our pleasure is even greater. Ultimately, personal involvement is the key to the joy of music. Just as David got involved musically with the congregation, we too must get involved personally in making music for the glory of God.

Personal prayer

Lord, I thank You for Your loyal love. Continue to build integrity and humility into my life as I place my trust in You.

Freedom

First Variation — Freedom from Fear

Exposition of theme

PSALM 27

The LORD is my light and my salvation — whom shall I fear? The LORD is the stronghold of my life — of whom shall I be afraid? When evil men advance against me to devour my flesh, when my enemies and my foes attack me, they will stumble and fall. Though an army besiege me, my heart will not fear; though war break out against me, even then will I be confident (vv. 1-3).

Development of theme

My wife, Karen, and I were with our beloved pastor, George Gardiner, when he lost his two-year bout with cancer and went to be with the Lord. Shortly before his homegoing, he shared with

> *"Fear can cripple us and keep us in bondage. Some of us allow anxiety, a type of fear common in modern culture, to dominate us and keep us from developing our full potential."*

me his paraphrase of Psalm 27:1-2: "The Lord is my light and my radiation — whom shall I fear? The Lord is the stronghold of my life — of whom shall I be afraid? When cancer advances against me to devour my flesh, even then will I be confident."

Fear can cripple us and keep us in bondage. Some of us allow anxiety, a type of fear common in modern culture, to dominate us and keep us from developing our full potential.

In two fitting and beautiful metaphors that de-

scribe the Lord, David gave the antidote to fear: light and salvation.

Light is an appropriate symbol for truth, goodness, and joy. When the Lord is our centerpiece, His light will dispel the darkness of our fear. Amen!

The Lord also *saves us* from our enemies. When they advance and attack, the Lord will make them stumble and fall. David built a crescendo in verse 3. He asserted his freedom from fear and his overwhelming confidence.

Like Pastor Gardiner, we can face courageously whatever confronts us if we remember that the Lord has already conquered fear. Worry will disintegrate if we remember that He is our light and salvation.

Personal prayer

Lord, instead of continuing to be overcome by fear, help me to find rest in perceiving You as my Light and my Salvation.

65

Freedom

Second Variation — Freedom to Praise

Exposition of theme

PSALM 27 CONTINUED

One thing I ask of the LORD, this is what I seek: that I may dwell in the house of the LORD all the days of my life, to gaze upon the beauty of the LORD and to seek him in his temple. For in the day of trouble he will keep me safe in his dwelling; he will hide me in the shelter of his tabernacle and set me high upon a rock. Then my head will be exalted above the enemies who surround me; at his tabernacle will I sacrifice with shouts of joy; I will sing and make music to the LORD (vv. 4-6).

Development of theme

Worship is another antidote for worry. David understood that praising the Lord was the one thing that could dispel fear (v. 4). There is safety and security in the Lord's sanctuary.

Filled with love for God's house, David used five different words to describe it: house, temple,

> *"We must not let the pressure of modern life squeeze the song out of our lives. A sure way to let that happen is to sing only when we feel like it — when we're inspired. We must learn to sing in the night, when we're hurting, and when we're afraid."*

dwelling, shelter, and tabernacle. From the simple tent in the wilderness to the glory of Solomon's temple, Israel had been preoccupied with worshiping Yahweh. David did not isolate him-

self. He did not face his troubles alone. He faced trial within the context of a community of believers. God's house was his place of safety and security.

David did not visit God's house merely to observe. He got personally involved in singing and making music to the Lord. His answer to deep,

> THE LANGUAGE OF MUSIC
> ## Variations
> *Modifications of a theme.*
>
> The form — theme and variations — is an apt musical picture of unity and diversity. The Trinity is the divine metaphor.

personal fear and insecurity was to make music for God's glory.

We must not let the pressure of modern life squeeze the song out of our lives. A sure way to let that happen is to sing only when we feel like it — when we're inspired. We must learn to sing in the night, when we're hurting and when we're afraid. Getting involved, moving on with your life, being forced out of yourself are the keys to transcending personal pain. Renewal and recovery come when we praise God for His sovereign control.

Then, the joy of the Lord will come flooding in, bringing with it His serenity and safety. Isaiah says it so beautifully, "You will keep in perfect peace him whose mind is steadfast, because he trusts in you" (Isaiah 26:3).

No matter what today may bring, "I will sing and make music to the Lord" (Psalm 27:6). This is the secret of tranquility in daily life.

Personal prayer

Lord, no matter what my circumstances turn out to be today, help me to sing and make music to Your holy Name!

Freedom

Third Variation — Freedom from Rejection

Exposition of theme

PSALM 27 CONTINUED

Hear my voice when I call, O LORD; be merciful to me and answer me. My heart says of you, "Seek his face!" Your face, LORD, I will seek. Do not hide your face from me, do not turn your servant away in anger; you have been my helper. Do not reject me or forsake me, O God my Saviour. Though my mother and father forsake me, the LORD will receive me. Teach me your way, O LORD; lead me in a straight path because of my oppressors. Do not turn me over to the desires of my foes, for false witnesses rise up against me, breathing out violence (vv. 7-12).

Development of theme

To David, ultimate rejection would be to have the Lord turn His face from him. Acutely aware of the gulf between his own impurity and God's absolute holiness, David appealed to God's mercy and pleaded to be spared from rejection.

Rejection is incredibly difficult to deal with,

> *"Rejection is incredibly difficult to deal with, especially when it comes from those ordinarily close to us. But even when rejected by loved ones, we can attain intimacy because the Lord never turns His face from those who seek Him."*

especially when it comes from those ordinarily close to us, such as family members or friends. This happens to many people, and it causes all kinds of emotional and psychological pain. But even when rejected by loved ones, we can attain intimacy because the Lord never turns His face from those who seek Him.

One of the keys to successful songwriting is to be able to handle rejection. Songs are subjective; unlike numbers, lyrics and music have nuances, so there can be a wide range of opinions about the value of a particular song. Perhaps it takes more courage than talent to be a songwriter. Rejection is painful, though, especially the personal rejection in a wife-husband, parent-child relationship.

David's point here is that even when we are rejected by those who are supposed to love us, the Lord will not reject us. Someone I love may push me off a cliff, but God has suspended Himself like a net to catch me. For believers, the Lord is always our safety net.

Personal prayer

Thank You, Lord, that You have suspended a safety net beneath me. Continue to deliver me from the fear of falling.

Freedom

Fourth Variation — Freedom to be Patient

Exposition of theme

PSALM 27 CONTINUED

I am still confident of this: I will see the goodness of the LORD in the land of the living. Wait for the LORD; be strong and take heart and wait for the LORD (vv. 13-14).

Development of theme

The final thought of this magnificent psalm is a statement of faith. David had the assurance that God was worth waiting for, and he had freely placed his confidence in the goodness and fairness of the Lord. He knew that the Lord would have the last word.

Relocation can be a traumatic experience for a family. Our move from Grand Rapids, Michigan, to Nashville, Tennessee, caused us to experience many conflicting emotions — sometimes feeling uprooted, confused, or excited! I believe it is possible to do the right thing yet feel strange doing it because of inward resistance to the Lord's will. The only way to gain perspective is to wait on the Lord.

"Fear can render us ineffective and lifeless. But God gives us the answer to this phantom of the night: Himself. He is our Light and our Salvation. Therefore, we need not be dominated by fear or rejection. We are free to praise and to be patient."

Fear can render us ineffective and lifeless. But God gives us the answer to this phantom of the night: Himself. He is our Light and our Salvation. Therefore, we need not be dominated by fear or rejection. We are free to praise and to be patient. Praise brings the shining light of His presence into our lives to replace darkness. And confidence in the Lord builds patience.

Faith stands in bold contrast to fear. When we seek the Lord, He delivers us from all our fears (Psalm 34:4).

Personal prayer

Lord, help me to place my complete confidence in You and to wait for You. Give me the ability to trust in Your overwhelming goodness.

Bursting Out in Song

A Mournful Melody

Exposition of theme

PSALM 28

To you I call, O Lord my Rock; do not turn a deaf ear to me. For if you remain silent, I will be like those who have gone down to the pit. Hear my cry for mercy as I call to you for help, as I lift up my hands toward your Most Holy Place. Do not drag me away with the wicked, with those who do evil, who speak cordially with their neighbors but harbor malice in their hearts. Repay them for their deeds and for their evil work; repay them for what their hands have done and bring back upon them what they deserve (vv. 1-4).

Development of theme

Forced to look into the eye of death, David pleaded for salvation. He asked the Lord to distinguish between himself and the wicked and requested that he not face a common death with

> *"What strength there is in placing our trust in the goodness and justice of God! Focusing our faith in the Lord and His righteousness answers a myriad of unsettling philosophical questions."*

them. He prayed specifically for three things: (1) that the Lord would hear him and help him; (2) that the Lord would not identify him with hypocritical sinners; (3) that the Lord would be fair in rendering judgment.

What strength there is in placing our trust in

Melody

A succession of tones, as opposed to harmony (tones sounded simultaneously).

Musical texture is comprised of both horizontal (melodic) and vertical (harmonic) elements. A melody can soar and deeply touch our soul.

the goodness and justice of God! When Abraham prayed for Sodom, he spoke profoundly when he said, "Will not the Judge of all the earth do right?" Focusing our faith in Yahweh and His righteousness answers a myriad of unsettling philosophical questions. One of the most profound is the question of our final destiny.

Personal prayer

Lord, I praise You that I can leave my eternal destiny in Your hands. I believe in Your righteousness and justice.

69

Bursting Out in Song

A Joyful Melody

Exposition of theme

PSALM 28 CONTINUED

Since they show no regard for the works of the Lord and what his hands have done, he will tear them down and never build them up again. Praise be to the Lord, for he has heard my cry for mercy. The Lord is my strength and my shield; my heart trusts in him, and I am helped. My heart leaps for joy and I will give thanks to him in song. The Lord is the strength of his people, a fortress of salvation for his anointed one (vv. 5-8).

Development of theme

In these verses, David expressed supreme confidence that the Lord would answer his prayer and would eventually overthrow the wicked.

This confidence put David in a mood to praise the Lord. He praised the Lord for three things: (1) for hearing his prayer; (2) for being his strength and shield; (3) for being the salvation of Israel.

David made these points with increasing intensity. Like a mighty musical crescendo climaxing with cymbals crashing, he burst out in song

"There is no better way to express ardent emotion than through music. I find that when I'm overburdened with melancholia, thinking about God's goodness helps me. I like to substitute praise songs for negative thoughts."

He Satisfies My Life

As I lift my voice in praise my heart sings,
For He satisfies my life with good things.
I can't describe the joy that He brings,
For He satisfies my life with good things.

Words and music by Don Wyrtzen © 1985

and praise. His heart leaped, and he was filled with thanksgiving. Convinced that the Lord was his strength, his salvation, and his song, David worshiped the Lord in the beauty of holiness.

There is no better way to express such ardent emotion than through the art form of music. Music allowed David to express the inexpressible.

I find that when I'm overburdened with my own melancholia (feeling "down"), thinking about God's goodness helps me. I like to substitute praise songs for negative thoughts, so I wrote a little chorus, "He Satisfies My Life" to concentrate on the theme: "God is good."

Personal prayer

May joy rise in my heart so that I may burst out in songs of praise to him! (Psalm 28:7, TLB).

Bursting Out in Song

An Entreating Melody

Exposition of theme

PSALM 28 CONTINUED

Save your people and bless your inheritance; be their shepherd and carry them forever (v. 9).

Development of theme

David was much more than an average citizen. He was the prototype of the Messiah. Because of his special position, David bestowed God's grace on the people. This concept reached full maturation in Christ of the New Testament "who has blessed us in the heavenly realms with every spiritual blessing" (Ephesians 1:3).

The final verse of this psalm is a prayer that has become part of the "Te Deum," a celebrated song of praise, rejoicing, and thanksgiving. In it, David importunes God for the salvation, blessing, and sustenance of his people. Using the shepherd motif again, David asked the Lord to lift up his people and carry them forever. Isaiah used similar comforting words: "In his love and mercy he redeemed them; he lifted them up and carried them all the days of old" (Isaiah 63:9).

David started in minor but ended in major. He began in the dark but ended in the light. He went

"David started in minor but ended in major. He began in the dark but ended in the light. He went from being low in spirit to being high with joy. He moved from lamentation to praise."

JOHN E. WALVOORD

A CONTEMPORARY LYRIC

Unbounded Grace

Unbounded Grace — it reached to me
When hope was gone from view;
In my despair, Christ came to me
As He alone could do.

Grace was for me the only way
My guilt could find relief;
My destiny was changed that day
I reached out in belief.

God's grace does not on me depend —
It's God who is my Stay;
His love is offered without end,
He walks with me each day.

The universe with joy will ring
When grace has won the day;
As all creation joins to sing,
"Praise God, who paid the way!"

Words by John E. Walvord. Music by Don Wyrtzen © 1971 Singspiration

from being low in spirit to being high with joy. He moved from lamentation to praise. What an appropriate model for worship and prayer!

Like David, I want to be able to honestly pour out my soul to my heavenly Father, trusting that He will carry me. What comfort this will bring when I feel stress from the complexity of modern life!

I am trying not to take for granted God's gifts of grace in my life. Grace involves even more than His gift of salvation. So a number of years ago, John Walvoord and I wrote a contemporary version of "Amazing Grace," which we titled "Unbounded Grace."

Personal prayer

Lord, I thank and praise You for Your grace, for Your salvation, for the blessing of Your inheritance, and for shepherding me forever.

72

Majesty
His Splendor

Exposition of theme
PSALM 29

Ascribe to the Lord, O mighty ones, ascribe to the Lord glory and strength. Ascribe to the Lord the glory due his name; worship the Lord in the splendor of his holiness (vv. 1-2).

Development of theme

Our Lord's absolute holiness, transcendence, and majesty are incomprehensible and unfathomable to mere mortals. For this reason, David threw logic and analysis to the wind, and allowed the flow of Hebrew poetry to take over in Psalm 29. Reminiscent of the Song of the Sea (Exodus 15), the oracles of Balaam (Numbers 23-24),

> *"It may be that we have a more intimate relationship with God than the angels do. Angels are awestruck by the greatness of God, but they do not experience the thrill of the gospel as we do."*

and the Song of Deborah (Judges 5), this psalm lets us feel through poetry the towering majesty of the Lord.

The scene opened with angels singing themes of true worship and adoration. In them we see that declaring the greatness of God involves the total personality.

It may be true that we have a more intimate relationship with God than the angels do. Angels are awestruck by the greatness of God, but they do not experience the thrill of the gospel as we do. God took the initiative to relate to us personally through Jesus Christ. Though we are "a little

lower than the angels" in God's hierarchy, we have a unique entrée to Him.

Like the angels, I am to be filled with love and wonder at the mention of His name. I am to worship Him for the splendor of His holiness. Through meditation, prayer, music, and poetry, I can do this. And because of who God is and what He does, I will do it. A.W. Tozer called worship "the missing jewel of evangelicalism." Instead of learning about worship from religious leaders, I need to learn about it from the angels who are uninhibited and unrestrained in their praise of God.

Personal prayer
Lord, make me aware of Your holiness and transcendence and teach me how to reflect them back to You.

A GOSPEL SONG LYRIC

Holy, Holy Is What the Angels Sing

Holy, holy is what the angels sing,
And I expect to help them make the
    courts of heaven ring;
And when they sing redemption's story,
They will fold their wings
For angels never felt the joy that our
    salvation brings.

Words by Johnson Oatman Jr. Music by John R. Sweney.

Majesty

His Storm

Exposition of theme

PSALM 29 CONTINUED

The voice of the LORD is over the waters; the God of glory thunders, the LORD thunders over the mighty waters. The voice of the LORD is powerful; the voice of the LORD is majestic. The voice of the LORD breaks the cedars; the LORD breaks in pieces the cedars of Lebanon. He makes Lebanon skip like a calf, Sirion like a young wild ox. The voice of the LORD strikes with flashes of lightning. The voice of the LORD shakes the desert; the LORD shakes the Desert of Kadesh. The voice of the LORD twists the oaks and strips the forests bare. And in his temple all cry, "Glory!" (vv. 3-9).

Development of theme

The magnificence of nature reflects the power and might of God (Romans 1:20). All of nature trembles at the sound of His voice. It calmed the raging sea of Galilee and caused Jesus' disciples to exclaim, "Who is this? He commands even the winds and the water, and they obey him" (Luke 8:25). And it made everyone in the temple shout, "Glory!"

In our day, we think of man as being bigger

> *"We major in minor issues when we reduce the mystery of the Godhead to a rationalistic system, when we get wrapped up in external behaviors rather than in internal reality."*

than he is and of God as being smaller than He is. This distortion makes us lose perspective on what is important and causes us to major on minor issues. We major in minor issues when we reduce the mystery of the Godhead to a rationalistic system, when we get wrapped up in external behaviors rather than in internal reality, and when we explain Christianity in numbers rather than by an intimate relationship with the Lord. We need to hear again the voice of Almighty God as it resounds like tympani rolling, cymbals crashing, and brass bands playing fanfares—all climaxing in one eruption of praise and a mighty crescendo of glory.

Personal prayer

Lord, give me an acute awareness of Your power and might. And give me a foretaste of heaven by letting me experience some of Your glorious presence now.

Majesty

His Salvation

Exposition of theme

PSALM 29 *CONTINUED*

The Lord sits enthroned over the flood; the Lord is enthroned as King forever. The Lord gives strength to his people; the Lord blesses his people with peace (vv. 10-11).

Development of theme

The Hebrew word for *flood* (v. 10) appears just one other time in the Old Testament—in Genesis 6. Psalm 29:10 means, therefore, that our Lord has the power to unleash the violent forces of nature just as He did during Noah's flood (Genesis 6—11).

The Lord Jesus, God-Incarnate, used His voice to display supernatural power. He said to the churning sea, "Quiet! Be still!" Then the wind died down, and it was completely calm (Mark 4:39). He also used His voice to raise Lazarus from the dead, "Lazarus, come out!" And the dead man obeyed (John 11:43-44). God speaks with awesome authority and might.

Verse 11 gives us a glimpse into the future. The Lord will give, and the Lord will bless. The Lord uses His voice not for a gratuitous show of force, but as an instrument of judgment and salvation.

Franz Delitzch, a brilliant nineteenth-century Old Testament scholar, viewed the closing words "with peace" as a rainbow arching over the psalm. We can either experience the *force* of God's wrath or the *peace* of His salvation. We can choose between the awesome power He uses against His enemies or the compassionate intimacy He offers to His children.

> *"We can either experience the force of God's wrath or the peace of His salvation. We can choose between the awesome power He uses against His enemies or the compassionate intimacy He offers to His children."*

Personal prayer

Lord, I am fully aware that You are enthroned as King forever. I praise You for giving me strength, blessing, and peace.

Joy Comes in the Morning

Outburst of Praise

Exposition of theme

PSALM 30

I will exalt you, O LORD, for you lifted me out of the depths and did not let my enemies gloat over me. O LORD my God, I called to you for help and you healed me. O LORD, you brought me up from the grave, you spared me from going down into the pit. Sing to the LORD, you saints of his; praise his holy name. For his anger lasts only a moment, but his favor lasts a lifetime; weeping may remain for a night, but rejoicing comes in the morning (vv. 1-5).

Development of theme

Restoration follows confession. David wrote Psalm 30 after experiencing this glorious truth.

Perhaps the most innovative, imaginative, and creative person in Scripture, David was vulnerable to the sin of pride. To chasten David for arrogantly numbering the fighting men of Israel (1 Chronicles 21), God allowed him to be placed near death.

David was aware of the contrasts between sorrow and joy, the momentary and the eternal, the troubles that weigh little and the glory that outweighs everything (2 Corinthians 4:16-18). He praised God that His anger lasts only for a moment but that His favor lasts for a lifetime (v. 5).

David experienced momentary personal pleasure with Bathsheba (2 Samuel 11). This affair produced unalterable consequences for David, Bathsheba, and their families. Yet because David had an intimate relationship with God, he confessed his sin (Psalm 51). God responded by restoring and renewing him (Galatians 6:1).

> *"Perhaps the most innovative, imaginative, and creative person in Scripture, David was vulnerable to the sin of pride."*

What an encouragement to those who have given in to temptation and are living with the inevitable stress! The answer is confession, which leads to restoration and praise.

Personal prayer

Lord, teach me how to keep short accounts with You. Teach me also to regularly praise Your precious Name.

Joy Comes in the Morning

Outburst of Confession

Exposition of theme

PSALM 30 CONTINUED

When I felt secure, I said, "I will never be shaken." O LORD, when you favored me, you made my mountain stand firm; but when you hid your face, I was dismayed. To you, O LORD, I called; to the LORD I cried for mercy: "What gain is there in my destruction, in my going down into the pit? Will the dust praise you? Will it proclaim your faithfulness? Hear, O LORD, and be merciful to me; O LORD, be my help" (vv. 6-10).

Development of theme

David had turned from God and was leaving Him out of his life. But when God turned His face from him, David felt cold, raw fear. He saw his unfaithfulness as frailty and his carefree lifestyle as carelessness.

Reciting his psychological disintegration, his personal destruction, and his feelings of deep insecurity, David cried out for mercy. At the end of himself, David abandoned his independence, his cleverness, and all his human resources, realizing that the solidarity of his kingdom depended on God's favor, not on his own ingenuity (vv. 6-7). Knowing that he had been out of tune with God, David tightened the strings of his life through a mighty outburst of confession.

In numerous ways my inadequacy comes to the surface every day. I reveal it when I'm threatened by competition, when I'm defensive with Karen, or when I desire to simplify the mysteries of life. I'm just learning to admit my inadequacy by not denying it. I'm even learning to rejoice in it, though a bit guardedly I admit, because Paul teaches us, "When I am weak, then I am strong"

"Knowing that he had been out of tune with God, David tightened the strings of his life through a mighty outburst of confession."

(2 Corinthians 12:9-10). Dependency on the Lord is the key to security.

Without the Lord we are dust (v. 9). David's artistic and administrative genius, apart from God's special touch, were no match for the pressures and complexities already apparent in the ancient world.

Personal prayer

Lord, forgive me for leaving You out of my life, for trying to "go it alone." I confess my tendency toward self-sufficiency and now thrust myself upon You for mercy and help.

Joy Comes in the Morning

Outburst of Joy

Exposition of theme

PSALM 30 *CONTINUED*

You turned my wailing into dancing; you removed my sackcloth and clothed me with joy, that my heart may sing to you and not be silent. O LORD my God, I will give you thanks forever (vv. 11-12).

Development of theme

David's richly textured personality and artistic temperament were expressed on many emotional levels. In this psalm he was as uninhibited in his praise as when he "danced before the Lord

with all his might" (2 Samuel 6:14). David wasn't shy about expressing the intensity of his joy.

In the first movement of this psalm, David felt the exuberance of praise (vv. 1-5). In the second movement, he felt the depression of guilt over his sin (vv. 6-10). In this movement, after a moving confession, David felt the exhilaration and

> *"What colorful contrasts David experienced: wailing to dancing; sackcloths of despair to garments of joy; sounds of silence to songs of joy; independence to dependence; disintegration to integration; cynicism to caring. I also feel stark contrasts, fluctuating mood swings, and mixed motives in my life."*

freedom of forgiveness, and it culminated in an outburst of joy (vv. 11-12).

What colorful contrasts David experienced: from wailing to dancing; sackcloths of despair to garments of joy; sounds of silence to songs of joy; independence to dependence; disintegration to integration; cynicism to caring; and from needing no one to trusting God. He exchanged a growing insecurity for unshakeable confidence. No wonder he vowed to praise the Lord and to give thanks to Him forever!

I also feel stark contrasts, fluctuating mood swings, and mixed motives in my life. I've conducted some of the finest musicians in the world, but I'm often plagued by self-doubts. I deeply desire to glorify God in writing this book. But I'm also conscious of my concern about how I'm coming across to you. Even though many would consider my life to be quite *successful*, I sometimes wonder how *significant* it has been. But I'm learning to persistently praise God in the midst of it all, and every once in a while, like C.S. Lewis, I'm surprised by joy.

Personal prayer

Dear Father, may I not continue to be content with my self-centered and self-contained life. May I not eat husks when I can feast at Your banquet table.

March PSALMS 31–39

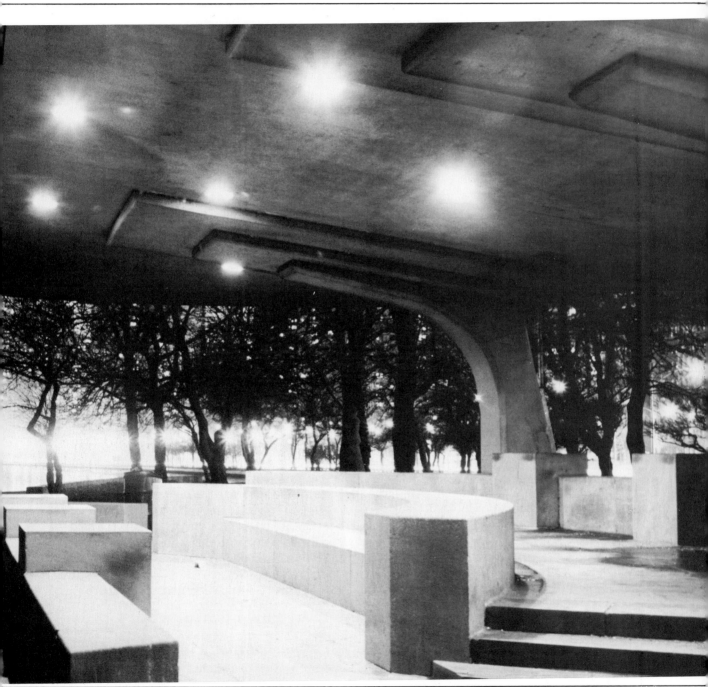

PANORAMA PHOTO BY GARY IRVING

David Faces Crisis

Rejection!

Exposition of theme

PSALM 31

Be merciful to me, O Lord, for I am in distress; my eyes grow weak with sorrow, my soul and my body with grief. . . . Because of all my enemies, I am the utter contempt of my neighbor; I am a dread to my friends — those who see me on the street flee from me. I am forgotten by them as though I were dead; I have become like broken pottery. . . . But I trust in you, O Lord; I say, "You are my God." My times are in your hands; deliver me from my enemies and from those who pursue me. . . . Love the Lord, all his saints! The Lord preserves the faithful, but the proud he pays back in full. Be strong and take heart, all you who hope in the Lord (vv. 9–24).

Development of theme

David knew what it was like to experience discouragement, despair, grief, and gloom. When he was depressed, he felt isolated and rejected. The picture he painted in Psalm 31:9–13 is black, and his use of graphic and descriptive nouns — distress, sorrow, grief, anguish, groaning, affliction, contempt, dread, and terror — helps us feel what he felt.

I'm certain that we all struggle with the pain of rejection. I feel rejected spiritually when I don't sense God's presence in my life. I feel rejected domestically when Karen and I disagree. And I

feel rejected professionally when someone doesn't like a new song I've written.

David's response to his rejection is a model for me today. Once again, he prayed and praised. After affirming his faith in the Lord and praying for deliverance from his enemies, for the shame and death of the wicked, and for his own purity, he moved again to a crescendo of praise (vv. 19–24). The first pair of verses speak eloquently of God's care for his own (vv. 19–20). The next pair personalize the message. David praised the Lord for his wonderful love and indescribable mercy (vv. 21–22).

Four brief, but powerful concepts end this psalm of crisis: Love the Lord! Be faithful! Be humble! Be strong and take heart!

Personal prayer

Lord, help me to wait for You! Help me to put my faith in what I know rather than in what I feel!

> *"Four powerful concepts end this psalm of crisis: Love the Lord! Be faithful! Be humble! Be strong and take heart!"*

Whiter Than Snow

Forgiveness

Exposition of theme

PSALM 32

Blessed is he whose transgressions are forgiven, whose sins are covered. Blessed is the man whose sin the Lord does not count against him and in whose spirit is no deceit. . . . Then I acknowledge my sin to you and did not cover up my iniquity. I said, "I will confess my transgressions to the LORD"—and you forgave the guilt of my sin (vv. 1–2, 5).

Development of theme

In the Psalter, David composed many variations on the theme of forgiveness. Psalm 32 zeroes in on the exhilarating emotional release that comes from forgiveness after confession.

David gave two reasons for personal contentment and happiness: First, we are happy (blessed) when our sins are forgiven; second, we are happy when we are counted righteous. The New Testament teaches that forgiveness and imputation of personal righteousness hinge on Christ's atonement for our sin. (David's faith prefigured Christ's sacrifice. See Romans 4:6–8.)

Like many of us, I too often choose short-term gratification over long-term benefits. My eating habits are an example. I'd rather have an ice cream cone now than be in great physical shape later. There is pleasure now but misery later when I feel guilty.

As David continued to sin, his bones wasted away but his conscience remained very much alive. He groaned all day long from the weight of God's heavy hand on him. He had all of the symptoms of guilt. But he confessed his sins, acknowledged his transgressions, and experienced complete forgiveness.

> *"David groaned all day long from the weight of God's heavy hand on him. But he confessed his sins and experienced complete forgiveness."*

Why do I sometimes continue in my sin? Why don't I listen to my conscience and follow David's example? When I face reality and acknowledge and confess my sin, I, like David, experience the exhilaration of forgiveness. I feel healthier too.

Personal prayer

Lord, wash me and I shall be whiter than snow.

Whiter Than Snow

Deliverance

Exposition of theme

PSALM 32 *CONTINUED*

Therefore let everyone who is godly pray to you while you may be found; surely when the mighty waters rise, they will not reach him. You are my hiding place; you will protect me from trouble and surround me with songs of deliverance (vv. 6–7).

Development of theme

When the mighty waters of trouble rise and I am about to go under, I can cry out, "Lord save me!" And He will. Peter also experienced deliverance in Matthew 14:28–33.

David was going through deep waters when he wrote Psalm 32. In danger of going under, he sought the Lord, and the Lord miraculously delivered him. Through this, David learned that trusting in the Lord was the only safe place to be and

---

"Music was the perfect vehicle of comfort and protection for me one day when I was flying in a small aircraft through vicious, clear-air turbulence.

---

his only real security. The Lord protected David from trouble and surrounded him "with songs of deliverance."

Music can be the perfect vehicle of comfort and protection. One day when I was flying in a small plane through vicious, clear-air turbulence, I had an anxiety attack and began hyperventilating. I started to sing to myself Joe Park's "He Holdeth Me." Then I remembered Moses' magnificent blessing, "The eternal God

is your refuge, and underneath are the everlasting arms" (Deuteronomy 33:27). As the Lord lovingly replaced my anxiety with the security of His arms, I became calm.

Saved from adversity, David composed his own songs of deliverance so that others could worship with him. How marvelous that he shared his discovery! What a motivation for me to make music that celebrates my deliverance.

Personal prayer

Lord, thank You that I am safe in You, and that You deliver me from the complex problems of life today!

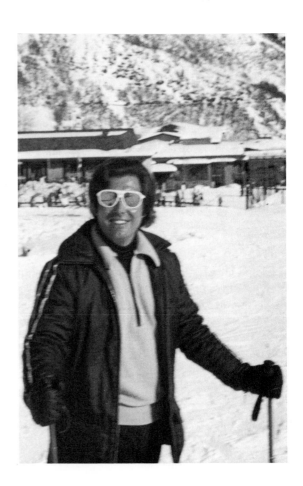

Whiter Than Snow

Joy

Exposition of theme

PSALM 32 CONTINUED

I will instruct you and teach you in the way you should go; I will counsel you and watch over you. Do not be like the horse or the mule, which have no understanding but must be controlled by bit and bridle or they will not come to you. Many are the woes of the wicked, but the LORD's unfailing love surrounds the man who trusts in him. Rejoice in the LORD and be glad, you righteous; sing, all you who are upright in heart! (vv. 8–11).

Development of theme

David progressed from sin to joy. Not only did he find exhilaration in forgiveness; he also found great joy in fellowship with the Lord. David felt God's chastening, then he experienced God's care.

Wicked people, because they don't understand or obey the truth, are like horses and mules; they can be controlled only by uncomfort-

> *"What a promise for us as we face life's day-to-day stresses. What a reason for celebration, singing, and joy!"*

able bits and bridles. Consequently, they experience many woes. In contrast, the righteous are surrounded by the Lord's unfailing truth and love. The Lord promises to instruct, counsel, and watch over us, which will keep us out of trouble. But we must depend on Him for guidance, which requires an intimate relationship with Him.

What a promise for us as we face life's day-to-

day stresses! What a reason for celebration, singing, and joy! The Lord's truth leads to personal freedom. And that freedom results in a deep sense of joy.

Personal prayer

Heavenly Father, I praise You for counseling me and watching over me. When I contemplate Your unfailing love, my heart is filled with joy and I want to make music.

A WONDERFUL OLD HYMN

Whiter Than Snow

Lord Jesus, I long to be perfectly whole,
I want You forever to live in my soul;
Break down every idol, cast out every
    foe —
Now wash me and I shall be whiter than
    snow.

Lord Jesus, for this I most humbly entreat,
I wait, blessed Lord, at Your crucified
    feet;
By faith, for my cleansing I see Your flood
    flow —
Now wash me and I shall be whiter than
    snow.

Lord Jesus, before You I patiently wait,
Come now and within me a new heart
    create;
To those who have sought You, You never
    said "No" —
Now wash me and I shall be whiter than
    snow.

Words by James Nicholson. Music by William G. Fisher

Hymn of Praise

Beauty

Exposition of theme

PSALM 33

Sing joyfully to the LORD, you righteous; it is fitting for the upright to praise him. Praise the LORD with the harp; make music to him on the ten-stringed lyre. Sing to him a new song; play skillfully, and shout for joy (vv. 1–3).

Development of theme

The psalmist starts this magnificent hymn of praise with a plea for music-making executed with excellence. The Lord wants to hear a *new* song, and He wants to hear it played *skillfully*. He despises frozen forms and sacred clichés because rituals lose their meaning and traditions turn stale.

Having reviewed hundreds of unsolicited music manuscripts, I can honestly say that most of them are imitative and derivative rather than truly creative and innovative. The Lord is unimpressed with echoes; He rewards uniqueness.

The very nature of music is to change—and

> *"Genuine art reflects the Lord's beauty and skill, so sincerity alone is never enough. The Lord wants freshness and good technique as well as fervor."*

true artists, by definition, grow steadily, change constantly, and create regularly. By doing so, they remain contemporary and relevant. Genuine art reflects the Lord's beauty and skill, so sincerity alone is never enough. The Lord wants

freshness and good technique as well as fervor.

When I sing a new song, play my instrument with skill, and shout for joy, the Lord will lift me out of my own small, circumscribed world, and I will join all true believers and heaven's angels in sacred song!

Praising God through artistic expression enhances my inner beauty the way a diamond tiara enhances the outward beauty of a lovely woman.

Personal prayer

Dear Lord, may I use my voice and my instrument to bring glory to Your Name today.

Hymn of Praise

Truth

Exposition of theme

PSALM 33 CONTINUED

Let all the earth fear the LORD; let all the people of the world revere him. For he spoke, and it came to be; he commanded, and it stood firm (vv. 8–9).

Development of theme

I find profound personal comfort in order and design. I observe it in nature when I drive up the Maine coast and when I scan a symphonic score by Mozart. Even though I admire the sensitivity of modern existentialists and can empathize with their despair — like the sweet psalmist of Israel, I find security in knowing that God has a specific plan for the universe — and one for my life too.

I cannot begin to understand the truth of God's power, but I see it in the wonder of creation and in the creative acts of history. Only the plans of the Lord are sure. They stand firm through all generations. The geopolitical manipulations of earth's rulers succeed or fail according to God's overarching plan. Nebuchadnezzar, Darius, Alexander the Great, Caesar, Napoleon, Hitler — all were mere instrumentalists contributing to God's score for the universe. The Lord is the Master Orchestrator of history.

The awesome truth of God's creative power stretches far beyond my imagination. God spoke and worlds came into being. And if He chose to do so, He could gather the majestic sea into a jar. The Lord's hallmark is faithfulness, and His Word is Truth. The only rational response is respectful fear and reverence.

Personal prayer

I praise you, Lord, for Your powerful Word. Thank You for using it to create the universe and to act in history.

> *"Only the plans of the Lord are sure. He is the Master Orchestrator of history."*

Hymn of Praise

Love

Exposition of theme

PSALM 33 *CONTINUED*

The Lord loves righteousness and justice; the earth is full of his unfailing love. . . .
But the eyes of the Lord are on those who fear him, on those whose hope is in his unfailing love (vv. 5, 18).

Development of theme

God not only sees all people and everything they do from His exalted position in the heavens, He also sees their inward thoughts and motives. No one can hide from Him! When God sees reliance upon self, rather than on Him, He withholds His reward. The use of huge armies, great personal strength, and the latest technology will lead to death, not victory.

The only hope for the arrogant and autonomous is for them to place their trust in the Lord, who watches over those who fear Him, and to place their hope in His love.

"If I place my confidence in my own cleverness, energy, charm, or other human resources, I will fail."

The Lord doesn't really need articulate people, as Joseph proved before Pharoah. The Lord doesn't really need strong people, as the young shepherd boy David proved before Goliath. And the Lord doesn't really need brilliant people. Paul tells us that God chooses "the foolish things of this world to shame the wise" (1 Corinthians 1:27).

If I place my confidence in my own cleverness, energy, charm, or other human resources, I will fail. Real inner strength to meet the challenges of my life will come only when I give the Lord reverence and when I trust totally in His unfailing love of righteousness.

Personal prayer

I praise You, Lord, that Your love for justice and righteousness will finally win and that I don't have to harbor bitterness and resentment over today's injustices.

Hymn of Praise

Holiness

Exposition of theme

PSALM 33 CONTINUED

We wait in hope for the LORD; he is our help and our shield. In him our hearts rejoice, for we trust in his holy name. May your unfailing love rest upon us, LORD, even as we put our hope in you (vv. 20–22).

Development of theme

The psalmist concluded this majestic hymn of praise by leading his congregation in asserting their faith in the holiness of the Lord!

They asserted their faith by waiting in hope for the Lord (v. 20), by rejoicing in Him (v. 21), and by praying for the Lord's loyal love (v. 22). Their finale is a promise that they have placed all of their hope in the Lord.

> *"Even a tiny glimpse of God's holiness can result in uninhibited praise and worship."*

Wait, rejoice, petition—what a paradigm for personal praise! Praise must be the top priority in our lives.

When Isaiah saw the Lord face-to-face, he trembled in fear because of his sins. In Isaiah 6, we can only imagine the utter majesty and glory of the Lord, which Isaiah saw. But even *this* tiny glimpse of God's holiness (Psalm 33) can result in our own trembling and sometimes terror; sometimes, in uninhibited praise and worship. "Through Jesus, therefore, let us continually offer to God a sacrifice of praise—the fruit of lips that confess his name" (Hebrews 13:15).

Personal prayer

Lord, I praise You for filling my heart with joy because I have trusted in Your holy Name.

Song of Exaltation
Extolling the Lord

Exposition of theme

PSALM 34

I will extol the LORD at all times; his praise will always be on my lips. My soul will boast in the LORD; let the afflicted hear and rejoice. Glorify the LORD with me; let us exalt his name together (vv. 1–3).

Development of theme

David knew how to praise the Lord. The rich texture of his highly sensitive personality made exaltation the focus of his life. As my mentor, he teaches me three facets of worship.

First, I am to extol the Lord. Praising Him must become second nature to me, part of the daily rhythm of my life. Praise must be an inner voice of worship, not a lifeless liturgy.

How do I do this? Sometimes, I paraphrase Scripture when I write poetry about the Lord and compose songs for His glory. I call upon His name in prayer and sing songs of praise to Him. No matter where I am, I try to glorify His name in simple, practical ways.

Second, I am to boast in the Lord. At dinner parties and other social occasions, my conversation must be dominated by stories of the great things God has done for me, not by what I have done for myself. Discussions about who I know, where I have been, and what I have done reveal my insecurity. Only by putting the spotlight on

> *"Discussions about who I know, where I have been, and what I have done reveal my insecurity."*

A CONTEMPORARY LYRIC

We Will Glorify

We will glorify the King of Kings,
We will glorify the Lamb,
We will glorify the Lord of Lord,
Who is the great I Am.

Lord Jehovah reigns in majesty,
We will bow before His throne,
We will worship Him in righteousness,
We will worship Him alone.

He is Lord of heaven, Lord of earth,
He is Lord of all who live,
He is Lord above the universe —
All praise to Him we give.

O hallelujah to the King of Kings,
Hallelujah to the Lamb,
Hallelujah to the Lord of Lords,
Who is the great I Am!

Words and Music by Twila Paris. © 1982 Singspiration

the Lord and focusing on Him will I find true security.

Third, I am to glorify the Lord. As C.S. Lewis observed, "to glorify is to enjoy." Ironically, the overstimulation of modern life leads to boredom. I need to move away from the emptiness the world offers to find the fulfillment of the Lord. Enjoying the Lord in the company of my brothers and sisters in Christ enhances this joy.

Personal prayer

Dear Lord, I extol You, I boast in You, and I glorify You. In Your precious Name, Amen!

Song of Exaltation

Seeking the Lord

Exposition of theme

PSALM 34 CONTINUED

I sought the LORD, and he answered me; he delivered me from all my fears. Those who look to him are radiant; their faces are never covered with shame. This poor man called, and the LORD heard him; he saved him out of all his troubles. The angel of the LORD encamps around those who fear him, and he delivers them (vv. 4–7).

Development of theme

The elusive monster of fear lurks in the shadows waiting to claw my soul to shreds. As one prone to melancholia, I see its ugly face often: when I'm struggling with the emotional stress of a difficult relationship, when I'm afraid failure is just around the corner, when success seems too hard to handle, and on days when free-floating anxiety is getting the best of me.

Ironically, the Lord delivers from fear all those who fear Him. So when I am afraid, I need to seek the Lord, who will hear me and save me from all my troubles.

Furthermore, the Lord promises me radiance. I can hold my head high and look straight ahead because He has covered my shame. Forgiveness leads to transparency, and transparency to intimacy. And, as if that were not enough, He gives me inner beauty that is reflected in outer radiance. Praise His holy Name!

Personal prayer

I praise You, Lord, for replacing fear and trouble with peace and radiance.

"The Lord replaces fear and trouble with peace and radiance."

Song of Exaltation

Tasting the Lord's Goodness

Exposition of theme

PSALM 34 CONTINUED

Taste and see that the LORD is good; blessed is the man who takes refuge in him. Fear the LORD, you his saints, for those who fear him lack nothing. The lions may grow weak and hungry, but those who seek the LORD lack no good thing (vv. 8–10).

Development of theme

Many who believe they have "tasted the Lord" have only a superficial knowledge of Him. They say they have tried Him, think they know all about Him, and claim they have been disappointed in Him. But "tasting the Lord" involves more than a casual glance, a brief encounter, or a simple, memorized formula. To taste the Lord, I need to embrace Him, to relate to Him with my whole being!

I need also to fear the Lord. To do this, I must concentrate on Him, not on myself. Narcissism

> *"Even the king of the jungle grows weak from hunger. But the one who seeks the Lord lacks no good thing."*

subtly kills spiritual intimacy. Because I am very sensitive, I tend to be neurotic. Instead of looking outside myself and to the Lord, I tend to turn inward, which leads to despair. I would do better to focus less on self, serve others, and trust the Lord more. When I respect Him as I should, I will lack nothing.

Even the king of the jungle grows weak from hunger. But the one who seeks the Lord lacks no good thing. Those who have the Lord have no need for anything else, for He alone is complete. As a result, the anxiety I feel about competitiveness will dissolve. And my struggles for power and prestige will be replaced by knowing intimately the One who holds all power and deserves all prestige.

Personal prayer

Help me to taste and see Your goodness, Lord. Help me to find all the power and prestige I need in my relationship with You.

MARCH 12

Song of Exaltation
Fearing the Lord

Exposition of theme
PSALM 34 CONTINUED

Come, my children, listen to me; I will teach you the fear of the LORD. Whoever of you loves life and desires to see many good days, keep your tongue from evil and your lips from speaking lies. Turn from evil and do good; seek peace and pursue it (vv. 11–14).

Development of theme

I am to reject the lie that there is fulfillment outside the will of God. Reverence for the Lord is the only way to personal enrichment. From David, I learn that two big changes will occur in my life when I reverence God.

First, I will speak the truth. Deception comes easily and naturally for me. I never had to learn

> *"When I reverence God, the fringe benefits will be personal fulfillment and spiritual enrichment."*

to lie. When I was a kid, I remember calling the operator just to say something rude and brash to her. When she called back, my Dad answered the phone. He asked me if I had made the call. I lied. Even though it was easy to lie, deceiving my Dad wasn't wise. As David says, if I commit myself to speaking the truth, I will have many good days and a long life.

Second, I will do good and pursue peace. The fringe benefits will be personal fulfillment and spiritual enrichment because my goals and behavior will be in harmony with the will of God.

Personal prayer

Lord, teach me to speak the truth and to turn from evil. I can't do it on my own, so empower me, that I may experience the fulfillment that comes from doing Your will.

93

Song of Exaltation

Crying out to the Lord

Exposition of theme

PSALM 34 CONTINUED

The eyes of the LORD are on the righteous and his ears are attentive to their cry; the face of the LORD is against those who do evil, to cut off the memory of them from the earth. The righteous cry out, and the LORD hears them; he delivers them from all their troubles. The LORD is close to the broken-hearted and saves those who are crushed in spirit (vv. 15–18).

Development of theme

A certain comfort comes from crying, and there is virtue in ventilation. Before I can really praise the Lord, I must lament honestly and deeply. I must be vulnerable enough to let my wife and children see me cry because genuine spirituality begins with honesty about my own feelings. Not long ago as Karen, Kathy, D.J., and I prayed for a bereaved family, I cried. I was so overcome

> *"I must be vulnerable enough to let my wife and children see me cry because genuine spirituality begins with honesty about my own feelings."*

with sadness for this good friend, I lost control in the middle of the prayer. I felt embarrassed and uncomfortable because I like to be in control. But crying was the best and most natural thing for me to do in order to give God complete control. I must remember that I do not live in exile, estranged from God, where there is darkness and no hope.

Though not denying the reality of sin, pain,

suffering, and death, I need to embrace the greater reality—that the Lord is Victor over these. He has conquered the negatives of my life. He is my Savior and Deliverer. When I begin to see this, laborious lament is transformed into uproarious praise.

Personal prayer

Thank You, Lord, that You are close to the brokenhearted and that You save those who are crushed in spirit.

MARCH 14

Song of Exaltation

Finding Safety in the Lord

Exposition of theme

PSALM 34 CONTINUED

A righteous man may have many troubles, but the LORD delivers him from them all; he protects all his bones, not one of them will be broken. Evil will slay the wicked; the foes of the righteous will be condemned. The Lord redeems his servants; no one will be condemned who takes refuge in him (vv. 19–22).

Development of theme

This promise was fulfilled beautifully after Jesus' death. Following Roman custom, the two condemned malefactors were removed from their crosses after having had their legs broken. But when they came to Jesus, "they did not break his legs" (John 19:33).

The Lord not only cares about me psychologically but physically as well. My psyche and my body reflect His image.

The Lord kept me safe on a particularly dangerous, icy road when I was in college. As I crested the hill, I saw two other cars had already collided at the bottom. Naturally I braked hard,

which was enough to propel me down the hill faster into the other two cars. Although I was badly shaken, no one was hurt. The Lord protected and delivered me that day.

David here vividly contrasts the wicked and the righteous. The wicked are slain by evil, but foes of the righteous are condemned. The Lord redeems His own. No one who finds refuge in the Lord is condemned. As a righteous person, I

> *"Although I was badly shaken, no one was hurt. The Lord protected and delivered me that day."*

may have many troubles, but the Lord will deliver me from all of them.

This great worship anthem, "Song of Exaltation," gives six specific steps toward personal fulfillment. I am to *extol* the Lord; *seek* the Lord; *taste* the goodness of the Lord; *fear* the Lord; *cry out* to the Lord, and *find safety* in the Lord. The key is in the object—the Lord! Faith in any person other than the Lord is foolishness.

Personal prayer

Lord, I praise You that no matter what my external circumstances will ever be, I am safe in Your care!

Limited Perspective

Impatience with God — First Movement

Exposition of theme

PSALM 35

May those who seek my life be disgraced and put to shame; may those who plot my ruin be turned back in dismay. . . . Then my soul will rejoice in the LORD and delight in his salvation. My whole being will exclaim, "Who is like you, O LORD? You rescue the poor from those too strong for them, the poor and needy from those who rob them" (vv. 4, 9–10).

Development of theme

David was impatient. The Lord, it seemed, was not listening to his prayers. While his enemies plotted against him, David tried to come to grips with God's seeming silence. The striking contrasts of his poetry reflect the ups and downs of his life.

David was being hassled and harassed, but his real problem was his limited perspective. One of the key issues in life is time. When we get

> *"How much time do I have left?*
> *Is what I'm doing important?*
> *Have I accomplished anything*
> *significant in my life?"*

preoccupied with "now," we lose perspective. When we get hung-up on the present, we lose sight of the future.

I'm in mid-life now. At times I become overly concerned about time. How much do I have left? Is what I'm doing important? Have I accomplished anything significant in my life? Since only God sees the big picture, we need to place complete trust in His will. His plan encompasses the whole universe, but it also includes me in detail as an individual.

Personal prayer

Dear Father, forgive me for being angry and impatient with You. Help me to place my complete faith in You and Your plan.

MARCH 16

Limited Perspective

Impatience with God — Second Movement

Exposition of theme

PSALM 35 CONTINUED

Yet when they were ill, I put on sackcloth and humbled myself with fasting. When my prayers returned to me unanswered, I went about mourning as though for my friend or brother. I bowed my head in grief as though weeping for my mother. I will give you thanks in the great assembly; among throngs of people I will praise you (vv. 13–14, 18).

Development of theme

The Lord had not yet answered David's prayer. Ruthless witnesses accused him. When he stumbled, they attacked maliciously. When he faltered, they gathered in glee. David had every human reason to get angry at God, but he responded by praising and thanking Him.

David went public with his confession. He worshiped in the company of believers, shared the reality of his plight, and told of his decision to trust God no matter what. His brothers and sisters participated in both his pain and his praise.

How often we hide when we are hurting! How often we pretend all is well when everything is falling apart! How often we try to maintain an image of stability when the foundation of our lives is crumbling! What emotional energy we waste building facades!

I come from a background that rewards performance. Consequently, even when my world seems to be falling apart around me, "the show" goes on. Even when I'm despondent and on the emotional brink, I still try to play or speak. But I'm learning to open-up to a few trusted friends. I'm gradually learning that being vulnerable is how we share our lives and our love.

David shared honestly and candidly. He wasn't afraid to cry in front of his family, and that was one of the secrets behind his powerful praise.

Personal prayer

Dear Father, I praise and thank You. I know You will answer my prayers in Your perfect time.

> *"I'm learning to open-up to a few trusted friends. I'm gradually learning that being vulnerable is how we share our lives and our love."*

Limited Perspective

Impatience with God — Third Movement

Exposition of theme

PSALM 35 *CONTINUED*

*Vindicate me in your righteousness, O L*ORD *my God; do not let them gloat over me. . . . May those who delight in my vindication shout for joy and gladness; may they always say, "The L*ORD *be exalted, who delights in the well-being of his servant." My tongue will speak of your righteousness and of your praises all day long (vv. 24, 27–28).*

Development of theme

Still grappling with the silence and distance of the Lord, David longed for vindication. He

---

> *"I am just beginning to pray when I'm sad, to give thanks when I'm grateful, and to praise God when I'm experiencing pain."*

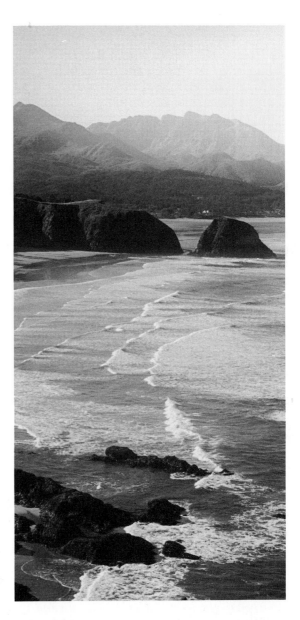

wanted to see his enemies defeated, disgraced, and put to confusion.

But instead of letting his sorrow get him down, David lifted up praise to the Lord. Though still concerned for his own acquittal, he concentrated on worship! And when he praised, his ambivalence melted away. I am just beginning to pray when I'm sad, to give thanks when I'm sorrowful or suffering, and to praise God when I'm experiencing pain. After praise and worship, David had a small problem and a big concept of God, instead of a big problem and a small concept of God.

Praise always brings with it a proper perspective, one that is unlimited.

Personal prayer

Lord, may my tongue speak of Your righteousness and Your praises all day long.

A Musical Play

Act One: Portrait of Wickedness

Exposition of theme

PSALM 36

An oracle is within my heart concerning the sinfulness of the wicked: There is no fear of God before his eyes (v. 1).

Development of theme

In this surprising oracle, David defined the wicked as those who lack the fear of God. In contrast to the righteous, who recognize their sin and fear God, the wicked flatter themselves too much to detect or hate their sin.

Their self-delusion and recklessness affects their communication, and they are deceitful. Even at night they plot evil schemes and sinful courses of action. They completely lack spiritual values. Their thoughts, wills, and feelings are all

> *"The thoughts, wills, and feelings of the wicked are corrupt. This interior rottenness leads to corrupt behavior."*

corrupt, and this interior rottenness leads to corrupt behavior.

I think of pornographers that exploit women and children for money and power. Of drug runners who pander to the needs of addicts. And of abusers of all types who use their strength to dominate innocent victims.

Apart from God, man is powerless to help himself. He doesn't even know he needs help. Wallowing in his own corruption, he desperately needs God's love and righteousness, but he doesn't know it.

Personal prayer

O God, I thank You that because of Your grace, I don't need to wallow in wickedness.

The Love of God

Could we with ink the ocean fill
And were the skies of parchment made.
Were every stalk on earth a quill.
And every man a scribe by trade.

To write the love of God above
Would drain the ocean dry,
Nor could the scroll contain the whole
Tho stretched from sky to sky.

Love Was When

Love was when God became a man
Locked in time and space
    without rank or place;
Love was God born of Jewish kin,
Just a carpenter with some fishermen.

Love was when Jesus walked in history—
Lovingly He brought a new life that's free;
Love was God nailed to bleed and die
To reach and love one such as I.

MARCH 19

A Musical Play

Act Two: Paradigm of Righteousness

Exposition of theme

PSALM 36 CONTINUED

Your love, O LORD, reaches to the heavens, your faithfulness to the skies. Your righteousness is like the mighty mountains, your justice like the great deep. O LORD, you preserve both man and beast (vv. 5–6).

Development of theme

When words are inadequate to define the love of

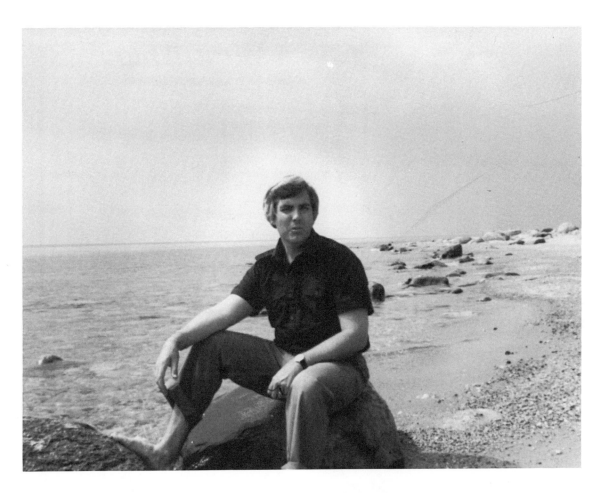

God, the music of poetry helps me express it. So do analogies. David used word pictures of finite things — the heavens, skies, mountains, and seas — to explain infinite things — love, faithfulness, righteousness, and justice. This description of the indescribable is more accurate than simple words could ever be.

Poets and lyricists revel in the use of vivid word pictures. An excellent example is Frederick Lehman's exquisite lyric, "The Love of God."

After describing God's unsearachable, inexhaustible, and unfathomable love, David becomes more intimate. He tells of the pricelessness of God's unfailing love and affirms that all men, whatever their station in life, can find security, "refuge in the shadow of your wings"; sustenance, "feast on the abundance of your house"; and satisfaction, "drink from your river of delights." He is the Fountain of life, the Source of all light and joy.

What cause for rejoicing and singing today! What themes to inspire magnificent music-making!

Personal prayer

O Lord, help me to feast at Your table and drink from Your fountain that I may be filled with eternal joy.

A Musical Play

Act Three: Prayer of Confidence

Exposition of theme

PSALM 36 CONTINUED

Continue your love to those who know you, your righteousness to the upright in heart (v. 10).

Development of theme

Overwhelmed by the stark contrast between human depravity and divine grace, David was driven to prayer. He pleaded for God's continued love and righteousness and for protection from arrogant and wicked men. Then he painted a word picture of the final doom of evil doers who lay fallen, thrown down, and unable to rise.

Ready to fight wickedness (Act One) and to embrace God's grace (Act Two), David get's caught up in urgent prayer (Act Three).

What are the lessons for me today? My life should be totally different from the person who has "no fear of God before his eyes." I don't want to be flippant about the holiness of God, casual about the grace of God, or unduly wise about evil. As Vance Havner so aptly said, "I don't want to be guilty of playing marbles with diamonds."

My life should be a paradigm of God's righteousness because my personality is being radically transformed by God's grace. Therefore, I can join David in this timeless prayer of confidence.

Personal prayer

O Lord, make me a paradigm of Your righteousness. May Your grace transform my life today.

> "I don't want to be flippant about the holiness of God, casual about the grace of God, or unduly wise about evil."

Harmonic Progressions

Harmony in Wisdom

Exposition of theme

PSALM 37

Trust in the LORD and do good; dwell in the land and enjoy safe pasture. Delight yourself in the LORD and he will give you the desires of your heart. Commit your way to the LORD; trust in him and he will do this: he will make your righteousness shine like the dawn, the justice of your cause like the noonday sun. Be still before the LORD and wait patiently for him; do not fret when men succeed in their ways, when they carry out their wicked schemes. Refrain from anger and turn from wrath; do not fret — it leads only to evil (vv. 3–8).

Development of theme

Jesus said, "Blessed are the meek, for they will inherit the earth" (Matthew 5:5). David taught the same truth in this psalm: "But the meek will inherit the land and enjoy great peace"(v. 11). The person who follows David's instruction will be wise.

> *"Those who follow these five imperatives will experience a deep peace and inner serenity."*

Like the flowers of the field, the wicked are only temporary; they eventually wither and die. Therefore, we are not to get upset over them. Instead, we are to concentrate on doing good, and David gives five steps to personal peace, wisdom, and tranquility:

First, we are "to trust in the Lord and do good."

When we do this, we will experience deep inner security.

Second, we are "to delight in the Lord." When we do, a spiritual metamorphosis takes place and His desires become ours.

Third, we are "to commit our way to the Lord." The Hebrew word for commit is *roll*— as though getting rid of a burden. We are to entrust our lives to our Lord's care.

THE LANGUAGE OF MUSIC

Harmony

Tones sounded simultaneously as opposed to melody which is a succession of tones.

Harmony can be either consonant (pleasant sounding) or dissonant (unpleasant sounding). "How good and pleasant it is when brothers live together in unity" (harmony) Psalm 133:1.

Fourth, we are "to be still before the Lord." We are to wait patiently for the Lord to work out His plans and not be impressed with the success of others.

Fifth, we are "to refrain from anger." We are to resist anger by turning away from it.

Those of us who follow these five imperatives will experience a deep peace and inner serenity, but not a total absence of upheaval in our personal lives. David teaches us that the storms of life are only on the surface; underneath is the calm of His security and strength. Those who obey the Lord will resist self-assertion and be following the path of patient faith. How do I know for sure? The Lord promises that they will inherit the earth and enjoy great peace.

Personal prayer

Dear Lord, I praise You for Your promise of deep personal security. Help me not to continue to search for it elsewhere.

Harmonic Progressions

Dissonance in Wickedness

Exposition of theme

PSALM 37 *CONTINUED*

Better the little that the righteous have than the wealth of many wicked; for the power of the wicked will be broken, but the LORD upholds the righteous (vv. 16–17).

Development of theme

Wise people are righteous; foolish people are wicked. They stand in bold contrast to each other in this psalm. David described the wicked vividly. They plot against the righteous. They attack by drawing the sword and bending the bow. They slay poor, needy, and righteous people. They are violent and hostile.

The Lord, however, will have the last word. He will laugh at the wicked. He knows their day is coming. He turns their own weapons against

---

"In the long run, it pays to serve the Lord and to live righteously. Personal fulfillment is a fringe benefit."

---

them. He breaks their power and renders their wealth useless. He predicts their final denouement. Like the flowers of the field, they will vanish and disappear. The righteous, on the other hand, will be upheld. Their inheritance will endure forever. Even in days of famine, they will enjoy plenty.

Though the wicked often prosper while the righteous suffer, in the end God will uphold His justice. He will destroy the wicked and bless the

righteous. In the long run, it pays to serve the Lord and to live righteously. Personal fulfillment is a fringe benefit.

Personal prayer

I praise You, Lord, for Your power and justice. I thank You that You will eternally reward personal righteousness.

Harmonic Progressions

Consonance in Righteousness

Exposition of theme

PSALM 37 *CONTINUED*

I was young and now I am old, yet I have never seen the righteous forsaken or their children begging bread. They are always generous and lend freely; their children will be blessed. . . . The mouth of the righteous man utters wisdom, and his tongue speaks what is just. The law of his God is in his heart; his feet do not slip (vv. 25–26, 30–31).

Development of theme

Would I like to give generously, experience the Lord's blessing, and look forward to an eternal inheritance? Would I like stability and steadiness in my personal life?

What would it be like to be blessed physically, materially, and to have inner security? Is it possible that I could speak wisdom, proclaim justice, and generally integrate God's truth into my personality? Could I ever be the focus of the Lord's delight? Because God's Word is my reference point for the nature of reality, the more I absorb

> *"Because God's Word is my reference point, the more I absorb and obey it, the more I fulfill my destiny."*

and obey it, the more I fulfill my destiny. Then I can become an accomplished, complete person.

These are the blessings and benefits the Lord gives to the righteous, to those who fill their hearts with the law of God. Their "feet do not slip."

What promises! My security and wealth don't lie in uncertain riches but in the Lord Himself. Therefore, I'm able to give and lend constantly, and I can be a lasting blessing to society through the family that I lead. What a comfort to know that even though I experience ups and downs, the Lord's hand holds me steady! The Lord Himself establishes my steps and delights in my way. He makes harmony out of my life.

Personal prayer

Lord, fill my heart with Your law so that my feet will not slip.

Harmonic Progressions

*Finale: Interplay Between
Harmony and Disharmony*

Exposition of theme

PSALM 37 CONTINUED

I have seen a wicked and ruthless man flourishing like a green tree in its native soil, but he soon passed away and was no more; though I looked for him, he could not be found. . . . The salvation of the righteous comes for the LORD; he is their stronghold in time of trouble. The LORD helps them and delivers them; He delivers them from the wicked and saves them, because they take refuge in him (vv. 35–36, 39–40).

Development of theme

In tying up the loose ends of this moving psalm, David lets us see the final end of the wicked and righteous person. The last verses are a moving finale, an exciting interplay between harmony and disharmony.

The wicked lie in wait for the righteous, but the Lord renders them impotent. The metaphor used to picture the wicked, ruthless man is a flourishing green tree. But that tree soon withers, dies, falls down, and rots. It vanishes without a trace.

Hitler, architect and Führer of Germany's Third Reich, became a broken man. On April 30, 1945 in a bomb shelter of the Chancellery, Hitler and his wife, Eva Braun, swallowed poison. Aides burned their bodies with gasoline.

In bold contrast, the righteous are exalted. They possess the land. They have a glorious future because their salvation comes from the Lord. The Lord helps them, protects them, and delivers them in times of trouble. He is their shelter and their refuge.

This uplifting psalm ends with peace, serenity,

> *"The wicked man withers, dies, falls down, and rots. He vanishes without a trace."*

and calm objectivity—a totally different mood from the fretful impatience and anxiety David expresses at the beginning of this psalm.

Personal prayer

Lord, I live in a frantic society and experience stress and pressure. Be my refuge and shelter.

106

Dirge of Discouragement

Guilt

Exposition of theme
PSALM 38

O LORD, do not rebuke me in your anger or discipline me in your wrath. For your arrows have pierced me, and your hand has come down upon me. Because of your wrath there is no health in my body; my bones have no soundness because of my sin. My guilt has overwhelmed me like a burden too heavy to bear (vv. 1–4).

Development of theme

Our heavenly Father is very attentive. He disciplines the children He loves (Proverbs 3:11–12). David was experiencing the profound, searing devastation of internal guilt. It gnawed away at him.

Since he feared God's anger and wrath, David cried out for mercy. Emotional tension erupted into physical illness because his guilt was so overwhelming.

> *"We must never assume that all sickness is punishment. But here we have a clear-cut case of illness resulting from sin."*

We must never assume that all sickness is a punishment, although I believe that sometimes physical illness is directly related to guilt over irresponsible behavior. Here we have a clear-cut case of illness resulting from sin. David said, "My wounds fester and are loathsome because of my sinful folly." He was paying the wages of sin with mental anguish and physical agony.

What is the bottom line of sinful behavior? David said, "I am feeble and utterly crushed. I groan in anguish of heart." Authentic lament almost always precedes genuine praise. I admire David's honesty. His life throbbed with reality and authenticity.

Personal prayer

I thank You, Lord, for giving me a sensitive conscience that serves as a spiritual gyroscope for my life.

Dirge of Discouragement

Isolation

Exposition of theme
PSALM 38 *CONTINUED*

All my longings lie open before you, O LORD; my sighing is not hidden from you. My heart pounds, my strength fails me; even the light has gone from my eyes. My friends and companions avoid me because of my wounds; my neighbors stay far away (vv. 9–11).

Development of theme

The more David needed the support of friends, the less attention he received from them because of his abnormality. He was caught in the same vicious cycle many of us find ourselves in. Sin has led to guilt; guilt has led to emotional and physical illness, illness has led to suffering and pain, and pain has led to isolation and loneliness. David was like a modern-day AIDS victim. He said, "My friends and companions avoid me

> "David was like a modern-day AIDS victim. He felt the effects of alienation. He was lonely and despondent—at a point where only the Lord could meet his incredible need."

because of my wounds; my neighbors stay far away" (38:11).

David felt the effects of alienation. Estranged from his heavenly Father as well as his community of friends, David—like many of us—was lonely and despondent. He was at a point where only the Lord could meet his incredible need. He was ready and open for a deep work of God in his life.

Personal prayer

I cry to You, Lord, out of my deep loneliness and despair. Please come to me, minister to me, and fully meet my need!

MARCH 27

Dirge of Discouragement

Patience

Exposition of theme

PSALM 38 CONTINUED

I wait for you, O LORD; you will answer, O LORD my God. For I said, "Do not let them gloat or exalt themselves over me when my foot slips" (vv. 15–16).

Development of theme

Despite David's instability and anxiety, he was able to wait on God. Though mired in a morass of sin, guilt, and suffering, he still exercised faith.

David faced his sin squarely and confessed his iniquity. His sensitivity to the inner voice of God's Spirit had not been seared, and he did not have a jaded conscience. Once Karen and I attended a bullfight in Mexico City. We were in a large stadium surrounded by thousands of very excited Latin people. We watched as the first bull was manipulated by the matador with his banderillas. In time, the bull was outmaneuvered and killed. Seeing blood flow the first time made

---

AN APT HYMN

Come Thou Fount

O to grace how great a debtor
Daily, I'm constrained to be!
Let Thy goodness like a fetter
Bind my wandering heart to Thee.
Prone to wander—Lord, I feel it—
Prone to leave the God I love.
Here's my heart—O take and seal it,
Seal it for Thy courts above.

Words by Robert Robinson. Music by John Wyeth.

> "Guilt is tacit evidence for the holiness of God, the absolute standard by which all ethics and values are measured."

us queasy. But after seeing ten bulls killed in a similar way, we weren't as queasy. I believe we can become anesthetized to sin in much the same way. David wasn't like this. He was still deeply troubled by his sin and was beyond making excuses or rationalizations for it.

All of this is testimony to the fact that David was God's child. Heathen people are not profoundly troubled by their sin. The fact that David felt God's chastening hand was one more proof that he was a son. Guilt is also tacit evidence for the holiness of God, the absolute standard by which all ethics and values are measured.

Personal prayer

Heavenly Father, I confess my sin before You today. Bind my wandering heart to You. Amen.

> *"I'm learning that I don't have to be so perfectionistic and that being vulnerable can be quite liberating."*

Dirge of Discouragement

Calling on God

Exposition of theme

PSALM 38 CONTINUED

O LORD, do not forsake me; be not far from me, O my God. Come quickly to help me, O LORD my Savior (vv. 21–22).

Development of theme

At the end of this penitential psalm, David cried out to God. He could no longer endure being alone.

David had an intimate knowledge of his Lord. He knew Him by His deepest, most personal name — *Yahweh.* He was also related to God by covenant. He knew the Lord as his Master and Savior, and addressed the Lord from these perspectives in verses 21–22.

David had three final requests: that the Lord would not forsake him; that the Lord would be close; and that the Lord would come quickly to help.

Being right all the time is really important to me. Therefore, saying "I'm sorry" isn't easy for me. But I'm learning that I don't have to be so perfectionistic and that being vulnerable can be quite liberating. I'm just beginning to learn how to be released through repentance. Apologizing brings real freedom to my life; repentance provides the only true resolution for my guilty conscience.

Personal prayer

Lord, I identify with David, the ancient King of Israel. Please don't forsake me; be close, and come quickly to help. To get right to the point: forgive my sin.

Aria on Anxiety

Verbalizing Feelings

Exposition of theme

PSALM 39

I said, "I will watch my ways and keep my tongue from sin; I will put a muzzle on my mouth as long as the wicked are in my presence." But when I was silent and still, not even saying anything good, my anguish increased. My heart grew hot within me, and as I meditated, the fire burned; then I spoke with my tongue (vv. 1–3).

Development of theme

David learned to verbalize his feelings, to communicate his anxiety, and to articulate his inner thoughts.

Silence and stillness had made David sick. Not facing reality had increased his anxiety. He had become a pressure cooker, and the lid was ready to blow off!

I'm a goal-oriented person. When my goal is blocked, I become angry. When my goal is uncertain, I become anxious. Often I deny or block out how I'm really feeling, which forces my feelings to escalate out of control. I have found that feelings, good or bad, must be acknowledged or they will destroy me.

David didn't acknowledge his feelings in front of the wicked. He restrained himself from venting them in the wrong company. Unrestrained ventilation could be misconstrued by unbelievers as disloyalty or even blasphemy.

> THE LANGUAGE OF MUSIC
>
> **Aria**
>
> *In contrast to songs, arias are complex, virtuoso solos.*
>
> Accompanied by instruments, they figure prominently in operas, oratorios, and cantatas.

He took his pent-up protest to the Lord. Lament as well as praise were an integral part of his prayer. His relationship with the Lord was honest and down-to-earth — the way I want mine to be today.

Personal prayer

Help me, Lord, to watch my ways and to keep my tongue from sin. Help me to bring my gravest concerns to You.

Aria on Anxiety

Assessing Life's Brevity

Exposition of theme

PSALM 39 *CONTINUED*

"Show me, O LORD, my life's end and the number of my days; let me know how fleeting is my life. You have made my days a mere handbreadth; the span of my years is as nothing before you. Each man's life is but a breath. Selah. Man is a mere phantom as he goes to and fro: He bustles about, but only in vain; he heaps up wealth, not knowing who will get it" (vv. 4–6).

Development of theme

Life is brief. Like a vapor, a mist, a breath, it is soon over. James says, "why, you do not even know what will happen tomorrow. What is your life? You are a mist that appears for a little while and then vanishes" (James 4:14).

Our busyness makes us think we are more important than we really are. Yet in all of our bustle and activity, we are still mere phantoms. We have little control over the destiny of our heaped-up wealth. Our lifespan is nothing before God. And life itself is empty without Him.

Mid-life is a time of critical evaluation for most of us. We are preoccupied with time. Accomplishments and achievements are carefully scrutinized as we look to the future. How much time do I have left? becomes a nagging question for us to answer. The dangerous temptation to live for false gods results in the emptiness we are so frantically fleeing. David, too, was aware of time's passing.

"What caused David to number his days? What made him suddenly look at things from God's point of view?"

112

What caused David to number his days? What made him suddenly look at things from God's point of view? The answer: *intense suffering.* Extreme pain opened David to a deep work of God in his life. Suffering is God's megaphone to reach those of us with deaf ears.

Personal prayer

Lord, help me to become aware of just how fleeting my life really is. Help me to make today really count for You.

MARCH 31

Aria on Anxiety

Experiencing Discipline

Exposition of theme

PSALM 39 CONTINUED

"But now, Lord, what do I look for? My hope is in you. Save me from all my transgressions; do not make me the scorn of fools. I was silent; I would not open my mouth, for you are the one who has done this. Remove your scourge from me; I am overcome by the blow of your hand. You rebuke and discipline men for their sin; you consume their wealth like a moth—each man is but a breath" (vv. 7–11).

Development of theme

After experiencing the shattering cruelty of friends (Psalm 38), David felt the crushing severity of the Lord.

Overcome by God's heavy-handed treatment, David prayed to be released from the pressure. Despondent, he cried out to God, pouring out his soul about how brief and fragile life is.

Though nearly overwhelmed by his own mortality, David knew that salvation came from the Lord. He affirmed that faith by crying but "My hope is in you!"

The year 1984 was one of profound loss for me. Norman Johnson, our senior editor at Singspiration Music, went to be with the Lord. Then shortly after his death, my mom died. A few months later, my pastor, Reverend George Gardiner, passed away. These losses caused me to realize how fleeting life is and how near eternity is. Just the timespan of the twinkling of an eye separates us from God. "Only one life, 'twill soon be past, only what's done for Christ will last!"

God isn't a sado-masochist, but He has built suffering and adversity into the mysterious nature of reality. God used pain and hardship to

> *"Dissonance is a necessary element of harmony. It is the tension between consonance and dissonance that creates music."*

give David perspective—on his transient life on earth and on his hope for eternity. In other words, dissonance is an essential element of harmony. For it is the tension between consonance and dissonance that creates music.

Personal prayer

Lord, no matter how dark and grave my circumstances become, help me to affirm my faith and trust in You. And I trust You to make music even out of the disharmony of my life.

My soul thirsts for God, for the living God. PSALM 42:2

PANORAMA PHOTO BY GARY IRVING

Aria on Anxiety

Petitioning God's Help

Exposition of theme

PSALM 39 CONTINUED

"Hear my prayer, O Lᴏʀᴅ, listen to my cry for help; be not deaf to my weeping. For I dwell with you as an alien, a stranger, as all my fathers were. Look away from me, that I may rejoice again before I depart and am no more (vv. 12–13).

Development of theme

David, feeling alienated and estranged from God, cries out for help. He even wonders if the Lord hears his weeping, for he feels like an out-cast—a foreigner in Israel, a mere passing guest or sojourner. For the moment, all he can see is his own death looming before him.

As a Christian music executive in a secular world, I have felt this kind of alienation. Then I remind myself that I'm just a pilgrim here and I

> **"The most natural thing for a believer to do, in times of despair and despondency, is to turn to the heavenly Father."**

think of the words of that old southern Gospel song, "This World Is Not My Home."

Despite David's desperation, alienation, and estrangement, he prays, and this prayer is a testimony of his bedrock faith and trust in God. Though he can't put his circumstances together rationally, he still clings to an existential relationship with God.

The most natural thing for a believer to do, in times of despair and despondency, is to turn to

the heavenly Father. All true spirituality begins with this basic kind of honest lament.

Personal prayer

Heavenly Father, I may be a stranger in this world, but I don't want to be a stranger to You. Don't let me blend with the voices of the world, but help me to sound a clear note of faith in the midst of doubt and disillusionment.

A SOUTHERN GOSPEL SONG

This World Is Not My Home

This world is not my home, I'm just a-passin' thru,
My treasures are laid up somewhere beyond the blue;
The angels beckon me from heaven's open door,
And I can't feel at home in this world anymore.

O Lord, You know I have no friend like You,
If Heaven's not my home, then, Lord, what will I do?
The angels beckon me from Heaven's open door,
And I can't feel at home in this world anymore.

Sonatina of Sacrifice

Joy

Exposition of theme

PSALM 40

I waited patiently for the Lord; he turned to me and heard my cry. He lifted me out of the slimy pit, out of the mud and mire; he set my feet on a rock and gave me a firm place to stand. He put a new song in my mouth, a hymn of praise to our God. Many will see and fear and put their trust in the Lord (vv. 1–3).

Introduction

In three magnificent movements treating the subjects of joy (vv. 1–4), thanksgiving, (vv. 5–10) and prayer (vv. 11–17), David has flawlessly crafted a sonatina on the sacrifice of praise.

Development of theme

Most likely the psalmist has recently been near death, for he uses the metaphor of a deep pit, lined with slime, to describe his precarious position. But the Lord hears his cry and delivers him — and what a deliverance! Now David's feet are firmly planted on a rock.

Released from distress, he moves quickly from anxiety to a joyous celebration of God's power. This fresh vision of God gives David exciting material for a "new song." He may have arranged an old hymn — and discovering its genius — added fresh color and new insights. Or perhaps, in the rush of creativity and exhilaration, he composed an entirely new song. Inner joy results in music!

This event, and other miraculous deliverances in David's life, have been the inspiration for many of his great hymns of praise, shared with his congregation and recorded for generations to come. As a result, thousands "fear and put their trust in the Lord." Worship becomes witness!

> *"I will be used of the Lord today to the extent that I trust in Him and lead others to do so. This is the source of my joy and my music."*

I also will be used of the Lord today to the extent that I place my faith and trust in Him and lead others to do so. This is the source of both my joy and my music.

Personal prayer

Lord, help me not to seek joy and happiness apart from You. And may the songs that come from the deep springs of my heart point others to the Source of all satisfaction.

THE LANGUAGE OF MUSIC

Sonatina

A brief sonata marked by simplicity and designed for instruction.

It is analogous to a good, brief three-point sermon.

Sonatina of Sacrifice

Thanksgiving

Exposition of theme

PSALM 40 CONTINUED

Many, O LORD my God, are the wonders you have done. The things you planned for us no one can recount to you; were I to speak and tell of them, they would be too many to declare. Sacrifice and offering you did not desire. . . . Then I said, "Here I am, I desire to do your will, O my God; your law is within my heart" (vv. 5–8).

Development of theme

Caught up in the vortex of an exhilarating experience with the Lord, David breaks forth with thanksgiving. As his imagination soars, he is reminded of many other miraculous works God has wrought in behalf of His people. David's whole being, permeated with God's truth, is

> "In music ministry it is easy to depend upon natural gifts, experience, and craftsmanship as a substitute for real inspiration."

turned to His will, and the psalmist discovers that God desires the sacrifice of a pure heart and attitude rather than external, and sometimes empty, liturgies.

In music ministry it is easy to depend upon natural gifts, experience, and craftsmanship as a substitute for real inspiration. But David's time with the Lord becomes the deep reservoir out of which flow his hymns of praise.

Elated with this discovery, David can't keep still in "the great assembly" (v. 9). His lips, unsealed, proclaim the righteousness of God

reigning in his heart, and he shares four major themes with the congregation: God's faithfulness, salvation, love, and truth. Suddenly David finds himself in the middle of a revival resulting from his own praise and thanksgiving!

Personal prayer

Lord, fill me with Your steadfast love and perfect truth so that the music I write will reflect my gratitude.

Sonatina of Sacrifice

Prayer

Exposition of theme

PSALM 40 CONTINUED

Do not withhold your mercy from me, O LORD; may your love and your truth always protect me. For troubles without number surround me; my sins have overtaken me, and I cannot see. They are more than the hairs of my head, and my heart fails within me.
Be pleased, O LORD, to save me; O LORD, come quickly to help me. . . . You are my help and my deliverer; O my God, do not delay (vv. 11–13, 17).

Development of theme

My sins always catch up with me. There is a ripple effect with sin. Like a pebble dropped into the water that creates ever widening circles, an act of sin has expanding consequences. The Lord forgives and erases the guilt, but He does not change history. Much of my pain emanates from the effects of sin that have continued past the original act.

David too is hurting. Overwhelmed by the number of his sins ("more than the hairs of my head") and the extent of his troubles, he is about ready to give up, to throw in the towel. Yet he cries out for mercy and for the protection of God's loyal love and flawless truth.

David may be down about his own sin, but he's very much aware of the sins of others as well, and he still has energy left to pray about the enemies who pursue him relentlessly. He petitions the Lord for their confusion, shame, and disgrace (vv. 14–15). In contrast, he also prays for the salvation, help, and deliverance of those who seek the Lord. This dual theme reminds us that, above all, God alone is worthy to be "exalted and magnified" (v. 16).

Though I am poor and needy, like David I recognize that the Lord is my "help and deliverance." David closes his exquisite "Sonatina of Sacrifice" by focusing on the majesty and glory of God.

Several years ago I was moved to set to music Paul's Doxology in Romans 11:33–36:

O the depth of the riches,
   the wisdom and knowledge of God!
How unsearchable his judgments,
   and his paths beyond tracing out.

Who has known the mind of the Lord
   or who has been his advisor?
Who has ever given to God,
   that God should repay him?

Personal prayer

Lord, may I seek You, rejoice and be glad in You, and may You always be exalted and magnified in my life and work.

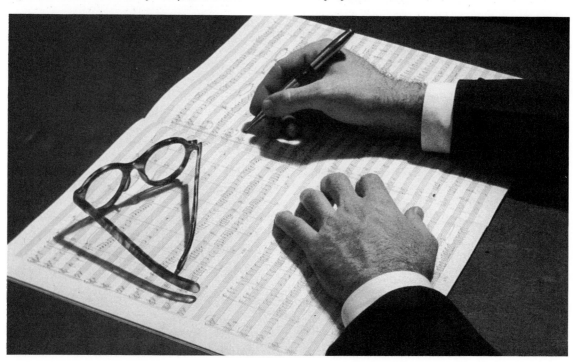

A Madrigal on Mercy

A Fundamental Principle Stated

Exposition of theme
PSALM 41

Blessed is he who has regard for the weak; the LORD delivers him in times of trouble. The LORD will protect him and preserve his life; he will bless him in the land and not surrender him to the desire of his foes. The LORD will sustain him on his sickbed and restore him from his bed of illness (vv. 1–3).

Development of theme

The message of these verses from Psalm 41 is found in miniature in Matthew 5:7 where the Lord Jesus says, "Blessed are the merciful for they will be shown mercy." David asserts the maxim of God's moral law that He will deliver the person who shows regard for the weak.

It is encouraging to see a growing response to human need. Many musicians donate the proceeds of their concerts to the underprivileged in cities where they perform. When motivated by

---

> *"David is very specific about the four blessings the Lord bestows on the compassionate person."*

---

love for the Lord, these merciful acts will not go unrewarded.

In fact, David is very specific about the four blessings the Lord bestows on the compassionate person: protection, security, strength, and good health. How practical and down-to-earth! The Lord protects and preserves the life of the

sympathetic and empathetic person. He also "blesses him in the land" and provides a profound sense of security. He further gives him strength over his foes; his enemies neither intimidate nor dominate him. Finally, He heals those who show compassion to the poor and needy.

Personal prayer

Lord, make me more sensitive to hurting people. Open my eyes and my heart to their needs and let me be a channel of Your blessing in their lives.

THE LANGUAGE OF MUSIC

Madrigal

A complex, polyphonic (many voices), unaccompanied vocal piece.

This form flourished from the 14th to 17th centuries.

A Madrigal on Mercy

A Fundamental Principle Supported

Exposition of theme
PSALM 41 CONTINUED

I said, "O LORD, have mercy on me; heal me, for I have sinned against you." My enemies say of me in malice, "When will he die and his name perish?" Whenever one comes to see me, he speaks falsely, while his heart gathers slander; then he goes out and spreads it abroad. All my enemies whisper together against me. . . . Even my close friend, whom I trusted . . . has lifted up his heel against me. But you, O LORD, have mercy on me (vv. 4–7, 9–10).

> *"A glorious doxology concludes this madrigal on mercy and serves as a fitting close to the First Book of Psalms."*

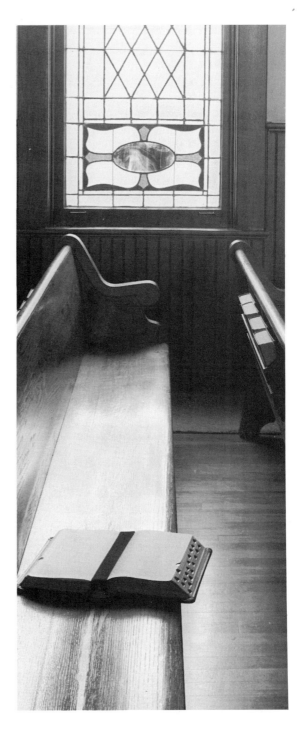

Development of theme

Most highly creative, artistic people are a bit fragile. Beneath the surface is a sea of insecurity. I have seen some of the top people in the industry demonstrate some pretty unChristlike characteristics when threatened by competition from within the ranks.

It's easy to understand why David is down in the pits again. Not only are his enemies hovering like vultures, just waiting for his death and denunciation, but he has just learned that he can't even count on his friends! Though they come to visit while he is on his sickbed, pretending concern, they spread malicious rumors about him the minute they leave. Even the friends with whom he has shared intimate confidences have betrayed him.

Though vengeance belongs to Jehovah alone, perhaps David is contemplating the punishment of traitors, one of the duties of a just monarch. David illustrates and supports God's principle that He will deliver those who are merciful. David believes his enemies have been held at bay because of his own integrity.

A glorious doxology concludes this madrigal on mercy and serves as a fitting close to the First Book of Psalms. It is a veritable outburst of praise comprising a double "Amen!"

Personal prayer

Dear Lord, it's tough to forgive those who deliberately set out to malign me. But because You have been merciful to me, I long to show mercy to others. Give me the grace to do it! Amen and Amen.

Longing and Lament

Thirsting for God

Exposition of theme

PSALM 42

As the deer pants for streams of water, so my soul pants for you, O God. My soul thirsts for God, for the living God. When can I go and meet with God? . . . These things I remember as I pour out my soul: how I used to go with the multitude, leading the procession to the house of God, with shouts of joy and thanksgiving among the festive throng (vv. 1–4).

Development of theme

This ancient temple singer, perhaps exiled in the north, has a deep longing for God and His house. His longing takes the form of an insatiable thirst, much like that of a deer foraging for water in a dry and arid land. He has been separated from God,

> **"My life resonates to the song this Levite is singing. How many times have I attempted to fill the vacuum of my life with substitutes for God?"**

estranged from the sanctuary, and is in desperate need of intimacy and fellowship.

His only solace is the memory of the great festivals in God's sanctuary. He remembers the pulsating excitement of public worship when throngs of worshipers filled the air with shouts of praise and songs of joy. He remembers being brought to the core of his own reality through his interaction with the Living God.

My life resonates to the song this Levite is singing. How many times have I attempted to fill the vacuum of my life with substitutes for God? How often have I felt emptiness deep inside my soul because I have become separated from Him? How typical of me to misuse God's precious gifts from a desire for sensual pleasure only to block deep personal intimacy! And what am I left with? A profound thirst and longing for the living God. Only He can satisfy my deepest longings. All the rest is a disappointingly empty cup.

Personal prayer

Lord, teach me to fill my life with You so that I will be fully satisfied.

A BEAUTIFUL OLD HYMN

Satisfied

All my life long I had panted
For a drink from some clear spring,
That I hoped would quench the burning
Of the thirst I felt within.

Feeding on the husks around me,
Till my strength was almost gone,
Longed my soul for something better,
Only still to linger on.

Well of water ever springing
Bread of life so rich and free,
Untold wealth that never faileth
My Redeemer is to me.

Hallelujah! I have found Him
Whom my soul so long has craved!
Jesus satisfies my longings —
Through His blood I now am saved.

Words by Clara Tear Williams. Music by Ralph E. Hudson.

Longing and Lament

Overwhelmed with Despair — I

Exposition of theme

PSALM 42 *CONTINUED*

Why are you downcast, O my soul? Why so disturbed within me? Put your hope in God, for I will yet praise him, my Savior and my God. . . . Deep calls to deep in the roar of your waterfalls; all your waves and breakers have swept over me. By day the LORD directs his love, at night his song is with me — a prayer to the God of my life (vv. 5, 7–8).

Development of theme

My soul is rooted in eternity, but my mind and body are often under severe pressures of the here and now. It is difficult to sustain creative energy over a long period of time. I live in fear of deadlines. I struggle with balancing my priorities, with handling money wisely, with proper investment of time, with handling difficult and demanding relationships. When I feel I'm in over my

> *"When I feel as if I'm sinking under unbelievable burdens, teach me to sing, to pray, and to feel Your inexhaustible love!"*

head, this psalm brings consolation.

David knew the debilitating effect of depression and despair. In verse 7, his mind must have been in turmoil as he portrays an alien scene. Perhaps churned by a spring storm, the Jordan River rages. As the troubled waters hiss and spew, the river becomes a metaphor for all that is overwhelming and uncontrollable in David's life,

> *"When I feel I'm in over my head, this psalm brings consolation."*

and he feels that he has lost his footing and is in danger of drowning.

Still, his hope is in God. Verse 8 is the centerpiece, the psalmist's confession of faith. The one ray of light in the darkness is his confidence that the Lord loves him. All of David's anxiety is channeled through prayer to the God of his life. The song of the Lord is with him — and with me — even in the deepest waters and through the darkest night.

Personal prayer

Lord, when I feel as if I'm sinking under unbelievable burdens, teach me to sing, to pray, and to feel Your inexhaustible love!

Longing and Lament

Overwhelmed with Despair — II

Exposition of theme

PSALM 42 *CONTINUED*

Why are you downcast, O my soul? Why so disturbed within me? Put your hope in God, for I will yet praise him, my Savior and my God. . . . You are God my stronghold. . . . Send forth your light and your truth, let them guide me. . . . Then will I go to the altar of God, to God, my joy and my delight. I will praise you with the harp, O God, my God (42:11; 43:2–4).

Development of theme

Just about the time I think I have gained the victory over some black mood, some writer's block, some unworthy goal, the whole thing comes crashing down around me, and I am back to square one. In this rut of defeat, my prayers

> *"In the sanctuary, in the presence of my fellow believers, I'll praise the Lord with acoustic and electric instruments, with sophisticated rhythms, with innovative harmonies and soaring melodies."*

sound very much like those of this psalmist: "Why have you rejected me? Why must I go about mourning, oppressed by the enemy?" (43:2)

David has a right to his depression. Ungodly people have accused him unjustly, and he prays to the Lord for vindication — for a declaration of his innocence.

But dark moods can give way to positive praying. Like the psalmist, I can't allow my mind to camp on negative ideas and feelings, but I can pray for God's light and truth to guide me. "Let them bring me to your holy mountain, to the place where you dwell" (43:3).

In the sanctuary, in the presence of my fellow believers, I'll praise the Lord with acoustic and electric instruments, with sophisticated rhythms, with innovative harmonies and soaring melodies — all reveling in the ineffable glory of God! In this way I, too, will be able to experience His transcending, transforming power.

Personal prayer

Lord, in the darkness of my circumstances, help me to be aware that consummate joy and delight are centered in You.

Longing and Lament

Overwhelmed with Despair — III

Exposition of theme

PSALM 43

Why are you downcast, O my soul? Why so disturbed within me? Put your hope in God, for I will yet praise him, my Savior and my God (v. 5).

Development of theme

Psalms 42 and 43 are actually one sadly beautiful poem. The two parts are unified by a plaintive refrain heard three times — 42:5; 42:11; 43:5. It is the lament of a temple singer in the ancient world. Its bitter-sweet song is startlingly relevant to our situation today.

This psalmist knew how to pray. He expresses his feelings honestly, admitting that his inner life is restless and insecure. Some deep longings have gone unmet, and he doesn't pretend otherwise, skimming over the surface of his personal needs.

But he doesn't stop with this candid appraisal of his life, refusing to wallow in his hopelessness. He utters a full-throated confidence in God and vows that he will again praise the Lord and will turn his whole being to face Him.

Unlike modern man, who gives up in despair or clings obstinately to some flimsy philosophy, this believer chooses to declare his faith in the one, true, living God of the universe. To pretend faith in an unworthy or imaginary object is foolishness. But to place our hope in God, no matter how uncertain and insecure we may be, is the path to praise.

Personal prayer

O Elohim, I pray that my hope will be in You, even when I feel most helpless. May I never turn my face away from You!

Unfailing Love

Then . . .

Exposition of theme

PSALM 44

We have heard with our ears, O God; our fathers have told us what you did in their days, in days long ago. With your hand you drove out the nations and planted our fathers; you crushed the peoples and made our fathers flourish. It was not by their sword that they won the land, nor did their arm bring them victory; it was your right hand, your arm, and the light of your face, for you loved them (vv. 1–3).

Development of theme

This psalm begins with a rousing recital of past victories in the history of Israel: Nations were driven out, peoples were crushed, enemies were pushed back, soldiers were victorious, foes were trampled. Israel's ancestors flourished as a theocracy — a nation united under the living God — in the midst of paganism and idolatry.

The psalmist articulates the secret of the overwhelming success of the armies of Israel: "I do not trust in my bow, my sword does not bring me victory; but you give us victory over our enemies, you put our adversaries to shame. In God we make our boast all day long, and we will praise your name forever" (44:6–8). They fought in the Name of the Lord. That Name alone empowered them!

Names or song titles are also pivotal in capsulizing the meaning and power of a lyric. The Chief Musician, David, would have loved "How Great Thou Art!" or "His Name Is Wonderful." There is incomparable force and energy in the Name of the Lord.

What is the secret of effectiveness and power for me today? I must choose not to live independently of God, but make Him central in my life. I must resist an easy, casual commitment to Christ, but reflect in my daily walk the personality of the One whose Name I bear. That Name will give me the power to withstand temptation, endure criticism, and witness boldly.

Personal prayer

O God, may I boast, not in my own gifts and abilities, but in You. And may I praise Your Name forever!

Unfailing Love

Now . . .

Exposition of theme

PSALM 44 CONTINUED

But now you have rejected and humbled us; you no longer go out with our armies. You made us retreat before the enemy, and our adversaries have plundered us. You gave us up to be devoured like sheep and have scattered us among the nations. . . . My disgrace is before me all day long (vv. 9–11, 15).

Development of theme

If ever there were a passage written in the minor key, it's this one. Hear the litany of defeat in the action words of these verses: *rejected, humbled, plundered, scattered, devoured.* Israel, God's favored nation, now faces demoralization and destruction.

Neighboring nations scoff and scorn; they gloat over the ill fortunes of Israel. They thumb their noses at these people who have apparently been abandoned by their God.

I heard my friend, Chuck Swindoll, give a moving message on integrity the other night. In it, he said that God tests His servants in two major ways—through adversity and through prosperity. Because we are children of the heavenly Father, He sometimes disciplines or chastens us. That's "tough love."

But how do we handle rejection and defeat? How do we react when our faith doesn't seem to be getting results? Is our relationship to God a hoax?

This psalm does not give us neat, tidy answers to those questions. The mystery of God's grand design looms in the distance. In the immediate situation God's people are suffering. Rather than causing them to forsake their faith, however, it drives them to their knees in profound prayer.

Personal prayer

O God, in the reversals and discordant moments of my life, help me to hear Your faithful love calling me to repentance and renewal.

APRIL 13

Unfailing Love
Why?

Exposition of theme
PSALM 44 CONTINUED

Awake, O LORD! Why do you sleep? Rouse yourself! Do not reject us forever. Why do you hide your face and forget our misery and oppression? Rise up and help us; redeem us because of your unfailing love (vv. 23–24, 26).

Development of theme

Why me, Lord? The psalmist reflects my own twentieth-century struggle to see God when the lights are turned out. The people of Israel are experiencing the crush of rejection, and they are as perplexed as I with the mysteries of my own life. Why has this happened? What have I done? I've been on the job, faithfully serving Him, laboring in the place He's assigned me. Doesn't He know I'm hurting? Doesn't He care? Is He asleep?

The history of God's people, both past and present, seems to fluctuate between periods of blessing and periods of defeat. At these times, is God really withdrawing in wrath or does He just refuse to be hurried? During a furious squall on

---

"Suffering may not be a punishment, only a battle-scar—the price paid for serving the Lord in a hostile environment, in a world at war with God."

---

the Sea of Galilee, as waves threatened to capsize the disciples' boat, Jesus slept peacefully on a cushion in the stern (Mark 4:37–38).

God's timetable is often different from ours. Suffering may not be a punishment, only a battle-scar—the price paid for serving the Lord in a hostile environment, in a world at war with God.

When it seems as if the boat is sinking, we can cling to the reality of His unfailing love. "Who shall separate us from the love of Christ? Shall trouble or hardship or persecution or famine or nakedness or danger or sword? . . . No, in all these things we are more than conquerors through him who loved us" (Romans 8:35, 37).

Personal prayer

O God, may my impatience not prevent me from constantly trusting in Your steadfast love no matter how bleak my circumstances appear.

The Love Song

Verses for A King

Exposition of theme

PSALM 45

My heart is stirred by a noble theme as I recite my verses for the king; my tongue is the pen of a skillful writer (v. 1).

Development of theme

No writer should write until a fire burns deep inside. If one feels no strong conviction, no genuine emotion, no real compulsion, there is nothing to say!

This verse gives us a glimpse of the process of composition in the ancient world. In this messianic psalm, the inscription tells us the name of the tune — "Lilies." The composers are the sons of Korah; their subject, the wedding of the King of kings.

No wonder this musical artist's heart is "stirred"! Moved by the most noble theme of all times — the marriage of Christ to His bride, the Church — the psalmist's words flow quickly and fluently. With consummate creativity he portrays Christ in all His beauty as a bridegroom arrayed for his bride.

Now deeply involved — intellectually, emotionally, and spiritually — the psalmist's tongue becomes "the pen of a skillful writer," and he articulates an eloquent lyric. As his heart responds and his thoughts are engaged, the sacrifice kindled upon his lips overflow upon the page. Truly, this is an inspired work, though crafted with great artistry. Sincerity, especially among biblical writers, is never a substitute for skill.

What a mandate for a Christian artist! What a mission statement for the Christian writer! What goals to live for! What a target to shoot toward! And all centering in a depiction of the Messiah that is intensely personal, beautiful, and artistic.

Personal prayer

Lord, give me a vision of Your Son that will set my heart on fire. Then my songs and my writing will burn with joy, praise, and beauty.

The Love Song

Verses for the Groom

Exposition of theme

PSALM 45 CONTINUED

You are the most excellent of men and your lips have been anointed with grace, since God has blessed you forever. Gird your sword upon your side, O mighty one; clothe yourself with splendor and majesty. In your majesty ride forth victoriously in behalf of truth, humility and righteous-

> "What a mandate for a Christian artist! What a mission statement for the Christian writer! What goals to live for!"

ness; let your right hand display awesome deeds. . . . You love righteousness and hate wickedness; therefore God, your God, has set you above your companions by anointing you with the oil of joy (vv. 2–4, 7).

Development of theme

When I read the words of this beautiful psalm, I'm reminded of my own marriage to Karen. July 14, 1963 was a spectacular day for an outdoor wedding on the lawn of Word of Life Inn. With Schroon Lake and the majestic Adirondack Mountains as our backdrop, we recited our vows from memory. This groom was typically nervous and apprehensive, but anticipated a glorious future with his beautiful bride.

The warrior King described by the psalmist is the "most excellent of men," the model for all

---

"July 14, 1963 was a spectacular day for an outdoor wedding on the lawn of Word of Life Inn. With Schroon Lake and the majestic Adirondack Mountains as our backdrop, we recited our vows from memory."

---

men of God. He is to ride forth in splendor and majesty, "in behalf of truth, humility, and righteousness."

His kingdom will be everlasting. It will be characterized by righteousness and justice. The King Himself is incomparable. He is anointed with the oil of joy; His robes are scented; His house is adorned with inlaid ivory; and His rooms are filled with the glorious music of strings. His honored women are the daughters of kings, the chiefest of whom is the royal bride beautified in robes of gold.

Hebrews 1 shows us that this is God's Son,

the "heir of all things" and the Creator of the universe. This King is the Son who is the "radiance of God's glory and the exact representation of his being, who sustains all things by his powerful word" (1:3). He is the model for all believers, but particularly for all who would aspire to be men of God.

Personal prayer

Lord, I worship You in all of Your magnificence and transcendent beauty. Make me more like You in truth, humility, and righteousness.

A GOSPEL SONG LYRIC

Ivory Palaces

My Lord has garments so wondrous fine,
And myrrh their texture fills;
Its fragrance reached to this heart of mine,
With joy my being thrills.

His life had also its sorrows sore,
For aloes had a part;
And when I think of the cross He bore,
My eyes with teardrops start.

His garments were in cassia dipped,
With healing in a touch;
Each time my feet in some sin have slipped,
He took me from its clutch.

In garments glorious He will come,
To open wide the door;
And I shall enter my heavenly home,
To dwell forevermore.

Out of the ivory palaces,
Into a world of woe,
Only His great eternal love
Made my Savior go.

The Love Song

Verses for the Bride

Exposition of theme

PSALM 45 CONTINUED

*Listen, O daughter, consider and give ear: Forget
your people and your father's house. The king is
enthralled by your beauty; honor him, for he is
your lord. . . . I will perpetuate your memory
through all generations; therefore the nations
will praise you for ever and ever (vv. 10–11, 17).*

Development of theme

The dignity of biblically ordained marriage in the
ancient world is certainly foreign to the psychology of many modern marriages. This scene from

the royal wedding depicts clearly the parting with
the old and the new beginning required of this
princess bride. The husband too must make a
break from his childhood home, separating both
physically and emotionally from parents, in order
to give himself fully to his wife (Genesis 2:24).

This is to be an all-encompassing relationship,
and no sacrifice is too great to ensure its success. Karen, for example, left her home and family in Topeka, Kansas to join me in New York.
She then accompanied me to Dallas so I could
further my education in both music and theology.
She moved our young family to Grand Rapids,
Michigan, and later to Nashville, Tennessee, to
pursue various ministry opportunities the Lord
opened up for us. None of these adjustments
has been easy or problem-free, but like her biblical sister, Sarah, she has chosen to honor her

> *"I recall that radiant young woman on our wedding day. I still have the newspaper clipping describing her gown. In my opinion, it rivals that of the royal bride in David's psalm."*

husband at great personal sacrifice (1 Peter 3:6).

This evidence of her love supports me daily, but I recall too that radiant young woman on our wedding day. I still have the newspaper clipping describing her gown. In my opinion, it rivals that of the royal bride in David's psalm. "Of white, silk organza, the bride's gown was fashioned with Alencon lace and seed pearls around the portrait neckline of the molded bodice and on the skirt which fell into a full cathedral-length train. On her head she wore a Swedish crystal crown and carried a bouquet composed of yellow roses, daisies, lily of the valley, and ivy." Like that royal procession in David's psalm, Karen was accompanied by friends and approached our improvised altar "with joy and gladness."

In conclusion, new glories are promised to couples who are yielded to the Lord. David's bride and groom will be blessed with sons who will become princes to "perpetuate their memory through all generations." This is a foretaste of the Messiah who will bring "many sons to glory" (Hebrews 2:10, 13) and who will "reign forever."

Personal prayer

Lord, I thank You for Karen and for the beautiful relationship of marriage which illustrates so clearly Your relationship to Your bride, the Church.

131

A Mighty Fortress

God's Power Over Nature

Exposition of theme

PSALM 46

God is our refuge and strength, an ever-present help in trouble. Therefore we will not fear, though the earth give way and the mountains fall into the heart of the sea, though its waters roar and foam and the mountains quake with their surging (vv. 1–3).

Development of theme

How does one face the possibility of world catastrophe? How does one guard against internal disintegration of the personality in view of pressure to conform to the false standards of society? The answer is found in God alone, not in God plus anything else.

In our lifetime we may never personally experience earthquake, volcanic eruption, or tornadic winds — all evidences of the physical universe in turmoil. While these natural calamities are devastating, equally distressing and disrupting are the more common upheavals caused by marital

"Worry is an inappropriate response for God's child. Anxiety, mental distress, and emotional agitation yield to trust in the unshakeable, immutable, omnipotent God of the universe."

conflict, financial reverses, illness, and death of friends or loved ones.

When that which seems unchangeable and impregnable falls, God is my stability. He is my refuge — "my shelter and protection from danger." He is my strength — "my vigor, mental and moral power, firmness and courage." He is my ever-present help in trouble.

As a high-strung, sensitive, emotional person, I need to be constantly reminded of these truths. Worry is an inappropriate response for God's child. Anxiety, mental distress, and emotional agitation yield to trust in the unshakeable, immutable, omnipotent God of the universe. He is the Master of all of nature, and I must make Him the Master of my troubled soul.

Personal prayer

O Lord, I praise You that I do not have to fear anyone or anything because You are my Refuge and Strength.

A HYMN LYRIC

A Mighty Fortress

A mighty fortress is our God,
A bulwark never failing;
Our helper He amid the flood
Of mortal ills prevailing.

Dost ask who that may be?
Christ Jesus it is He —
Lord Sabaoth His name,
From age to age the same,
And He must win the battle

Words and music by Martin Luther

APRIL 18

A Mighty Fortress

Part 1 — God's Protection of His City

Exposition of theme

PSALM 46 CONTINUED

There is a river whose streams make glad the city of God, the holy place where the Most High dwells. God is within her, she will not fall; God will help her at break of day. Nations are in uproar, kingdoms fall; he lifts his voice, the earth melts. The LORD Almighty is with us; the God of Jacob is our fortress (vv. 4–7).

Development of theme

The city of God is a rich metaphor, a symbol of peace, tranquility, and contentment. It denotes Jerusalem, Zion, any place where God dwells. The New Testament vision is of a heavenly community, rather than an earthly locality, where believers praise the Lord forever. God fills that

> *"How do I live now with daily stresses and nightly fears that claw at my soul? How do I cope with anxieties and pressures that keep me restless and uneasy?"*

place with His glory and peace. Fear, darkness, and vulnerability will be foreign there.

But how do I live now with daily stresses and nightly fears that claw at my soul? How do I cope with anxieties and pressures that keep me restless and uneasy? I must latch on to the exciting reality that the Lord is with me *now!* The God of Jacob is my fortress *now!*

Personal prayer

O Lord, may I catch a vision of that city of God where there is no anxiety, no fear, no stress and may I realize that I may dwell with You — now — in peace.

A Mighty Fortress

Part 2 — God's Omnipotence

Exposition of theme

PSALM 46 CONTINUED

Come and see the works of the LORD, the desolations he has brought on the earth. He makes wars cease to the ends of the earth; he breaks the bow and shatters the spear, he burns the shields with fire. "Be still, and know that I am God; I will be exalted among the nations" (vv. 8–10).

Development of theme

Christ commanded the violent surging waters, "Peace, be still!" When the last chapter of world history has been written, in the same way God will put an end to violence, war, and to all of the effects of sin in the universe.

In this vision of the end of time, desolations have been brought on the earth, wars have ceased, and instruments of war have been eliminated. God's judgment has prevailed and the world has become forcibly disarmed. At that time He will be exalted among the nations and in the

"God is my fortress, my shelter, my protection. In the end, He is all that matters in time and eternity."

earth. Man's hopes will be dashed, but God will be exalted in all of His majesty and glory.

What should be my response to this vision? Once fully aware that God is my fortress, my shelter, my protection, I must learn to be still and know that God is God and that He has provided our redemption through Christ.

In the end, He is all that matters in time and eternity.

Personal prayer

O Lord, as You will finally be exalted among the nations and in the earth, be exalted in my life now and help me to be still before You.

Exultation!

Exposition of theme

PSALM 47

Clap your hands, all you nations; shout to God with cries of joy. . . . God has ascended amid shouts of joy, the LORD amid the sounding of trumpets. Sing praises to God, sing praises; sing praises to our King, sing praises (vv. 1, 5–6).

Development of theme

This psalm, a hymn to the Great King, gives us a graphic picture of drama in worship. These ancient believers allowed themselves to be caught

---

A HYMN LYRIC

A Mighty Fortress CONTINUED

For still our ancient foe,
Doth seek to work us woe —
His craft and power are great,
And armed with cruel hate,
On earth is not His equal.

Did we in our own strength confide
Our striving world be losing,
Were not the right Man on our side,
The Man of God's own choosing.

Words and music by Martin Luther

up in worship. They praised the Lord with every aspect of their being — intellectually, emotionally, and physically. They learned how to worship God with each of the five senses — sight, sound, smell, taste and touch. This psalm pulsates and resonates with excitement!

Note the verbs which give movement and power to this psalm: "Clap your hands!" "Shout to God with cries of joy!" "Sing praises!" (Note too that these verbs are in the imperative. Lackluster worship is not acceptable.) Why such jubilation? Because the King has "subdued nations" (v. 3); He has chosen our inheritance" (v. 4), and now He "has ascended amid shouts of joy" (v. 5).

This is a royal procession. As God ascends, accompanied by trumpet fanfares, the people form a great choir of highly involved worshippers, all praising the Lord in song and with musical instruments.

We need to attend church as dynamically involved worshippers rather than spectators. Church services are not sit-coms which "couch potatoes" view for entertainment. They should

> **"Church services are not sit-coms which 'couch potatoes' view for entertainment. They should be dynamic encounters with God."**

be dynamic encounters with God — challenging, convicting, and somewhat uncomfortable!

I want to lay aside personal inhibition and apathy and catch the spirit of these ancient worshippers. When I see God as they saw Him, high and lifted up, I will be euphoric in my praise and will long to exalt Him with every means at my disposal.

Personal prayer

Dear Lord, I long to praise You with vigor and unrestrained passion. Unfetter my personality, enhance my sensitivity, and enlarge my creativity so that I can be profoundly involved in lifting You high!

135

Chorus of Praise

The King in Zion

Exposition of theme
PSALM 48

Great is the LORD, and most worthy of praise, in the city of our God, his holy mountain. It is beautiful in its loftiness, the joy of the whole earth. Like the utmost heights of Zaphon is Mount Zion, the city of the Great King. God is in her citadels; he has shown himself to be her fortress (vv. 1–3).

Development of theme
The Glory of the Lord . . .

Something has happened which has inspired the psalmist to exude praise. Perhaps the Lord has once again miraculously delivered the nation from annihilation. He sings out lustily and full-throatedly, "Great is the Lord, and most worthy of praise!" What a motif for today!

The songwriter revels in encomiums of praise to Zion, the city of our God. Nothing less than the

---

> *"I must allow Him to become the hub, the center, the fulcrum of my life, just as Jerusalem is the spiritual crossroads of all nations on earth."*

---

most majestic expressions of highest praise will suffice in this setting — a city that is lofty and magnificent, "the joy of all the earth." God Himself is her fortress, her sure defense.

Why are all nations charmed by this city of Jerusalem? Why is it pivotal and strategic? Because it represents the place where God dwells. Blessings flow forth from her to all the earth.

What is here for me to learn today? First, that the best place for me is where God is. I will discover my identity, security, and stability in Him. Second, the source of personal blessing is God Himself. I must allow Him to become the hub, the center, the fulcrum of my life, just as Jerusalem is the spiritual crossroads of all nations on earth.

Personal prayer
Dear Lord, You are most worthy of my praise. Nothing charms me like the irresistible picture of the New Jerusalem where I will someday dwell with You.

Chorus of Praise

The Nations in Retreat

Exposition of theme
PSALM 48 *CONTINUED*

When the kings joined forces, when they advanced together, they saw her and were astounded; they fled in terror. Trembling seized them there, pain like that of a woman in labor.

You destroyed them like ships of Tarshish shattered by an east wind. As we have heard, so have we seen in the city of the LORD Almighty, in the city of our God: God makes her secure forever (vv. 4–8).

Development of theme

The protection of the Lord . . .

Assyrian warriors were renowned for their iron courage and enormous strength. Yet, at the sight of Jerusalem, the city of God, Sennacherib's vassals trembled! Even with their awesome power, they were no match for this impregnable fortress, defended by God Himself.

Strong metaphors describe their panic: "Pain like that of a woman in labor"; "like ships of Tarshish shattered by an east wind" (vv. 6–7). There is no rational explanation for such a disas-

> *"The same God who routed the Phoenician armies and battered their ships at sea is available to me today to set my anxious heart at rest."*

ter — only the terrible majesty and strength of God, who provided supernatural protection and providence for His people.

How frail I am in my humanity. I must not let myself be intimidated by minor fears or even by problems of more significant proportions. The same God who routed the Phoenician armies and battered their ships at sea is available to me today to set my anxious heart at rest. "If [that] God be for [me], who can be against [me]?" (Romans 8:31)

Personal prayer

O Lord, I come to You as a little child, thanking You once again for Your protection and care.

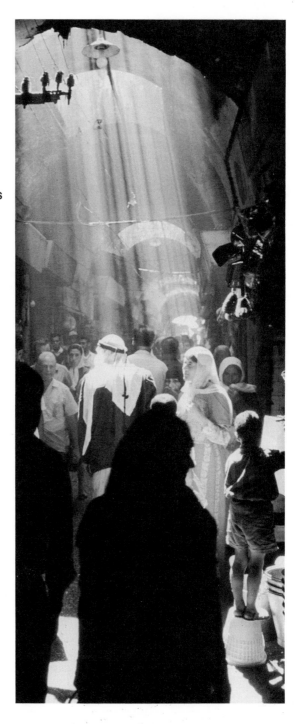

137

Chorus of Praise

Exposition of theme

PSALM 48

Within your temple, O God, we meditate on your unfailing love. Like your name, O God, your praise reaches to the ends of the earth; your right hand is filled with righteousness. Mount Zion rejoices, the villages of Judah are glad because of your judgments (vv. 9–11).

Development of theme

The praise of the Lord . . .

What a beautiful model for a praise song. The psalmist ponders the unfailing love of the Lord. The Hebrew word *hesed* is a magnificent Old Testament word for God's loyal, covenant love.

A CONTEMPORARY LYRIC

Stubborn Love

Funny me . . . just couldn't see
Even long before I knew You, You were
    loving me.
Sometimes I cry . . . You must cry too.
When You see the broken promises I've
    made to You.
I keep saying that I'll trust You, though I
    seldom do.
Yet You stay and say "I love you still"
Knowing someday I'll be like You

It's your stubborn love
That never lets go of me.
I don't undertand how You could stay—
Perfect love embracing the worst in me.
I can't live without Your stubborn love.

Words and music by Amy Grant, Gary Chapman, Sloan Towner, Brown Bannister, Michael W. Smith. © Meadowgreen Music Co. / Handrail Music.

> *"It is refreshing to know that the real world of the spirit is governed by a God of grace and stubborn love.*

Much like the Greek word *agape* in the New Testament, it describes the fact that God loves us no matter what, no strings attached. His love is unconditional and persistent.

In our self-centered society—where even love must often be earned through good performance, wealth, beauty, or status—it is refreshing to know that the real world of the spirit is governed by a God of grace and stubborn love.

Supporting me today are the pillars of God's loyal love and His eternal faithfulness. When I meditate on that, I am encouraged and strengthened. I have a choice. Either I can succumb to fears of rejection and failure, or I can lean against God's promises.

Personal prayer

O God, I praise You for Your great faithfulness and stubborn love, even when I am tempted to try to "earn" my place with You and with my peers.

Chorus of Praise

The Review of Zion

Exposition of theme

PSALM 48 CONTINUED

Walk about Zion, go around her, count her towers, consider well her ramparts, view her citadels, that you may tell of them to the next generation. For this God is our God for ever and ever; he will be our guide even to the end (vv. 12–14).

Development of theme

The posterity of the Lord . . .

Because the Lord has delivered Israel, they celebrate and worship with exuberance. Having been confined within the walls of the city, they are now free to walk outside. There, in the exhilaration of new-found freedom, they behold and admire the city's undamaged towers, walls, and pristine palaces.

Reviewing the city, they are reminded that the Lord is their high tower forever. He will continually protect and deliver them and will guide them forever. More importantly, they are to "tell of [these things] to the next generation."

What a responsibility! Through the medium of music, I have God's mandate to share my faith and my gifts with those who will come after me.

New music inevitably builds on what has gone before. Bach, the epitome of artistic genius and craftsmanship in the Baroque period, has inspired many musicians centuries after his death. I praise the Lord for other church musicians who have been my mentors—Don Hustad, John W.

"Now, maybe it's my turn. There is a 'musical discipleship' involved. I must contribute to the lives of younger composers, arrangers, and orchestrators. I must pass the baton of God's truth and values to generations to follow."

Peterson, Ralph Carmichael, and others.

Now, maybe it's my turn. There is a "musical discipleship" involved. I must contribute to the lives of younger composers, arrangers, and orchestrators. As a communicator seasoned in the faith and in the medium, I must pass the baton of God's truth and His values to generations to follow.

Personal prayer

Dear Lord, help me to be faithful, through the witness of my music, to "tell the next generation" of Your protection and guidance all the days of their lives.

139

Meaning in Wealth?

Exposition of theme

PSALM 49

Hear this, all you peoples; listen, all who live in this world, both low and high, rich and poor alike. . . . Why should I fear when evil days come, when wicked deceivers surround me — those who trust in their wealth and boast of their great riches? . . . For all can see that wise men die; the foolish and the senseless alike perish; and leave their wealth to others. . . . But man, despite his riches, does not endure; he is like the beasts that perish (vv. 1–2, 5–6, 10, 12).

"The Christian music scene has suffered many excesses: inflated budgets, out-of-control production expense, political hype, unreasonable contracts, outrageous lifestyles."

Development of theme

The futility of trusting in wealth . . .

I've talked to a lot of secular musicians, and most of them say the same thing: When success comes, big money is at first a turn-on; after that, it can be real trouble. The Christian music scene has also suffered many excesses: inflated budgets, out-of-control production expense, political hype, unreasonable contracts, outrageous lifestyles, etc. This psalmist agrees and shoots down the theory that the acquisition of wealth guarantees happiness and immortality.

He begins with a solemn introduction in which he proposes to grapple with this age-old problem of meaning in life. Then he asks a question: Why should I fear an enemy who trusts in wealth? No man can buy human life. Life is so valuable and the price so high that no amount of money can buy off death. In the end all men, whatever their station, die and leave their accumulation of possessions behind.

In our blatantly materialistic society, many of us expend a lot of time and energy chasing "the bucks" while denying the reality of our own appointment with death. Since money cannot buy my life or happiness, I need to discover the true Source.

Personal prayer

O Mighty One, Lord, God, help me not to buy into the world view that money and status bring meaning to life when that is Satan's lie, his counterfeit proposal, camouflaging the profound truth that You are our only real meaning.

APRIL 26

Meaning in Wealth

Exposition of theme
PSALM 49 CONTINUED

This is the fate of those who trust in themselves, and of their followers, who approve their sayings. Like sheep they are destined for the grave, and death will feed on them. The upright will rule over them in the morning; their forms will decay in the grave, far from their princely mansions. But God will redeem my life from the grave; he will surely take me to himself (vv. 13–15).

Development of theme

The final end of those who trust in wealth . . .

What a graphic picture of death the psalmist paints! Those who are trusting "in themselves"—in their own resources—for salvation are destined for the grave. At the moment of death, even wealthy, influential persons will be as helpless as sheep herded together. According to one poet, "death pastures them," and their ultimate resting place is "far from their princely mansions."

What a contrast with the godly and upright! I'm impressed by three promises in this passage: (1) The godly will have dominion—"the upright will rule over them" (v. 14). (2) The souls of the upright will be ransomed from the place of the dead—"God will redeem my life from the grave" (v. 15). (3) The Lord Himself will receive the righteous—"he will surely take me to himself" (v. 15). When phobias and fears about death assail me, these verses are a comfort and a lifeline.

Enoch walked with God on a regular basis and, one day, he continued walking right into His presence. Elijah was caught up in a chariot of fire. Our Lord ascended into the clouds. One day, each one of us who knows the Lord will walk through a door into eternity. We will be "absent from the body, but present with the Lord" (2 Corinthians 5:8).

Personal prayer

Lord, I thank You that because you have conquered death, I don't need to live in fear of it. I'm looking forward to the day when You will take me to Yourself.

Meaning in Wealth?

Exposition of theme
PSALM 49 CONTINUED

Do not be overawed when a man grows rich, when the splendor of his house increases; for he will take nothing with him when he dies, his splendor will not descend with him. Though while he lived he counted himself blessed — and men praise you when you prosper — he will join the generation of his fathers, who will never see the light of life. A man who has riches without understanding is like the beasts that perish (vv. 16–20).

Development of theme

The finite nature of wealth . . .

I must admit that I, along with many others, have been charmed by "Tinseltown." The accouterments of success seem so appealing that it's pretty easy to fall for those less-than-subtle advertising ploys touting fancy foreign engineering or the architectural wonders of some luxury house. Even in church we sometimes focus on the trappings — lavish sanctuaries, fine pipe organs, plush carpeting. When materialism and

> **"When materialism and personal pride fuse together, we're all in grave danger of neglecting or even forgetting God!"**

personal pride fuse together, we're all in grave danger of neglecting or even forgetting God!

Thoughts of death and the prospect of eternity, however, can abruptly change one's focus, perspective, and priorities. The psalmist reminds us that, no matter how imposing the wealthy and powerful may appear, "they can't take it with them."

In this life the wealthy often inspire awe, admiration, and praise. But this adulation will be short-lived. The possessions that are the basis of their pride and self-aggrandizement will not survive past the grave. Verse 20 describes the final state of the man who leaves God out of his life. Without understanding, he is like the beasts that perish. His power, influence, and wealth won't carry any weight in eternity.

Personal prayer

Lord, may I learn to live always, not for this life only, but with "eternity's values in view."

APRIL 28

True Worship

Exposition of theme

PSALM 50

The Mighty One, God, the LORD, speaks and summons the earth from the rising of the sun to the place where it sets. From Zion, perfect in beauty, God shines forth. Our God comes and will not be silent; a fire devours before him, and around him a tempest rages. He summons the heavens above, and the earth, that he may judge his people: "Gather to me my consecrated ones, who made a covenant with me by sacrifice." And the heavens proclaim his righteousness, for God himself is judge (vv. 1–6).

Development of theme

The Lord appears . . .

Through the words of the psalmist, can we see the Lord in the beauty of His holiness? He is transcendent — beyond and above us. He is the Mighty One, who spoke the world into existence and orders the universe. He is the Perfect One. He is the Righteous One. He is also *Yahweh*, un-

changeable and faithful. It is this One who is coming to judge the earth.

From Zion, the glorious place where God dwells, he comes, surrounded by fire and fierce

---

"Our worship practices, like our relationship with the Lord, should reflect both majesty and intimacy."

---

energy. He does not remain silent, for He comes to judge His covenant people who have been negligent in their worship. He sees their hearts and knows that their practices have been deficient and their attitudes, flippant.

Our worship practices, like our relationship with the Lord, should reflect both majesty and intimacy. Unfortunately, we usually emphasize one or the other. We worship God in His majesty, but are not intimate with Him. or we cultivate intimacy and neglect reverence. There is a holy balance toward which we should strive. In our services, there should be times of fervor in which we may even loudly proclaim His praises with clapping of hands. At other times, deeply moved by God's holiness, we approach Him in quiet meditation.

Our Lord is absolutely holy. He is also jealous. He covets genuine worship and praise. He is very serious about His Personhood and disdains my inattentiveness and casual approach to my relationship with Him. As He addresses His people Israel, He is also speaking to me.

Personal prayer

Dear Lord, help me to sense Your absolute holiness and transcendence. And may this glorious vision of You lead me to fall at Your feet in total adoration.

143

True Worship

Exposition of theme

PSALM 50 CONTINUED

"Hear, O my people, and I will speak, O Israel, and I will testify against you: I am God, your God. I do not rebuke you for your sacrifices or your burnt offerings, which are ever before me. I have no need of a bull from your stall or of goats from your pens, for every animal of the forest is mine, and the cattle on a thousand hills. . . . Sacrifice thank offerings to God, fulfill your vows to the Most High, and call upon me in the day of trouble; I will deliver you, and you will honor me" (vv. 7–10, 14–15).

Development of theme

The Lord speaks against empty liturgy . . .

I stand amazed in His presence! This transcendent Lord, this Sovereign God, who is beyond us and above us is also around us and within us and desires fellowship with us!

Ritualism can never take the place of relationship. Obedience, faithfulness, and calling on God in trouble all flow from an intimate relationship with Him. Now, God comes into court to ar-

---

"Adoration of God is not scoring brownie points with Him. He is eternally self-existent and does not need our puny offerings, our gifts, our talents."

---

raign His own covenant people, intellectually strong and orthodox in their beliefs, but faulty in their motives and attitudes.

While Israel has practiced sacrifice and observed the Law, she has assumed that her offerings benefited God, as if He were somehow in debt to them. They have grown independent and cold, and their fervor has cooled. In point of fact, God owns everything, including the cattle on a thousand hills.

Adoration of God is not scoring brownie points with Him. He is eternally self-existent and does not need our puny offerings, our gifts, our talents. But wonder of wonders, He longs to have us know Him well, closely, intimately and to worship Him—not for what He gets out of it, but because He is waiting to bless and deliver us!

Personal prayer

O Lord, You are high and holy, yet You invite me into Your presence. You tell me to call on You in trouble. Lord, You are my Friend!

APRIL 30

True Worship

Exposition of theme
PSALM 50 CONTINUED

But to the wicked, God says: "What right have you to recite my laws or take my covenant on your lips? You hate my instruction and cast my words behind you. . . . You use your mouth for evil and harness your tongue to deceit. . . . These things you have done and I kept silent. . . . But I will rebuke you and accuse you to your face." Consider this, you who forget God. . . . He who sacrifices thank offerings honors me, and he pre-

pares the way so that I may show him the salvation of God" (vv. 16–17, 19, 21–23).

Development of theme
The Lord speaks against hypocrisy . . .

Sometimes I'm guilty of going through the motions—responding automatically to expectations when my mind is preoccupied with other concerns.

But God's indictment against the people in this

> "If I don't cultivate intimacy with the Lord, all I will have is an empty religion rather than a transforming relationship."

passage involved more than a warning against simple preoccupation. Israel was engaged in full-fledged disobedience! While Israel was giving verbal assent to the law, she was in reality breaking it right and left. In fact, she went beyond disobedience to the point where she defended dishonesty (v. 19), condoned adultery (v. 18), and participated in slander, speaking against their own brothers and sisters and despising familial ties (v. 20).

Because the Lord has been silent to this point, Israel assumed that He was satisfied with mere lip service. But God's outlook isn't like man's. Man places a high premium on outward appearance, but God looks at the attitude of the heart.

It isn't enough for me to have a thorough knowledge of the truth. I must cultivate intimacy with the Lord. Otherwise, all I will have is an empty religion rather than a transforming relationship.

Personal prayer

Dear Lord, transform my mind and heart. May Your Truth not just spring automatically from my lips, but may it transfigure my life.

PANORAMA PHOTO BY GARY IRVING

Fugue on Forgiveness

Subject: Prayer of Confession

Exposition of theme

PSALM 51

Have mercy on me, O God, according to your unfailing love; according to your great compassion blot out my transgressions. Wash away all my iniquity and cleanse me from my sin. For I know my transgressions, and my sin is always before me. Against you, you only, have I sinned and done what is evil in your sight (vv. 1–4).

Development of theme

The background of this splendid poem on forgiveness is David's sin of adultery with Bathsheba (2 Samuel 11). Bold phrases showcase the intensity of David's confession: "blot out my transgressions" (v. 1); "wash away all my iniquity" (v. 2); "cleanse me from my sin" (v. 2). David is crying out for full forgiveness. Aware that he does not deserve God's mercy, he nevertheless appeals to God's unfailing love and compassion.

David feels the crushing weight of his guilt. Further compounding the problem is the fact that

> *"Anyone — man or woman, peasant or potentate — may appeal to God for forgiveness and be restored to a life of joy and service."*

he has been engaged in a cover-up for at least a year. The death of the child conceived out of wedlock and the prophet Nathan's confrontation are the catalysts for his confession, and David

acknowledges that his sin is ultimately against God and God alone.

The thesis of this remarkable outpouring from the heart of a king is that anyone — man or woman, peasant or potentate — may appeal to God for forgiveness and be restored to a life of joy and service.

I too am painfully aware that intimacy with God comes only when I am brutally honest with the Lord about specific sins in my life. I start making headway when I give up self-deception and stop playing games with myself and the Lord. Reality, not rationalization, leads to growth.

Personal prayer

Lord, deliver me from impotence and guilt. On the basis of Your unfailing love and grace, set me free and fill my life with Your joy.

A PERTINENT HYMN

Are You Washed in the Blood?

Have you been to Jesus for the cleansing
   power?
Are you washed in the blood of the Lamb?
Are you fully trusting in His grace this hour?
Are you washed in the blood of the Lamb?

Lay aside the garments that are stained with
   sin —
O be washed in the blood of the Lamb;
There's a fountain flowing for the soul un-
   clean —
Are you washed in the blood of the Lamb?

Are you washed in the blood,
In the soul-cleansing blood of the Lamb?
Are your garments spotless?
Are they white as snow?
Are you washed in the blood of the Lamb?

Words and music by Elisha A. Hoffman.

Fugue on Forgiveness

Counter-Subject: Prayer of Petition

Exposition of theme

PSALM 51 CONTINUED

Cleanse me with hyssop, and I will be clean; wash me, and I will be whiter than snow. Let me hear joy and gladness; let the bones you have crushed rejoice. Hide your face from my sins and blot out all my iniquity. Create in me a pure heart, O God, and renew a steadfast spirit within me. Do not cast me from your presence or take your Holy Spirit from me. Restore to me the joy of your salvation and grant me a willing spirit, to sustain me (vv. 7–12).

Development of theme

Nearly three thousand years after David's downfall, we don't have to look far to find his successors — fallen leaders dragged down by their sin nature into moral bankruptcy. Unfortunately this condition is no longer limited to the secular world. In the Christian arena too we have been concerned with image rather than reality. We have evaluated success on the basis of external symbols rather than on internal purity. We have some Christian leaders who look great on the

outside, but are dying inside.

In this very personal petition to the Lord, David acknowledges that he can't possibly correct his basic sin nature. Only the God who created him can cleanse, renew, and restore. David's body, wracked with physical and emotional pain, must learn how to rejoice again. His crushed spirit

> **"We have some Christian leaders who look great on the outside, but are dying inside."**

longs to hear, once more, the music of God's joy and gladness. He asks to become a new creation, both psychologically and judicially, and prays, in this Old Testament context, that the Holy Spirit not be taken from him. Likely he is remembering Saul, who had lived as such an exile, deposed from God's blessing.

I also need a deep work of God in my life. Like David, I yearn for radical spiritual surgery — cleansing, restoration, a purified heart, the transforming power of the Holy Spirit, and the antidepressant of being filled with the joy of my salvation!

Personal prayer

Lord, cleanse me from sin today and fill my crushed spirit with the joy of the Holy Spirit.

THE LANGUAGE OF MUSIC

Lugue

A polyphonic musical composition in which one or two themes are imitated by successively entering voices.

Themes are developed contrapuntally (one or more independent melodies added above or below a given melody).

Fugue on Forgiveness

Answer: Prayer of Praise

Exposition of theme

PSALM 51 *CONTINUED*

Then I will teach transgressors your ways, and sinners will turn back to you. Save me from bloodguilt, O God, the God who saves me, and my tongue will sing of your righteousness. O LORD, open my lips, and my mouth will declare your praise. You do not delight in sacrifice, or I would bring it; you do not take pleasure in burnt offerings. The sacrifices of God are a broken spirit; a broken and contrite heart, O God, you will not despise (vv. 13–17).

Development of theme

You can feel the beat of David's heart in this deeply personal interaction with the Lord. He has been locked into a pattern of deceit, God has allowed him to be crushed, and now he pleads

---

"In exchange for mercy and forgiveness, David pledges himself to three actions."

---

for mercy and forgiveness.

Yet David knows that the justice and honor of the heavenly Father demand nothing less than His child's utter brokenness. You can hear the resonant chords of his broken heart as he pleads, "Save me from bloodguilt, O God, the God who saves me!" (v. 14)

In exchange for mercy and forgiveness, David pledges himself to three actions: (1) to teach sinners the ways of God so convincingly that they will repent; (2) to praise God in song. Genuine praise always springs from honest, heart-

wrenching lament; (3) to worship God through the sacrifice of contrition. David offers up his broken heart.

David concludes this magnificent fugue on forgiveness with a prayer for prosperity. He believes that meaningful worship leads to national prosperity, beginning with the purity and righteousness of its leaders.

Personal prayer

Lord, my heart breaks when I consider my own willfulness and waywardness. Teach me to teach others about You, to praise You, and to sacrifice. Above all, lead me into a genuinely honest relationship with You. May sin not be a veil separating us.

A CONTEMPORARY LYRIC

Something Beautiful

Something beautiful, something good,
All my confusion He understood;
All I had to offer Him was brokenness and
　　strife,
But He made something beautiful of my life.

Words by Gloria Gaither. Music by William J. Gaither.
© 1971 by Wiliam J. Gaither. All rights reserved. Used by permission.

Fantasia on Faith

In Minor: Deceit's Discord

Exposition of theme

PSALM 52

Why do you boast of evil, you mighty man? Why do you boast all day long, you who are a disgrace in the eyes of God? Your tongue plots destruction; it is like a sharpened razor, you who practice deceit. You love evil rather than good, falsehood rather than speaking the truth. . . . Surely God will bring you down to everlasting ruin. . . . The righteous will see and fear; they will laugh at him, saying, "Here now is the man who did not make God his stronghold but trusted in his great wealth and grew strong by destroying others!" (vv. 1–3, 5, 6–7).

Development of theme

This psalm was written because of the treachery of a man named Doeg (1 Samuel 21–22), who was an informer during the reign of David. Doeg's career as a terrorist was built on slander,

> *"How much easier it is to be critical rather than creative, to put down rather than to build up."*

deceit, and intrigue. The tongue of this self-satisfied, clever man revealed his evil, corrupt character. His words, sharp as a razor, were used to destroy people and bring disgrace to God.

God will not put up with this kind of behavior forever, then or now. The unsaved can learn a lesson from Doeg. Their ruin, like his, is inevitable. In an act of final judgment, God will bring them to "everlasting ruin" (v. 5) and they'll learn, too late, that great wealth, obtained at the expense of destroying others, will not buy a reprieve in the day of judgment.

Probing my own often deceitful heart, I find that his psalm stirs my conscience. I'm so often controlled by mixed motives and false goals. This affects my speech. How much easier it is for me to be critical rather than creative, to put down rather than to build up, to be a troublemaker rather than a peacemaker. Deceit always creates discord. Only a truthful tongue can sing in harmony!

Personal prayer

O Lord, purify and purge me of deceit. Cleanse me on the inside so that my tongue sings only truth.

THE LANGUAGE OF MUSIC

Fantasia

Italian term meaning "fantasy."

(French, "fantaisie"; German, "fantasie"). As you would think, it is an instrumental piece involving "fantasy." This is accomplished in different ways: improvisation, romanticism, or use of rather free forms.

Fantasia on Faith

In Major: Faith's Fantasy

Exposition of theme

PSALM 52 CONTINUED

But I am like an olive tree flourishing in the house of God; I trust in God's unfailing love for ever and ever. I will praise you forever for what you have done; in your name I will hope, for your name is good. I will praise you in the presence of your saints (vv. 8–9).

Development of theme

What a difference between Doeg, the traitor, and David, the man of faith! What bold contrasts exist in the psalms: the wicked versus the righteous, the transient versus the permanent, adversity versus prosperity.

David uses the metaphor of a flourishing olive tree to depict God's blessing on his life. His faith is strong because his roots go down deep into the soil of God's unfailing love. Because of this inner security, David is able to praise God *for what He has done.* He is also freed to praise

God *for who He is,* for His incomparable attributes, His "good name." In that Name David places his eternal hope.

I love David's last statement in this psalm: "I will praise you *in the presence of your saints.*" For ancient worshipers, private praise always led to public worship. Individualism did not obliterate their sense of community.

> *"Isolation, alienation, and aloneness result in weakness. The fellowship of brothers and sisters in Christ lends strength."*

So many of us are loners, but how we need each other! Isolation, alienation, and aloneness result in weakness. The fellowship of brothers and sisters in Christ lends strength. God doesn't want us to be spiritual "Lone Rangers."

Personal prayer

Your unending, unfailing love, O God, inspires me to proclaim my faith in You wherever your saints gather for worship.

Sonatina on Wickedness

Exposition of theme

PSALM 53

The fool says in his heart, "There is no God." They are corrupt, and their ways are vile: there is no one who does good. Will the evildoers never learn — those who devour my people as men eat bread and who do not call on God? Oh, that salvation for Israel would come out of Zion? When God restores the fortunes of his people, let Jacob rejoice and Israel be glad! (vv. 1, 4, 6).

Development of theme

"The fool says in his heart, 'There is no God.' " This recurring theme is hammered home in the irreverent lyrics of heavy metal and punk rock musicians as well as in the various pseudo-religious movements so prevalent today. And if it isn't blatant atheism, it is passively leaving God out of our lives. Many live today as if God didn't exist!

The thesis of this psalm, almost identical to Psalm 14, is that people are universally corrupt.

> **"How refreshing to find many godly people in the music industry!"**

(Paul further elaborates on this theme in Romans 3 — his theological masterpiece.) What a contrast to modern-day humanism which boasts of the inherent goodness of man!

In the first movement (vv. 1–3), David describes the human race as "fools," "corrupt," "vile," "turned away." He further grieves, "There is no one who does good, not even one" (v. 3).

How refreshing to find many godly people in the music industry. One such musician is Steve Green, who is known not only for his soaring voice, but also for his strong conviction and personal holiness. David wishes he could find "even one"!

The second movement (vv. 4–5) portrays the wicked as ultimately "overwhelmed by dread" and despised by God. David can't believe the ignorance of those who persecute the righteous.

In the third and final movement David utters a plea for the salvation of Israel and declares his faith that God will restore the fortunes of His people. David has a deep, inner longing for the coming of God's kingdom.

As I think about the fact that Christ is coming back to this sinful world, my whole perspective changes. When people leave God out of their lives, they sour and become corrupt. I want to warn them that He may come today! But without spiritual reality at the core of my personhood, I too will sour and become corrupt. What will keep me pure and fresh today? Closeness and intimacy with the Lord and the eager expectation of His return.

Personal prayer

O God, act as my preservative from corruption. As I interact with unbelievers in my world, may I be salt and light. Come, Lord Jesus!

153

Hymn of Confidence

Exposition of theme
PSALM 54

Save me, O God, by your name; vindicate me by your might. Surely God is my help; the LORD is the one who sustains me (vv. 1, 4).

Development of theme

How do I respond under pressure? Am I paralyzed by fear? Do I panic? Do I try to escape? Do I withdraw? Do I become depressed? Do I use medication?

David, hotly pursued by his enemies, knows that he is in mortal danger. He has been betrayed by the Ziphites — ungodly, ruthless men — and even threatened by one who has loved him, King Saul. With his life on the line, David doesn't panic, but cries out to God.

His prayer is in two parts: "Save me, O God, by your name; vindicate me by your might." In the second part of this hymn, David asserts his trust in God: "Surely God is my help; the LORD is the one who sustains me."

Under fire, David faced the hard facts of his dilemma with confidence, but he was not alone. Nor does God abandon me to sort out my problems alone. The same Lord who delivered David "from all [his] troubles" is able to deliver me!

Personal prayer

O God, when I am experiencing unbelievable pressure, help me to trust in Your name and in Your power — not in human solutions.

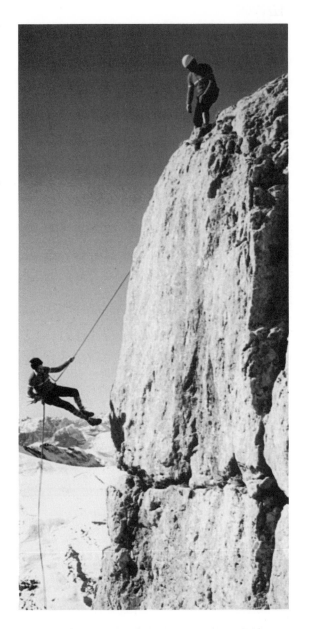

"With his life on the line, David doesn't panic, but cries out to God."

Ballad of Betrayal

First Motif: Rejection

Exposition of theme

PSALM 55

If an enemy were insulting me, I could endure it; if a foe were raising himself against me, I could hide from him. But it is you, a man like myself, my companion, my close friend, with whom I once enjoyed sweet fellowship as we walked with the throng at the house of God (vv. 12–14).

Development of theme

One of the most painful experiences in life is betrayal by a close and trusted friend, one "with whom [you] once enjoyed sweet fellowship." Insult and persecution from enemies is to be expected; rejection by a beloved companion is almost unendurable! And this happens because human relationships are never free from impure motivations. It is human nature to use, exploit, and manipulate people for our ends. Often, all of this is denied until the association sours, the

> **"But the ultimate blow is the rejection rendered by an intimate friend."**

communication ceases, and the friendship dies. Then, when we see this person in the mall, we turn and go the other way!

As a warrior, David was often in danger. He had learned to live with "the terrors of death" (v. 4), "horror" (v. 5), "violence and strife" (v. 9), "threats and lies" (v. 11). But the ultimate blow is the rejection rendered by an intimate friend.

Destructive forces are loose in the city of David. Anarchy and confusion are the result of the betrayal of his trusted confidant who has become a traitor. To make matters worse, David has even worshiped with this rogue!

What do I learn from David's desperate cry? I learn to expect the unexpected, to stand firm in my belief that the Lord is orchestrating my life — its highs and lows, its dissonance and consonance. Further, I learn from my own suffering and anguish something of what Christ endured for me, and that redemption comes at a terribly high price.

Personal prayer

O God, help me to be honest with You about my feelings of injustice and unfairness. May times of persecution give me insight into the compassion and suffering of my Lord and Savior.

THE LANGUAGE OF MUSIC

Ballad

From the Latin, "ballare" "to dance."

A ballad is now a popular song involving romantic, adventurous, and narrative elements.

Ballad of Betrayal

Second Motif: Affirmation

Exposition of theme

PSALM 55

Cast your cares on the LORD and he will sustain you; he will never let the righteous fall. But you, O God, will bring down the wicked into the pit of corruption; bloodthirsty and deceitful men will not live out half their days. But as for me, I trust in you (vv. 22–23).

Development of theme

In the midst of his gut-wrenching betrayal by a close friend, David feels the affirming hand of God on his life. I am reassured today, knowing that God has not changed and that He ministers to me in the same ways.

He hears my cry of distress—morning, noon, or night (v. 17). He is able to save me just as he saved David (v. 16). He is aware of the violence

---

> "Help me not to get so wrapped up with rejection that I miss the liberating power of Your affirmation."

---

of the wicked because "men . . . never change their ways" (vv. 18–19). Even before I suspect treachery, the Lord knows the intent of the heart (v. 21).

The rich metaphors used in this psalm aptly depict a modern-day Judas. David's friend uses speech "as smooth as butter," but beneath the surface lies a ruthless, violent man. His words, "more soothing than oil," are "drawn swords." This situation is not new to David, for he mentions it on at least three other occasions (57:4, 59:7, 64:3).

What a God! He will not forsake the righteous (v. 22). I can "cast my cares" on the Lord and He will see me through my own Gethsemanes. David's final words in this psalm echo the song of my heart: "But as for me, I trust in you!"

Personal prayer

O God, help me not to get so wrapped up emotionally with rejection that I miss the liberating power of Your affirmation.

Polyphony of Pressure

David's Plight

Exposition of theme

PSALM 56

Be merciful to me, O God, for men hotly pursue me; all day long they press their attack. My slanderers pursue me all day long; many are attacking me in their pride. When I am afraid, I will trust in you. In God, whose word I praise, in God I trust; I will not be afraid. What can mortal man do to me? (vv. 1–4).

Development of theme

The publishing world is a pressure cooker. But all of twentieth-century life, whether in the corporate world or the kitchen, is a cauldron of frenetic

> **"How I respond under pressure reveals my true character. My neighbors are watching!"**

activity, vigorous competition, and pressing decisions. We're all on the run. Seldom, however, are Christians in America running for their lives, though many are quietly dying inside.

In this psalm David is acutely aware of his fight for survival. (See 1 Samuel 21 and Psalm 34.) During a visit to Gath, he faces the possibility of daily attack. His enemies, all conspirators and killers, twist his words and plot to harm him. simply speaking, David is on the run. He is a fugitive, living like a scavenger on the edge of society. He is fighting for his life. He even has to pretend insanity! But because of his intimate relationship to the Lord, his response isn't typical. Instead of giving in to fear, he chooses faith.

As I face the stresses and tensions of modern life, I want to respond like King David. Instead of groveling in fear and intimidation, I choose to pray, to trust, to exercise faith, and to praise the Lord. How I respond under pressure reveals my true character. My neighbors are watching!

Personal prayer

O God, may I not be intimidated by other people. When I'm afraid, let me learn to trust more in You, for "what can mortal man do to me"?

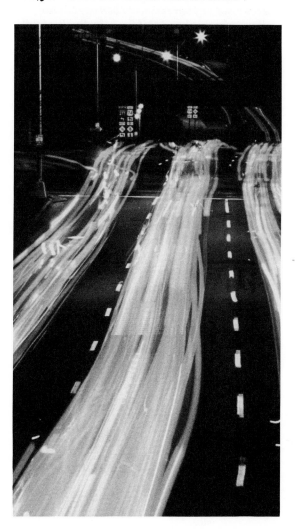

Polyphony of Pressure

God's Protection

Exposition of theme

PSALM 56 *CONTINUED*

Record my lament; list my tears on your scroll — are they not in your record? Then my enemies will turn back when I call for help. By this I will know that God is for me. In God, whose word I praise, in the LORD, whose word I praise — in God I trust; I will not be afraid. . . . For you have delivered my soul from death and my feet from stumbling (vv. 8–11, 13).

Development of theme

Every tear we shed is recorded "on God's scroll"! What a comfort to David, whose back was to the wall! The king was a brilliant soldier

---

"Like a highly competent recording engineer who uses digital sampling, God accurately records every sigh, every whisper, every heartbeat, every tear. He knows me intimately."

---

and a military genius who exuded power and strength. But he wasn't afraid to cry!

Like a highly competent recording engineer who uses digital sampling, God accurately records every sigh, every whisper, every heartbeat, every tear — from the moment of my birth cry to the present. He knows me intimately. He is the complete and perfect Engineer, always attuned to my condition.

Though under severe stress, David is a real model for me. He places his complete trust in the

Lord and in His Word. He is so confident of deliverance that he speaks in the past tense: "You *have delivered* my soul from death and my feet from stumbling" (v. 13).

David wasn't victimized by his circumstances. He didn't let pressure overwhelm him. His conscious choice made all the difference. He chose to praise the Lord and to trust His supernatural powers of protection. David's decision drove away his fear and enabled him to see his deliverance as an accomplished fact.

Personal prayer

Father, I am moved, not only by Your vigilant protection, but by Your tenderness. Not a whisper goes unheard! What can I do but praise Your Name?

THE LANGUAGE OF MUSIC

Polyphony

Greek for "many voiced."

There are three basic musical textures: monophonic (a single, melodic line unaccompanied), homophonic (a single, melodic line accompanied), and polyphonic (two or more melodic lines). Polyphony is synonymous with counterpoint. (Romans 8:28 shows how God, the Master Composer, controls the counterpoint of our lives around the theme of His own glory).

Triumphant Song
Prayer of Deliverance

Exposition of theme
PSALM 57

I cry out to God Most High, to God, who fulfills his purpose for me. He sends from heaven and saves me, rebuking those who hotly pursue me; Selah God sends his love and his faithfulness. Be exalted, O God, above the heavens; let your glory be over all the earth (vv. 2–3, 5).

Development of theme

Again I see myself reflected in David. This time he has fled from King Saul and is hiding in a cave (1 Samuel 22, 24). There are times when I feel like escaping from the world and going into hiding "until the [present] disaster has passed."

In fact, when I was attending a Christian high school, I was under pressure to be a campus leader. Secretly I wanted to blend in with the crowd or, better still, to be left alone. I still struggle with feelings of shyness and social ineptitude, so I can relate to David's cave.

Instead of giving up or giving in, David prays in that dark hiding place. His prayer is a harmony in four parts.

Part One: "Lord, have mercy!" He calls on the mercy of God and huddles under "the shadow of his wings" (v. 1).

Part Two: He believes that God has a plan, uniquely designed for him, and that He will "fulfill his purpose" (v. 2).

Part Three: He acknowledges his helpless state and describes his adversaries as predators with teeth like "spears and arrows" and tongues like "sharp swords" (v. 4).

Part Four: Seeing beyond his present plight, David looks forward to a time when he will be vindicated and avenged and to that day when the

> *"I still struggle with feelings of shyness and social ineptitude, so I can relate to David's cave."*

Lord will establish His righteousness and glory over the earth! (v. 5).

When David finds himself in hot water, he prays. When he is between a rock and a hard place, he prays. When he is under extreme pressure, he prays. I'd like to be more like this warrior who prayed!

Personal prayer

My prayer, O God Most High, is that Your purpose will be fulfilled in my life and that Your glory may shine through my personality.

Triumphant Song
Prayer Celebrating God's Love and Faithfulness

Exposition of theme
PSALM 57 CONTINUED

My heart is steadfast, O God, my heart is steadfast; I will sing and make music. Awake, my soul! Awake, harp and lyre! I will awaken the dawn. I will praise you, O LORD, among the nations. I will sing of you among the peoples. For great is your love, reaching to the heavens; your faithfulness reaches to the skies. Be exalted, O God, above the heavens; let your glory be over all the earth (vv. 7–11).

Development of theme

David is counting on victory, so he celebrates God's love and faithfulness. As the chief musician in Israel, he can't conceive of a better way to

159

> *"On a crescendo of praise,*
> *David's imagination soars as*
> *he exults in purest praise of his*
> *Lord."*

adore his Lord than through music and song. Because his faith is steadfast, he feels no fear, but plans to "awaken the dawn" with singing. How interesting, since depression and despair are most acutely felt by many people in the early morning hours.

On a crescendo of praise, David's imagination soars as he exults in purest praise of his Lord.

He vows to sing of Him to all peoples. He eloquently proclaims the greatness of God's love and worshipfully celebrates His faithfulness which reaches to the skies. "Be exalted, O God, above the heavens; let your glory be over all the earth" (v. 5).

David didn't bow down in defeat to his intolerable circumstances. Instead, he made an artistic choice to lift his voice in song, celebrating God's incomparable love and faithfulness!

Personal prayer

O God, I praise You for giving me reason to awaken the dawn. May I start each day with You, sharing the melody of your love and faithfulness with others I meet today.

Appassionata for Justice

The Charge

Exposition of theme

PSALM 58

Do you rulers indeed speak justly? Do you judge uprightly among men? No, in your heart you devise injustice, and your hands mete out violence on the earth. Even from birth the wicked go astray; from the womb they are wayward and speak lies. Their venom is like the venom of a snake, like that of a cobra that has stopped its ears, that will not heed the tune of the charmer, however skillful the enchanter may be (vv. 1–5).

Development of theme

Many of us struggle with bitterness over dishonesty, injustice, and unfairness in life. From the perspective of the immediate, life *is* often unfair. I know what it's like to be set up for humiliation in a public business meeting — to feel like a sheep

---

> *"David's haunting questions linger like an unwelcome refrain. Am I honest and aboveboard in all my dealings? As a husband and father, do I give Karen and the kids a fair hearing?"*

---

among wolves because of the surprise element.

Our God is a God of righteousness and justice. Moses correctly assumes that the "Judge of all the earth" will do right (Genesis 18:25). On this basis David poses two critical questions: "Do you rulers indeed speak justly?" and "Do you judge uprightly among men?" (v. 1).

The questions are obviously rhetorical and intended to cause self-assessment in the hearers. A scathing denunciation follows. David's accusation rings out: "You devise injustice!" (v. 2). "Your hands mete out violence!" (v. 2). [You] "speak lies!" (v. 3). And there is more. These judges are as venomous as snakes and as indifferent to correction as cobras who pay no heed to their charmers.

David is right in denouncing these ancient judges. God places a high premium on justice, since this is an aspect of His own character. Still, Jeremiah 17:9 reminds us that the human heart is desperately deceitful.

David's haunting questions linger in my mind like an unwelcome refrain. Am I honest and aboveboard in all my dealings? Am I a just executive? As a husband and father, do I give Karen and the kids a fair hearing? I'm glad our God is a just — and merciful — Judge!

Personal prayer

Dear Lord, search my heart and, by the power of Your Holy Spirit, point out any wicked way in me. I want to reflect Your character with integrity.

THE LANGUAGE OF MUSIC

Appassionata

Italian for "impassirued."

It is the nickname for Beethoven's Piano Sonata in F minor, op. 57 (1806). It is the dark companion piece to the Waldstein Sonata. Beethoven wrote the most magnificent piano sonata of all time.

Appassionata for Justice

The Verdict

Exposition of theme

PSALM 58 CONTINUED

Break the teeth in their mouths, O God; tear out, O LORD, the fangs of the lions! Let them vanish like water that flows away; when they draw the bow, let their arrows be blunted. Like a slug melting away as it moves along, like a stillborn child, may they not see the sun. Before your pots can feel the heat of the thorns—whether they be green or dry—the wicked will be swept away (vv. 6–9).

Development of theme

I know just how David feels! How often have I been tempted to judge others as they have judged me. It's especially easy to spot a weakness in someone else when I too am guilty—like knocking lack of discipline in overeating when I've put on a few pounds myself.

David doesn't check his emotions here. He pronounces his verdict on these unjust judges, using bold strokes and vivid imagery. He demands that their teeth be smashed and their fangs pulled out so they will not be able to communicate their lies. He hopes they will vanish like water on a hot day. He wants their words to be as ineffectual as blunted arrows. He desires that they simply melt away like slugs (snails) in a

> *"It's easy to spot a weakness in someone else when I too am guilty—like knocking overeating when I've put on a few pounds myself."*

drought. He wants them to die suddenly like a stillborn child who never sees the light of day. He wants their destruction to be swift. Maybe they will even be swept away like astronauts in a blinding explosion!

In anticipating the fulfillment of a geopolitical kingdom on earth, David expects that all enemies who threaten the establishment of God's kingdom on earth will be destroyed swiftly and violently. Here he savors the sweet taste of revenge.

The New Testament, however, gives us an entirely different perspective. We are to leave the final judgment of scoundrels to God and wait patiently for His kingdom to be established on earth. "Vengeance is mine. I will repay, says the Lord" (Hebrews 10:30).

Personal prayer

Lord, may I entrust the ultimate end of my enemies to You. Remove from me the bitterness of revenge.

Appassionata for Justice

The Vindication

Exposition of theme

PSALM 58 CONTINUED

The righteous will be glad when they are avenged, when they bathe their feet in the blood of the wicked. Then men will say, "Surely the righteous still are rewarded; surely there is a God who judges the earth" (vv. 10–11).

Development of theme

Immanuel Kant, noted German philosopher, believed that the universal notion of justice was proof of God's existence. He also believed it was proof of a literal heaven. Why? Because he didn't observe justice being fully fulfilled on this earth. It is also tacit evidence for a place of eternal punishment. Why? Because Hitler, for example, never got the punishment he deserved during his lifetime.

David is encouraged that God's justice will be

> *"Someday God will set all things straight. The finale of a Beethoven symphony will seem inconsequential by comparison!"*

carried out. In these verses he resorts to wild, strong imagery to carry the intensity of his thoughts. He longs to see the righteous "bathing their feet in the blood of the wicked." Such a military coup would bring him great satisfaction.

David is also convinced that injustice will not prevail forever. The righteous will be rewarded. Men will see that God does judge the earth finally and righteously. So ends David's passionate plea for justice and vindication.

What personal comfort and intellectual solace I can derive from the fact that God will someday set all things straight! The finale of a Beethoven symphony will seem inconsequential in comparison to this!

Personal prayer

Dear Lord, I thank You that by definition You are just. Help me to leave final judgments with You.

Ein' Feste Burg
("A MIGHTY FORTRESS")

Conspiracy and Treachery

Exposition of theme
PSALM 59

Deliver me from my enemies, O God; protect me from those who rise up against me. Deliver me from evildoers and save me from bloodthirsty men. O my Strength, I watch for you; you, O God, are my fortress, my loving God (vv. 1–2, 9).

Development of theme

As I read these hymns penned by David, the greatest warrior-king Israel ever produced, I'm reminded that my own life seems somewhat tame by comparison. While David, the shepherd boy, was stalking and killing fierce predators that threatened his flock, I struggle with fierce competition in the music industry. Still a lad, he fought the giant Goliath with a slingshot, five smooth stones, and the Name of the Lord. Some of the giants in my life loom large to me, but budget hassles, contract negotiations, and balancing priorities are not so dramatic. Assuming

> *"In my routine, it isn't 'fierce and bloodthirsty men' who conspire against me and rob me of life and vitality, but tight schedules, family crises, and creative dry spells."*

manhood, David seemed forever engaged in the fight for survival, while I attempt to keep creative energy alive and wrestle with significance and meaning in life.

Inspired by yet another attempt on his life, this time by crazed and jealous King Saul, David prays for deliverance from the treachery of evildoers. As is so often the case in an assassination attempt, conspiracy is involved (v. 3). But David's wife, Michal, foils the plan, warns David, and helps him escape through a window.

In my daily routine, it isn't often "fierce and bloodthirsty men" who conspire against me and rob me of life and vitality, but tight schedules, family crises, and creative dry spells. In these mundane moments too God provides an "open window" of deliverance, a way out.

Personal prayer

O God, I praise You for "open windows" and that You continue to stand as my Strength and Fortress in every circumstance of my life.

MAY 18

Ein' Feste Burg

("A MIGHTY FORTRESS")

Justice and Peace

Exposition of theme

PSALM 59 CONTINUED

But do not kill them, O LORD our shield, or my people will forget. In your might make them wander about, and bring them down. . . . But I will sing of your strength, in the morning I will sing of your love; for you are my fortress, my refuge in times of trouble. O my Strength, I sing praise to you; you, O God are my fortress, my loving God (vv. 11, 16–17).

Development of theme

While David expects justice to be done, he is motivated by more than revenge and vindication. He longs for the punishment of his enemies to *reflect God's sovereignty.* Is this the same David

---

"Do I desire that God be glorified . . . even more than I desire to see my competitors get their deserts?"

---

who envisioned a blood bath of the wicked (58:10), exhorted God to defang the lions and blot them up like water that evaporates in the sun (58:6–7)?

Now the psalmist implores God to stay His hand of execution (v. 11), but allow his enemies to wander as fugitives so that "it will be known to the ends of the earth that God rules over Jacob" (v. 13).

I pause to reflect: Do I desire that God be glorified . . . even more than I desire to see my competitors get their deserts? Am I motivated by pride to seek credit for peacemaking, or do I point others to Him?

Notice the bold contrast in verse 16. David is carried away into paeans of praise. So moved is he by His Sovereign Lord that he promises to extol His virtures "in the morning." And, to emphasize his intent, David repeats his promise: "I will sing of your strength, in the morning I will sing of your love; for you are my fortress, my refuge in times of trouble" (v. 16).

Personal prayer

O Lord God Almighty, You are King of kings, my All in all. May I never be guilty of seeking revenge for injustices, but desire to point all people — even my opponents — to You.

Military March

Deliverance

Exposition of theme

PSALM 60

But for those who fear you, you have raised a banner to be unfurled against the bow. Save us and help us with your right hand, that those you love may be delivered (vv. 4–5).

Development of theme

Being a passionate person, I'll have to admit that there have been times when I've been angry with God. When bad things happen, when my goals are blocked, when nothing seems to work out, I feel angry! In turn, my attitude is displeasing to

---

"Battling with God is no contest. To withdraw or to move farther away is to prolong healing and intimacy with Him."

---

my heavenly Father, and he deals with me like the obstinate child I am.

David is keenly aware that God is sovereign and has absolute control over victories and defeats. The big threat here is probably the nation of Edom, which invaded Judah while David was fighting in the north (2 Samuel 8, 1 Kings 11, and 1 Chronicles 18).

This major defeat is the result of God's anger kindled against His people. The very earth has been shaken and David pleads with the Lord to "mend its fractures" (v. 2). "You have been angry—now restore us!" he cries.

When God is angry with me and I have felt the earthquake of His displeasure, there is only one hope—to ask for restoration and renewal. Bat-

tling with God is no contest. To withdraw or to move farther away is to prolong healing and intimacy with Him. "Let [me] draw near to God with a sincere heart in full assurance of faith, having [my] heart sprinkled to cleanse me from a guilty conscience" (Hebrews 10:22).

Personal prayer

O God, continue to save me and help me with Your right hand. I am so grateful that Your great love and mercy outweigh Your anger.

Military March

Triumph

Exposition of theme

PSALM 60 CONTINUED

God has spoken from his sanctuary: "In triumph I will parcel out Shechem and measure off the Valley of Succoth. Gilead is mine, and Manasseh is mine; Ephraim is my helmet, Judah my scepter. Moab is my washbasin, upon Edom I toss my sandal; over Philistia I shout in triumph" (vv. 6–8).

Development of theme

When I moved my family from Grand Rapids, Michigan, to Nashville, Tennessee, feelings of disorientation, dislocation, and disruption were almost overwhelming. Yet I felt the move was part of God's plan for our lives. Perhaps He wanted us to face our deepest soul longings that can only be fulfilled in Him, not in friends or familiar surroundings. He puts us in the place where He wants us!

The psalmist reminds us that because the tribes of Israel belong to God, He will deliver His own and subjugate their enemies. They will be

> *"Perhaps He wanted us to face our deepest soul longings that can only be fulfilled in Him, not in friends or familiar surroundings."*

put in their place. God, the Lord of the manor, will parcel out the lands precisely as it suits Him.

To Israel, he assigns the lands of Shechem, the Valley of Succoth, Gilead, Manasseh, Ephraim (His helmet of defense), and Judah (His place of rule).

Israel's enemies will become their slaves.

Moab will be reduced to the level of a washbasin! God will toss His sandal to Edom! Philistia will hear God's shout of triumph!

Note that all of these lands already belong to God. The Israelites are merely sojourners, tenants, and stewards of all that the Lord has given to them. This gives them both security and an awesome responsibility.

Personal prayer

O God, I thank You for providing our home, for which we are only "tenants" for the time You have given us on this earth. May I never forget that, whatever my address, my real dwelling place is with You!

Military March

Trust

Exposition of theme

PSALM 60 CONTINUED

Who will bring me to the fortified city? Who will lead me to Edom? Is it not you, O God, you who have rejected us and no longer go out with our armies? Give us aid against the enemy, for the help of man is worthless. With God we will gain the victory, and he will trample down our enemies (vv. 9–12).

Development of theme

In the ancient world, David believes that supernatural power supercedes natural resources. Divine victory comes through trusting and praising God. Human defeat is the result of fearing man and cowering before him. The answers to David's problems almost always come through prayer and praise — a recognition of God's sovereignty.

This is a reminder to me when I'm intimidated by obstacles to success and tempted to depend solely upon human resources — my mind, my talent, the corporation, the weekly paycheck, the marketing team, the sales force, and the professional musicians with whom I work.

In this passage, David asks some questions I might ask myself: "Who will lead me to this heathen, fortified city?" *(Am I intimidated by the size and strength of the opposition, or do I trust God to make up for my inadequacies?)* "Who will lead me to Edom?" *(Dare I face my competition without prayer for direction?)* "Is it not You, O God?" *(Are You on my side, Lord? Or, more importantly, Am I on Your side?).*

David then declares that human help is worthless and ends this military psalm by pleading with God for aid against the enemy. His faith is strong. God *will* give the victory.

> "*Technology and human ingenuity are no match for the incomparable power of God.*"

Technology and human ingenuity are no match for the incomparable power of God. Without His inspiration, no matter how well-trained or gifted or knowledgeable I may be, I'll fail. Under his banner, I march to sure and certain victory!

Personal prayer

Lord, help me neither to trust in my own abilities and connections nor to flinch in the face of overwhelming obstacles, but to depend upon Your supernatural power.

Hiding in Thee

"Lead me to the rock that is higher than I"

Exposition of theme

PSALM 61

Hear my cry, O God; listen to my prayer. From the ends of the earth I call to you, I call as my heart grows faint; lead me to the rock that is higher than I (vv. 1–2).

Development of theme

Far from home, David is feeling overwhelmed, inadequate, and insecure. Isolation makes one an easy target for discouragement and depression.

From time to time, I've felt this way on a business trip. Differences in time zones, jet lag, and unfamiliar surroundings exacerbate those feelings. And calling home isn't always the answer, since problems crop up there too! It's not easy to be God's man in today's world.

Nor was it easy for David. But he didn't allow himself the luxury of sliding into despair. He called on God who "neither slumbers nor sleeps

---

> *"Isolation makes one an easy target for discouragement. Sometimes on a business trip zones, jet lag and unfamiliar surroundings have made me feel lonely. It's not easy to be God's man in today's world."*

(Psalm 121:4). He asked the Lord to led him to a place of safety, a high refuge—one that he could never attain by himself. Only then will he feel truly safe.

Though I may travel to "the ends of the earth"

on business for my company, I'm as close to my Lord as my next prayer.

Personal prayer

Lead me today, Father to "the Rock that is higher than I"!

A GOSPEL HYMN LYRIC

Hiding in Thee

O safe to the Rock that is higher than I,
My soul in its conflicts and sorrows would
    fly;
So sinful, so weary—Thine, Thine would I
    be:
Thou blest "Rock of Ages," I'm hiding in
    Thee.

Hiding in Thee, Hiding in Thee,
Thou blest "Rock of Ages," I'm hiding in
    Thee.

Words by William O. Cushing. Music by Ira D. Sankey.

Hiding in Thee

"I long to dwell in Your tent forever."

Exposition of theme
PSALM 61 CONTINUED

For you have been my refuge, a strong tower against the foe. I long to dwell in your tent forever and take refuge in the shelter of your wings. For you have heard my vows, O God; you have given me the heritage of those who fear your name (vv. 3–5).

Development of theme

There are times when even strong men feel weak and undone. Such a time was in 1984, when a series of losses changed my life radically and decimated my emotional energy.

David candidly admits his weakness—both physically and emotionally. Now he simply wishes to retreat for a time into the sanctuary of the tent of the Lord. He is likely referring to the Tabernacle, that magnificent portable temple of God, built of acacia wood overlaid with gold and hung with blue, purple, and scarlet curtains of

> **"In 1984, a series of losses changed my life radically and decimated my emotional energy."**

finest linen. It was here that God's shekinah Glory dwelt in the Holy of Holies, His presence abiding with David's forebearers during their sojourn in the wilderness. Now, so far from home, David longs for such a physical manifestation of his Lord.

David has made his vows before God, just as I dedicated my life to His service on Word of Life Island when I was a kid. I share David's spiritual

inheritance—unlimited and inalienable. In reality, then, I already possess the power of God's attributes, if I lay claim to them, confessing my own unworthiness and weakness.

In these times of retreat, when I'm at the end of myself, I find Him in a fresh experience of worship. The 1984 episode had the positive effect of causing me to reevaluate my life critically and forced me to face "false gods" squarely. It was the beginning of a turning point in my ministry!

Personal prayer

O God, may I dwell in Your place of safety forever. There, may I experience the profound fulfillment of my deepest longings.

Hiding in Thee

"Increase the days of the king's life."

Exposition of theme
PSALM 61 CONTINUED

Increase the days of the king's life, his years for many generations. May he be enthroned in God's presence forever; appoint your love and faithfulness to protect him. Then will I ever sing praise to your name and fulfill my vows day after day (vv. 6–8).

Development of theme

When David prays, "Increase the days of the king's life, his years for many generations," I understand his concern. America is a nation preoccupied with aging.

It's uncomfortable to reach midlife. Because I have prematurely silver hair, some people think

Karen is my daughter instead of my wife! Even my Dad, who is now in his seventies, likes to tell people that he's my brother. Not only that, but I'm surrounded by highly talented, young musicians in an industry dominated by youth.

While much of Western society worships at the shrine of youth, touting wrinkle creams, beauty spas, and fitness clubs as the secret to its preservation, King David knows that there is only one lasting solution. I know it too. To abide in the presence of God forever is to enjoy eternal life — both in duration and in quality. What an answer to deep personal fears and insecurities!

Since this psalm most likely also alludes to the coming Messiah, these blessings will be fulfilled to overflowing in the Person of the King of kings and Lord of lords!

No wonder David's intense emotion erupts in exuberant praise. "Then will I ever sing praise to Your name" (v. 8). He pledges his faithfulness "day after day." The mandate for the believer is a deep, abiding sense of the Lord's love and faithfulness.

Personal prayer

O Lord, You have numbered my days. Don't let me be so concerned with my own aging process that I miss the blessings of intimate relationship with You, now and in the life to come.

Hymn in Three Stanzas

First Stanza: Waiting in Silence

Exposition of theme

PSALM 62

My soul finds rest in God alone; my salvation comes from him. He alone is my rock and my salvation; he is my fortress, I will never be shaken. How long will you assault a man? Would all of you throw him down—this leaning wall, this tottering fence? They fully intend to topple him from his lofty place; they take delight in lies. With their mouths they bless, but in their hearts they curse (vv. 1–4).

Development of theme

David's life wasn't a bed of roses. He faced an inordinate amount of adversity. He learned, however, to be still under stress—to rest in the Lord.

Rests in music are crucial. A musical rest is a sign that, for a specified time, the music ceases. Contrasts in the arts are highly significant; hence, rests are often as important as the notes. Intervals of silence between tones enhance the beauty and texture of the music. So, also, in life!

The psalmist's calm security and implacable stability come from God. David perceives his Lord as his Rock, his Salvation, his impregnable Fortress. Therefore, he cannot be moved or distracted by the taunts of the wicked.

His enemies, of course, see him in a different light. They view him as vulnerable—"a leaning wall," "a tottering fence" (v. 3). Shouting curses and lies, they will attempt to topple David from his lofty position.

Unbelievable strength is drawn, however, in rest—waiting in silence which implies utter trust that the rope will hold, the fortress will stand, the walls won't cave in. Not only does salvation come from God, but He gives me those still moments when I gain strength for the battle.

Personal prayer

O God, I thank You for intervals of silence when, if my soul really listens, I can hear, not the mockery of the world, but Your still, small voice.

THE LANGUAGE OF MUSIC

Stanza

A stanza is a verse, measure, or refrain.

Songs are made up of stanzas. David is called "Israel's singer of songs (2 Samuel 23:1)."

> "Rest is that waiting in silence, trusting that the rope will hold, the fortress will stand, the walls won't cave in."

Hymn in Three Stanzas

Second Stanza: Trusting in God

Exposition of theme

PSALM 62 CONTINUED

Find rest, O my soul, in God alone; my hope comes from him. He alone is my rock and my salvation; he is my fortress, I will not be shaken. My salvation and my honor depend on God; he is my mighty rock, my refuge. Trust in him at all times, O people; pour out your hearts to him, for God is our refuge (vv. 5–8).

> *"This biblical picture of man is in sharp contrast to the bleak portrait painted by secular existentialism."*

Development of theme

David has a very personal relationship with God. This intimacy is observed in his use of the pronoun *my*. Note the phrases: "*my* soul," "*my* hope," "*my* rock," "*my* salvation," "*my* fortress," "*my* honor," "*my* mighty rock," and "*my* refuge." God was not an abstract theological concept to David, but his source of hope, safety, deliverance, and unshakeable faith.

On the basis of his experiential knowledge of God, David pleads with other believers to trust in God, to pour out their hearts to Him, and to rely on Him as their shelter from danger.

This biblical picture of man is in sharp contrast to the bleak portrait painted by secular existentialism. Yes, *apart from God,* I am fragile and vulnerable. But *in union with God,* I am complete and fulfilled!

Personal prayer

O God, my Rock and my Refuge, once again I express my trust in You. I pour out my heart to You. I thank You for filling the vacuum of my soul with the hope of Your salvation.

A BELOVED GOSPEL HYMN

Rock of Ages

Rock of Ages, cleft for me,
Let me hide myself in Thee;
Let the water and the blood,
From Thy riven side which flowed
Be of sin the double cure,
Cleanse me from its guilt and power.

Nothing in my hands I bring,
Simply to Thy cross I cling;
Naked, come to Thee for dress,
Helpless, to look to Thee for grace;
Foul, I to the fountain fly,
Wash me, Savior, or I die!

Words by Augustus M. Toplady.   Music by Thomas Hastings

Hymn in Three Stanzas

Third Stanza: Expecting His Reward

Exposition of theme

PSALM 62 CONTINUED

Lowborn men are but a breath, the highborn are but a lie; if weighed on a balance, they are nothing; together they are only a breath. . . . Though your riches increase, do not set your heart on them. One thing God has spoken, two things have I heard: that you, O God, are strong, and that you, O LORD, are loving. Surely you will reward each person according to what he has done (vv. 9–12).

Development of theme

I have a tendency to be impressed with a person's status, his level of achievement, her impeccable credentials. David shows us how futile it is to place too much emphasis on human ac-

---

"Both human ingenuity and material prosperity are meaningless when weighed against the majesty and might of God."

---

complishment. Why? Because all people, regardless of rank or position, are "but a breath."

Another common fallacy in affluent America is our fascination with money-making. We have only to watch the stock market to see that money is an inadequate object for our faith. In a rollercoaster economy, a person who sets his heart on getting rich is skating on thin ice. Both human ingenuity and material prosperity are meaningless when weighed against the majesty and

might of God.

Where, then, is the real power in life, the real rewards? David shows us the answer in two facets of God's diamond-like character: "You, O God, are strong. . . . You, O LORD, are loving." On the basis of these two attributes, He will control events so that perfect justice prevails in the end. We can trust that kind of God to reward us accordingly.

Personal prayer

O God, I thank You that, though I am so weak, You are strong. Even more astounding is that You love me and are planning to reward me "according to what [I] have done."

A CONTEMPORARY LYRIC

Secret Ambition

Young man on the hillside
Teaching new ways,
Each word winning them over;
Each heart a kindled flame.

Some say, "Death to the radical
He's way out of line!"
Some say, "Praise be the miracle!
God sends a blessed sign—
A blessed sign for troubled times!"

Nobody knew his secret ambition,
Nobody knew His claim to fame;
He broke the old rules steeped in tradition,
He tore the holy veil away.
Questioning those in powerful position,
Running to those who called His name;
But nobody knew His secret ambition,
Was to give His life away.

Words by Amy Grant and Wayne Kirkpatrick.
Music by Michael W. Smith.
© 1988 by O'Ryan Music, Emily Booth, and Fred & Ethel.

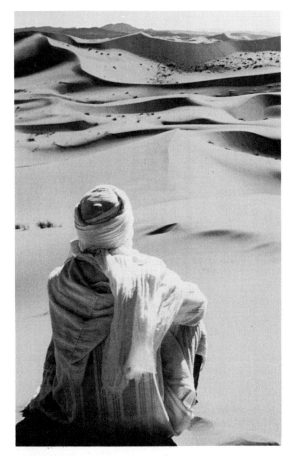

Development of theme

The desert sands are hot, the heat excruciating, the land parched and dry. David is thirsty. His mouth is as dry as a potsherd. This experience

---

"Much like David, my song 'Longing for God' was born out of the hunger and thirst of my soul."

---

prompts him to reflect on his deep thirst for God.

This first verse of his song is an affirmation of David's faith: "O God, You are my God." The prayer that follows is expressed in three motifs: "Earnestly *I* seek you." "My *soul* thirsts for you." "My *body* longs for you." His whole being is in touch and in love with God. Nothing that "dry and weary land" can provide will satisfy the driving hunger and thirst of his soul.

Much like David my song "Longing for God" was born out of the hunger and thirst of my soul.

A CONTEMPORARY LYRIC

Longing for God

Like a dry and thirsty land,
I long for You, O Lord!
My parched and hungry soul
Longs for Your quenching Word!

May I find You in sweet fellowship,
May I see You in great preaching;
May my heart be moved with Your love,
May Your Spirit work in teaching!

In the shadow of Your wings
I sing songs in the night;
In the darkness of this world
I cling to You for light.

Words and music by Don Wyrtzen. © 1980 Singspiration Music.

MAY 28

Plainsong of Praise

"My soul thirsts for you."

Exposition of theme
PSALM 63

O God, you are my God, earnestly I seek you; my soul thirsts for you, my body longs for you, in a dry and weary land where there is no water (v. 1).

176

Personal prayer

Dear Lord, my whole being longs for You today. Please come and let me drink deeply of the living water.

MAY 29

Plainsong of Praise

"I will praise you as long as I live."

Exposition of theme

PSALM 63 CONTINUED

I have seen you in the sanctuary and beheld your power and your glory. Because your love is better than life, my lips will glorify you. I will praise you as long as I live. . . . My soul will be satisfied as with the richest of foods; with singing lips my mouth will praise you. . . . Because you are my help, I sing in the shadow of your wings (vv. 2–5, 7).

Development of theme

Once David had beheld the power and glory of his Lord, he was never the same again. Deeply moved by the presence of God in the sanctuary,

> *"Like David, I know the deep satisfaction of composing praise music—a satisfaction much like that of rich food that satisfies physical hunger."*

he was inspired to write some of the loftiest and most sublime praise music ever written.

Because the love of God also means more to me than life itself, I will praise Him "as long as I live."

Like David, I know the deep satisfaction of composing praise music—a satisfaction much like that of rich food that satisfies physical hunger.

I long for the kind of divine obsession that drove David to meditate on the name of the Lord through the watches of the night. As "my soul clings" to Him, whether in the sanctuary or in the shadows of my life, I pray that my music will be a reflection of His power, glory, and love.

Personal prayer

Dear Lord, I want to praise You as long as I live! Kindle in me a fire of passion until the words and music flow through my purified soul.

A CONTEMPORARY LYRIC

As Long As I Live

As long as I live, He will be supreme,
As long as I live, He will be my theme;
As long as I live, this will be my dream—
Jesus, the Source of lasting joy.

Jesus, the Source of lasting joy,
Giving life abundantly;
Jesus, the Source of lasting joy,
He's my only security.

Words and music by Don Wyrtzen. © 1982 Singspiration Music.

Plainsong of Praise

"They who seek my life will be destroyed."

Exposition of theme

PSALM 63 *CONTINUED*

They who seek my life will be destroyed; they will go down to the depths of the earth. They will be given over to the sword and become food for jackals. But the king will rejoice in God; all who swear by God's name will praise him, while the mouths of liars will be silenced (vv. 9–11).

Development of theme

There is more than one way to "destroy" life. A sarcastic comment can cut like a sword. When it is premeditated, the wound is even deeper. Gossip, often without basis in fact, can be a lethal weapon. "The tongue is a small part of the

---

"The church needs to become much more tolerant of creative people. Art doesn't flourish in the harsh winds of criticism. A bitter spirit can't break forth into beautiful song."

---

body. . . . Consider what a great forest is set on fire by a small spark" (James 3:5).

It's much easier to be a critic than a creator — to pick apart someone's work rather than to put together something new. How insidious we are with our criticism! "So and so is terrific, *but . . .*" These negative evaluations tear down those who are made in God's image and destroy the creative process as well. The church needs to become much more tolerant of creative people. Art doesn't flourish in the harsh winds of criti-

cism. A bitter spirit can't break forth into beautiful song.

King David knew all about verbal swordplay as well as physical attack. His enemies were ever lurking in the shadows. In this psalm he has been personally absorbed in praising God until some incident or memory triggers his thoughts about his enemies, and he is forced to contemplate the judgment of the wicked. The destroyers will themselves be destroyed and swallowed up into the depths of the earth. They will be devoured by the sword and their bodies will be thrown to the jackals. "The mouths of liars will be silenced" (v. 11). It seems a fitting punishment for the crime.

What a contrast for King David and contemporary Christians as well! We, who have been delivered, spontaneously burst forth into affirmations of belief in God's Name and songs of praise. When the Lord meets our needs, as He works in our lives, when He defuses the venomous words and deeds of our critics, we praise Him!

Personal prayer

Dear Lord, I rejoice in Your holy Name and thank You for helping me deal with criticism. Turn the words of my critics into praises to You!

Drone-Pipe of Judgment

Drone of Complaint

Exposition of theme

PSALM 64

Hear me, O God, as I voice my complaint; protect my life from the threat of the enemy. Hide me from the conspiracy of the wicked, from that noisy crowd of evildoers. They sharpen their tongues like swords and aim their words like deadly arrows. They shoot from ambush at the innocent man; they shoot at him suddenly, without fear. They encourage each other in evil plans, they talk about hiding their snares; they say, "Who will see them" They plot injustice and say, "We have devised a perfect plan!" Surely the mind and heart of man are cunning (vv. 1–6).

Development of theme

A drone-pipe is the lowest tone on the bagpipe, used for accompaniment. It is often used as a pedal point, a long sustained bass note against which changing harmonies sound.

Like so many of David's psalms, my prayers often take on the monotonous tone of complaint Here David is overwhelmed by the malicious schemes of that "noisy crowd," the wicked. "They shoot from ambush at the innocent man!" (v. 4). What a natural tendency it is to counter-attack — to "sharpen our tongues like swords" and to "aim our words like deadly arrows!" (v. 3).

Yet beneath the apparent bitterness and complaining is a ground bass, an insistent pedal

> "Like so many of David's psalms, my prayers often take on the monotonous tone of complaint."

point: "Hear me, O God. . . . Hear me, O God. . . . Hear me, O God." David's emphasis is not on his grumbling, but on God!

Caught in the crossfire of slanderous speech and hidden snares, he acknowledges the Sovereign Lord as his ultimate Arbiter, the supreme Peacemaker. David may drone on indefinitely about his woes, but he always turns to the Lord for protection and justice.

Personal prayer

Hear me, O God! If I must be monotonous, let it be in singing Your praises!

THE LANGUAGE OF MUSIC

Drone-Pipe

The lowest tone used for accompaniment on the bag-pipe.

It can refer to any long sustained bass note. It is often used as a pedal-point (a long-held bass note against which changing harmonies sound). God's judgment is like a drone-pipe underneath the rapidly changing textures of human history.

June PSALMS 64–74

PANORAMA PHOTO BY GARY IRVING

Drone-Pipe of Judgment

Prophecy of Praise

Exposition of theme

PSALM 64 CONTINUED

But God will shoot them with arrows; suddenly they will be struck down. He will turn their own tongues against them and bring them to ruin; all who see them will shake their heads in scorn. All mankind will fear; they will proclaim the works of God and ponder what he has done. Let the righteous rejoice in the LORD and take refuge in him; let all the upright in heart praise him! (vv. 7–10).

Development of theme

When I'm tempted to question certain inequities in my world, I need to be reminded that the administration of a just God promises perfect objectivity and lack of prejudice . . . *someday.* Such a God can be counted on to balance the scales.

Ironically the very people who are bringing me the most grief, those who dare to wage war against God, will be brought down by their own words and schemes. God is in control!

Over and over again, I read the psalmist's litany of grievances, his pleas for protection, and, at last, his songs of praises. I've wondered, sometimes, just why God felt it necessary to be quite so repetitious in recording His Word.

In music, repetition is vital! Beethoven was a master at taking a little bit of material — sometimes just one short theme — and repeating it in a kaleidoscope of musical variations. The psalmists did the same thing. They hammered away at similar motifs and themes repeatedly. Perhaps the ancient Israelites were like us — slow learners! Like the ocean, music is cyclical — it thrives

"Beethoven was a master at taking a short theme and repeating it in a kaleidoscope of musical variations. The psalmists did the same thing."

on thematic repetition, development, and variety.

God is teaching me — pounding out the truth in every heartbeat, in every rhythmic cycle of nature, in the echoes of His love — that He is the Sovereign Lord of my life. *Someday* He will be feared and respected by all mankind because of His swift enactment of justice. *Someday* all the righteous will rejoice and take refuge in Him. *Someday* "at the name of Jesus every knee [will] bow . . . and every tongue confess that Jesus Christ is Lord" (Philippians 2:10–11).

Personal prayer

O Lord, I rejoice in You today. My heart leaps in recognition of another continuous theme — the insistent, steady reminder of Your love!

THE LANGUAGE OF MUSIC

Drone-Pipe

The lowest tone used for accompaniment on the bag-pipe.

It can refer to any long sustained bass note. It is often used as a pedal-point (a long-held bass note against which changing harmonies sound). God's judgment is like a drone-pipe underneath the rapidly changing textures of human history.

Concerto of Gratitude

His Blessing

Exposition of theme

PSALM 65

Praise awaits you, O God, in Zion; to you our vows will be fulfilled. O you who hear prayer, to you all men will come. When we were overwhelmed by sins, you forgave our transgressions. Blessed is the man you choose and bring near to live in your courts! We are filled with the good things of your house, of your holy temple (vv. 1–4).

Development of theme

"God is so good; God is so good; God is so good . . . He's so good to me."

The words of this contemporary chorus reflect the view of ancient believers who celebrated this life-sustaining affirmation in conjunction with the barley harvest (Leviticus 23). This psalm holds the key to the "utter fulfillment, blissful happiness, and complete contentment" available to modern-day believers as well.

In meditation, I review God's blessings on my life—salvation, answered prayer, Christian fellowship. I'll never forget the night my Mom led me to the Lord as a kid of seven. I was afraid and upset. She comforted me with Christ's words in John 6:37: "All the Father giveth me shall come to me; and him that cometh to me I will in no wise cast out" (KJV). Upon accepting that promise, peace and serenity displaced my childish fears. Since then, I have felt God's hand of provision—once when Karen and I were down to our last nickel and an unexpected royalty check put food on our table! And we continue to grow in Christ with other brothers and sisters—Larry, Jan, Dick, Carol, Don, Shay, and Stan—as we meet together weekly for prayer.

Finally, like the temple-worshipers, I have been *chosen* and brought "near to live in [his] courts!" What sublime happiness awaits me for the rest of my life and through all eternity. "All the good things of [his] house" are mine! Where will I experience real happiness and a rich, inner satisfaction? Only in the presence of the Lord.

> *"I'll never forget the night my Mom led me to the Lord. I was afraid and upset, but when she comforted me with Christ's words in John 6:37, peace and serenity displaced my childish fears."*

Personal prayer

O God, my Savior, thank You for saving me, for sustaining me, and for giving me all the good things of Your house.

Concerto of Gratitude

His Power

Exposition of theme

PSALM 65 CONTINUED

You answer us with awesome deeds of righteousness, O God our Savior, the hope of all the ends of the earth and of the farthest seas, who formed the mountains by your power, having armed yourself with strength, who stilled the roaring of the seas, the roaring of their waves, and the turmoil of the nations. Those living far away fear your wonders; where morning dawns and evening fades you call forth songs of joy (vv. 5–8).

Development of theme

We Americans are obsessed with power. We want to climb higher, run farther, move faster than any other generation in history. We'd like to climb on board the Concorde at lunch and arrive in London in time for dinner. Our psychologists delve into the recesses of inner space, while our

scientists explore outer space. All America held its breath when Neil Armstrong stepped onto the moon! Sometimes, when I take the express elevator to the top of the World Trade Center in New York or the Sear's Tower in Chicgao, I wonder if we are even guilty of erecting our own twentieth-century Towers of Babel.

As a kid I used to watch the Atlantic Ocean roar off the New Jersey coastline. I've observed Niagara Falls many times from different vantage points (including the excursion boat at the foot of the Falls)! And I've peered into the crater atop Mt. St. Helens via videotape, helicopter, and television. God's omnipotence evidenced in nature dwarfs even the most splendid of man's puny achievements.

But this God of might and majesty is also intensely personal. He is intimate as well as infinite. He who "formed the mountains" and "stilled the roaring of the seas" hears every whispered prayer.

Such a God inspires me to hope. He "calls forth songs of joy" from my soul until I can hardly wait to transpose them to paper!

Personal prayer

O God, my Savior, thank You for Your power which, not only formed the world, but keeps my spirit alive with joy!

JUNE 4

Concerto of Gratitude

His Provision

Exposition of theme

PSALM 65 CONTINUED

You care for the land and water it; you enrich it abundantly. The streams of God are filled with water to provide the people with grain, for so you have ordained it. You drench its furrows and level its ridges; you soften it with showers and bless its crops. You crown the year with your bounty, and your carts overflow with abundance. The grasslands of the desert overflow; the hills are clothed with gladness. The meadows are covered with flocks and the valleys are mantled with grain; they shout for joy and sing (vv. 9–13).

Development of theme

Human striving and struggle to attain is often disappointing. Always wanting more and never being satisfied feeds on itself and produces greed, lust, and discontent. What a waste of energy!

In these exalted verses the psalmist tells us a simpler way to be happy. He points us to God who answers prayer, not in the abstract, but specifically and in intricate detail. Look at the exqui-

site lines in verses 9 through 13. He waters the land, enriches it abundantly, drenches its furrows, levels its ridges, softens it with showers, and blesses its crops. The carts are filled to overflowing with grain. Even the desert flourishes, and the hills are "clothed with gladness."

God is not only the consummate Husbandman; He knows all about the music business too! He knows what it takes to take a song from its germ idea—often a title, sometimes a "hook," a chorus, or a musical phrase—through the various stages of development. Fine craftsmanship is imperative. Then comes reevaluating, rewriting, polishing. Once the song is complete, other musical disciplines come into play: making a demo, song plugging, arranging, orchestrating, and recording. No detail must escape our attention.

Nothing escapes His notice either. There is no matter too trivial to take to the Lord in prayer. Whatever my need—whether shepherding a single song through the recording process, developing a major new recording artist, or fulfilling my role as husband and father—my God has all the answers. His concern for every minute detail of my work and existence prompts me to shout for joy!

Personal prayer

O God, my Savior, thank You for caring about every aspect of my life and answering my smallest prayer with Your bounty.

Call to Remembrance

"Come and see what God has done!"

Exposition of theme
PSALM 66

Shout with joy to God, all the earth! Sing to the glory of his name; offer him glory and praise! . . . Come and see what God has done, how awesome his works in man's behalf! . . . For you, O God, tested us; you refined us like silver. You . . . laid burdens on our backs . . . but you brought us to a place of abundance (vv. 1–2, 5, 10–12).

Development of theme

"Come and see what God has done," exhorts the psalmist. Israel is encouraged to remember past victories and to join in a song of deliverance. Strong verbs signal the personal involvement of surrounding nations: "Shout with joy!" "Sing to the glory of his name!" "Offer him glory and praise!"

Israel has reason to rejoice. God has performed "awesome works"—the parting of the Red Sea, the routing of rebels and the overthrow of dangerous enemies, the provision of His presence in times of severe testing and trial. The Israelites have come through a painful process of purification much like the refining of silver. ("You, O God, tested us; you refined us like silver" v. 10.) To remove impurities, the smelter must fire his furnace to at least 1,761 degrees F.

"I too have known the Refiners fire. Out of my grief I wrote 'When Thou Passest Through the Waters,' a spiritual based on Isaiah 43:2."

According to Pliny in his *Historia Naturalis*, "the ore was washed and sieved five times, fused with lead and then cupelled for pure silver."

I too have known the Refiner's fire. The loss of my Mom, my pastor, and a close friend in a single year was a devastating experience. Out of my grief I wrote "When Thou Passest Through the Waters," a spiritual based on Isaiah 43:2.

God is faithful to lead us through the fire and water to a "place of abundance" (v. 12). Jesus says, "I have come that they may have life, and have it to the full" (John 10:10). I find a place of fullness and intimacy with my Lord when I follow where He leads.

Personal prayer

Dear Lord, I praise You for walking with me through the fire and water of purification so that I may enjoy You forever in the "place of abundance."

A SONG BORNE OF GRIEF

When Thou Passest Through the Waters

When thou passest through the waters, I will be with thee,
When thou passest thru the waters, I will be with thee;
And thru the rivers, they shall not overflow thee,
When thou walkest thru the fire, thou shalt not be burned.

When thou passest thru the waters, I will be with thee,
When thou passest thru the waters, I will be with thee;
And thru dark trials, they shall not overwhelm thee,
When suffering for His sake, thou art glorified.

Words and music by Don Wyrtzen. © 1979 by Singspiration Music.

Call to Remembrance

"Come and listen!"

Exposition of theme

PSALM 66 CONTINUED

Come and listen, all you who fear God; let me tell you what he has done for me. I cried out to him with my mouth; his praise was on my tongue. If I had cherished sin in my heart, the LORD would not have listened; but God has surely listened and heard my voice in prayer. Praise be to God, who has not rejected my prayer or withheld his love from me! (vv. 16–20).

Development of theme

What did an Old Testament believer do when he was in the furnace of God's testing, when he was on a "guilt trip"? He fulfilled his vows to the Lord. He went to the temple to present burnt offerings—animals "without spot or blemish"—as a sacrifice for sin. Why? Because "without the shedding of blood there is no forgiveness" (Hebrews 9:22).

Karen and I once had an interesting conversation with a well-known songwriter. He was having a hard time accepting the Gospel. The Old Testament blood sacrifices seemed primitive and barbaric to him, and he could not conceive of a loving God sacrificing His own Son!

Each time a choice animal was killed and the white wool was stained crimson with its life's blood, the worshiper received a graphic message of substitutionary death. God's refrain echoed again and again: "I love you. I love you. I love you." Because of God's great love, that ancient believer saw with his own eyes the staggering cost of sin and the amazing grace that guarantees our redemption.

God's full forgiveness follows *sincere* repen-

tance. "If I had cherished sin in my heart, the Lord would not have listened" (v. 18). But the Lord does listen to the psalmist's heartfelt confession and pours out His love in response.

Twenty centuries later, you and I have the benefit of the Gospel message that was foretold in those Old Testament rites: "For God so loved the world that He gave his one and only Son, that whoever believes in him shall not perish but have eternal life" (John 3:16). Therefore, I am filled with joy and thanksgiving because I am forgiven, cleansed, and absolved from guilt! I am now free to accept myself because the Lord accepts my prayer and does not withhold His love from me.

Personal prayer

O Lord, I can't keep silent! You inspire me to write and to sing songs of thanksgiving for the miracle of Your love and forgiveness!

"Karen and I once had an interesting conversation with a well-known songwriter. He could not conceive of a loving God sacrificing His own Son!"

Shine on Me

Exposition of theme
PSALM 67

May God be gracious to us and bless us and make his face shine upon us, that your ways may be known on earth, your salvation among all nations. May the peoples praise you, O God; may all the peoples praise you (vv. 1–3).

Development of theme

The Lord bless you and keep you;
   the Lord make his face shine upon you
     and be gracious to you;
The Lord turn his face toward you
     and give you peace (Numbers 6:24–26).

So Aaron and his sons blessed the Israelites in ancient times. This familiar benediction has been blessing people for generations.

In this passage the composer uses the metaphor of light: "May God . . . make his face shine upon us" (v. 1), followed by a trio of eternal themes: God's grace (vv. 1–2), praise of the peoples (vv. 3–5), and God's blessing (vv. 6–7).

I can envision a scenario in which the worship

> *"I can envision a scenario in which the worship leaders, the congregation, and God all play vital roles. See it with me."*

leaders, the congregation, and God all play vital roles. See it with me. It could go something like this:

Pastor or worship leader: O God, may Your unmerited favor rest upon us and may the light of Your countenance flood our hearts and minds with all spiritual understanding. Then we can be Your witnesses, Your living letters, bringing

proof of Your salvation and love to all nations on earth.

Congregation: In this praise gathering, we lift our voices to You, O God! We are but one tribe, one nation among many who rejoice to see justice and perfect leadership. We express the utmost joy and gladness in You today.

God's blessing: "If my people, who are called by my name, will humble themselves and pray and seek my face and turn from their wicked ways, then will I hear from heaven and will forgive their sin and will heal their land" (2 Chronicles 7:14).

God is speaking. We must listen. As He shines upon us, we'll reflect His glory.

Personal prayer
Joyful, joyful, I adore You, God of glory, Lord of light!

Celebration of Conquest
Extolling God

Exposition of theme
PSALM 68

But may the righteous be glad and rejoice before God; may they be happy and joyful. Sing to God, sing praise to his name, extol him who rides on the clouds—his name is the Lord—and rejoice before him. A father to the fatherless, a defender of widows, is God in his holy dwelling. God sets the lonely in families, he leads forth the prisoners with singing (vv. 3–6).

Development of theme

The more intimately I come to know God, the more I am awed by His grace and goodness. Through David's eyes, I see even more clearly God's compassionate nature as well as His majesty and power.

This song accompanied a ritual procession

> *"My friend, Margaret Clarkson, hymn writer par excellence, never knew her father, and I can read the depth of her pain in her lyrics."*

celebrating God's conquests and victories in behalf of Israel. David begins by praying that God will show His awesome power to the wicked by "blowing them away" (v. 2). Then he moves almost immediately to praise, urging his followers to honor and extol the Lord for His tender care. He is the Father of the fatherless, the Defender of widows, the Caring One who sets the lonely in families, the Deliverer of prisoners.

I have a Dad whom I respect and admire, so I

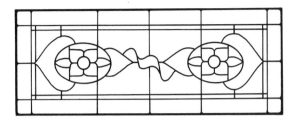

don't know what it's like to be fatherless. But my friend, Margaret Clarkson, hymn writer par excellence, never knew her father, and I can read the depth of her pain in her lyrics. I will never be a widow, but my mother-in-law, Ruth Parr, lost her husband some time ago. I don't know exactly how she feels, but I hear her crying sometimes. I have a friend who has been in prison and, while I haven't served a jail sentence, I imprison myself sometimes behind bars of isolation and remoteness, even with my family around me! But I know our heavenly Father can meet every one of these needs and so many more, if we let Him, for He is our source of consummate security, shelter, and safety.

When I experience God is His gentleness, I am compelled to join in the chorus of praises to His Name. He is my Father, my Defender, my Provider, my Redeemer!

Personal prayer

O God, I rejoice before You today. May I continue to see You, not only as the omnipotent Rider of the Clouds, but as the tender Shepherd.

THE LANGUAGE OF MUSIC
Celebration
The public performance of sacraments or ceremonies with appropriate rites.

A festive, religious ceremony or worship service where the Lord is acclaimed and extolled.

Celebration of Conquest

Remembering the Conqueror

Exposition of theme

PSALM 68 CONTINUED

The mountains of Bashan are majestic mountains: rugged are the mountains of Bashan. Why gaze in envy, O rugged mountains, at the mountain where God chooses to reign, where the LORD himself will dwell forever? The chariots of God are tens of thousands and thousands of thousands; the LORD has come from Sinai into his sanctuary. When you ascended on high you led captives in your train; you received gifts from men, even from the rebellious—that you, O LORD God, might dwell there (vv. 15–18).

Development of theme

Sometimes I need to step back and take a look at where I've been before I can discern where I'm going or how I'm going to get there. These times of inventory are not always preplanned, but it oc-

> *"This psalm brings to mind some of my own wilderness wanderings. It's easy to get lost on the pilgrim journey when you tend to live in a fog. Creative people are like that."*

curs to me that midway through the year is a natural time to take stock.

David must have felt much the same way, since so many of his psalms review Israel's glorious history—from her trek through the wilderness to her conquest of the Promised Land (vv. 7–10). The psalmist then describes the occupation of Canaan where wicked kings were routed and driven out (vv. 11–14).

This psalm brings to mind some of my own wilderness wanderings. It's easy to get lost on the pilgrim journey when you tend to live in a fog. Creative people are like that. Maybe I'm too laid back—not decisive enough. Or maybe I don't always discipline myself enough. But I'm thankful that even at these times, my Lord knows the way!

The climax of the passage comes in the form of exquisite poetry (vv. 15–18), depicting God ascending Mt. Zion—a mighty conqueror with "thousands of thousands" (v. 17) of chariots, and leading "captives in [His] train" (v. 18). The Apostle Paul uses this metaphor to illustrate the spiritual victory that believers experience in Christ (Ephesians 4:8). This song also recalls the siege of Jerusalem by David's army and his establishing the Ark of the Covenant there.

My life gains fresh perspective when I count my victories, not my losses, and focus on the Conqueror. God Himself has escorted me through the wastelands, has cared for me tenderly when I am troubled and tired, and has even conquered death (vv. 19–20) as a guarantee of my eternal life in Him. Such a Conquering Savior demands my highest praise and adoration!

Personal prayer

O God, thank You for reminding me of Your comforting presence through some tangled times. I praise You, my Savior, for rescuing me and leading me to the mountaintop where I will dwell with You forever!

Celebration of Conquest

Assessing His Victory

Exposition of theme

PSALM 68 CONTINUED

Your procession has come into view, O God, the procession of my God and King into the sanctuary. In front are the singers, after them the musicians; with them are the maidens playing tambourines. Praise God in the great congregation; praise the LORD in the assembly of Israel. . . . You are awesome, O God, in your sanctuary; the God of Israel give power and strength to his people. Praise be to God! (vv. 24–26, 35).

Development of theme

I love a parade! I remember taking our kids, D.J. and Kathy, when they were small to the Fourth of July parade in Cascade, a suburb of Grand Rapids, Michigan. There were homemade floats, decorated bikes (with streamers in the wheels), and even an old fire tender with water spewing forth in all directions. Parades are exciting!

God's triumphal entrance into Zion is pictured as a victory parade, complete with singers, dancers, and musicians. Led by the little tribe of Benjamin, they are all praising God in the assembly.

David ends this celebration psalm with a moving call to praise the God who "rides the ancient skies" and "thunders with mighty voice" (v. 33). God's power is awesome and He bestows strength on His people.

"El Shaddai," one of the most magnificent of the contemporary praise songs by my friends, Michael Card and John Thompson, celebrates praise to God for our generation.

May my vision of the Lord increase to the magnitude of David's vision! May I resonate with the awareness that if I open up to Him and cultivate spiritual receptivity, I will receive more of His awesome power and strength in my life. Praise be to God!

Personal prayer

O Lord, I join the artists, musicians, and singers of the ancient world in worshiping You in all of Your power, majesty, and glory!

"I remember taking D.J. and Kathy to a Fourth of July Parade. There were homemade floats, bikes with streamers, even an old fire tender with water spewing forth in all directions!"

A CONTEMPORARY PRAISE SONG

El Shaddai

El Shaddai, El Shaddai,
El Elyon na Adonai
Age to age You're still the same
By the power of the name;
El Shaddai, El Shaddai,
er kamka na Adonai—
We will praise and lift You high,
El Shaddai.

Thru Your love and thru the ram
You saved the son of Abraham,
Thru the power of Your hand
You turned the sea into dry land;
And by Your might You set Your children free.

Your most awesome work was done
Thru the frailty of Your Son,
I will praise You till I die,
El Shaddai.

Words by Michael Card. Music by John W. Thompson.
© 1981 and arr. © 1983 Whole Armor Publishing Company.

Ode to Hope

David feels low . . .

Exposition of theme

PSALM 69

Save me, O God, for the waters have come up to my neck. . . . I am worn out calling for help; my throat is parched. My eyes fail, looking for my God. Those who hate me without reason outnumber the hairs of my head; many are my enemies without cause, those who seek to destroy me. I am forced to restore what I did not steal (vv. 1–4).

Development of theme

There is nothing more disconcerting than being unjustly accused, since denial is the weakest form of defense. David finds himself in just such a no-win situation in this psalm.

His enemies, some of whom are important city officials, despise him, and even his own relatives have disowned him. He feels like a drowning man! "The waters have come up to my neck" (v. 1); "I sink in the miry depths" (v. 2); "I have come into deep waters; the floods engulf me!" (v. 2).

> *"Following Him sometimes leads me into uncomfortable circumstances. But I'm in good company!"*

His enemies sing cynical songs about him and mock him.

What's significant here is that David is suffering, not because of sin, but as a consequence of zealously following the Lord. He puts on sackcloth, signifying mourning, and pours out his heart to the Lord.

Music is probably the richest of all art forms because it speaks to all levels of the personality simultaneously. One doesn't relate to a powerful piece of music cognitively only, but emotionally and physically as well. Hence, we use music to speak the unspeakable, to express the inexpressible — sorrow, discouragement, anger, bitterness, joy. And we use it when words are not enough.

David uses poetic lament to vent his sense of personal injustice. I'm encouraged by his honesty. I am made aware again that not all suffering is the result of sin. Christ Himself suffered the greatest injustice of all, precisely because He was pure and righteous. Following Him sometimes leads me into uncomfortable circumstances. But I'm in good company!

Personal prayer

Dear God, teach me how to embrace Your sufferings so I can share in the delights of Your kingdom and may I use the gift of music to share the secrets of Your caring with others.

JUNE 12

Ode to Hope

David prays . . .

Exposition of theme

PSALM 69 CONTINUED

But I pray to you, O LORD, in the time of your favor; in your great love, O God, answer me with your sure salvation. . . . Answer me, O LORD, out of the goodness of your love; in your great mercy turn to me. Do not hide your face from your servant; answer me quickly, for I am in trouble. Come near and rescue me; redeem me because of my foes (vv. 13, 16–18).

Development of theme

No one has ever prayed with more fervor than David. His intensity is equal to his need, graphi-

cally described in these phrases: "Rescue me from the mire, do not let me sink; deliver me . . . Do not let the floodwaters engulf me or the depths swallow me up or the pit close its mouth over me" (v. 15).

Ninety-nine out of a hundred persons will not go through the hard work of letting the Lord ex-

> *"When I'm in trouble, I need to pray for His Name to be magnified through my circumstances, in His timing, for the salvation of souls."*

cise the pain from their lives. Denial, changing external behaviors, and maintaining proper images are attempted shortcuts to maturity for most people.

David refuses to resort to that kind of evasive maneuver. He is facing reality here, and I can learn something from his prayer. He appeals to the Lord on the basis of (1) His timing — "in the time of your favor." (v. 13); and (2) His purposes — "your sure salvation" (v. 13). Yet his overriding desire seems to be that God's justice prevail (v. 18). Maybe this is the secret to power in prayer. When selfish desires are yielded to the Lord, His Name is glorified and His purposes fulfilled.

So often I try to hurry God, or attempt to manipulate Him for my own ends. I need to be aware that I limit His work in my life when I confine Him to the present moment rather than the time-span of eternity. When I'm in trouble, I need to pray for His Name to be magnified *through* my circumstances, *in* His timing, *for* the salvation of souls.

Personal prayer

Dear Lord, You are the Giver of life, but You are also my Lifesaver in times of deep trouble.

193

Ode to Hope

The Lord Hears . . .

Exposition of theme

PSALM 69 CONTINUED

I will praise God's name in song and glorify him with thanksgiving. This will please the LORD more than an ox, more than a bull with its horns and hoofs. The poor will see and be glad — you who seek God, may your hearts live! The LORD hears the needy and does not despise his captive people (vv. 30–33).

Development of theme

Our Lord is like the shepherd who knows each individual sheep intimately and by name. He is also like the symphony conductor who not only hears the grand ensemble of the orchestra, but can also single out each individual part as well.

The ear of the Lord is tuned to the hearts of His people. "When he cries out to me, I will hear, for I am compassionate" (Exodus 22:27).

David is counting on that compassion. He comes before the Lord with singing, knowing that the sounds of thanksgiving will be more pleasing than burnt offerings — "an ox . . . or a bull with its horns and hoofs" (v. 31). In turn, this sacrifice of praise will be heard by all in the assembly, and the hearts of the people will be encouraged.

As the psalmist gains personal strength and hope in the very process of praising the Lord, he

urges others to join him in the glad chorus. All is not lost! We are not alone in our pain and distress. He hears! He hears!

Personal prayer

O God, You know the sounds of my distress. You hear me when I sing Your praises. May I never fail to hear Your voice — comforting, guiding, instructing, warning.

> *"Our Lord is like the symphony conductor who not only hears the grand ensemble of the orchestra, but can also single out each individual part as well."*

Petition

O God, save me!

Exposition of theme

PSALM 70

*Hasten, O God, to save me; O L*ORD*, come quickly to help me. May those who seek my life be put to shame and confusion; may all who desire my ruin be turned back in disgrace. May those who say to me, "Aha! Aha!" turn back because of their shame (vv. 1–3).*

Development of theme

For years I've dreaded deadlines. Enormous pressure builds when there is a full symphony recording session booked for tomorrow, and the scores aren't done — even though there has been pacing and discipline. Often, there is only time for a hasty "Help, Lord!"

David is again in dire straits. His life is in danger and his reputation at stake (v. 2). God must act quickly, or David's adversaries will press their advantage. With his enemies breathing down his neck, he cries, "O God, save me!"

The Apostle Peter had a similar experience in New Testament times. Like his Lord, he walked on the water. "But when he saw the wind, he was afraid and, beginning to sink, cried out, 'Lord, save me!'"

Along with David and Peter, I can praise the Lord for responding to life's emergencies with His grace and deliverance.

"For years I've dreaded deadlines. Along with David and Peter, I can praise the Lord for responding to life's emergencies with His grace and deliverance."

Personal prayer

Hurry, Lord! I need the strength of Your presence right now . . . this hour . . . this minute! And hasten the coming of Your kingdom on earth, as it is in heaven.

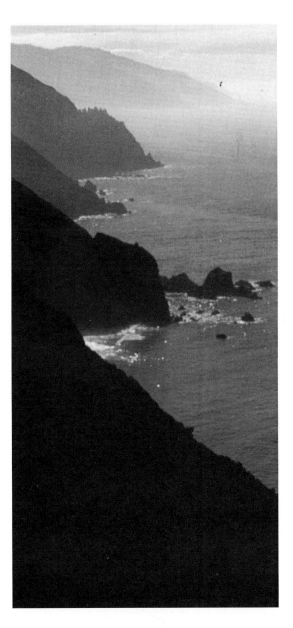

Petition

Let God Be Exalted!

Exposition of theme

PSALM 70 CONTINUED

But may all who seek you rejoice and be glad in you; may those who love your salvation always say, "Let God be exalted!" yet I am poor and needy; come quickly to me, O God. You are my help and my deliverer; O LORD, do not delay (vv. 4–5).

Development of theme

There is no trumped-up worship experience here — no empty ritual or phony liturgy. David is brutally honest with himself and with God in fac-

---

"There is no trumped-up worship experience here — no empty ritual or phony liturgy. David is brutally honest with himself and with God in facing the reality of his plight."

---

ing the reality of his plight. But he doesn't stay in the doldrums. He shifts his focus from problems to praise.

He revels in exalting the Lord and in expressing the love he feels for Him. The Lord is his Help and Deliverer. Though David is poor and needy, surely the Lord will come to his aid without delay.

As I actively seek the Lord, I find great joy in Him. I delight in my salvation, in the help and deliverance He offers. Thank You, Lord.

Personal prayer

O God, may You be lifted to the highest position of praise, honor, and power in my life!

Praise My Soul, the King of Heaven

Praise my soul, the King of heaven.
To His feet thy tribute bring;
Ransomed, healed, restored, forgiven,
Evermore His praises sing.

Praise Him for His grace and favor
To our fathers in distress;
Praise Him, still the same as ever,
Slow to chide, and swift to bless.

Fatherlike, He tends and spares us;
Well our feeble frame He knows;
In His hands He gently bears us,
Rescues us from all our foes.

Words by Henry F. Lyte. Music by Henry Smart.

Lifestyle of Dependence

Confidence

Exposition of theme

PSALM 71

In you, O LORD, I have taken refuge; let me never be put to shame. Rescue me and deliver me in your righteousness; turn your ear to me and save me. Be my rock of refuge, to which I can always go; give the command to save me, for you are my rock and my fortress. Deliver me, O my God, from the hand of the wicked, from the grasp of evil and cruel men (vv. 1–4).

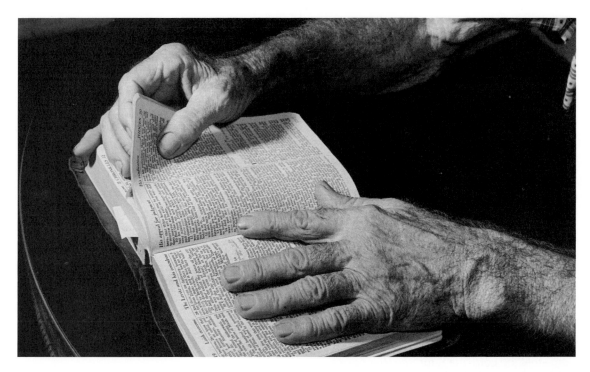

Development of theme

This psalmist is most likely an older person who has experienced the marvelous faithfulness of

---

"The practice of praise produces inner beauty, seasons the spirit, develops prayer muscle. Older saints have learned that dependence upon the Lord is the secret to perfect freedom!"

God for a lifetime. He knows his psalter well, for he quotes Psalms 22, 31, 35, and 40, and vows to continue praising God. He also asks for deliverance from the wicked men who seek to harm him and who mock him for his faith.

He has supreme confidence in the Lord's ability to save. He pictures the Lord as his Refuge, his Rock, and his Fortress. He knows that the only reliable place of safety and security is with the Lord.

I have observed some benefits of growing older in the Lord. For example, there is nothing so full of character as the time-worn, wrinkled face of one of God's prayer warriors, glowing with a radiance that no cosmetic on earth can bestow. The practice of praise produces inner beauty, seasons the spirit, develops prayer muscle. Older saints have learned the paradox that dependence upon the Lord is the secret to perfect freedom! Like the great hymns of the faith, these dear men and women of God grow more precious as time goes by.

Personal prayer

O Lord, You are my refuge, my Rock, and my Fortress. May I learn to lean on You more completely.

Lifestyle of Dependence

Hope

Exposition of theme

PSALM 71 CONTINUED

For you have been my hope, O Sovereign LORD, my confidence since my youth. From birth I have relied on you; you brought me forth from my mother's womb. I will ever praise you. I have become like a portent to many, but you are my strong refuge. My mouth is filled with your praise, declaring your splendor all day long. Do not cast me away when I am old; do not forsake me when my strength is gone (vv. 5–9).

Development of theme

This psalmist believes in the sovereignty of God—that the Lord, the Supreme Ruler of the universe, has everything under His control. Not only is He sovereign, but He *sustains*. From birth, through youth, into the middle years and beyond, the psalmist has felt His sustaining grace.

In music, we use the fermata (musical pause

> *"As I grow older, I need to build my confidence on my own life history with the Lord. He has never failed to meet my needs. He has always taken care of me."*

or hold) to indicate that a note is to be sustained or held. Breaking the rhythmic pace of a piece adds texture and variety. Sustained notes have emphasis because of their staying power. A person can likewise exhibit strong character

through endurance, persistence, and continuance in habits of holiness.

Now that the psalmist is growing older, however, he is afraid. He fears losing his strength (v. 9). He fears his enemies (v. 10). He even fears the possibility that the lord will forsake him (v. 11). Still, he is honest and forthright about his anxieties and cries out to God who has always been his safe haven. He prays for "staying power" as he faces the challenges of aging.

As I grow older, I need to build my confidence on my own life history with the Lord. He has never failed to meet my needs. He has always taken care of me. He has proven Himself faithful and has been my confidence and hope "since my youth." I know I can rely on Him to take care of me today . . . and tomorrow.

Personal prayer

O Lord, You are fully trustworthy. I rest myself in You for the remaining days of my life and into all eternity!

Lifestyle of Dependence

Praise

Exposition of theme

PSALM 71 CONTINUED

I will praise you with the harp for your faithfulness, O my God; I will sing praise to you with the lyre, O Holy One of Israel. My lips will shout for joy when I sing praise to you—I, whom you have redeemed. My tongue will tell of your righteous acts all day long, for those who wanted to harm me have been put to shame and confusion (vv. 22-24).

> *"Musicians have a divine mandate to live a lifestyle of praise. Worship begins with the imagination and the heart, but it must expand outward until our very nerve endings tingle with praise. Like the elderly psalmist, I've experienced some dissonant moments when it appeared there was no resolution, only to find that God was orchestrating these events for my good."*

Development of theme

Repetition teaches and reinforces. This psalmist has learned how to praise the Lord by praising — repeatedly, continually, for a lifetime. He revels in the subject of his praise — God's faithfulness and righteousness (v. 16). He delights in the act of praise — "with the harp" (v. 22); "with the lyre" (v. 22); with "my lips" (v. 23); with "my tongue" (v. 24).

Musicians have a divine mandate to live a lifestyle of praise. I thrill to the variety of musical instruments mentioned in the Book of Psalms and to the parts of the body used in praising the Lord. Hands clap and strum; lips shout; vocal cords resonate and sing; tongues confess and testify; feet dance! Our very bodies are created to perform a symphony of praise! As temples of the Holy Spirit, our bodies are sacred sanctuaries, to be used for His glory, not for our selfish desires. Worship begins with the imagination and the heart, but it must expand outward until our very nerve endings tingle with praise.

The longer I live, the more evidence I gather of God's grace and glory. As I practice praise, I become more proficient in expressing my love and gratitude to Him. Like the elderly psalmist, I've experienced some dissonant moments when it appeared there was no resolution, only to find that God was orchestrating these events for my good. "And we know that in all things God works for the good of those who love him, who have been called to his purpose" (Romans 8:28).

Personal prayer

O Lord, teach me how to praise You and remind me to practice until my heart sings in perfect harmony with Your will.

Solomon's Song

His Justice

Exposition of theme
PSALM 72

Endow the king with your justice, O God, the royal son with your righteousness. He will judge your people in righteousness, your afflicted ones with justice. . . . He will defend the afflicted among the people and save the children of the needy; he will crush the oppressor. He will endure as long as the sun, as long as the moon, through all generations (vv. 1–2, 4–5).

Development of theme

Solomon most likely composed both Psalm 72 and Psalm 127. In this first psalm, he is probably describing his reign as well as the millennial reign of Christ, for he speaks of righteousness, peace, and long-term prosperity.

While he has the good judgment to ask God's blessing on his own administration — "Endow the king with your justice, O God!" (v. 1), it seems clear that Solomon is referring also to the coming messianic kingdom that will "endure as long as the sun, as long as the moon, through all generations" (v. 5).

As a musician and businessman, what can I learn from Solomon? First, I admire his verbal artistry. "He [Jesus] will be like rain falling on a mown field, like showers watering the earth. In his days the righteous will flourish; prosperity will abound till the moon is no more" (vv. 6–7).

But I am also deeply moved by Solomon's personal ethics. "He will judge your people with righteousness. . . . He will defend the afflicted among the people and save the children of the needy; he will crush the oppressor" (vv. 2, 4). Solomon is worthy of emulation in my business dealings and in the practice of my faith.

Without Christ's love in my heart, I might be tempted to lapse into neglect of the talented people who come through my office. But I operate my business on Christian principles, nurturing musical gifts for the glory of God, not for selfish gain. I look for opportunities to hear the unheard and to stand firmly against outside influences that would dilute the Christian message of our music. Living a life of integrity may not promote material rewards, but it promises spiritual prosperity!

Personal prayer

Lord, reign in my heart and bring Your justice and righteousness to every area of my life!

> *"I look for opportunities to hear the unheard and to stand firmly against outside influences that would dilute the Christian message of our music."*

Solomon's Song

His Rule

Exposition of theme
PSALM 72 CONTINUED

All kings will bow down to him and all nations will serve him. For he will deliver the needy who cry out, the afflicted who have no one to help. He will take pity on the weak and the needy and save the needy from death. He will rescue them from oppression and violence, for precious is their blood in his sight (vv. 11–14).

Development of theme

Solomon's reign was lengthy and far-reaching, extending from sea to sea and from the Euphrates River to the ends of the earth (v. 8). He received tribute from the kings of Tarshish and

> *"I would love to be remembered for some of the songs I've written, the passion with which I approach music — attempts at soaring melodies, sophisticated harmonies, and unusual voicings. But to be known as a competent musician with a servant's heart would be the highest accolade of all!"*

gifts from the kings of Sheba and Seba (v. 10). He was widely worshiped and revered.

One might imagine that mighty Solomon would have become corrupted and drunk with pride because of his great power and influence. Instead, he had a heart of compassion for the needy, the afflicted, and the helpless. He rescued them from oppression and violence. Motivated by a lofty concept of the worth of the individual, he was a great king with a servant heart much like that of One who came much later — our Savior, who knelt to wash His disciples' feet (John 13:5).

I would love to be remembered for several things: some of the songs I've written, the passion with which I approach music — attempts at soaring melodies, sophisticated harmonies, and unusual voicings. I love to communicate, to feel as if I'm playing an audience like a Stradivarius. But to be known as a competent musician with a servant's heart would be the highest accolade of all!

Personal prayer

O Lord, may I lay aside my hang-ups with success and model myself after You, who willingly laid down Your crown and took up a cross . . . for me!

Solomon's Song

His Adoring Subjects

Exposition of theme

PSALM 72 CONTINUED

Long may he live! May gold from Sheba be given him. May people ever pray for him and bless him all day long. . . . May his name endure forever; may it continue as long as the sun. All nations will be blessed through him, and they will call him blessed. Praise be to the LORD God, the God of Israel, who alone does marvelous deeds. Praise be to his glorious name forever; may the whole earth be filled with his glory. Amen and Amen (vv. 15, 17–19).

Development of theme

I barely remember the coronation of Queen Elizabeth II of England, only that there was a lot of pomp and pageantry and that some magnificent music was played in Westminister Abbey. I loved the majesty of the pipe organ, combined with brass fanfares and undergirded by the strength and power of rolling timpani and clashing cymbals. And I'll never forget seeing the telecast showing the smiling faces and waving flags of the English subjects who lined the streets to celebrate her coronation day.

King Solomon was held in the highest esteem. He was blessed with personal gifts, agricultural prosperity, a solid, enduring reputation, and the respect of his peers. The Queen of Sheba alone brought him massive amounts of gold (1 Kings 10:10). The common folk praised him for paving the way for flourishing trade, peaceful alliances with neighboring nations, and the blessing of God on their land, which yielded unprecedented crops and herds.

Solomon's response to all of this takes the form of a majestic doxology. It is the second doxology in the book of Psalms and is a fitting close for Book II (Psalms 41–72). "Praise be to the Lord God, the God of Israel, who alone does marvelous deeds. Praise be to his glorious name forever; may the whole earth be filled with his glory. Amen and Amen" (vv. 18–19).

In 1741, at the London premiere of Handel's *Messiah*, King George II rose to his feet during the glorious "Hallelujah Chorus" in worshipful recognition of his Supreme Sovereign. Later, it was Queen Victoria who said, "Someday it shall be my joy to lay my crown at His feet!"

> *"I loved the majesty of the pipe organ, combined with brass fanfares and undergirded by the strength and power of rolling timpani and clashing cymbals."*

Personal prayer

Lord, whatever honors or accolades come to me in this life I will gladly lay at Your feet!

Prelude to True Prosperity

Stating the Paradox

Exposition of theme
PSALM 73

Surely God is good to Israel, to those who are pure in heart. But as for me, my feet had almost slipped; I had nearly lost my foothold. For I envied the arrogant when I saw the prosperity of the wicked. They have no struggles; their bodies are healthy and strong. They are free from the burdens common to man; they are not plagued by human ills (vv. 1–5).

Development of theme
If the Christian life promises blessing, why do godly people struggle while unbelievers enjoy prosperity? Some, in attempting to answer that question, have considered turning away from God.

Sheldon Vanauken, noted author of *A Severe Mercy*, was tempted to disown God when his wife was dying of cancer. My Dad has a friend, a highly articulate, gifted evangelist who abandoned his ministry after becoming disillusioned. And when I was in college, I too experienced some disharmony between mind and spirit and came close to a decision to get along without God in my life.

> *"Sheldon Vanauken, noted author of A Severe Mercy, was tempted to disown God when his wife was dying of cancer. When I was in college, I came close to a decision to get along without God in my life."*

This psalm wrestles with those issues poignantly and poetically. Asaph, one of the chief singers, percussionists, and ministers in the ancient temple, almost walked away from God. He was one of the Lord's major spokesmen and a charismatic leader; yet he seriously considered packing it all in.

I believe spirituality begins with honesty. Part of that is being objective about one's true feelings. This psalm is a beautiful catharsis for Asaph. He pours out his hurting soul before his heavenly Father. The Lord, in His marvelous mercy and imcomprehensible grace, hears.

Personal prayer
O Father, how can I ever be objective about my feelings? I'm hurting, confused, and very frustrated. Please minister to me out of Your vast storehouse of grace.

Prelude to True Prosperity

Viewing Life From What Is Seen

Exposition of theme

PSALM 73 CONTINUED

Therefore pride is their necklace; they clothe themselves with violence. From their callous hearts comes iniquity; the evil conceits of their minds know no limits. They scoff, and speak with malice; in their arrogance they threaten oppression. . . . Therefore their people turn to them and drink up waters in abundance. They say, "How can God know? Does the Most High have knowledge?" (vv. 6–11).

Development of theme

Has the Lord called us to happiness or to holiness? Is it possible to have harmony in life without dissonance? Asaph, in attempting to come to grips with adequate answers to those questions, is tempted to wander away from the Lord.

First, he draws his view of life from what he *sees:* The wicked are prospering and the godly are afflicted. To Asaph and to many modern wor-

> *"Behavioral conformity without spiritual renewal leads to performance without intimacy, breeds doubt rather than faith, and stresses illusion rather than reality."*

shipers, this seems contrary to the moral teaching of the Scriptures, since the Law and Proverbs boldly promise blessing for obedience (Deuteronomy 28; Proverbs 3). The more Asaph observes these apparent contradictions, the more his faith is shaken.

I too suffered from cognitive dissonance while in college. I believed what I saw—that the external symbols of success equaled success itself. Nor did I observe enough internal consistency and reality in Christendom. (It's easier to build a flourishing Christian empire than to nurture a sensitive, beautiful marriage, for example.) Behavioral conformity without spiritual renewal leads to performance without intimacy, breeds doubt rather than faith, and stresses illusion rather than reality.

Secular society and the media can also impact upon our Christian beliefs. For many people, newspapers and television—indeed, the whole non-Christian milieu—carry more clout than God's Word! Yet the Scriptures present the big picture, the long-term view. My own limited perspective often leads to an incorrect translation of God's meaning for my life. I don't want to be guilty of making the mistake Asaph almost made—selling the Lord short.

Personal prayer

O Father, help me to have complete confidence in the authority of Your Word even if it seems to contradict what I see with my eyes. You alone know my tomorrows and how the minor chords of my life can be used to produce a pleasant and harmonious melody.

JUNE 24

Prelude to True Prosperity

Becoming Consumed by Envy

Exposition of theme

PSALM 73 CONTINUED

This is what the wicked are like—always carefree, they increase in wealth (v. 12).

> *We might as well admit, along with Asaph, that we don't have it all together. Some things just don't add up."*

Development of theme

How perplexing! Asaph takes the second step down the ladder of faith when he allows envy to dominate his thoughts. How easy to be drawn into this tangled web spun by the Master Deceiver. Sometimes the grass *does* seem greener on the other side of the fence!

Envy is sin. It's as simple as that. Yet I know of no more subtle addiction to which Christians, living in a highly commercialized world, can fall prey. We see the same ads as the wicked—the posh luxury resorts, the high-tech cars and gadgets, the designer clothing—and wonder why some who seem so undeserving get all the breaks—particularly when prosperity for obedience was promised in the Law! We might as well admit, along with Asaph, that we don't have it all together. Some things just don't add up!

In Isaiah 55:8–9, I receive a gentle rebuke: "For my thoughts are not your thoughts, neither are your ways my ways. For as the heavens are higher than the earth, so are my ways higher than your ways, and my thoughts than your thoughts." The Apostle Paul echoes this truth and adds the dimension of his own reaction: "We are hard pressed on every side, but not crushed; *perplexed*, but not in despair" (2 Corinthians 4:8).

Apparently the proper response to perplexity, at least for the Christian, is to trust in the Lord . . . anyway!

Personal prayer

O Father, I bring my perplexities and unresolved conflicts to You. Help me not to envy the unrighteous who prosper but to put my trust in You.

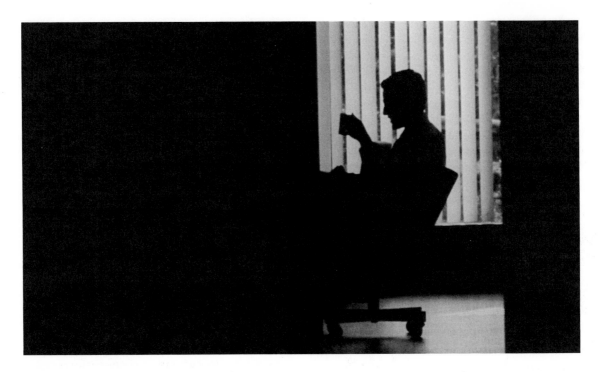

JUNE 25

Prelude to True Prosperity

Almost Dropping Out

Exposition of theme

PSALM 73 CONTINUED

Surely in vain have I kept my heart pure; in vain have I washed my hands in innocence. All day long I have been plagued; I have been punished every morning (vv. 13–14).

Development of theme

What's the use? I can almost hear Asaph's rationale as he takes the third step down the ladder of faith to defection. "All day long I have been plagued; I have been punished every morning"

(v. 14). "But as for me, my feet had almost slipped; I had nearly lost my foothold" (v. 2).

In Hebrew, the word *foot* includes the area from the knee to the sole. The picture is this: "My knees nearly buckled. My steps almost slipped out from under me." In effect, Asaph is saying, "I can't take it anymore!" He's about to take mat-

> *"John DeLorean was bright, pragmatic, energetic, and innovative. But without Christ at the helm of his life, his empire came crashing down."*

ters into his own hands and remove the Lord from the throne of his life.

In some ways John DeLorean, before his conversion to Christ, was the paradigm of the modern American man. One of the "beautiful people," he was bright, pragmatic, energetic, and innovative. But without Christ at the helm of his life, without his sights set on Christian values, without a proper perspective of the value of people, his empire came crashing down.

Fortunately for John, Asaph—and me—God is merciful and longsuffering, "not willing that any should perish, but that all should come to repentance" (2 Peter 3:9, KJV).

Personal prayer

O Father, when everything in me screams, "I can't take it any more," help me to hold on!

JUNE 26

Prelude to True Prosperity

Returning to the Lord

Exposition of theme

PSALM 73 CONTINUED

If I had said, "I will speak thus," I would have betrayed your children. When I tried to understand all this, it was oppressive to me till I entered the sanctuary of God; then I understood their final destiny (vv. 15–17).

Development of theme

Asaph now begins his journey back to the Lord by pondering "all this" (v. 16) and rejecting materialism—what is *seen*. Materialism is seriously flawed. It can put food *on* the table, but will never guarantee fellowship *around* the table. It can provide a *house*, but not a *home*. It can adorn a woman with fine jewels, but never promises love. Materialism generates the notion of loving things and using people. Christianity produces love for people and subordinates things.

Asaph takes a second rung up the ladder of faith when he enters the sanctuary (v. 17). In that

> *"Materialism can only put food on the table, but will never guarantee fellowship around the table. It can provide a house, but not a home."*

place of shelter and serenity, he experiences fellowship and he hears God's Word. With the temple as his support system, he's no longer trying to go it alone.

All Christians, including leaders, speakers, writers, and recording artists, need that kind of support. Since true prosperity is spiritual in nature, we find it only in fellowship with other "becomers." In concert, we give and receive empathy, accountability, inquiry, and care. The Enemy would love to encourage the "star syndrome" which places the "star" in a class by himself, above the limitations and restrictions governing everyone else. When that person becomes isolated in an ivory tower, when he believes his own stuff, when he becomes charmed by the press releases and his own notoriety, he is set up for a big fall. There is only one Superstar, the Lord Jesus Christ.

Asaph too begins to get the picture when he encounters God. The terminology used in this magnificent psalm stresses God's holiness, His "everlastingness," His transcendence. When Asaph finally sees God as He really is, the stunning revelation gives him a whole new perspective on life.

Personal prayer

O Father, give me a fresh revelation of Yourself. May I not neglect my worship experience, but gladly seek the fellowship of other believers in Your sanctuary.

JUNE 27

Prelude to True Prosperity

Encountering the Living God

Exposition of theme

PSALM 73 CONTINUED

When my heart was grieved and my spirit embittered, I was senseless and ignorant; I was a brute beast before you. Yet I am always with you; you hold me by my right hand. You guide me with your counsel, and afterward you will take me into glory. Whom have I in heaven but you? And earth has nothing I desire besides you (vv. 21–25).

Development of theme

After Asaph's encounter with the living God, he sees *himself* as he is: "senseless . . . ignorant . . . a brute beast" — hardly the picture of success as we know it. That's always the case. Meeting God and coming to know Him intimately exposes our limitations, our inadequacies, our weaknesses.

> *"Meeting God and coming to know Him intimately exposes our limitations, our inadequacies, our weaknesses."*

And now Asaph begins to understand the ultimates of life. Because he has caught a glimpse of God in His glory, his perspective is changed on everything, including death. "And afterward you will take me into glory" (v. 24). The alternative is to see life as the brutes or animals, who are locked by instinct into the material world.

Asaph then "lets go and lets God." He invites God to meet his needs for love and meaning. "My flesh and my heart may fail, but God is the strength of my heart and my portion forever" (v. 26). He concludes by fully committing himself to the Lord. In turn, God stamps upon Asaph His own character, heart and mind.

Personal prayer

O Father, give me Your thoughts, Your mindset, and Your perspective on my life. Please meet my profound longings for meaning and love as I commit myself fully to You.

A CONTEMPORARY LYRIC

Come Thou Fount of Every Blessing

O to grace how great a debtor
Daily I'm constrained to be!
Let Thy goodness like a fetter
Bind my wandering heart to Thee.

Prone to wander — Lord, I feel it —
Prone to leave the God I love;
Here's my heart — O take and seal it,
Seal it for Thy courts above.

Words by Robert Robinson. Music by John Wyeth.

Asaph's Lament

Devastation: No Leaders in the Land

Exposition of theme

PSALM 74

Why have you rejected us forever, O God? Why does your anger smolder against the sheep of your pasture? Remember the people you purchased of old, the tribe of your inheritance, whom you redeemed — Mount Zion, where you dwelt. . . . They burned your sanctuary to the ground; they defiled the dwelling place of your Name. They said in their hearts, "We will crush them completely!" They burned every place where God was worshiped in the land. We are given no miraculous signs; no prophets are left, and none of us knows how long this will be (vv. 1–2, 7–9).

Development of theme

"No prophets are left . . ." This mournful theme delivers Asaph's message of devastation. A nation or an individual without "prophets" — spiritual counsel — is a prime target for the Enemy. What Israel needed most was Solomon's dictum: "Plans fail for lack of counsel, but with many advisors they succeed" (Proverbs 15:22).

Asaph groans over the fate of his people, who are suffering at the hands of enemy invaders. He describes, in graphic detail, the demolition of the sanctuary — the seat of worship and God's dwell-ing place. The aggressors have roared in like renegade lumbermen raping a forest (v. 5). They have "smashed all the carved paneling," looted, and pillaged. The final act of blasphemy is the burning of the sanctuary and the dispersion of the prophets. God's Word is not heard in the land, and no one knows how long the devasta-tion will continue.

Though our church buildings are not in immi-nent danger of being razed at this time in our his-tory, we might well ask ourselves why our pulpits and our people are not evidencing more power. Is it because we fail to lift up our spiritual leaders in our prayers? Do we criticize instead of encour-age? Or is it that so many of our churches are "Laodicean" — neither hot nor cold (Revelation 3:15). We coast along apathetically, satisfied with the status quo.

What is needed? Honest, courageous facing of our sin as God's people — individually and cor-porately. Repentance — crying out to God with contrite hearts. Forgiveness — accepting the covering of Christ's precious blood shed on the Cross. Renewal — allowing His Spirit to change our lives to conform to His image. Witness — sharing the Gospel with the unsaved world.

God's dwelling place in my neighborhood is safe. No marauding army has invaded it. But when we fail in any one of these areas, then we might as well post a "Closed" sign on the door.

Personal prayer

O God, may I be faithful to be in Your house, worshiping, praising, thanking You for our free-dom to gather. Anoint Your servant, my pastor, with Your grace and blessing.

> *"Though our church buildings are not in imminent danger of being razed at this time in our history, we might well ask our-selves why our pulpits and our people are not evidencing more power."*

Asaph's Lament

Disorientation: God's Tempo or Mine?

Exposition of theme

PSALM 74 CONTINUED

How long will the enemy mock you, O God? Will the foe revile your name forever? Why do you hold back your hand, your right hand? Take it from the folds of your garment and destroy them! But you, O God, are my king from of old; you bring salvation upon the earth (vv. 10–12).

Development of theme

Unlike the impotent gods of the ancient world, Asaph's God is fully involved, fully in control of His creation. Still, He doesn't move fast enough to suit the psalmist, for God does not bow to man's demands nor adhere to his timetable.

We are often like the trumpet player in an orchestra who wants to set his own tempo (rate of movement) instead of following the conductor.

> **"We are often like the trumpet player in an orchestra who wants to set his own tempo instead of following the conductor. What Asaph needed to learn and what I need to remember is that God's tempo is perfect."**

We'd like for God to work *presto* (at a rapid rate) when the tempo of His plan may be *largo* (slow and dignified). A major aspect of being a world-class conductor, such as Herbert Von Karajan or Georg Solti, is to be in perfect control of the orchestra, setting the appropriate tempo to enhance the master score. As a virtuoso percussionist in Israel, Asaph should have known that.

But Asaph has had it with waiting on God.

"Why do you hold back your hand, your right hand?" he complains. He'd be much happier if the Lord would assert Himself and destroy the adversary—quickly and decisively.

As if to refresh His memory, Asaph outlines God's sovereign acts of the past: "You split open" the Red Sea; "You broke the heads" of sea monsters; "You crushed" Leviathan (a reference to Egypt); "You opened up springs" for the

Israelites; "You set all the boundaries of the earth!" (vv. 13–17). Asaph wonders how such an active God can sit passively by and why He doesn't strike back in behalf of His people with dramatic force and energy.

But God always moves to accomplish His purposes . . . with precise timing. What Asaph needed to learn and what I need to remember is that God's tempo is perfect. "But when the time had fully come, God sent His Son, born of a woman, born under law, to redeem those under law, that we might receive the full rights of sons" (Galatians 4:4).

Personal prayer

O God, forgive my impetuous nature, my desire to rush things. Teach me that the greatest gifts come to those who wait patiently for You.

JUNE 30

Asaph's Lament

Deliverance: The Grand Finale

Exposition of theme

PSALM 74 CONTINUED

Remember how the enemy has mocked you, O LORD, how foolish people have reviled your name. Do not hand over the life of your dove to wild beasts; do not forget the lives of your afflicted people forever. Have regard for your covenant, because haunts of violence fill the dark places of the land. Do not let the oppressed retreat in disgrace; may the poor and needy praise your name. Rise up, O God, and defend your cause; remember how fools mock you all day long. Do not ignore the clamor of your adversaries, the uproar of your enemies, which rises continually (vv. 18–23).

Development of theme

Everything in this psalm is building to a grand finale, a glorious resolution of the woes of these prophetless people.

The glory of a finale was mastered by Beethoven. He was able to build enormous tension be-

> *"A note of triumph soars high above Asaph's lament, heralding God's grand finale of deliverance."*

fore the final ending. He would often seesaw back and forth between tonic and dominant, throwing in a neopolitan sixth to build even more intensity. All of that energy set up an incredibly satisfying final chord. Today, in contemporary Christian music, David Clydesdale is a master of the big ending. Asaph's lament is moving toward such a climax here.

Pleading the cause of Israel, Asaph pours out his soul before God. He asks the Lord to remember His promise to His covenant people — "your dove" — who have suffered affliction. He argues a strong case in defense of the poor, the needy, and the oppressed. When God hears, defends, and delivers them from disgrace, then His people will be able to praise His Name.

The Apostle James reminds us that "the prayer of a righteous man is powerful and effective" (James 5:16). Asaph is such a man, interceding for the helpless children of Israel. A note of triumph soars high above Asaph's lament, heralding God's grand finale of deliverance.

Personal prayer

O God, I take my stand with Asaph, a musician who interceded for his people. Deliver us from the clamor and uproar of sin in our lives as we anticipate Your glorious finale!

211

How lovely is your dwelling place, O LORD Almighty! PSALM 84:1

PANORAMA PHOTO BY GARY IRVING

Victory Celebration

Praise to God

Exposition of theme
PSALM 75

We give thanks to you, O God, we give thanks, for your Name is near; men tell of your wonderful deeds. . . . As for me, I will declare this forever; I will sing praise to the God of Jacob. I will cut off the horns of all the wicked, but the horns of the righteous will be lifted up (vv. 1, 9–10).

Development of theme

Asaph's cup is overflowing. He is profuse in his praise and his thanksgiving, singling out the nearness of God's Name and his wonderful deeds as cause for celebration. In fact, in his

---

"Those of us who feel the sting of injustice and inequality understand the joy of God's intervention in our relationships."

---

ecstasy, he vows to praise the God of Jacob forever!

It is possible that God Himself is speaking in verse 10. He promises to cut off the defiance of the wicked and to lift up and exalt the righteous. Those of us who feel the sting of injustice and inequality understand the joy of God's intervention in our relationships.

I learn a couple of crucial things from these verses. First, I need to praise the Name of the Lord regularly. Second, I need to give thanks to Him for His sovereign acts in my life. Third, I need to rest in the fact that God will judge evil. Things are not careening out of control. My Lord, the Divine Arbiter, is the eternal evaluator of all things.

Personal prayer

O Lord, I adore You and find exquisite comfort in the security of knowing You have everything under control.

A CONTEMPORARY HYMN

Celebrate

Look and see in awesome wonder
People coming without number
From ev'ry tribe and nomad band,
From ev'ry sea and bound'ried land:

See them marching, singing, swaying!
Can't you hear the people saying,
"Salvation is our God's alone,
The Lamb is now upon the throne."

Ev'ry tongue and ev'ry nation
They will join our celebration,
Our God is great!
So celebrate, celebrate!

Words by John E. Walvoord. Music by Don Wyrtzen.
© 1971 by Singspiration Inc.

Victory Celebration

Judgment of God

Exposition of theme
PSALM 75 CONTINUED

You say, "I choose the appointed time; it is I who judge uprightly. When the earth and all its people quake, it is I who hold its pillars firm. To the arrogant I say, 'Boast no more,' and to the wicked, 'Do not lift up your horns; do not speak with outstretched neck.' " No one from the east or the west or from the desert can exalt a man. But it is

God who judges: *He brings one down, he exalts another. In the hand of the* LORD *is a cup full of foaming wine mixed with spices; he pours it out, and all the wicked of the earth drink it down to its very dregs (vv. 2–8).*

Development of theme

When you're on a roll, and every song seems destined for the charts, it's easy to take the credit and forget the One who wrote the music!

"The Lord despises arrogance! People in the music industry are especially vulnerable to pride."

The Lord despises arrogance! People in the music industry are especially vulnerable to pride. Caught up in their own self-importance, the proud are pictured in this passage as animals who strut about, lifting up their horns in "stiff-necked" rebellion.

God Himself will judge our performance. It is He who promotes and demotes, exalts and diminishes. It is only by His touch that any life produces the kind of music that is pleasing to His ear. Those who are consistently "out of tune" will find themselves confronting His wrath. It will be administered like a cup of strong, foaming wine which they will be forced to drink to the last dregs!

At the "appointed time," every person will stand before this righteous Judge. He shows no favoritism, nor is He impressed with credentials or sales records or hit tunes. He will judge "uprightly," with absolute integrity.

Personal prayer

O Lord, I will never stop speaking of You. I will never stop singing of You. And I'm grateful that You will judge my performance in this life with utter fairness.

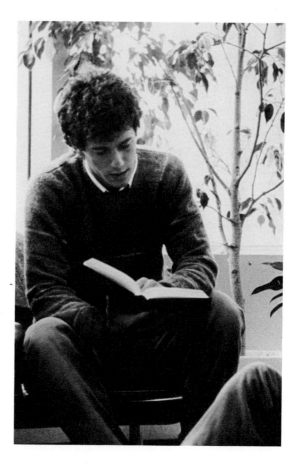

Psalm of Sovereignty

Exposition of theme
PSALM 76

In Judah God is known; his name is great in Israel. His tent is in Salem, his dwelling place in Zion. There he broke the flashing arrows, the shields and the swords, the weapons of war. You are resplendent with light, more majestic than mountains rich with game. (vv. 1–4).

Development of theme

In these stirring lines, Asaph plays on two physical characteristics of the countryside to describe God — the "resplendent light" of the desert sun and the majestic mountains surrounding Jerusalem.

God's majesty and light have inspired hymnists through the ages. Think of the lexicon of praise hymns used in our worship: "Joyful, Joyful, We Adore Thee," "The Lord Is My Light and My Salvation," "Praise, My Soul, The King of Heaven," "How Great Thou Art," "Sing Praise to God Who Reigns Above," "Praise the Lord!

> **"Light the dark corners of my life and give me a fresh vision of Your majesty!"**

Ye Heavens, Adore Him," "The Light of the World," "My Tribute," "Bless His Holy Name," and on and on. We can never exhaust the majesty and glory of His Name.

God displays His majestic power in His sovereign judgment of the wicked; "He broke the flashing arrows, the shields and the swords" (v. 3). "Valiant men . . . sleep their last sleep"

(v. 5). "Both horse and chariot are still" (v. 6). What a prophecy! One day all weapons of war will be obsolete (Isaiah 2:4).

I am moved by reverent awe for this God of ours to vow my allegiance to Him. He is capable of using His terrible might and majesty to chasten His children as well as to rout the Enemy. But there is another reason. He is also a God of infinite and unconditional love, dazzling radiance and light, and my only place of shelter is in the shadow of His mountain.

Personal prayer

How majestic is Thy Name, O Lord! Light the dark corners of my life and give me a fresh vision of Your majesty!

A Song in the Night
Feeling Abandoned

Exposition of theme
PSALM 77

When I was in distress, I sought the LORD; at night I stretched out untiring hands and my soul refused to be comforted. I remembered you, O God, and I groaned; I mused, and my spirit grew faint. You kept my eyes from closing; I was too troubled to speak. I thought about the former days, the years of long ago; I remembered my songs in the night (vv. 2–6a).

Development of theme

Why is it that one's troubles seem so much worse at night? There have been times when I've been so disturbed I couldn't sleep. Tossing and turning, I've asked the same questions the psalmist asked so long ago: Does God still love me? Has He forgotten me? Can He hear my

A POEM OF REMEMBRANCE

Then I Remembered

Troubled, I couldn't speak
Worried, I couldn't sleep;
Rejected, unloved, my longings were
    unfulfilled.
I prayed to God for help,
"O Lord, Don't You hear me?"
Distressed, I reached out my hands to Him,
His voice said, "Peace be still!"

Then I remembered how He touched me
And He made me His heir,
How He's led me like a Shepherd
I'm a wonder of His care;
When I remembered all He had done for
    me,
I was lifted from despair —
He heard me, He touched me
And He answered my prayer.

Words and music by Don Wyrtzen. © 1988 Singspiration Music.

prayer? Is He mad at me? Has He turned His back on me forever?

Asaph feels utterly abandoned by God and cries out, but finds no comfort for his churning emotions. Recalling times in the past when God has acted in his behalf, he is puzzled now by God's silence. The Lord seems distant, remote, even angry. Asaph is experiencing deep, personal pain and begins a downward spiral on a decrescendo of depression (vv. 7–9).

Rejection breeds deep inner fear that can hold the spirit in a vice-like grip. In my midnight hours, irrational emotions sweep over me like waves in a turbulent sea.

My fellow musician did the right thing in venting his feelings. Asaph was learning some of the deep mysteries of life in God's school of suffering. He was learning to wait patiently for the Lord. He was learning that honesty precedes spirituality, and that lament almost always precedes praise.

> *"Rejection breeds deep inner fear that can hold the spirit in a vice-like grip. Honesty precedes spirituality, and lament almost always precedes praise."*

Personal prayer

Lord, I'm hurting. Right now, in the soul-deep darkness of my night, I cry out for relief. Let me hear some note of hope.

A Song in the Night

Remembering God's Miracles

Exposition of theme

PSALM 77 *CONTINUED*

Then I thought, "To this I will appeal: the years of the right hand of the Most High." I will remember the deeds of the LORD; yes, I will remember your miracles of long ago. I will meditate on all your works and consider all your mighty deeds. Your ways, O God, are holy. What god is so great as our God? You are the God who performs miracles; you display your power among the peoples (vv. 10–14).

Development of theme

Asaph's deliverance from despair comes when he remembers that his God is a God of miracles, past and present. Asaph's joy erupts in this pen-

---

"Lord, You have never let me down! Remembering Your work in my behalf, I praise You more for Your sustaining power."

---

etrating question: "What god is so great as our God?" (v. 13).

He recalls the astonishing events of the Exodus: Rain cascades in sheets; thunder rumbles; lightning rips the sky; the earth quakes; the waters writhe and convulse and are at last swept back into trembling walls, forming a conduit for the teeming masses of Israelites escaping Egyptian tyranny (vv. 16-20).

Meditation on these miracles prompt him to praise God for His incomparable holiness and majesty.

Asaph's conclusion is based on a critical evaluation of the past. The Lord has consistently met the needs of His people. The implication is that He will again rescue and deliver them. Hence, Asaph moves from a diatribe of despair to a doxology of hope.

Personal prayer

O Lord, why do I ever worry and fret? Yesterday You died for me. Today You live for me. Tomorrow You come for me.

A CONTEMPORARY LYRIC

Yesterday, Today, and Tomorrow

Yesterday He died for me, yesterday,
   yesterday,
Yesterday He died for me, yesterday,
Yesterday He died for me, died for me —
This is history.

Today He lives for me, today, today,
Today He lives for me, today,
Today He lives for me, lives for me —
This is victory.

Tomorrow He comes for me, He comes, He
   comes,
Tomorrow He comes for me, He comes,
Tomorrow He comes for me, comes for
   me —
This is mystery.

O friend do you know Him? know Him?
   know Him?
O friend do you know Him? know Him?
O friend do you know Him? you know Him?
Jesus Christ the Lord.

Words by Jack Wyrtzen. Music by Don Wyrtzen.
© 1966 by Singspiration, Inc.

Chords of Rebellion

Disobedience

Exposition of theme

PSALM 78

He decreed statutes for Jacob and established the law in Israel, which he commanded our forefathers to teach their children, so the next generation would know them, even the children yet to be born, and they in turn would tell their children. Then they would put their trust in God and would not forget his deeds but would keep his commands (vv. 5–7).

Development of theme

Teach the children . . . "so the next generation would know them . . . and they in turn would tell their children. . . ."

I'll never forget the first Scripture verses I learned as a child: John 3:16, John 1:12, Romans 3:23 and 6:23. Or the first songs: "Jesus Loves Me," "For God So Loved the World," "Deep and Wide," "The Happy Day Express," and so many others.

Hundreds of generations after God gave that command to teach the children, my parents obeyed! Mom taught us most of the time, since Dad was a traveling evangelist. But when he was home, we kids got the whole nine yards—Bible

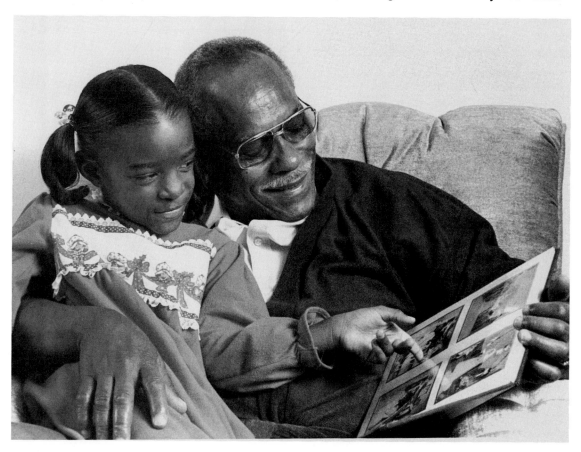

reading, Scripture memory, singing, and prayers around the world!

Just as my parents warned me, Asaph now warns his audience about personal rebellion against God and disobedience of His Law. He tells of ancestors who forgot God and were slain in the wilderness because of His anger. He also tells of a nation graciously delivered when its people learned to obey.

As an example of disobedience, he relates the case history of the tribe of Ephraim. They broke God's covenant and spurned His law. Intoxicated by self-confidence and human independence, they forgot God's miracles and spurned His law. Though armed to the teeth with bows and arrows, in battle they turned back.

What is the message for me from these verses? Once committed to the Lord, I must not turn back or I set myself up for personal disaster.

If I rebel, He will crush me. If I allow a pattern of disobedience to develop, God will respond in anger — not because He has that right as my Creator, but because He cannot bear to see me destroy myself. I must go all the way with Him — the whole nine yards!

Personal prayer

Dear Lord, so soon I forget Your wonderful works. Forgive my poor memory, my rebellion, and my disobedience. Don't let me stray from Your side.

A GOSPEL SONG

Trust and Obey

When we walk with the Lord
In the light of His Word,
What a glory He sheds on our way!
While we do His good will
He abides with us still,
And with all who will trust and obey.

Then in fellowship sweet
We will sit at His feet,
Or we'll walk by His side in the way;
What He says we will do,
Where He sends we will go —
Never fear, only trust and obey.

Trust and obey —
For there's no other way
To be happy in Jesus
But to trust and obey.

Words by John H. Sammis. Music by Daniel B. Towner.

Chords of Rebellion

Disloyalty

Exposition of theme

PSALM 78 CONTINUED

He did miracles in the sight of their fathers in the land of Egypt, in the region of Zoan. . . . But they continued to sin against him, rebelling in the desert against the Most High. They willfully put God to the test by demanding the food they craved. . . . But then they would flatter him with their mouths, lying to him with their tongues; their hearts were not loyal to him, they were not faithful to his covenant (vv. 12, 17–18, 36–37).

Development of theme

So often I'm like these willful wanderers of Israel. Instead of being grateful for God's gracious provision in the wilderness, they griped!

When they demanded food, "he rained down manna for the people to eat, he gave them the grain of heaven. . . . He sent them all the food they could eat. . . . He rained meat down on them like dust. . . . They ate till they had more than enough, for he had given them what they craved" (vv. 24–25, 27, 29).

Despite all this, the children of Israel behaved

> ### "So often I'm like these willful wanderers of Israel."

like spoiled brats. They were negative, critical, and rebellious. When God chastised them, they returned to Him briefly before lapsing back into flattery and deceit. Yet He was merciful and chose not to destroy them, remembering "that they were but flesh, a passing breeze that does not return" (v. 39).

Yet who am I to condemn? I'm as ambivalent as they. The Lord calls me to consistency, but my walk with Him is cluttered with behavioral highs and lows. He asks that I be thankful for unexpected mercies and daily gifts of grace, but I demand more. Lord, forgive me!

Personal prayer

Father, deliver me from the sins of ingratitude and greed. Above all, don't let me take Your goodness for granted!

Chords of Rebellion

Desertion

Exposition of theme

PSALM 78 CONTINUED

But they put God to the test and rebelled against the Most High; they did not keep his statutes. Like their fathers they were disloyal and faithless, as unreliable as a faulty bow. They angered him with their high places; they aroused his jealousy with their idols. When God heard them, he was very angry; he rejected Israel completely. . . . He chose David his servant and took him from the sheep pens; from tending the sheep he brought him to be the shepherd of his people Jacob, of Israel his inheritance. And David shepherded them with integrity of heart; with skillful hands he led them (vv. 56–59, 70–72).

Development of theme

Asaph continues to describe his rebellious people. They put God to the test, did not keep His statutes, and engaged in idolatry and spiritual adultery. Their heavenly Father reacted in anger and rejection. He abandoned the tabernacle of Shiloh and allowed the ark (covenant box) to be captured by the enemy. Young men were killed in war, leaving eager maidens with no one to marry; priests died violently, and widows were not able to mourn.

Then the Lord awoke "as from sleep" and saved them. He rejected the tribes of Joseph, Manasseh, and Ephraim in favor of Judah's Zion for the place of His sanctuary. He also reached down into the sheep pens and chose the country boy, David, to shepherd people instead of sheep. The young man was chosen because of two outstanding personality traits — skill and integrity. His hands were proficient and his heart was pure.

What a model King David is for me! I covet the delicate balance between a high level of professional skill and a deep sense of personal integrity. I admire his roots, his country values, and his poet's vision which he took with him all the way to the throne of Israel!

Personal prayer

Dear Lord, bless my life with skill and integrity so that I can aspire to leadership with distinction.

Lamentation Over Jerusalem

The Holy City Defiled

Exposition of theme
PSALM 79

O God, the nations have invaded your inheritance; they have defiled your holy temple, they have reduced Jerusalem to rubble. They have given the dead bodies of your servants as food to the birds of the air, the flesh of your saints to the beasts of the earth. They have poured out blood like water all around Jerusalem, and there is no one to bury the dead. We are objects of reproach to our neighbors, of scorn and derision to those around us (vv. 1–4).

Development of theme

Despite the animated promises of modern media evangelists, life sometimes delivers blows instead of blessings, even for the godly.

> **"Life sometimes delivers blows instead of blessings, even for the godly."**

This psalm recaps the theme of Psalm 74 — the devastation of the Holy City. The temple had been defiled. Saints had been slaughtered, the corpses left to be scavenged by the birds of the air. Blood was flowing like water around Jerusalem and there was no one left to bury the dead. The heathen nations, filled with profane people, mocked and blasphemed the name of God.

Moved by the plight of his people, Asaph prayed with deep feeling that the Lord would not remember their sins, but would come to their aid once again. This was not a time of booming prosperity, but a time of national agony and personal suffering. The only hope was God's supernatural intervention.

This very day I can expect to encounter at least three obstacles that cause pain or distress — from mild discomfort and irritation to deep, personal anguish. And I will probably compound the trauma by adding guilt. It encourages me to learn that Asaph faced trouble, just as I do, yet was faithful to his commitment to the Lord.

Personal prayer

O God, my life is a mess! I've come to the end of myself, and I don't know which way to turn. But I know that, wherever I might go, You are there!

Lamentation Over Jerusalem

Prayer and Praise

Exposition of theme
PSALM 79 *CONTINUED*

How long, O LORD? Will you be angry forever? How long will your jealousy burn like fire? Pour out your wrath on the nations that do not acknowledge you, on the kingdoms that do not call on your name; for they have devoured Jacob and destroyed his homeland. . . . Before our eyes, make known among the nations that you avenge the outpoured blood of your servants. May the groans of the prisoners come before you; by the strength of your arm preserve those condemned to die. . . . Then we your people, the sheep of your pasture, will praise you forever; from generation to generation we will recount your praise (vv. 5–7, 10–11, 13).

Development of theme

Asaph is fed up! I sympathize with his frustration over the heathen nations who mock God. Christians in the marketplace constantly hear such complaints from skeptical colleagues and neighbors: "Where was God when the stock market crashed?" "How can a loving God let innocent people suffer?" Or even from Christians themselves: "Why did the Lord let this happen to me . . . after all I've done for Him?!"

Still, Asaph doesn't lose faith here. He implores God to hear the "groans of the prisoners" and "avenge the outpoured blood of [his] servants" (vv. 10–11). This plea is not motivated by duty, but out of a sense of "desperate need." He longs to see the Lord glorified *through the affliction of the people.*

Joni Eareckson Tada is physically disabled because of a diving mishap when she was a kid. She is paralyzed from the neck down. Yet the

---

"*Joni Eareckson Tada is a very special person whose life has touched literally millions around the world!*"

Lord has graced Joni with profound insight and faith and has given her a far-reaching ministry that she didn't have before the accident. She's a very special person whose life has touched literally millions around the world!

This is the kind of answer Asaph and I long to hear from the Lord. Crippled by painful loss, emotional and psychological trauma, lack of love and acceptance, we cry out for ourselves and other sufferers: "Lord, I am weak, but You are strong!"

Personal prayer

O Lord, help me to hear Your voice above the din of human confusion. Teach me that Your strength is made perfect in my weakness and let me praise You forever.

Refrain of Restoration

Please listen!

Exposition of theme

PSALM 80

Hear us, O Shepherd of Israel, you who lead Joseph like a flock; you who sit enthroned between the cherubim, shine forth before Ephraim, Benjamin and Manasseh. Awaken your might; come and save us. Restore us, O God; make your face shine upon us, that we may be saved (vv. 1–3).

Development of theme

A choir containing one person singing off-key is distracting and displeasing to the ear. But when the "out of tuneness" is between an individual and God, the very melody of life is destroyed!

For too long the children of Israel have been off-key with the Lord. They have lost their reference point and have strayed into some atonal musical wilderness. Now the psalmist pleads for his people to be restored to God's favor. "Hear us! . . . Wake up! . . . Restore us, O God!" he cries out in spiritual agony. "Bring us back to our former condition with You!"

Hope is implied in the psalmist's plaintive refrain. While Asaph is addressing the Eternal God who "sits enthroned between the cherubim," he preceives Him also as the tender "Shepherd of Israel."

Shepherds often soothed their restless flocks

"When there is disharmony between an individual and God, the very melody of life is destroyed!"

---

with music. David himself got his start singing his folk songs to sleepless sheep out in the desert on many a Mediterranean night.

Asaph and I long to hear harmony restored once more in the life of the flock and in our own hearts.

Personal prayer

Shepherd of Israel, please listen! And let me hear the tender melody of Your love so I can tune my life to Your perfect pitch.

THE LANGUAGE OF MUSIC

Refrain

A regularly recurring phrase or verse repeated at the end of each stanza.

Similar to "chorus," the basic structure is: (a, v, b, v, c, v . . .) or verse-chorus.

Refrain of Restoration

Please don't be angry!

Exposition of theme

PSALM 80 *CONTINUED*

O LORD God Almighty, how long will your anger smolder against the prayers of your people? You have fed them with the bread of tears; you have made them drink tears by the bowlful. You have made us a source of contention to our neighbors, and our enemies mock us. Restore us, O God Almighty; make your face shine upon us, that we may be saved (vv. 4–7).

Development of theme

I like the emotional openness of these verses, since I tend to deny a lot of emotion. Like my ancient brothers and sisters, I need to become more transparent and vulnerable. Toughing it out with the aid of denial and pretense is dis-

---

> *"Though I seldom cry, I know that tears are often therapeutic."*

---

honest and self-defeating. Beyond that, it's not biblical.

Here, in stunning hyperbole, Asaph portrays the response of Israel to the disciplining hand of God. "You have fed them with the bread of tears;

you have made them drink *tears by the bowlful*" (v. 5)!

Though I seldom cry, I know that tears are often therapeutic. They give emotional release. They also cleanse and lubricate the ducts of the eye, and they can even dislodge foreign objects. Perhaps the faithless children of Israel are dislodging the foreign object of sin from their hearts as they weep tears of repentance. As a result of their penitent state, God will not be angry forever, but will restore them to full favor (v. 7).

When I recall that even "Jesus wept" (John 11:35), I am encouraged to allow the healing tears to flow!

Personal prayer

Shepherd of Israel, please don't be angry with me! Open me up emotionally and show me how my deepest needs can be met in You.

Refrain of Restoration

Please restore prosperity!

Exposition of theme

PSALM 80 CONTINUED

Your vine is cut down, it is burned with fire; at your rebuke your people perish. Let your hand rest on the man at your right hand, the son of man you have raised up for yourself. Then we will not turn away from you; revive us, and we will call on your name. Restore us, O LORD God Almighty; make your face shine upon us, that we may be saved (vv. 16–19).

Development of theme

In this psalm, the metaphor of a flourishing vine is used to picture Israel. At one time the vine was so abundant that it spread to the southern mountains, to the northern cedars of Lebanon, to the eastern Euphrates River, and to the western

---

> *"Secular success, apart from God's hand on my life, is a hollow victory."*

Mediterranean Sea. But now it has withered and died after being trampled by wild beasts and boars.

For the third time Asaph reiterates the refrain, "Restore us, O LORD God Almighty; make your face shine upon us, that we may be saved (v. 19). He promises faithfulness in exchange for restoration and salvation.

I need to remember that prosperity finds its genesis in the Lord. Secular success, apart from God's hand on my life, is a hollow victory. Without His blessing, life has no meaning. I want to be very much aware of how much my personal effectiveness depends on Him.

Personal prayer

Shepherd of Israel, please prosper my soul and make my life a flourishing vine.

Music for the Feast of Tabernacles

Let's celebrate!

Exposition of theme

PSALM 81

Sing for joy to God our strength; shout aloud to the God of Jacob! Begin the music, strike the tambourine, play the melodious harp and lyre. Sound the ram's horn at the New Moon, and when the moon is full, on the day of our Feast; this is a decree for Israel, an ordinance of the God of Jacob (vv. 1–4).

Development of theme

This psalm celebrates God's miraculous deliverance of His people from Egyptian bondage. In the wilderness He had met every need. On one occasion He had answered out of a thundercloud (Exodus 16:10). On another, He tested His people at Meribah (Numbers 20).

Now Asaph calls the people to a glorious festival which will memorialize these events. He commands them to sing joyfully and loudly. The choir is to be accompanied by an orchestra of tambourines, melodious harps, and lyres. The ram's horn will deliver its fanfare at the New Moon to usher in the Feast. God Himself has decreed this worship service as an ordinance and statute.

> *"I need to get creatively involved in praising the Lord — reading Scripture aloud, praying the Word back to the Lord, or sharing the work of the Holy Spirit in my life with another person."*

What do I learn from this joyous festival? I learn that part of my worship should memorialize God's supernatural acts in my life, such as the most recent time His truth set me free in my inner person. I learn that I need to get creatively involved in praising the Lord — reading Scripture aloud, praying the Word back to the Lord, or sharing the work of the Holy Spirit in my life with another person.

And one of the best ways to do this is through music.

Personal prayer

God of Jacob, teach me to make music for Your glory today. Set me free to play skillfully, to sing worshipfully, and to dance joyfully.

Music for the Feast of Tabernacles

Hear, O my people

Exposition of theme

PSALM 81 *CONTINUED*

"Hear, O my people, and I will warn you — if you would but listen to me, O Israel! You shall have no foreign god among you; you shall not bow down to an alien god. I am the Lord your God, who brought you up out of Egypt. . . . But my people would not listen to me; Israel would not submit to me. So I gave them over to their stubborn hearts to follow their own devices. . . . If Israel would follow my ways, how quickly would

I subdue their enemies and turn my hand against their foes!" (vv. 8–14).

Development of theme

Without the responsive ear of the listener, there is no music! There is a marked difference between passive hearing and active listening. Music depends on involved listeners: Choir members must hear their director's instructions; soloists must listen for their musical cues; symphony conductors must listen critically to

---

"What Israel missed by refusing to listen is parallel to my own loss if I miss God's cues for my life."

---

create balance and ensemble in their orchestras. Audiences too must learn how to listen.

In this psalm God is saying, "Listen, my people, let me warn you." But the people are willful and independent. *They will not listen!* And God "gave them over to their stubborn hearts to follow their own devices" (v. 12).

What Israel missed by refusing to listen is parallel to my own loss if I miss God's cues for my life: freedom from enemies (v. 14), food for the table (v.16). In fact, if I worship God in an exclusive relationship, I will be abundantly blessed with "the finest of wheat; with honey from the rock."

Unfortunately for the Israelites, God's hands were tied. Because of their stubborn rebellion, He could not bring the prosperity and peace they craved. How sad that so often I too go unrewarded because I don't listen.

Personal prayer

God of Jacob, I'm much like those other people of Yours in my stubbornness and refusal to listen to Your instructions for abundant life. Speak loudly so your servant will hear and obey.

Psalm of Justice

God Indicts Human Judges

Exposition of theme
PSALM 82

"How long will you defend the unjust and show partiality to the wicked? Defend the cause of the weak and fatherless; maintain the rights of the poor and oppressed. Rescue the weak and needy; deliver them from the hand of the wicked. They know nothing, they understand nothing. They walk about in darkness; all the foundations of the earth are shaken" (vv. 2–5).

Development of theme

God is speaking here. And when God speaks, we'd do well to listen! The question He asks probes my own twentieth-century conscience: "How long will you defend the unjust and show partiality to the wicked? . . . Rescue the weak and needy!"

Though God is addressing the legal magistrates He Himself has appointed over Israel, I need to assess my own attitudes and actions toward the oppressed, the weak, the fatherless, and the poor. As I encounter these needs in my daily life, do I turn a deaf ear, or do I respond with

> **"God's structure of law and order is undermined when His people don't respond to the needs of others; His kingdom is advanced when they do!"**

compassion and mercy?

It is the rare person who really shows compassion for needy, hurting people. In this society we're programmed to expect a person to shape up, take control, solve his or her own problems.

We applaud self-reliance and scorn any show of dependence. But Bob MacKenzie, well-known music executive, brought a struggling young musician to Nashville at his own expense. That young man, Greg Nelson, is now one of the most outstanding producers in the industry!

God's structure of law and order is undermined when His people don't respond to the needs of others; His kingdom is advanced when they do!

I may not be an "elected official," but I am God's official representative within my own sphere of influence. And I'm accountable to Him to reflect not only His justice, but His mercy also.

Personal prayer

O God, I thank You for allowing me the privilege of representing You in my world. Help me to emulate Your righteousness and kindness to all I meet.

Psalm of Justice

God Is the Only Righteous Judge

Exposition of theme
PSALM 82

God presides in the great assembly; he gives judgment among the "gods. . . ." Rise up, O God, judge the earth, for all the nations are your inheritance (vv. 1, 8).

Development of theme

God is the Judge of human judges. He created justice, equity, and objectivity. Judges who practice law deceitfully, without awareness of God's

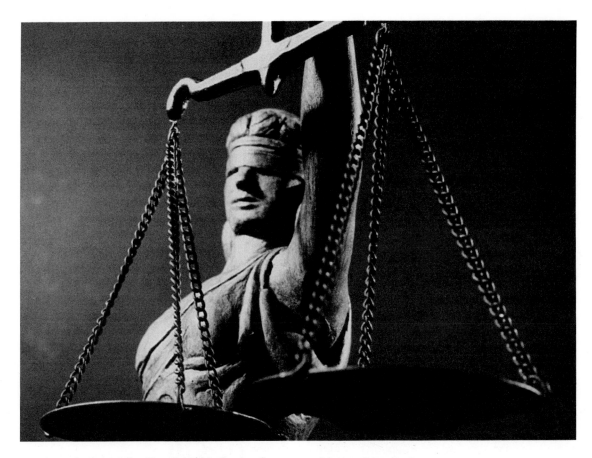

solemn appointment will perish. It is the Lord who presides in the great assembly.

Not only will God come down on the heads of human judges, but He will also judge all the earth. The nations of the world belong to God, who holds the inhabitants responsible for their ethics and conduct.

All of this confirms that I am not just a statistic in a cold, indifferent universe, nor merely part of the flow in an environment resulting from chance. I am a human being who fits into God's plans for all eternity. Therefore, I have rare value. Because I am precious to Him, my behavior has significance. I am responsible, so I must learn to live responsibly. Beyond that, I am unique because I am made in God's image. He has created me, saved me, and sealed me with His Spirit. What encouraging thoughts for today!

> *"I am not just a statistic in a cold, indifferent universe. I fit into God's plans for all eternity. Therefore, I have rare value. My behavior has significance. I am unique because I am made in God's image."*

Personal prayer

O God, I thank You that You are impartial and just and that I can rest my case with You.

Asaph's Lament for Judah

O God, do not keep silent!

Exposition of theme
PSALM 83

O God, do not keep silent; be not quiet, O God, be not still. See how your enemies are astir, how your foes rear their heads. With cunning they conspire against your people; they plot against those you cherish. "Come," they say, "let us destroy them as a nation, that the name of Israel be remembered no more" (vv. 1–4).

Development of theme

Groaning is good! One of the keys to dispelling pain is to face it head on. Lament almost always precedes praise.

Asaph is in pain. Troubled by a coalition of disgruntled nations who are plotting to overthrow tiny Judah, he takes his complaints to God once again. Edomites, Ishmaelites, Moabites, Ammonites, Amalekites, and Philistines have allied themselves and, with the support of mighty Assyria, are threatening to roll over Judah like a tidal wave. Total annihilation is their objective.

The psalmist doesn't mince words. He wants God to get involved: "Do not keep silent! . . . Be not quiet! . . . Be not still!" In reverse order, he seems to be saying, "It's your move, Lord. Don't just speak to our enemies. Shout, if you have to!"

Still, Asaph has pled before, and his words

> **"The psalmist doesn't mince words. He seems to be saying, 'It's your move, Lord. Don't just speak to our enemies. Shout if you have to!' "**

alone seem impotent to produce the desired effect.

In facing personal pain, I've learned that, when words fail me, I can trust the Holy Spirit to help me. "[I] do not know what [I] ought to pray, but the Spirit Himself intercedes for [me] with groans that words cannot express" (Romans 8:26).

Personal prayer

Holy Spirit, speak for me. My own words are weak and powerless, but Your groans in my behalf will be heard and interpreted by the Father.

Asaph's Lament for Judah

Do it to them!

Exposition of theme
PSALM 83 *CONTINUED*

Do to them as you did to Midian, as you did to Sisera and Jabin at the river Kishon, who perished at Endor and became like refuse on the ground. Make their nobles like Oreb and Zeeb, all their princes like Zebah and Zalmunna, who said, "Let us take possession of the pasturelands of God." . . . May they ever be ashamed and dismayed; may they perish in disgrace. Let them know that you, whose name is the LORD — that you alone are the most High over all the earth (vv. 9–12, 17–18).

Development of theme

Asaph is a consummate lyricist. He uses vivid, picturesque imagery to express his feelings. What haunting Israeli melody accompanied this powerful lament? We can only imagine what it sounded like — plaintive, vigorous, intense!

The angrier Asaph grows, the more moving

> **"The God I worship is the God of fire and storm as well as green pastures and still waters."**

---

and dramatic his imagery! His lyric captures the intensity of his lament to the Lord: "Do to them as you did to Midian . . . to Sisera and Jabin at the river Kishon . . . to Oreb and Zeeb, Zebah and Zalmunna." Here, Asaph is referring to specific historical events: When the Lord delivered the Midianites into Gideon's hand (Judges 7), when Sisera met a grisly death through Deborah and Barak (Judges 4–5), and when Oreb and Zeeb (Midianite warriors) and Zebah and Zalmunna; (Midianite kings) were crushed because they dared to oppose Him (Judges 8).

The next phrases shimmer with excitement. Asaph asks God to make the enemy hosts like "tumbleweed . . . like chaff before the wind. As fire consumes the forest or a flame sets the mountains ablaze, so pursue them with your tempest and terrify them with your storm" (vv. 13–15).

The God I worship is the God of fire and storm as well as green pastures and still waters. He alone inspires the intricate composition of my life and it involves tension along with release.

Personal prayer

O God, with the power of Asaph's pen, I would compose rhapsodies to Your Name. I want the world to know that You alone are the Most High over all the earth!

Pilgrim's Song
Longing for God

Exposition of theme
PSALM 84

How lovely is your dwelling place, O Lord Almighty! My soul yearns, even faints, for the courts of the Lord; my heart and my flesh cry out for the living God. Even the sparrow has found a home, and the swallow a nest for herself, where she may have her young—a place near your altar, O Lord Almighty, my King and my God. Blessed are those who dwell in your house; they are ever praising you. Blessed are those whose strength is in you, who have set their hearts on pilgrimage. As they pass through the Valley of Baca, they make it a place of springs; the autumn rains also cover it with pools. They go from strength to strength, till each appears before God in Zion (vv. 1–7).

Development of theme

How easy it is for contemporary society to accept the view that this life is all there is! We tend to put down as many roots as possible and pretend that this world is really our home.

The writer of this psalm has discovered his permanent roots. Driven by a deep, inner compulsion to know God, he is drawn to the temple. He longs to make his home in the place "where God is." Just as the lark and the swallow—birds known for their sweet songs—have found nests for themselves, this unknown psalmist

desires to "settle in," to nestle near the altar close to his God, where he can sing His praises continually.

Other believers, on pilgrimage to Jerusalem, must pass through the Valley of Baca, a once-arid region where the Lord has caused springs of water to flow. Refreshed and strengthened, these pilgrims move on to complete their journey.

I too must remember that I'm only a pilgrim. "This world is not my home." Instead of putting down roots in a particular city or community or vocation, I must keep in mind my eternal destination. My roots are in eternity, not in this life. But I need frequent renewal in God's refreshing springs and the fellowship and loving support of other pilgrims. I love the church because it is my place of stability, security, and sustenance as I continue the journey.

Personal prayer

O Lord Almighty, help me to love Your place and Your people. May I draw strength from my fellow pilgrims, my brothers and sisters in Christ.

> **"Instead of putting down roots in a particular city or community or vocation, I must keep in mind my eternal destination. My roots are in eternity, not in this life."**

Pilgrim's Song
Praying to God

Exposition of theme

PSALM 84 CONTINUED

Hear my prayer, O LORD God Almighty; listen to me, O God of Jacob. Look upon our shield, O God; look with favor on your anointed one. Better is one day in your courts than a thousand elsewhere; I would rather be a doorkeeper in the house of my God than dwell in the tents of the wicked. For the LORD God is a sun and shield; the LORD bestows favor and honor; no good thing does he withhold from those whose walk is blameless. O LORD Almighty, blessed is the man who trusts in you (vv. 8–12).

Development of theme

These verses are both a comfort and a challenge. I know I've been "set apart" to Christian service in the ministry of music, but sometimes low-grade motivation obscures my vision. The enchantment of conducting a professional orchestra for the first time, seeing my first published song, listening to my first record have faded, and I'm faced with the daily grind. I must work harder to keep the excitement and creative-energy level high.

The psalmist has no such fears or insecurities. His rock-solid devotion to God supercedes all other concerns. He knows he has been set apart ("anointed") by the Lord, and he is utterly committed to his calling (v. 9). In fact, if necessary, he is willing to serve in some menial position ("a doorkeeper") in the house of the Lord rather than to live in the lavish tents of the wicked (v. 10).

In verse 11 we learn the reason for such devotion. The Lord is pictured as a "sun and shield." He offers warmth, blessing, protection, and prosperity. He does not withhold anything good

> *"Out of the rich texture of meaningful human relationships come songs that touch the heart."*

from those whose walk with Him is *blameless*— "a spotless walk, conduct ordered according to God's will, and a truth-loving mode of thought."

Now that the musical honeymoon is over, I need to be more committed, to persist and persevere in practicing my craft. I need to exercise discipline as I'm enjoying inspiration. I also need to follow the example of my ancient colleague— turn to my Source and spend more time in meaningful interaction with His people. Out of the rich texture of meaningful human relationships come songs that touch the heart.

Personal prayer

O Lord, today I rededicate my life to Your service. Be my Sun and Shield, and give me the satisfaction of knowing that my walk is worthy of my calling.

Rhapsody on Renewal

Prayer for Revival

Exposition of theme

PSALM 85

You showed favor to your land, O LORD; you restored the fortunes of Jacob. You forgave the iniquity of your people and covered all their sins. You set aside all your wrath and turned from your fierce anger. Restore us again, O God our Savior, and put away your displeasure toward us. Will you be angry with us forever? Will you prolong your anger through all generations? Will you not revive us again, that your people may rejoice in you? Show us your unfailing love, O LORD, and grant us your salvation (vv. 1–7).

Development of theme

Life is often difficult and depressing for me. Work and family priorities go askew. I feel stressed out, disoriented, unbalanced. Why? Because I'm trying to make it on my own, taking God for

> **"Sometimes I feel stressed out, disoriented, unbalanced. Why? Because I'm trying to make it on my own, taking God for granted, failing to follow His master score."**

granted, failing to follow His master score.

In art, as in life, balance and symmetry of form are crucial both in the creation and the reception of the work. Sir Georg Solti, maestro of the Chicago Symphony, is a master at juggling the intricacies of complex works and fashioning them into a glorious musical melange. Our lives need

A GOSPEL HYMN

Revive Us Again

Revive us again—fill each heart with Thy love;
May each soul be rekindled with fire from above.

Hallelujah, Thine the glory!
Hallelujah, amen!
Hallelujah, Thine the glory!
Revive us again.

Words by William P. Mackay.   Music by John J. Husband.

to be lived as art forms for God's glory.

This psalm, written by the Sons of Korah, begins by reciting ways in which the Lord has restored Israel—He has forgiven and covered their sins; He has set aside His wrath and turned from (changed His mind about) His anger toward them (v. 3).

The people need revival once again. They have failed to stay in tune with His will. They are out of sync with His plan. They need to right themselves, to shift their position until they are restored to harmony and balance in Him.

No one needs revival more than I. When the Lord dominates and controls my life, then and only then will I feel His incredible love and lasting joy . . . again!

Personal prayer

O God my Savior, let me experience a renewal of my soul today so that Your love breaks out in every word and action of my life.

Rhapsody on Renewal

Harvest Time

Exposition of theme

PSALM 85 CONTINUED

I will listen to what God the LORD will say; he promises peace to his people, his saints — but let them not return to folly. Surely his salvation is near those who fear him, that his glory may dwell in our land. . . . The LORD will indeed give what is good, and our land will yield its harvest. Righteousness goes before him and prepares the way for his steps (vv. 8–9, 12–13).

Development of theme

When a dying church is rekindled, when a spirit is revived, when harmony is restored — there is a blend of elements that produces a symphony of grace. "Love and faithfulness meet together; righteousness and peace kiss each other" (v. 10).

Though I have a tendency to pretend that pain

> *"When the Holy Spirit convicts me of some sinful attitude and I'm willing to repent, I know the ecstasy of freedom and release."*

doesn't exist in my close relationships, when the Holy Spirit convicts me of some sinful attitude and I'm willing to repent, I know the ecstasy of freedom and release.

The psalmist is looking forward to this kind of answered prayer, because he knows God always keeps His promises. For those who choose faith instead of folly, He will grant "harvest." Blessing is the effect of Gods' character colliding with culture (v. 12).

This kind of harmony is perfectly illustrated in the life of Christ. As God in human flesh, He dwelt among us "full of grace and truth" (John 1:14). Further, He was a walking revelation of God's glory, and lives today in repentant hearts.

Presently, my spirit wrestles with many hindrances to lasting revival — among them, a powerful and sometimes shaky ego. I need to let go and let God take full control. I need to be a "miniature Christ," reflecting His glory. When I die to self, He will assume His rightful place as Conductor of my life, and I will hear the full symphony of His favor, promised to the faithful!

Personal prayer

O God, my Savior, reflect Your glory in me today. May my ego decrease as Your attributes increase in my life today!

David's Prayer

For Mercy

Exposition of theme
PSALM 86

Hear, O LORD, and answer me, for I am poor and needy. Guard my life, for I am devoted to you. You are my God; save your servant who trusts in you. Have mercy on me, O LORD, for I call to you all day long. Bring joy to your servant, for to you, O LORD, I lift up my soul. You are forgiving and good, O LORD, abounding in love to all who call to you. Hear my prayer, O LORD; listen to my cry for mercy. In the day of my trouble I will call to you, for you will answer me (vv. 1–7).

Development of theme

I really admire David. Here is a man who doesn't mind admitting his weaknesses, and in doing so, demonstrates his strength. Three times in these few verses, the verb *call* is used (vv. 3, 5, 7). David doesn't just pray; he calls to God, "crying out in a loud voice."

When I'm under intense pressure, I tend to question God rather than call out to Him. My life gradually becomes layered with anxiety. Before long, fear has a firm grip on my soul, and my prayer is more a pathetic whimper than a strong plea.

Not David! He speaks to the Lord with all the authority of his convictions and in the expecta-

tion of an affirmative answer: "Hear," "Answer," "Guard," "Save," "Have mercy." Then he congratulates the Lord for His kindness and forgiveness, His abounding love and His tender mercy.

David's song is a perfect balance of petition and praise. This form provides a model, not only for my meditations, but for the full measure of my days. How very simple! How profoundly rewarding!

Personal prayer

Hear my prayer, O Lord, as You heard King David's. Give me the same bold conviction, the same simple faith, the same childlike trust. May I never petition until I've taken time to praise!

David's Prayer

For an "Undivided" Heart

Exposition of theme
PSALM 86 *CONTINUED*

Among the gods there is none like you, O LORD; no deeds can compare with yours. All the nations you have made will come and worship before you, O LORD; they will bring glory to your name. For you are great and do marvelous deeds; you alone are God. Teach me your way, O LORD, and I will walk in your truth; give me an undivided heart, that I may fear your name. I will praise you, O LORD my God, with all my heart; I will glorify your name forever. For great is your love toward me; you have delivered me from the depths of the grave (vv. 8–13).

> **"David's song is a perfect balance of petition and praise. This form provides a model, not only for my meditations, but for the full measure of my days. How very simple! How profoundly rewarding!"**

Development of theme

Though David sometimes prays and writes in bold strokes, this passage has an almost ethereal quality. How magnificently he expresses God's sovereignty! How tenderly he caresses the name of the Lord who loves him and preserves his life!

In these lines I hear traces of the impressionists—Debussy, Ravel, Delius, I hear muted

---

> **"I know that line—that hauntingly familiar refrain. I understand so well how a heart can be ripped open and laid bare, fragmented, broken."**

---

strings and harp glissandi. I hear transparency, sheen, and range of mood, from turbulence to serenity.

With all the verbal artistry at his command, David pours out his love song to the Lord. But for me, the climax of the piece comes in verse 11, when he prays, "Give me an undivided heart."

Suddenly I am startled out of my reverie, brought up short, reduced to tears. I, who never cry! "An undivided heart"! I know that line—that hauntingly familiar refrain. I understand so well how a heart can be ripped open and laid bare, fragmented, broken. Yet I rarely share this kind of intimate pain, but bury it beneath a façade of cool indifference.

So David knows that agony too! Yet there is no hint of self-pity. From the heights of ecstasy to the "depths of the grave," he keeps on singing!

Personal prayer

Hear my prayer, O Lord. Make my life an artistic statement that magnifies and glorifies Your Name and celebrates Your incomparable greatness.

David's Prayer

For Strength

Exposition of theme

PSALM 86 *CONTINUED*

The arrogant are attacking me, O God; a band of ruthless men seeks my life—men without regard for you. But you, O Lord, are a compassionate and gracious God, slow to anger, abounding in love and faithfulness. Turn to me and have mercy on me; grant your strength to your servant and save the son of your maidservant. Give me a sign of your goodness, that my enemies may see it and be put to shame, for you, O Lord, have helped me and comforted me (vv. 14–17).

Development of theme

I must admit I'm sometimes morose and unpredictable. David too is a man of many moods. Like most creative people, he shifts quickly from passion to pathos, from biting sarcasm to tender lyricism.

Harmony directly affects the emotions. Try watching a suspenseful program on television . . . with the sound turned down! Much of

---

> **"Like most creative people, David shifts quickly from passion to pathos, from biting sarcasm to tender lyricism."**

---

the edge, the drama, is lost. John Williams, composer of the scores for "Star Wars," "E.T." and "Superman," is a master of film scoring. Here is a lyric full of potential for a Christian composer.

- *Forte*—In loud and positive terms, David, here profiles the "ruthless" enemies who oppose him and defy everything for which he stands for. Not only do these "arrogant" men attack David,

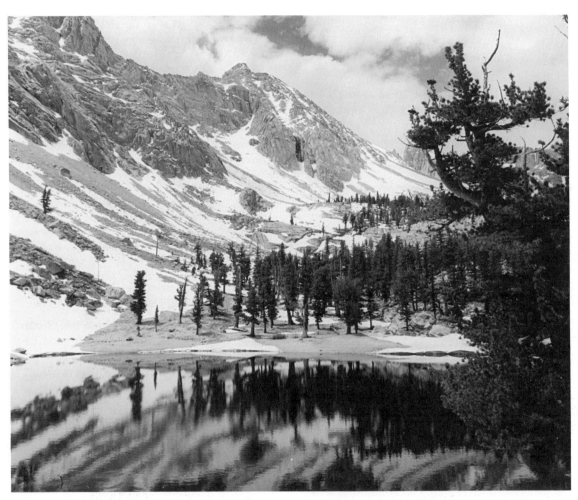

they have utter contempt for the Lord as well (v. 14).

● *Affetuoso* — The mood changes to one of warmth and affection as David catalogs the virtues of his Lord — compassion, grace, slow to anger, love, faithfulness, mercy, strength, goodness. Such a God will not fail him in this time of imminent danger (vv. 15–16).

● *Spiritoso* — With rising vigor and a sense of urgency, David cries out for mercy and for "a sign . . . that my enemies may see it and be put to shame" (v. 17).

● *Rallentando* — As the tempo slows, there is implicit trust in David's final words; "You, O LORD, have helped me and comforted me" (v. 17). Whether David was anticipating God's early response to his request or whether he is reflecting on past favors, he's confident that God acts in his behalf.

Personal prayer

● *Largo — My Lord and my God, I bow in acknowledgment of Your mercies. Come to my rescue today and deliver me as much from myself as from false friends and enemies.*

Processional to Zion

Exposition of theme
PSALM 87

*He has set his foundation on the holy mountain;
the LORD loves the gates of Zion more than all the
dwellings of Jacob. Glorious things are said of
you, O city of God. . . . As they make music
they will sing, "All my fountains are in you"
(vv. 1–3, 7).*

Development of theme

I love to hear people really sing — so that the
walls vibrate and the air currents get moved
around! I remember hearing some kids sing like
I'd never heard before. About a hundred of them
were jammed into a small, white brick chapel at
Hampden DuBose Academy. Under the baton of
Miss Dorothy Hill and accompanied by two
grand pianos, they lifted the roof! There have
been other memorable times and places . . . the
Praise Gathering in Indianapolis, Indiana . . .
Christian Artists' Retreat at Estes Park,
Colorado. . . .

But the music we'll hear in the celestial city will
far surpass anything we'll ever hear on this
earth. "The city of God" mentioned in these
verses written by the Sons of Korah is both a
geographical location — Jerusalem — and a symbolic one — heaven.

Zion, which encompasses Jerusalem and surrounding hills, was the earthly dwelling place of

God — the chosen object of His love (Psalm
78:68). With its towers, gates, bulwarks, and
palaces, it stood too as proof of eternal reconcili-
ation with God. The very enemies who pursued
David most of his life — Rahab (Egypt), Babylon,
Philistia, Phoenicia, Tyre — will be recorded by
the Lord Himself in His register (v. 6).

In the New Jerusalem, that heavenly city, the
population will be composed of peoples from all
nations and ages. Music will be the language of
praise!

As a Christian whose name is recorded in the
Lamb's Book of Life, I look forward to that glorious reunion. I will become part of the music and
dancing of eternity. I will sit down with the saints
at God's banquet table. Today I march onward
and upward to Zion!

Personal prayer

*O Lord, keep my eyes firmly fixed on my future
home. Don't let the hindrances and strongholds
of the Enemy rob me of rewards and joy in that
great day when I will see You face to face.*

> **"The music we'll hear in the
> celestial city will far surpass
> anything we'll ever hear on this
> earth."**

A ROUSING GOSPEL HYMN

We're Marching to Zion

Come, we that love the Lord,
And let our joys be known;
Join in a song with sweet accord,
And thus surround the throne.

Then let our songs abound,
And ev'ry tear be dry;
We're marching through Immanuel's
    ground,
To fairer worlds on high.

We're marching to Zion,
Beautiful, beautiful Zion;
We're marching upward to Zion,
The beautiful city of God.

Words by Isaac Watts, Chorus: Robert Lowry. Music by Robert Lowry.

Song of Suffering
Heman's Complaint

Exposition of theme
PSALM 88

O Lord, the God who saves me, day and night I cry out before you. May my prayer come before you; turn your ear to my cry. For my soul is full of trouble and my life draws near the grave. I am counted among those who go down to the pit; I am like a man without strength. I am set apart with the dead, like the slain who lie in the grave, whom you remember no more. . . . You have taken from me my closest friends and have made me repulsive to them. I am confined and cannot escape; my eyes are dim with grief (vv. 1–5, 8–9a).

Development of theme

Physical suffering, the irrational emotions that accompany it, and the seeming injustice of "bad things happening to good people" is a bewildering reality. Sensitive scholars have grappled with these questions. (See *The Problem of Pain*, C.S. Lewis; *Why Me, Lord?*, Warren Wiersbe; *Where Is God When It Hurts?*, Philip Yancey.)

This psalmist isn't afraid to ask hard, penetrating questions. Heman the Ezrahite, a gifted and sensitive musician (1 Chronicles 25:1), has composed one of the saddest passages in all the Bible. Since youth, he has been afflicted with some kind of debilitating disease that has not only sapped his strength (v. 4), but has separated him from the comfort of his closest friends. He is actually "repulsive to them" (v. 8). In his lonely isolation, he feels like a forgotten man.

He handles his pain by praying day and night. "O Lord, the God who saves me . . . turn your ear to my cry!" (vv. 1–2).

I'm reminded of another Man who suffered not only physical torture, but also bore the weight of

---

"Jesus, though sinless and perfect, experienced unimaginable shame and agony . . . for me."

my sin. He too cried out in His pain: "My God, my God, why have you forsaken me?" (Mark 15:34). Jesus, though sinless and perfect, experienced unimaginable shame and agony . . . for me.

Personal prayer

Father, when I'm called upon to suffer, may I cry out to You in patient prayer. Deliver me from bitterness and remind me always of the One who suffered so cruelly in my behalf!

JULY 29

Song of Suffering
Heman's Conclusion

Exposition of theme
PSALM 88 *CONTINUED*

I call to you, O Lord, every day; I spread out my hands to you. Do you show your wonders to the dead? Do those who are dead rise up and praise you? Is your love declared in the grave, your faithfulness in Destruction? . . . But I cry to you for help, O Lord; in the morning my prayer comes before you. Why, O Lord, do you reject me and hide your face from me? From my youth I have been afflicted and close to death; I have suffered your terrors and am in despair (vv. 9b–10, 13–15).

Development of theme

Like many a modern-day counterpart, this ancient psalmist is full of mind-boggling questions about his condition: If I die, can I praise God

> **"Personal introspection is not the total answer. Personal projection in faith toward the Lord is the beginning of divine resolution."**

from the grave? Why have I suffered so long? Is God deaf? Why have my friends and loved ones been taken from me?

This deeply emotional psalm is a mini-version of the Book of Job. As in that masterpiece, Heman's questions are left unanswered. Yet I'm convinced that Job — and perhaps Heman too — found comfort in the very process of prayer. Job concluded, "Though he slay me, yet will I hope in him" (Job 13:15)! Not being in control, they were driven to trust in God's sovereignty.

God alone knows the answers to the puzzling circumstances of life, though prayer itself, as an act of worship, does bring a measure of relief. *Personal introspection* is not the total answer. *Personal projection* in faith toward the Lord is the beginning of divine resolution.

Personal prayer

O Lord, I thank You for the release I find in prayer and for the fact that I am not overwhelmed by my pain in any final sense. Help me to continually choose to exercise faith in You . . . even when I see no visible solutions.

Covenant-Maker

God's Promises

Exposition of theme
PSALM 89

I will sing of the love of the Lord forever; with my mouth I will make your faithfulness known through all generations. . . . You said, "I have made a covenant with my chosen one, I have sworn to David my servant, 'I will establish your line forever and make your throne firm through all generations. . . . If his sons forsake my law and do not follow my statutes, if they violate my decrees and fail to keep my commands, I will punish their sin with the rod, their iniquity with flogging; but I will not take my love from him (vv. 1, 3–4, 30–33a).

Development of theme

In the music industry, contracts are vital for spelling out the agreement between the publisher and the artist. Will the artist retain all rights to the music, or will the artist and publisher share equally? What responsibilities will each party be expected to fulfill? What will be the percentage of royalty and how often will it be paid?

In one of the greatest contracts ever written, the agreement is between two parties, God and His servant David. "I have made a covenant with my chosen one," God says. "I have sworn to David my servant, 'I will establish your line forever and make your throne firm through all generations.' " (vv. 3–4).

In legal parlance, the party of the first part is

> **"If only my faith could soar on such wings! 'Lord, You haven't answered all my prayers yet . . . but I believe You will!' "**

God; the party of the second part is David and his descendants. Still, a contract is only as valid as the integrity of the persons negotiating it. God is faithful and trustworthy (v. 1), while He acknowledges that the human weakness of David and his line will cause them to be capable of violating the terms of the agreement. Further promises in the form of warnings are made: "If his sons forsake my law and do not follow my statutes . . . I will punish their sin with the rod . . . but I will not take my love from him [David]!" (v. 33). This covenant of love, faithful-

ness, and blessing is inviolable, eternal, and based on God's holiness.

Ethan, the wise man who wrote this psalm, grapples with one apparent contradiction in God's contract with King David. God has promised blessing to future generations, yet the king is in imminent danger of death from his enemies almost daily! The succession does not appear secure.

The psalmist moves quickly to remind the Lord of His own nature and character. In essence he says, "Lord, I believe You are loving and faithful. You haven't delivered David from his enemies *yet*, but I believe You will!" (v. 1).

If only my faith could soar on such wings! "Lord, You haven't answered all my prayers *yet* . . . but I believe You will!"

Personal prayer

O Lord, I cling to Your precious promises, fully confident that You who made the promises are able to keep them!

Covenant-Keeper

God's Faithfulness

Exposition of theme

PSALM 89 CONTINUED

I will declare that your love stands firm forever, that you established your faithfulness in heaven itself. . . . The heavens praise your wonders, O LORD, your faithfulness, too, in the assembly of the holy ones. For who in the skies above can compare with the LORD? Who is like the LORD among the heavenly beings? . . . You are mighty, O LORD, and your faithfulness surrounds you. . . . "Nor will I ever betray my faithfulness. I will not violate my covenant or alter what my lips have uttered. Once for all, I have sworn by my holiness—and I will not lie to David—that his line will continue forever and his throne endure before me like the sun; it will be established forever like the moon, the faithful witness in the sky" (vv. 2, 5–6, 8b, 33b–37).

Development of theme

Contracts are no longer taken very seriously. Legal loopholes are found and exercised every day. Marriage vows are violated and families

> *"The Lord doesn't approve of broken promises and casual contracts."*

ripped apart. Promises between friends are broken.

Only One can be counted on to keep His Word. "His [David's] throne will endure before me like the sun; it will be established forever like the moon, the faithful witness in the sky" (vv. 36–37). Even the heavens bear witness to His faithfulness!

The Lord doesn't approve of broken promises and casual contracts. I long to uphold my part of His covenant of grace and follow Him faithfully.

Personal prayer

O Lord God Almighty, may I honor all vows and keep all contracts, remembering that You consider such agreements sacred and binding.

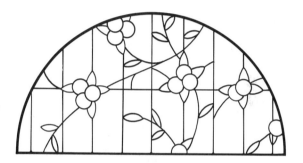

A WONDERFUL GOSPEL HYMN

Great Is Thy Faithfulness

Great is Thy faithfulness, O God my Father,
There is no shadow of turning with Thee;
Thou changest not, Thy compassions, they
    fail not;
As Thou hast been Thou forever wilt be.

Summer and winter, and springtime and
    harvest,
Sun, moon, and stars in their courses above
Join with all nature in manifold witness
To thy great faithfulness, mercy, and love.

Great is Thy faithfulness!
Great is Thy faithfulness!
Morning by morning new mercies I see;
All I have needed Thy hand hath provided;
Great is Thy faithfulness, Lord, unto me!

Words and music by Thomas O. Chisholm.
(Based on Lamentations 3:22-23).
© 1923, renewal 1951 (ext.) by Hope Publishing Co.

August *PSALMS 89–105*

The LORD is upright; he is my Rock. PSALM 92:15

PANORAMA PHOTO BY GARY IRVING

Covenant-Breaker

God's Memory

Exposition of theme

PSALM 89 CONTINUED

How long, O LORD? Will you hide yourself forever? How long will your wrath burn like fire? Remember how fleeting is my life. For what futility you have created all men! What man can live and not see death, or save himself from the power of the grave? O LORD, where is your former great love, which in your faithfulness you swore to David? Remember, LORD, how your servant has been mocked, how I bear in my heart the taunts of all the nations, the taunts with which your enemies have mocked, O LORD, with which they have mocked every step of your anointed one. Praise be to the LORD forever! Amen and Amen (vv. 46–52).

Development of theme

There are times when I'm tempted, like the writer of this psalm, to wonder if God has forgotten His promises. Surely the Lord will remember His covenant to King David, Ethan agonizes, though it seems doubtful at the moment. Despite God's promises, the king has suffered humiliating defeat — rejection, anger, renunciation, plunder, scorn, and shame.

Ethan, the Levite musician renowned for his

> **"If I take only the immediate point of view, life often appears unfair and futile."**

remarkable wisdom, writes of divine wrath and holy anger. He is moved by the futility of life and the inevitability of the grave. He appeals to God's infinite love and great faithfulness. He asks God to honor His word, then ends his prayer with a

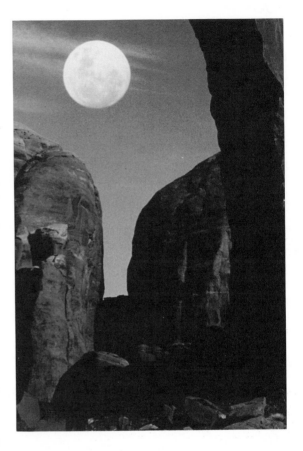

moving doxology which concludes Book III (Psalms 73–89).

If I take only the immediate point of view, life often appears unfair and futile. But if I appeal to God's love and faithfulness, I begin to approach life from the divine perspective. The final step is to follow Ethan's lead in praising God for *everything that happens.* "Praise be to the Lord forever! Amen and Amen."

Personal prayer

O Lord God Almighty, I know You keep Your promises, but time passes and I can't always see the answers to my prayers. Give me steadfastness and faith to believe in Your perfect faithfulness. The only covenant-breakers are Your people!

Moses' Masterpiece

Contrasting Images:
Transitory Man Versus the Everlasting God

Exposition of theme

PSALM 90

*L*ORD, *you have been our dwelling place throughout all generations. Before the mountains were born or you brought forth the earth and the world, from everlasting to everlasting you are God. You turn men back to dust. . . . For a thousand years in your sight are like a day that has just gone by, or like a watch in the night. . . . You have set our iniquities before you, our secret sins in the light of your presence. All our days pass away under your wrath; we finish our years with a moan. The length of our days in seventy years — or eighty, if we have the strength; yet their span is but trouble and sorrow, for they quickly pass, and we fly away. . . . Teach us to number our days aright, that we may gain a heart of wisdom (vv. 1–4, 8–10, 12).*

Development of theme

When I was just a little kid, I enjoyed blowing those bubbles made of soapsuds. They would appear in the atmosphere like iridescent Christmas ornaments, only to disappear a second

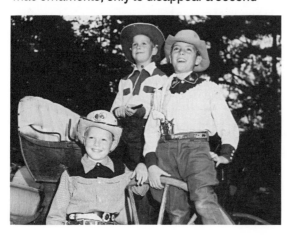

later. I had a similar experience with cotton candy. With great expectation, I would bite into the tantalizing pink bouquet of candy, only to have it dissolve in my mouth almost immediately. I learned early how many things in life are merely beautiful illusions, quickly passing away.

In this masterful blend of contrasting images, Moses teaches us that our earthly existence is like that sparkling bubble or that frothy confection. Human beings are "dust" that is soon swept away in "the sleep of death" or new grass that springs up in the morning, but withers away by nightfall (v. 5).

Though mankind is transitory, God is eternal. "Before the mountains were born . . . you are God" (v. 2). Man may be finite, but God is infinite,

> *"I learned early how many things in life are merely beautiful illusions, quickly passing away."*

"from everlasting to everlasting" (v. 2). Nor does He measure time as we do, for "a thousand years . . . are like a day that has just gone by, or like a watch in the night" (v. 4).

Moses pleads with his fellow mortals to recognize the fleeting quality of life, "to number their days" (v. 12). Since the normal lifespan is generally only seventy or eighty years at most, each moment is precious. Wisdom comes with an objective awareness of time that results in a changed perspective.

I must reorder my priorities and plan strategically so that every moment of every day will be spent wisely and in preparation for the glorious life to come!

Personal prayer

Lord, I praise You for Your infiniteness and constancy. I thank You that, even though my days on this earth are brief, I will sing Your praises for eternity!

Moses' Masterpiece

Contrasting Images:
Affliction Versus Affirmation

Exposition of theme

PSALM 90 CONTINUED

Relent, O LORD! How long will it be? Have compassion on your servants. Satisfy us in the morning with your unfailing love, that we may sing for joy and be glad all our days. Make us glad for as many days as you have afflicted us, for as many years as we have seen trouble. May your deeds be shown to your servants, your splendor to their children. May the favor of the LORD our God rest upon us; establish the work of our hands for us—yes, establish the work of our hands (vv. 13–17).

Development of theme

The human mind can only conceive of things in contrasts. For example, love would be unintelligible if there were no such thing as indifference. Francis Schaeffer, noted theologian, used to refer to this idea as "a" and "non-a," or the law of contradiction. The arts use contrasts in a similar fashion. The tension between unity and diversity produces high art.

In the same way, we can't fully appreciate the splendor of a sunrise without the darkness of night (v. 14), or vibrant good health without a little pain (v. 15), or the satisfaction of a job well done without some failures (v. 17).

Living out the changing textures of my life, I discover new depth in my growing relationship with my Lord. As He meets my deepest needs for love and acceptance, for healing, for relief from persecution, for meaningful work, I find inspiration for music-making. Out of a heart filled with gladness and gratitude, I will write, sing, and play songs of praise to Him.

When I am plagued by uncertainty about the future, insecurity about the present, and guilt about the past, I need to focus on the unchanging nature of God. My moods may shift like quicksilver, but God remains ever the same—omnipotent, infinite, and eternal. I rest on these granite peaks of His personality.

Personal prayer

O Lord, I long to compose a masterpiece to You. Against the drab backdrop of my own sin, sickness, and despair, I am inspired to write of Your everlasting, unfailing love!

> **"My moods may shift like quicksilver, but God remains ever the same—omnipotent, infinite, and eternal. I rest on these granite peaks of His personality."**

Song of Shelter and Security

Promise of Protection

Exposition of theme

PSALM 91

He who dwells in the shelter of the Most High will rest in the shadow of the Almighty. I will say of the LORD, "He is my refuge and my fortress, my God, in whom I trust." . . . For he will command his angels concerning you to guard you in all your ways; they will lift you up in their hands, so that you will not strike your foot against a stone. You will tread upon the lion and the cobra; you will trample the great lion and the serpent. "Because he loves me," says the LORD, "I will rescue him; I will protect him, for he acknowledges my name. He will call upon me, and I will answer him; I will be with him in trouble, I will deliver him and honor him. With long life will I satisfy him and show him my salvation" (vv. 1–2, 11–16).

Development of theme

Because I live in a fallen world, I am constantly exposed to violence, corruption, and raw, ugly evil. If it's not the blatant assault of the temporal world on my five senses, it's a more subtle blitz of Satan on my spirit. Seen and unseen dangers lurk in every shadow.

This magnificent psalm is a testimony to the security found only in the "Most High," the Sovereign God of the universe. The Creator has posted a guard of angels around the psalmist to protect him "in all [his] ways" (v. 11).

Some angelic beings are created to praise God continually (i.e., seraphim). Whole choirs of angels, like those who appeared to the shepherds on the night of Christ's birth, sing "Holy, holy, holy." (See Isaiah 6:3; Revelation 4:8; 5:9–12.) Others are assigned to guard duty (Psalm 91:11). Still others serve God as agents of His mighty works (Job 38:7; Acts 7:53). Some are ministering spirits sent to defend God's people (Psalm 34:7). Another special ministry of angels is to assist the saints at the time of death. Angels carried Lazarus to Abraham's bosom (Luke 16:22). What security in knowing about these very practical ministries of angels!

Verses 14–16 are precious promises from God Himself. Seven times He uses the verb form "I will." By His divine authority, God declares, "I will rescue . . . protect . . . answer . . . be with him in trouble . . . deliver and honor . . . satisfy with long life . . . and show him my salvation."

Everything I need for a full and prosperous life is promised "because [I] love [Him] . . . and acknowledge [His] name" (v. 14). I can heave a big sigh of relief. I'm safe in Him!

> **"This magnificent psalm is a testimony to the security found only in the 'Most High,' the Sovereign God of the universe."**

Personal prayer

O Most High, the Almighty, help me to become fully aware that I have complete safety and security because You are my hiding place and I dwell in the shadow of Your wings.

251

More Secure Is No One Ever (Tryggare Kan Ingen Vara)

More secure is no one ever
Than the loved ones of the Saviour—
Not yon star on high abiding
Nor the bird in homenest hiding.

God His own doth tend and nourish,
In His holy courts they flourish;
Like a father kind He spares them,
In His loving arms He bears them.

Neither life nor death and ever
From the Lord His children sever,
For His love and deep compassion
Comfort them in tribulation.

Little flock, to you than yield thee!
Jacob's God will ever shield thee;
Rest secure with this Defender—
At His will all foes surrender.

What He takes or what He gives us
Shows the Father's love so precious;
We may trust His purpose wholly
'Tis His children's welfare solely.

Translated from Swedish by Lina Sandell Berg
Music—Swedish folk melody.

Song of Shelter and Security

Freedom From Fear

Exposition of theme

PSALM 91 CONTINUED

Surely he will save you from the fowler's snare and from the deadly pestilence. He will cover you with his feathers, and under his wings you will find refuge; his faithfulness will be your shield and rampart. You will not fear the terror of night, nor the arrow that flies by day, nor the pestilence that stalks in the darkness, nor the plague that destroys at midday. A thousand may fall at your side, ten thousand at your right hand, but it will not come near you. You will only observe with your eyes and see the punishment of the wicked. If you make the Most High your dwelling—even the LORD, who is my refuge—then no harm will befall you, no disaster will come near your tent (vv. 3–10).

Development of theme

Can it be true? As a believer, will I really be spared suffering? Will the "deadly pestilence" (disease) and "plague" pass over my house and strike my unsaved neighbor? Can I avoid the "fowler's snare"—those insidious attempts to damage my reputation—just because I'm a Christian? How do I trust in the Lord when pain and death and treachery are real?

The key to my understanding lies in verses 4 and 5: "He will cover you with his feathers, and under his wings you will find refuge. . . . You will not fear. . . ."

Does this passage mean, then, that I will never suffer pain or loss? I don't think so, though I choose to believe the truth of this psalm. Through the power of the Holy Spirit, I believe that, if I take refuge in the Lord, I will not be afraid

"Pressure and pain give me an opportunity to flex my spiritual muscles. I can choose to trust the Lord to deliver me from fear, or I can be victimized by it."

in spite of my circumstances. I become aware that the deep inner core of my personality — the real me — cannot be touched or harmed by evil unless I permit it. Pressure and pain also give me an opportunity to flex my spiritual muscles. I can choose to trust the Lord to deliver me from fear, or I can be victimized by it.

In time, I experience the miracle of triumph through my tears, peace in the midst of the storm.

Personal prayer

O Most High, the Almighty, I praise You for protecting my real self — the part of me that will live forever — from all danger including death. I can live unafraid, knowing that You are with me always.

Doxology of Praise

Declaration

Exposition of theme

PSALM 92

It is good to praise the LORD and make music to your name, O Most High, to proclaim your love in the morning and your faithfulness at night, to the music of the ten-stringed lyre and the melody of the harp. For you make me glad by your deeds, O LORD; I sing for joy at the works of your hands. How great are your works, O LORD, how profound your thoughts! The senseless man does not know, fools do not understand, that though the wicked spring up like grass and all evildoers flourish, they will be forever destroyed (vv. 1–7).

Development of theme

This psalm is music to a musician's ears! The psalmist declares that it is *good* to praise the Lord, from morning till night (v. 2). I am to make music to His name, an outpouring of praise to be

---

"I don't need to play semantic games or to psych myself into a fake piety or phony joy. I want my life to be captivated by His greatness and grandeur. What cause for singing, playing, and dancing!"

---

accompanied by the ten-stringed lyre and the melody of the harp.

A contemporary song that grew out of two hearts united in praise to their Lord is often performed in concert on the synthesizer, to the beat of drums and fanfares of brass. But it is equally effective for a great choir, accompanied by a

---

Great is the Lord

Great is the Lord,
He is holy and just,
By His power we trust
In his love.

Great is the Lord,
He is faithful and true,
By His mercy He proves
He is love.

Great is the Lord
And worthy of glory.
Great is the Lord
And worthy of praise.
Great is the Lord —
Now lift up your voice!
Now lift up your voice!
Great is the Lord!

Words by Deborah D. Smith.
Music by Michael W. Smith.
© 1982 Meadowgreen Music.

---

symphony orchestra with a full string section. What motivates me to praise is the impact of the Lord's works — not only His acts in history but also His personal supernatural work in my life. I don't need to play semantic games or to psych myself into a fake piety or phony joy. The Lord really has done some profound and amazing things! His thoughts are infinite and astonishing. I want my life to be captivated by His greatness and grandeur. What cause for singing, playing, and dancing!

Personal prayer

Great are You, Lord! I want to make music to Your name all day long!

Doxology of praise

Exaltation

Exposition of theme
PSALM 92 CONTINUED

But you, O LORD, are exalted forever. For surely your enemies, O LORD, surely your enemies will perish; all evildoers will be scattered. You have exalted my horn like that of a wild ox; fine oils have been poured upon me. My eyes have seen the defeat of my adversaries; my ears have heard the rout of my wicked foes. The righteous will flourish like a palm tree, they will grow like a cedar of Lebanon; planted in the house of the LORD, they will flourish in the courts of our God. They will still bear fruit in old age, they will stay fresh and green, proclaiming, "The LORD is upright; he is my Rock, and there is no wickedness in him" (vv. 8–15).

Development of theme

Can you imagine "winter without Christmas?" Yet that's exactly how C.S. Lewis described the state of the unsaved. The enemies of God have

---

"I can choose to live solo — apart from God, independent and autonomous. Or I can draw near Him and develop a finely tuned intimacy, vulnerability, and dependence."

---

nothing to look forward to!

Boldly contrasting with this bleak metaphor is the eternal condition of the believer. The righteous will flourish like a stately palm tree or like a cedar of Lebanon, remaining "fresh and green" into old age and still bearing fruit.

So life is perceived in simple, basic terms. I can choose to live solo — apart from God, independent and autonomous. Or I can draw near Him and develop a finely tuned intimacy, vulnerability, and dependence. He lets me play my instrument in my own style. But as I follow Him, the Master Conductor, I become part of His score.

One person follows the path to self-destruction; another follows the way to mature, productive faith and exquisite harmony!

Doxology

Praise God, from whom all creatures flow;
Praise Him, all creatures here below;
Praise Him above, ye heavenly host;
Praise Father, Son, and Holy Ghost. Amen.

From the Genevan Psalter. Music attr. to Louis Bourgeois.
Words by Thomas Kerr.

Personal prayer

O Lord, Most High, You are exalted forever. I confess my utter dependence and vulnerability before You. Satisfy my thirst for You today.

Our God Reigns

Exposition of theme

PSALM 93

*The LORD reigns, he is robed in majesty; the LORD
is robed in majesty and is armed with strength.
The world is firmly established; it cannot be
moved. Your throne was established long ago;
you are from all eternity. The seas have lifted up,
O LORD, the seas have lifted up their voice; the
seas have lifted up their pounding waves. Mightier than the thunder of the great waters, mightier
than the breakers of the sea—the LORD on high
is mighty. Your statutes stand firm; holiness
adorns your house for endless days, O LORD
(vv. 1–5).*

Development of theme

I remember being overwhelmed the first time I
heard Beethoven's "Hallelujah" from *The Mount
of Olives* when I was still in high school. I'll never
forget the power, the majesty, the dignity of that
piece. I wondered if the music of heaven would
sound like that!

Psalm 93 echoes that immortal music, celebrating the day when the Lord will reign forever
and ever. This poetic form—the enthronement

> *"I need have no fear of the awe-
> inspiring forces of nature, but
> can exult in them as evidence of
> the power of Almighty God."*

psalm or theocratic psalm—was used in temple
worship to extol God's sovereignty. It soars ma-
jestically to the Lord, "robed in majesty" and
"armed in strength" (v. 1), whose throne is high
above the oceans.

The ancients—the Canaanites in particular—
were terrified of the sea. Baal, their god, was au-

thenticated by struggling with and overcoming
Yam, the sea god in Canaanite mythology. But in
verses 3–4 the sea is a metaphor of God's
strength and might—"pounding waves," "thunder of the great waters," "mightier than the
breakers of the sea."

I can live today in anticipation of His future
reign on this earth when final justice will prevail.
In the meantime, I need have no fear of the awe-
inspiring forces of nature, but I can exult in them
as evidence of the power of Almighty God. Such
incredible beauty and might are but a reflection
of His character and strength.

Personal prayer

*Dear Lord, I worship You whose voice thunders
above the crashing waves and rolling breakers.
Please focus Your power on solving my small
problems today as I wait in eager expectation of
that day when all nature sings.*

Soliloquy on Security

My Inheritance — God's Award

Exposition of theme

PSALM 94

O LORD, the God who avenges . . . shine forth. Rise up, O Judge of the earth; pay back to the proud what they deserve. . . . Does he who disciplines nations not punish? Does he who teaches man lack knowledge? The LORD knows the thoughts of man; he knows that they are futile. Blessed is the man you discipline, O LORD; the man you teach from your law; you grant him relief from days of trouble, till a pit is dug for the wicked. For the LORD will not reject his people; he will never forsake his inheritance. Judgment will again be founded on righteousness, and all the upright in heart will follow it (vv. 1–2, 10–15).

Development of theme

It is with great ambivalence that I attend award ceremonies. Admittedly, it's a thrill to be nomi-

---

> *"It seems so innocent — this compulsion we have to prove ourselves, to earn recognition, to accumulate awards."*

---

nated and win. After all, peer approval is something to be appreciated at any age! But if I don't win or, worse, if I'm not even nominated, I feel a certain rejection.

It seems so innocent — this compulsion we have to prove ourselves, to earn recognition, to accumulate awards. Yet, at the root of these ambitions is that subtle and seductive monster,

pride, that seeks to elevate self rather than God.

Selfish ambition has no place in the life of the believer, nor is it necessary, for I am already guaranteed a precious legacy. As Christ's co-heir, I will share in His glory (Romans 8:18). Instead of gold medallions and lavish trophies conferred by my peers, I'd rather work for the "prize for which God has called me heavenward in Christ Jesus" (Philippians 3:14). On that day of judgment and reward, I want to receive His "Well done!" Such a commendation will far surpass all the tarnished gold the world has to offer.

Personal prayer

Dear Lord, forgive my preoccupation with trivialities — the recognition of my peers and the acclaim of the world. Crush any proud place in me and help me focus on receiving an award of merit from You, bestowed after the grand finale of time.

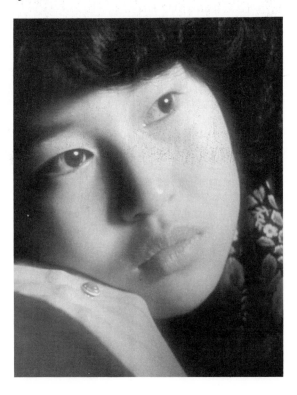

Soliloquy on Security

My Consolation — God's Loyal Love

Exposition of theme

PSALM 94 CONTINUED

Who will rise up for me against the wicked? Who will take a stand for me against evildoers? Unless the LORD had given me help, I would soon have dwelt in the silence of death. When I said, "My foot is slipping," your love, O LORD, supported me. When anxiety was great within me, your consolation brought joy to my soul (vv. 16–19).

Development of theme

I can relate to this psalmist whose foot is "slipping" and whose knees are buckling beneath him. He is weighted down with performance pressure and negative criticism. At such times even the godly can stumble.

I remember vividly the first time I had a memory lapse in a public performance. I was playing Mendelssohn's "Rondo Capriccioso" as a piano solo at Word of Life Island. Up to that time I'd never gone blank in my life! But here, before an audience of five hundred people, I forgot the notes. That sinking sensation came flooding back as I watched Debi Thomas stumble on the ice during the Olympic figure skating competition. It takes a lot to be able to get up and go on

with your career after than kind of public embarrassment!

In this psalm the psalmist is outnumbered and overpowered. Human resources are inadequate. He has no back-up. . . .

In music, back-up is critical. Once, while conducting several hundred Baptist teenagers in John Peterson's and my musical," I Love America," to the accompaniment of a tape track, someone accidently kicked out the plug! I was mortified, but we continued *a cappella*.

At last the psalmist remembers the Lord — His help (v. 17), His love (v. 18), His consolation (v. 19). Belief in one's own ability alone produces a false sense of security. Faith in God results in consolation, comfort and inner strength.

Personal prayer

Dear Lord, I thank You for lifting me up when I stumble. When I'm filled with anxiety and "stage fright," I'm a prime candidate for Your comfort!

> **"Belief in one's own ability alone produces a false sense of security. Faith in God results in consolation, comfort and inner strength."**

Invention of Praise

First Part — Praising God's Sovereignty

Exposition of theme
PSALM 95

Come, let us sing for joy to the LORD; let us shout aloud to the Rock of our salvation. Let us come before him with thanksgiving and extol him with music and song. . . . Come, let us bow down in worship, let us kneel before the LORD our Maker; for he is our God and we are the people of his pasture, the flock under his care (vv. 1–2, 6–7).

Development of theme

The psalmist almost explodes with praise in this stirring enthronement psalm. He sings for joy to the Lord and worships the One who provides security and deliverance. He moves on to celebrate God's marvelous wide-ranging creativity, for He is the "great King above all gods" who made the mountain peaks, the sea, and the depths of the earth.

Moved by the same great theme, I composed this song of praise:

> O come, let us sing to the Lord,
> The Rock of our salvation;
> With joyous shouts of love and praise
> We'll sing a psalm for endless days:
> In vibrant jubilation,
> Come, let us sing to the Lord!
>
> We come to Him, the great God-King,
> With joyful noise our voices sing;
> He takes His throne of royalty
> And reigns above in sovereignty;
> In notes of exaltation,
> Come, let us sing to the Lord!
>
> We come to Him, the Creator,
> The one Illuminator;
> He made the sea and formed the land,
> And He shaped the earth with His
>   mighty hand:
> With songs of appreciation,
> Come, let us sing to the Lord!
>
> We come to Him, our Shepherd
> Our consummate Provider;
> He tends His flock with surety
> And blesses us with security:
> With comfort and consolation,
> Come, let us sing to the Lord!

Words and music by Don Wyrtzen.   © 1974 by Singspiration.

In the tradition of Abraham and other spiritual forefathers, I am compelled to fall facedown before my Lord. Merely bowing or kneeling will just begin to express my heart's adoration in the presence of such majesty. Yet He is also my tender Shepherd and desires to have intimacy with the people of His pasture.

Personal prayer

O Great King and Gentle Shepherd, I can scarcely believe that You who created the world desire fellowship with one of Your lowly sheep. Praise your Name forever!

Invention of Praise

Second Part — Warning Against Unbelief

Exposition of theme

PSALM 95 *CONTINUED*

Today, if you hear his voice, do not harden your hearts as you did at Meribah, as you did that day at Massah in the desert, where your fathers tested and tried me, though they had seen what I did. For forty years I was angry with that generation; I said, "They are a people whose hearts go astray, and they have not known my ways." So I declared on oath in my anger, "They shall never enter my rest" (vv. 8–11).

Development of theme

As the first movement in this symphony of praise ends, bringing the believer to his knees in worshipful adoration, there is an abrupt change of pace.

I can almost hear the rich, somber tones of the horns here. God is issuing a stern ultimatum: "Do not harden your hearts!" He is referring, of course, to the obstinate children of Israel who had murmured in the wilderness, sounding like the random notes of an orchestra tuning up. But His warning has my name on it. I often become

> **"I can almost hear the rich, somber tones of the horns here. God is issuing a stern ultimatum."**

critical and negative, and my whining sounds like a kid learning to play the violin!

The names of key geographical locations in Israel tell the story: "Meribah" (strife—like the fuzzy tones on an electric guitar); "Massah" (testing—like the critical shaping of the oboe's

double reed). At those memorable sites, His rebellious children pushed the Lord to the limits of His patience. As a result, they never made it to the Promised Land. This whole episode feels romantic, German, and Wagnerian to me—so intense, so sad, so earthy.

Suddenly I hear a trumpet fanfare signaling God's desires for me: "Be warned! I will give you abundant opportunity to follow where I lead, but you must obey—instantly and without argument or complaint!"

This warning, in stark and striking measures, climaxes the symphony, and the lingering cadences resonate in my heart and mind: Unbelief and resistance cost the children of Israel their promised rest in the land flowing with milk and honey. Will I be faithful to the end? Will my performance disintegrate, or will I reach the finale?

Personal prayer

O Great God King, soften my heart toward You and turn my murmurings into a melody of praise.

Greater Is He

All the earth praises His majesty . . .

Exposition of theme

PSALM 96

Sing to the LORD a new song; sing to the LORD, all the earth. Sing to the LORD, praise his name; proclaim his salvation day after day. Declare his glory among the nations, his marvelous deeds among all peoples. For great is the LORD and most worthy of praise; he is to be feared above all gods. For all the gods of the nations are idols, but the LORD made the heavens. Splendor and majesty are before him; strength and glory are in his sanctuary (vv. 1–6).

Development of theme

What makes a song publishable? First the content must be fresh and biblical—presenting God's truth in a new way. Too many songs are imitative and derivative and seem to be cloned from secular sources.

A wonderful song should be eternal, dealing with a universal theme that has cosmic significance and presented in a form that is contemporary and natural.

Certain themes are especially pleasing to the Lord: salvation (v. 2), His glory (v. 3), His marvel-

> *"Powerful, life-changing music will never be initiated by monetary concerns or ego needs, for human genius without a focus on God is sterile."*

ous deeds (v. 3). Thematically, in both life and music, we must declare His attributes and His acts, reflect His majesty, and celebrate history— *His* story!

Pondering His majesty, splendor, strength , and glory should lead us to spiritual ecstasy. *Our Lord made the heavens and spun the galaxies into space!* Out of this should come art that is worthy of His praise. The alternative is the lifeless, toneless sounds of the pagan world.

Powerful, life-changing music will never be initiated by monetary concerns or ego needs, for human genius without a focus on God is sterile. Until He does a deep work in our lives, we really don't have anything to write about!

Personal prayer

I worship You, Sovereign Lord, with all the creativity at my command. Inspire me to write and sing Your praises and to live my song!

261

Greater Is He

Nations and nature praise His majesty . . .

Exposition of theme

PSALM 96 CONTINUED

Say among the nations, "The LORD reigns." The world is firmly established, it cannot be moved; he will judge the peoples with equity. Let the heavens rejoice, let the earth be glad; let the sea resound, and all that is in it; let the fields be jubilant, and everything in them. Then all the trees of the forest will sing for joy; they will sing before the LORD, for he comes, he comes to judge the earth. He will judge the world in righteousness and the peoples in his truth (vv. 10–13).

Development of theme

When I was still in graduate school, I had a marvelous opportunity to participate in a revival in Mexico City. The evangelist was Luis Palau, the Billy Graham of Latin America; the song leader was Bruce Woodman, the Cliff Barrows of that continent; the organist was yours truly. I can still hear those thousands of Latin people singing God's praises in their own language. Because I don't speak fluent Spanish, I recognized only a few phrases, but the name of "Je-sus" provided a common denominator. What a preview of the music of heaven!

The Apostle Paul tells of a day, perhaps very soon, when Christ will be exalted and every creature from every nation on earth will acknowledge Him. Today's reading from the Psalms is the Old Testament counterpart of a magnificent passage in Philippians: "Therefore God exalted him to the highest place and gave him the name that is above every name, that at the name of Jesus every knee should bow, in heaven and on earth and under the earth, and every tongue confess that Jesus Christ is LORD, to the glory of God the Father" (2:9–11).

> *"If even inanimate objects are moved to praise, how much more should my tongue be loosed to join in the universal chorus!"*

On that day, the curse on nature will be lifted, and God will pour out His blessing. As harmony and balance is restored to the universe, the heavens and earth will be glad, and all of creation will tremble with joy and music. The sea will "resound, and all that is in it" (v. 11); the fields will be jubilant (v. 12), and "all the trees of the forest will sing for joy" (v. 12).

If even inanimate objects are moved to praise, how much more should my tongue be loosed to join in the universal chorus! It will be "love in any language" — Spanish, English, Russian, Chinese. . . .

Personal prayer

Dear Lord, I sing Your precious Name, for "Jesus is the sweetest Name I know!" I rejoice with people of all nations and with all of nature in the majesty and glory of that Name.

Epiphany of Glory

Vision of the Lord's Glorious Coming

Exposition of theme

PSALM 97

The LORD reigns, let the earth be glad; let the distant shores rejoice. Clouds and thick darkness surround him; righteousness and justice are the foundation of his throne. Fire goes before him and consumes his foes on every side. His lightning lights up the world; the earth sees and trem-

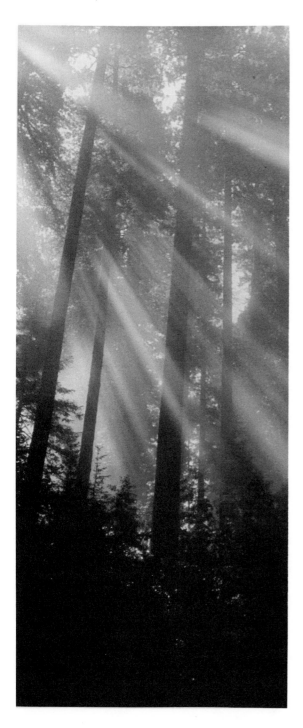

bles. The mountains melt like wax before the LORD, before the LORD of all the earth. The heavens proclaim his righteousness, and all the peoples see his glory (vv. 1–6).

Development of theme

Reading the prophetic words of this psalm excites my imagination. My Lord is coming again to rule and to reign! In light of that dynamic truth, all the petty frustrations of this life seem ridiculously unimportant.

The sublime poetry of these verses describe in figurative language the Lord's glory. In their broadest interpretation, they also depict His coming reign and remind me of prophecies in both Old and New Testaments. When He comes, He will be surrounded by clouds. (See Revelation 1:7.) "Fire goes before him and consumes his foes." (See Isaiah 66:15–16.) Not only do men fear Him, but nature trembles as well. "His lightning lights up the world." (See Luke 17:24.) "The mountains melt like wax." (See Micah 1:4.) "The heavens proclaim his righteousness, and all the peoples see his glory" (v. 6).

If I knew Jesus were coming one week from

> *"If I knew Jesus were coming one week from today, how would I change my life and ministry? I'd go on a crash course to know my Lord a lot better."*

today, how would I change my life and ministry? I'd go on a crash course to know my Lord a lot better. I'd put house-hunting on hold and wait for that mansion in glory! I'd double-check with certain relatives about their relationship with the Lord and if necessary I'd share the gospel more honestly and passionately with them. I'd spend more time in the Word, allow the Holy Spirit to control me more completely, and draw closer to my brothers and sisters in Christ. If I had any extra time, I'd concentrate on making some music to the praise and glory of God!

Personal prayer

O Lord, I feel like a child at Christmas when I anticipate Your coming again! Order my priorities to conform to Your plan for my role in Your kingdom. Give me a fresh vision!

AUGUST 16

Epiphany of Glory
A Call to Righteous Living and Faithfulness

Exposition of theme

PSALM 97 CONTINUED

All who worship images are put to shame, those who boast in idols—worship him, all you gods! Zion hears and rejoices and the villages of Judah are glad because of your judgments, O LORD. For you, O LORD, are the Most High over all the earth; you are exalted far above all gods. Let those who love the LORD hate evil, for he guards the lives of his faithful ones and delivers them from the hand of the wicked. Light is shed upon the righteous and joy on the upright in heart. Rejoice in the LORD, you who are righteous, and praise his holy name (vv. 7–12).

Development of theme

How do we define idolatry in contemporary terms? The "images" mentioned in biblical times refer to physical objects made with hands. But idolatry also means "clinging attachment or devotion." In Christian terms idolatry refers to anything or anyone that comes "between God and me." It takes many subtle forms—making heroes out of celebrities, getting carried away with my own gifts, being unduly impressed with personal status symbols, education, or expertise.

> *"Idolatry takes many subtle forms—making heroes out of celebrities, getting carried away with my own gifts, being unduly impressed with personal status symbols, education, or expertise."*

The emptiness and foolishness of idolatry is exposed when the radiant glory of God penetrates the fog. This super ego that blinds us to our own sin, these works of our own hands are then laid bare, and we recognize the "Most High over all the earth" (v. 9).

With the Lord of Glory as my reference point and His righteous reign as my context, I need to learn how to discern idolatry—especially in myself—and hate it as much as He does. I need to trust in His deliverance from wickedness, then rest secure because "he guards the lives of his faithful ones."

On this—my birthday—I want to celebrate by creating a new work of praise to His glory. He is the Author of life, the Composer of the music of my days, my Songmaker!

Personal prayer

Dear Lord, trample any idols I may have foolishly erected. As You crush them, may the sweet perfume of my love and gratitude rise before You and may the melody of my heart be a sacrifice of praise.

Sing to the Lord a New Song

"The Lord has made His salvation known."

Exposition of theme

PSALM 98

Sing to the LORD a new song, for he has done marvelous things; his right hand and his holy arm have worked salvation for him. The LORD has made his salvation known and revealed his righteousness to the nations. He has remembered his love and his faithfulness to the house of Israel; all the ends of the earth have seen the salvation of our God (vv. 1–3).

A SONG

Joy to the World

Joy to the world! the Lord is come!
Let earth receive her King;
Let every heart prepare Him room,
And heaven and nature sing.

Joy to the earth! the Savior reigns!
Let men their songs employ;
While fields and floods, rocks, hills, and
   plains
Repeat the sounding joy.

No more let sins and sorrows grow,
Nor thorns infest the ground;
He comes to make His blessings flow
Far as the curse is found.

He rules the world with truth and grace,
And makes the nations prove
The glories of His righteousness
And wonders of His love.

Words by Isaac Watts (adapted from Psalm 98).
Music adapted from George F. Handel.

Development of theme

When I read of God's covenant with Israel, His loyal love and faithfulness to His chosen people, I don't feel excluded, but greatly blessed. Spiritually I too am Jewish — part of the spiritual seed of Abraham (Galatians 3:28–29)!

As that concept impacts my life, I am moved to make music to this God who has included me in His marvelous plan. Saved and sealed by His

---

"As nonbelievers overhear my songs of praise, they will be drawn to His irresistible love."

Spirit, I sing and proclaim His salvation to "all the ends of the earth." As nonbelievers overhear my songs of praise, they will be drawn to His irresistible love.

This psalm motivated Isaac Watts to write the familiar carol "Joy to the World" that is sung each Christmas to Frederick Handel's heroic melody.

Personal prayer

O Lord, I long to compose carols of joy, celebrating the marvelous things You have done in my life.

Sing to the Lord a New Song

"He will judge the world in righteousness."

Exposition of theme

PSALM 98 CONTINUED

Shout for joy to the LORD, all the earth, burst into jubilant song with music; make music to the LORD with the harp, with the harp and the sound of singing, with trumpets and the blast of the ram's horn—shout for joy before the LORD, the King. Let the sea resound, and everything in it, the world, and all who live in it. Let the rivers clap their hands, let the mountains sing together for joy; let them sing before the LORD, for he comes to judge the earth. He will judge the world in righteousness and the peoples with equity (vv. 4–9).

Development of theme

There is nothing subdued or restrained about the message of this psalm! It's a toe-tapper! How can we be still when we are exhorted to "burst

> *"There is nothing subdued or restrained about the message of this psalm! It's a toe-tapper!"*

into jubilant song" (v. 4), "shout for joy before the Lord" (v. 6), and "make music . . . with trumpets and the blast of the ram's horn" (v. 6)!

My former neighbor, Dr. Bill Reus, has hunted long-horn rams on all the major continents of the world. When I first saw these fierce-looking horns mounted over his fireplace, I was reminded of the ancient orchestra. At the inauguration of Solomon's Temple, 120 priests blew rams' horns, accompanied by other Levites, singing

and playing cymbals, harps, and lyres (2 Chronicles 5). No wonder the Lord says, "Make a joyful noise!"

All of nature joins in a cacophony of sound and motion. "Let the sea resound. . . . Let the rivers clap their hands. . . . Let the mountains sing together for joy" (vv. 7–8).

What inspires this explosion of joy? What induces this liberated worship in song? The Lord is coming! And when I think of all that will mean, I am inspired to mix all the rich colors available to me in this palette of praise and pour out my own "new song."

Personal prayer

Dear Lord, unleash my spirit today and set me free to create music worthy of Your praise. Let my imagination soar as I lift up Your Name!

A CONTEMPORARY LYRIC

Sing to the Lord a New Song

Sing to the Lord a new song,
Sing to the Lord all day long;
Break out in praise and sing the refrain;
Our Lord will come to rule and reign.

He saved us with His holy hand,
Announced His truth to every land;
In love and truth He watched His own,
To all the earth His grace was shown.

With shouts of joy before your King,
With happy voices, anthems sing;
Join all in rapturous symphony,
And worship Him in harmony.

Vast seas and oceans roar with acclaim,
People of earth, His worth proclaim;
Let rivers clap their hands in glee,
And hills sing songs spontaneously.

Words and music by Don Wyrtzen. © 1974 Singspiration Music.

Holy, Holy, Holy
The Lord is Holy

Exposition of theme
PSALM 99

The LORD reigns, let the nations tremble; he sits enthroned between the cherubim, let the earth shake. Great is the LORD in Zion; he is exalted over all the nations. Let them praise your great and awesome name—he is holy. The King is mighty, he loves justice—you have established equity; in Jacob you have done what is just and right. Exalt the LORD our God and worship at his footstool; he is holy (vv. 1–5).

Development of theme

Dr. Karl Menninger, internationally celebrated psychiatrist, has asked the question: "Whatever became of sin?"

The ugly reality of sin fades away when we lose our vision of the dazzling holiness of God (Isaiah 6). In our modern perception, the shed blood seems cannibalistic and barbaric, the price of forgiveness is cheapened, and the Good News is relegated to the "religion" section of the local newspaper.

This psalm inspires us to recover the truth of God's character. He alone is holy—"perfectly pure and worthy of profound reverence." This is the pillar—the *sine qua non*—upon which everything in Christianity rests!

Personal prayer

Dear Lord, I praise Your great and glorious Name because You alone are holy.

> **"The ugly reality of sin fades away when we lose our vision of the dazzling holiness of God."**

Holy, Holy, Holy
The Lord Answers Prayer

Exposition of theme
PSALM 99 CONTINUED

Moses and Aaron were among his priests, Samuel was among those who called on his name; they called on the LORD and he answered them. He spoke to them from the pillar of cloud; they kept his statutes and the decrees he gave them. O LORD our God, you answered them; you were to Israel a forgiving God, though you punished their misdeeds. Exalt the LORD our God and worship at his holy mountain, for the LORD our God is holy (vv. 6–9).

Development of theme

The Lord has dramatically steered my passage through life. In high school I wanted to attend a particular college, but God chose Moody Bible Institute. (If I hadn't listened to His voice, I probably wouldn't have met Karen!) After Moody, I planned to study at Juilliard, but God wanted me at King's. (If I hadn't obeyed, I probably wouldn't be involved in the world of Christian music.) After college I had my sights set on graduate school at Columbia University, but God led me to Dallas Theological Seminary. (If I had followed my own inclination, I probably wouldn't have written this book!) These career turning points all came out of wrestling matches with the Lord. It is only as I look back that I can see the providential hand of God on our lives.

Our Lord has a history of answering the prayers of His saints. In ancient times, Moses

---

> *"It only takes one turning point like mine, one gigantic crisis, one moment of unresolved conflict to realize how frail and vulnerable we are."*

(Exodus 3, 4), Aaron (Exodus 4:27–31; 7:6), Hannah (1 Samuel 2), Samuel (1 Samuel 3), and Nehemiah (Nehemiah 1) called on the name of the Lord, and He answered. They were rewarded for their obedience. Though God punished Israel for misdeeds, He also forgave them and regularly answered their prayers.

Why don't more people pray more often, believing that God really hears and answers? Maybe it's because they have bought into the system that claims we are self-sufficient beings, perfectly capable of taking care of ourselves and, at the extreme, that we're even evolving into gods! Yet it only takes one turning point like mine, one gi-

gantic crisis, one moment of unresolved conflict to realize how frail and vulnerable we are. We need Him every hour!

Personal prayer

Dear Lord, I know You hear and answer today just as You did in the days of Moses, Aaron, and Samuel. May I always call on You rather than relying on my puny human resources.

A WONDERFUL OLD HYMN

Holy, Holy, Holy

Holy, holy, holy! Lord God Almighty!
Early in the morning our song shall rise to
 Thee;
Holy, holy, holy! merciful and mighty!
God in three persons, blessed Trinity!

Holy, holy, holy! all the saints adore Thee,
Casting down their golden crowns around
 the glassy sea;
Cherubim and seraphim falling down
 before Thee,
Who wert and art and evermore shalt be.

Holy, holy, holy! Though the darkness hide
 Thee,
Though the eye of sinful man Thy glory may
 not see;
Only Thou art holy — there is none beside
 Thee,
Perfect in pow'r, in love and purity.

Holy, holy, holy! Lord God Almighty!
All Thy works shall praise Thy name in earth
 and sky and sea;
Holy, holy, holy! merciful and mighty!
God in three persons, blessed Trinity!

Words by Reginald Heber. Music by John B. Dykes.

The Old One-Hundredth

Exposition of theme

PSALM 100

Shout for joy to the LORD, all the earth. Worship the LORD with gladness; come before him with joyful songs. Know that the LORD is God. It is he who made us, and we are his; we are his people, the sheep of his pasture. Enter his gates with thanksgiving and his courts with praise; give thanks to him and praise his name. For the LORD is good and his love endures forever; his faithfulness continues through all generations (vv. 1–5).

Development of theme

A brilliant example of an ancient musician at his best is contained in this enduring psalm. Perhaps only the Twenty-third is more widely known and loved in all of Christendom.

The things that are most familiar to us, however, often lose their deepest meaning. To rediscover the rich mother lode of treasure in these verses, I've asked myself why this passage has remained one of the best-loved in all the Bible.

There are at least five reasons: First, the Lord is God—Creator, Sustainer, Redeemer (v. 3). Second, He made me and I belong to Him. My identity is in Him. I'm not a faceless nonentity, floating through the impersonal cosmos, but *a child of God*, "the sheep of his pasture" (v. 3).

> "To rediscover the rich mother lode of treasure in these verses, I've asked myself why this passage has remained one of the best-loved in all the Bible."

Sing Joyfully Before the Lord!

Sing joyfully before the Lord,
Obey Him gladly on the earth;
Rejoicing, take Him at His Word,
Before Him sing with joy and mirth!

Go through His open gates with joy,
Go to His courts with deepest praise;
Let grateful songs your tongue employ,
And bless His name for endless days!

Because the Lord is always good,
His faithfulness forever sure,
His truth for endless ages firmly stood,
And will for ages still endure.

Words and music by Don Wyrtzen. © 1971 Singspiration Music.

Third, the Lord is good. He wishes me well, not evil (v. 5). Fourth, He loves me with an endless love because I am infinitely precious to Him (v. 5). Finally, His covenant of love extends to my children—D.J. and Kathy—and to any grandchildren they may give me someday! (v. 5)

Such good news fills me with joy and a desire to "enter His gates with thanksgiving and His courts with praise."

Personal prayer

Dear Lord, help me to shout for joy today, to worship You with gladness, and to come before You with joyful songs.

Psalm of Integrity

Exposition of theme
PSALM 101

I will sing of your love and justice; to you, O LORD, I will sing praise. I will be careful to lead a blameless life—when will you come to me? I will walk in my house with blameless heart. I will set before my eyes no vile thing. . . . No one who practices deceit will dwell in my house; no one who speaks falsely will stand in my presence. Every morning I will put to silence all the wicked in the land; I will cut off every evildoer from the city of the LORD (vv. 1–3, 7–8).

Development of theme

I've given a lot of thought lately to the question of personal and professional ethics. Rumors of corruption in government have always been rife; business empires crumble in the face of fraud and embezzlement at the level of top management; politicians and peachers alike succumb to greed and lust. How can I guard my own integrity in these perverse times?

David's psalm gives me some cues to managing my personal and professional life. Unique among the rulers of the ancient Near East, David was a man whose lifestyle and reign were marked by integrity. He was scarred, fallen, and flawed like the rest of us, yet he submitted to God's authority over his life. Here is the character by which he ruled.

First, he pledged himself to be "careful to lead a blameless life," realizing that the attitude of

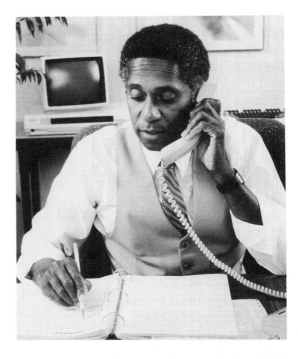

one's heart dictates his actions (vv. 2–3). Second, he warned the people that he would tolerate no shady deals, no under-the-counter maneuvers, no ethical hanky-panky (vv. 4–6). More than that, he threatened to deal sternly with those who violated sound principles of moral conduct (vv. 7–8), and then God allowed David to experience the consequences of his own actions!

David chose justice over popularity, integrity over peace at any price. He boldly confronted evil in his empire and set the standard by his strong commitment to personal purity.

Nor can I abdicate my responsibility as God's man in my own world. He calls me to authenticity—not just image—both in the office and at home.

Personal prayer

O Lord, keep me pure and blameless as I move from the realm of my business dealings to my God-ordained position as head of my home.

> **"God calls me to be His man in my world. He calls me to authenticity—not just image—both in the office and at home."**

Ballad of Burnout

Burned Out

Exposition of theme

PSALM 102

Hear my prayer, O Lord; let my cry for help come to you. Do not hide your face from me when I am in distress. Turn your ear to me; when I call, answer me quickly. For my days vanish like smoke; my bones burn like glowing embers. My heart is blighted and withered like grass; I forget to eat my food. . . . All day long my enemies taunt me; those who rail against me use my name as a curse. . . . My days are like the evening shadow; I wither away like grass (vv. 1–4, 8, 11).

Development of theme

I know what it's like to run dry, both spiritually and creatively. The symptoms the psalmist describes in these verses are all too familiar. One day blends, facelessly, into another, with nothing to show for it. Unbridled emotions produce almost physical pain before plunging me into a state of feeling almost nothing at all. I have no heart for my work, no inspiration. To top it all off, I suffer from periodic insomnia and, occasionally, even loss of appetite!

Psychologists diagnose this problem as "burnout." Authors call it the "blank page syndrome." Musicians sometimes refer to it as a creative dry spell. I call it low-grade motivation or no motivation at all. The psalmist feels that life itself is over.

But there's a flip side to this record of griefs.

"Inspiration for victorious living and for creative music-making have a common source—intimacy with the Lord."

This afflicted believer is doing the only thing he knows to do, thereby setting the pace for every depressed believer who has ever lived. He calls on the Lord! He cries out to him and groans in His presence.

Inspiration for victorious living and for creative music-making have a common source—intimacy with the Lord. One way to nurture intimacy with Him and beat the cycle of despair is to begin with an uninhibited outpouring of raw and honest emotion. To deny these overwhelming feelings is to concede defeat. Pretending is fantasy; honesty produces reality. The psalmist's way, though painful, is the only sure route to healing, wholeness, and renewed creativity.

Personal prayer

Hear my prayer, O Lord. I'm burned out, dried up, and spiritually depleted. I turn to You—Savior, fellow Sufferer, Songmaker.

AUGUST 24

Ballad of Burnout

Worn Out

Exposition of theme

PSALM 102 CONTINUED

The nations will fear the name of the LORD, all the kings of the earth will revere your glory. For the LORD will rebuild Zion and appear in his glory. He will respond to the prayer of the destitute; he will not despise their plea. . . . "In the beginning you laid the foundations of the earth, and the heavens are the work of your hands. They will perish, but you remain; they will all wear out like a garment. Like clothing you will change them and they will be discarded. But you remain the same, and your years will never end. The children of your servants will live in your presence; their descendants will be established before you" (vv. 15–17, 25–28).

Development of theme

My wife Karen is an astonishingly beautiful lady whose clothes make an artistic statement. A person with a strong sense of style and color, her tastes run from sporty and classic to elegant and sophisticated. With her fair Nordic coloring, I love to see her in pink. In any gathering she stands out, and I'm always proud of her. Whatever the occasion, she's always appropriately dressed.

But clothing, no matter how fine the fabric or how well-constructed, eventually wears out or becomes outdated. In this passage, the psalmist calls our attention to the fact that even the heavens, that vast canopy covering the earth, will "wear out like a garment" (v. 26). The Lord will change them (heaven and earth) "like clothing" and "they will be discarded" (v. 26).

Karen is no clotheshorse. While she enjoys dressing in good taste and with a kind of flair, she's a person of great spiritual sensitivity and depth. She knows as well as this psalmist that the only covering that will endure is Jesus Christ, who clothes us in His righteousness.

We can have confidence that the Lord knows the deepest needs and desires of our heart and will respond accordingly. Styles may change—in fashion and in other art forms, including music! Only our great God remains the same, from generation to generation, world without end!

Personal prayer

Lord, Karen and I bring our pitiful wardrobe to You. In Your sight our garments are as filthy rags. We rejoice that we will be dressed in Your righteousness throughout all eternity!

AUGUST 25

Bless the Lord, O My Soul!

Praising the Lord for His Benefits

Exposition of theme
PSALM 103

Praise the LORD, O my soul; all my inmost being, praise his holy name. Praise the LORD, O my soul, and forget not all his benefits—who forgives all your sins and heals all your diseases, who redeems your life from the pit and crowns you with love and compassion, who satisfies your desires with good things so that your youth is renewed like the eagle's (vv. 1–5).

Development of theme

This exalted work is the definitive answer to the problems so honestly enumerated in Psalm 102.

David's artistic soul erupts in uninhibited praise. From the core of his being, from the focal point of his soul, he praises the holy name of the Lord. And he has good reason to celebrate!

The Lord has given David a cornucopia over-flowing with gifts of His grace. He has forgiven David's sins (v. 3). He has healed his sickness (v. 3). He has delivered David from the grave (v. 4). He has enriched David's life with gifts of loyal love and tender compassion (v. 4). He has satisfied David's deepest desires with good things (v. 5).

Instead of being grounded by despair, David can now soar like an eagle. Instead of a weak, anemic faith, he is blessed with vigorous spiritual health which vibrates in his songs of praise.

Personal prayer

I praise You and thank You, O Lord, for all of Your blessings to me: Your forgiveness, Your healing, Your deliverance, Your love, Your compassion, and for fully satisfying my inner being with Yourself.

AUGUST 26

Bless the Lord, O My Soul!

Praising the Lord for His Compassion

Exposition of theme
PSALM 103 CONTINUED

The LORD . . . made known his ways to Moses, his deeds to the people of Israel: The LORD is compassionate and gracious, slow to anger, abounding in love. He will not always accuse, nor will he harbor his anger forever; he does not treat us as our sins deserve or repay us according to our iniquities. For as high as the heavens are above the earth, so great is his love for those who fear him; as far as the east is from the west, so far has he removed our transgressions from us. As a father has compassion on his children, so the LORD has compassion on those who fear him; for he knows how we are formed, he remembers that we are dust. . . . But from everlasting to everlasting the LORD's love is with those who fear him, and his righteousness with their children's children—with those who keep his covenant and remember to obey his precepts (vv. 6–14, 17–18).

Development of theme

Whenever I read this psalm cataloging the virtues of God, I feel like Moses must have felt

---

"Of all the divine attributes, the one that resounds in my spirit like the clash of cymbals is His love. It is incomprehensible and inexhaustible."

---

when standing in His presence on Mt. Sinai (Exodus 34:6–7). Moses was allowed to view the back of God and, in that intimate exposure, the great man of God found out what our Lord is like!

He is compassionate and not only feels our pain and sorrow, but stands ready to alleviate it. He is gracious, choosing not to punish our sins in proportion to their seriousness (v. 10). He is loving and even-tempered (vv. 7–8). He does not hold grudges (v. 9). His love is infinite; His forgiveness, totally effective and complete (vv. 11–12).

Of all these divine attributes, the one that resounds in my spirit like the clash of cymbals is His love. It is incomprehensible and inexhaustible. It is "wide and long and high and deep," and when I begin to grasp it, my inner being is strengthened by the Holy Spirit (Ephesians 3:16-21). I am changed from the inside out.

My imagination fired, I want to write a concerto, using God's incomparable love as my theme!

Personal prayer

I am grateful, Lord, that Your mercy, love, and compassion temper the anger and judgment that should rightfully fall on me. Praise be to the Lord of love and grace!

Bless the Lord, O My Soul!

Praising the Lord for His Dominion

Exposition of theme

PSALM 103 CONTINUED

The LORD has established his throne in heaven, and his kingdom rules over all. Praise the LORD, you his angels, you mighty ones who do his bidding, who obey his word. Praise the LORD, all his heavenly hosts, you his servants who do his will. Praise the LORD, all his works everywhere in his dominion. Praise the LORD, O my soul (vv. 19-22).

Development of theme

At various stages of my life I have exercised authority in a number of arenas. I have been a church music director, head of a music department in a Christian college, editor-in-chief of a music company, and instructor in a theological seminary. Musicians and writers sometimes consult me for musical and theological advice. At home, God has assigned me to the role of husband to Karen and father to D.J. and Kathy.

But God's domain has no such limitations or restrictions. The entire universe is under His dominion. All of creation is obligated to bow before Him. "Angels and mighty ones . . . do his bidding and obey his word" (vv. 20–21). Heavenly hosts praise Him and servants do His will.

If the whole creation is expected to worship the Lord, then I must bless the Lord in my per-

---

"Neglecting worship and praise will shrink my soul and reduce the margins of my life and influence."

---

sonal life as well. Neglecting worship and praise will shrink my soul and reduce the margins of my life and influence. If I desire fulness, richness, and abundance, I'll spend my days adoring the King of the universe — the only One worthy of concentrated service and worship.

Personal prayer

I praise You and thank You, O Lord, for Your sovereignty and authority over all creation. I want to join the heavenly hosts in praising Your name today. Teach me some "melodious sonnet."

His Glorious Creation

The Glory of the Creator

Exposition of theme

PSALM 104

Praise the Lord, O my soul. O Lord my God, you are very great; you are clothed with splendor and majesty. He wraps himself in light as with a garment; he stretches out the heavens like a tent and lays the beams of his upper chambers on their waters. He makes the clouds his chariot and rides on the wings of the wind. He makes winds his messengers, flames of fire his servants. He set the earth on its foundations; it can never be moved. You covered it with the deep as with a garment; the waters stood above the mountains. . . . He makes springs pour water into the ravines; it flows between the mountains (vv. 1–6, 10).

Development of theme

Psalm 104 focuses on the glory of the Creator revealed in His majesty, His care of creation, and His rule.

The exalted poetry of these verses portray God as light. He wraps Himself in a garment of radiance. The skies over the earth are envisioned as a tent, covering nomadic dwellers. His personal dwelling place is pictured above the waters of the sky, attended by the elements — winds and flames of fire.

God's glory is also observed in His perfect maintenance of creation. He waters the animals

> **"As the seasons change and as each day fades into night, I'm continually reminded of God's glory in creation."**

from freshly made springs. He provides grassy meadows for cattle to graze in and for men to cultivate. Out of the rich resources of the ground come wine, oil, and bread. He provides stately trees as a home for birds and majestic mountains as havens for wild goats.

He established the intricacies of the vernal equinox and the summer solstice, and marked out the precise pathway of all the stars. He allows the sun and moon to rule the days, the nights, and the seasons. The circadian rhythms of men and animals, predetermined by these heavenly bodies, give meaning and variety to life, and further indicate the glory and imagination of the Creator.

Personal prayer

Praise the Lord, O my soul! I praise You for Your majesty, Your creativity, Your care, and Your rule. As the seasons change and as each day fades into night, I'm continually reminded of Your glory in creation.

His Glorious Creation

The Glory of His Creation

Exposition of theme

PSALM 104 CONTINUED

How many are your works, O Lord! In wisdom you made them all; the earth is full of your creatures. There is the sea, vast and spacious, teeming with creatures beyond number — living things both large and small. There the ships go to and fro, and the leviathan, which you formed to frolic there. These all look to you to give them their food at the proper time. . . . I will sing to the Lord all my life; I will sing praise to my God as long as I live. May my meditation be pleasing to him, as I rejoice in the LORD. But may sinners vanish from the earth and the wicked be no more. Praise the LORD, O my soul. Praise the LORD (vv. 24–27, 33–35).

Development of theme

The psalmist bursts into passionate praise, celebrating God's creation. An earth full of creatures, teeming seas, and overarching heavens were brought into being where nothing had existed before! Only God can do that.

> *"The composer must fashion the building blocks of music into ideas, themes, and melodies that become vehicles of praise."*

Dr. Harold Best, dean of Wheaton College Conservatory, says, "Creativity is the ability both to imagine (think up) something and to execute it." He feels that creativity, craftsmanship, technique, and skill are often confused. The *special* quality of creativity "lies in the thinking up, the *imagining*."

Man takes raw materials which God has made and fashions them into useful items (i.e., trees become lumber; lumber becomes houses or furniture). In the same way a Christian musician uses the laws of nature (i.e., the harmonic series) to produce music. The composer must fashion the building blocks of music into ideas, themes, and melodies that become vehicles of praise.

The psalmist is so stirred by these lofty thoughts that he vows to sing praise to the Lord as long as he lives, *in a manner pleasing to the Lord.* I too want to please God — not my colleagues or my competition — through the works of my mind and my hands. Though I have written approximately two hundred anthems and songs, only those will endure that have been inspired by the heart of God.

I echo the psalmist who concludes with a mighty "Hallelujah!" and "Amen!"

Personal prayer

I praise You, Lord, for Your creativity and Your artistic control over creation. I, like every other living creature of earth, am totally vulnerable and dependent upon You for inspiration and for life itself! Hallelujah!

How Great Thou Art!

His Greatness

Exposition of theme
PSALM 105

Give thanks to the LORD, call on his name; make known among the nations what he has done. Sing to him, sing praise to him; tell of all his wonderful acts. Glory in his holy name; let the hearts of those who seek the LORD rejoice. Look to the LORD and his strength; seek his face always. Remember the wonders he has done, his miracles, and the judgments he pronounced. O descendants of Abraham his servant, O sons of Jacob, his chosen ones. He is the LORD our God; his judgments are in all the earth (vv. 1–7).

Development of theme

Throughout the entire history of Israel, God has revealed His greatness through His loyal, covenant love. The psalmist inspires his audience to call on the name of the Lord and to give thanks. He urges them to proclaim to the nations the Lord's mighty miracles in history.

> **"I tend to take for granted the Lord's continual intervention in my life and to get so wrapped up in myself that I forget how great He is!"**

I need this kind of spiritual motivation. I need a stirring preacher to remind me that the Lord has worked miraculously in my behalf. Why? Because I tend to take for granted His continual intervention in my life and to get so wrapped up in myself that I forget how great His is!

Personal prayer

Dear Lord, prod my memory when I forget Your miracles! Write them on my heart and stir me to sing about Your goodness!

How Great Thou Art!

His Faithfulness

Exposition of theme
PSALM 105 *CONTINUED*

He remembers his covenant forever, the word he commanded, for a thousand generations, the covenant he made with Abraham, the oath he swore to Isaac. . . . He brought out Israel, laden with silver and gold, and from among their tribes no one faltered. Egypt was glad when they left, because dread of Israel had fallen on them. He spread out a cloud as a covering, and a fire to give light at night. They asked, and he brought them quail and satisfied them with the bread of heaven. He opened the rock, and water gushed out; like a river it flowed in the desert (vv. 8–9, 37–41).

Development of theme

Certain key words leap from the pages of the Psalms — words used repeatedly to speak of the enduring quality of God's covenant with His people — words and phrases such as "forever," "for a thousand generations," "everlasting" (vv. 8–10).

In this psalm the musician is praising the Lord for taking His promises seriously. Unfortunately, we contemporary Christians use these words and phrases pretty casually. They have a certain ring that makes them attractive to songwriters

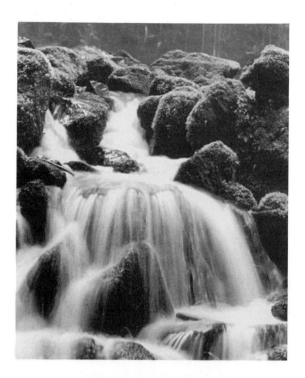

and poets. In fact, our list of synonyms is extensive: eternal, always, evermore, unending, endless, ceaseless, continual, perpetual. But do we really grasp the meaning of *forever*?

In reviewing this passage, I see again the "forever" faithfulness of God in keeping His covenant with Israel. First, He protected them as aliens in foreign lands, keeping His eye on Abraham wherever he went—Chaldea, Haran, Canaan, Egypt, and the Negev (vv. 12–15). Second, the Lord guided His people to Egypt and promoted Joseph to rule over them (vv. 17–22). Third, the Lord blessed His oppressed people with productivity (v. 14). Fourth, the Lord used Moses and Aaron to deliver them from Egypt (vv. 26–36). Finally, the Lord was faithful in providing for them while they were in the wilderness (vv. 39–41). So even when Israel was "following afar off," God was faithful in meeting their needs (vv. 42–45).

If I were to trace the steps of my own pilgrimage, there would be many parallels, because God's character never changes. It is this kind of endless love and provision He promises me today.

Personal prayer

Dear Lord, I thank You for providing for Israel's needs in the ancient world. Because Your character never changes, I know You will care for me unceasingly, always, forever!

A GLORIOUS GOSPEL SONG
How Great Thou Art

Then sings my soul, my Savior God, to Thee:
How great Thou art, how great Thou art!

O Lord my God, when I in awesome wonder
Consider all the worlds Thy hands have made,
I see the stars, I hear the rolling thunder,
Thy power throughout the universe
    displayed!

When thru the woods and forest glades I
    wander
And hear the birds sing sweetly in the trees,
When I look down from lofty mountain
    grandeur
And hear the brook and feel the gentle breeze.

And when I think that God His Son not
    sparing,
Sent Him to die, I scarce can take it in—
That on the cross, my burden gladly bearing,
He bled and died to take away my sin!

When Christ shall come with shout of
    acclamation
And take me home, what joy shall fill my heart!
Then I shall bow in humble adoration
And there proclaim, my God, how great Thou
    art!

Words by Carl Boberg. Music—Swedish Folk Melody.
(Arr. and trans. by Stuart K. Hine.) © 1953, 1955 by Manna Music, Inc.

PANORAMA PHOTO BY GARY IRVING

How Great Thou Art!

Freedom

Exposition of theme

PSALM 105 CONTINUED

For he remembered his holy promise given to his servant Abraham. He brought out his people with rejoicing, his chosen ones with shouts of joy; he gave them the lands of the nations, and they fell heir to what others had toiled for — that they might keep his precepts and observe his laws. Praise the LORD (vv. 42–45).

Development of theme

This shrinking world of ours has given me a new appreciation for this passage from Psalm 105. America has never fallen into enemy hands, nor has any other nation stormed the streets of our cities and carried our people into captivity. Still, I read newspaper accounts and see telecasts of this kind of tyranny in the world today.

> " *'It is dangerous to talk about God. Each word must be a sacrifice — filled to the brim with authenticity.'* "

When the Lord remembered His "holy promise" to Abraham, He "brought out" His people from the bondage of Egypt to the security of the Holy Land "that they might keep his precepts and observe his laws" (v. 45). The bottom line of deliverance is freedom to obey and praise His holy Name.

How ironic that "captives" are often freer than many Americans who practice shallow and casual Christianity. Tatiana Goricheva, author of

Talking About God Is Dangerous: Diary of a Russian Dissident, is a recent emigrant who claims, "My life only began when God found me." Even in atheistic Russia, her faith was growing strong and vibrant before her arrival in this country. Upon viewing a Western TV evangelist for the first time, however, she observed, "What this man said on the screen was likely to drive more people out of the church than the clumsy chatter of our paid atheists. Dressed up in a posh way . . . he was a boring, bad actor with mechanical and studied gestures. . . . For the first time I understand how dangerous it is to talk about God. Each word must be a sacrifice — filled to the brim with authenticity. Otherwise it is better to keep silent." God demands our praise, but it must be genuine!

Personal prayer

O Lord, may every word I write and every song I sing be a sacrifice of praise to Your holy Name!

Chaconne of Confession

Confessing Inconsistency

Exposition of theme

PSALM 106

Praise the LORD. Give thanks to the LORD, for he is good; his love endures forever. Who can proclaim the mighty acts of the LORD or fully declare his praise? Blessed are they who maintain justice, who constantly do what is right. Remember me, O LORD, when you show favor to your people, come to my aid when you save them, that I may enjoy the prosperity of your chosen ones, that I may share in the joy of your nation and join your inheritance in giving praise (vv. 1–5).

Development of theme

In Baroque music, a composition consisting of the repetition of a short theme or succession of harmonies in slow triple meter was called a "chaconne." Johann Sebastian Bach said, "The end and goal of thorough bass is nothing but the honor of God." Here we have the psalmist's chaconne of confession.

Musically speaking, confession is the ground-bass around which this psalm is structured. Far from "constantly doing what is right," Israel was more often ungrateful and rebellious. Depraved humanity exhibited itself regularly in her history. The ancient prophets, including Ezekiel and Isa-

THE LANGUAGE OF MUSIC

Chaconne

In Baroque music a composition consisting of the repetition of a short theme in slow, triple meter.

The theme, rather than being a tune, is a succession of harmonies (i.e., I-IV-I¼—V) repeated many times. Another term for chaconne is *"passacaglia.*

iah, sounded a stern warning, urging her to confess and forsake her evil ways. (See Nehemiah 9, Isaiah 63, and Ezekiel 20.)

The psalmist strikes a major chord by praising God's goodness and constancy, as evidenced in the mighty acts He has performed in Israel's behalf. On that same note he moves on to pronounce a blessing on those who are consistently just and fair, progressing to a chord of concern for his personal accountability before the Lord.

Emotionally I'm capable of pretty severe mood swings, but I worship the living God of the universe who never changes. Sunrise and sunset, summer and winter, in adversity and prosperity—He parades past me the evidence of His unchanging nature. Even when the unthinkable happens and I'm caught off guard by crisis or tragedy, He is there to blend those dissonant chords into the musical pattern of His plan.

Personal prayer

I praise You, Lord, today for Your constancy. When all of life crumbles in around me, I can count on Your faithful love to orchestrate a symphony of joy.

> **"Even when I'm caught off guard by crisis or tragedy, He is there to blend those dissonant chords into the musical pattern of His plan."**

Chaconne of Confession

Confessing Sin

Exposition of theme

PSALM 106 CONTINUED

We have sinned, even as our fathers did; we have done wrong and acted wickedly. When our fathers were in Egypt, they gave no thought to your miracles; they did not remember your many kindnesses, and they rebelled by the sea, the Red Sea. Yet he saved them for his name's sake, to make his mighty power known. . . . But they soon forgot what he had done and did not wait for his counsel. . . . They defiled themselves by what they did; by their deeds they prostituted themselves (vv. 6–8, 13, 39).

Development of theme

It has been said that the curse of Christianity is a short memory! Why can't we learn? Why must we continue to make the same mistakes? Don't we know the consequences of following our spiritual ancestors who sinned in the very same ways as their fathers before them?

I listen to the psalmist's litany of sins and feel deep empathy with those ancient brothers and sisters who stumbled through the wilderness. Over and over again—at the Red Sea, at Peor, at Meribah—they resisted God's guidance. How could they have made such arrogant demands to be fed, then complain when the menu never

varied? How could they forget all those miracles so soon and begin their murmuring and complaining? How dared they to provoke God to anger, so much so that He would have killed them had it not been for Moses' intercession? Yet Moses himself was no paragon of virtue. His disobedience cost him the dream of his life—entering the Promised Land.

Pride, arrogance, complaining, disobedience. Guilty as charged—my spiritual forebears . . . and me! I stand condemned before the God of Abraham and Moses "without one plea, but that Thy blood was shed for me."

Personal prayer

I'm just like my fathers, Lord! Those people just couldn't learn. Neither can I. My soul is also a litany of disobedience and rebellion, but I'm glad 1 John 1:9 is still in the Book!

"I listen to the psalmist's litany of sins and feel deep empathy with those ancient brothers and sisters who stumbled through the wilderness."

A BELOVED HYMN

Just As I Am

Just as I am, and waiting not,
To rid my soul of one dark blot,
To Thee whose blood can cleanse each
    spot,
O Lamb of God, I come! I come!

Just as I am, Thou wilt receive,
Wilt welcome, pardon, cleanse, relieve,
Because Thy promise I believe,
O Lamb of God, I come! I come!

Words by Charlotte Elliott. Music by William B. Bradbury.

Chaconne of Confession

Seeking Forgiveness

Exposition of theme

PSALM 106 CONTINUED

Therefore the LORD was angry with his people and abhorred his inheritance. He handed them over to the nations, and their foes ruled over them. Their enemies oppressed them and subjected them to their power. Many times he delivered them, but they were bent on rebellion and they wasted away in their sin. But he took note of their distress when he heard their cry; for their sake he remembered his covenant and out of his great love he relented. . . . Praise be to the LORD, the God of Israel, from everlasting to everlasting. Let all the people say, "Amen!" Praise the LORD (vv. 40–45, 48).

Development of theme

God is neither distant nor deaf. He did not turn His face from faithless Israel, nor does He fail to hear our cries of distress, though it may seem that way sometimes.

In His anger, God turned Israel over to heathen nations for punishment. Under their foreign taskmasters, the chosen people soon cried out for deliverance, and God answered.

Suddenly a majestic fanfare soars above the confessional—the harmonic changes for which I've been listening: "For their sake he remembered his covenant and out of his great love he relented" (v. 45). Despite their stiff-necked rebellion and the pitiful waste of their lives, God still loved them and wouldn't let them go!

Time after time He sent judges to lead them back to Him. Time after time they were faithful for a season and then fell back into their old ways. He was forced to discipline these delinquent children. "Those I love I rebuke and discipline" (Revelation 3:19).

At last! The great resolution! The people of God will return to Him, where they will remain in His presence "from everlasting to everlasting." The psalmist ends Book IV of the Psalter with a doxology of praise to the God of Israel. And all the people said, "Amen!"

Personal prayer

O Lord my God, I thank You for not closing the door permanently when I sin. Like my ancient brothers and sisters, I can approach You with a contrite heart and find forgiveness and restoration.

SEPTEMBER 5

Descant of Deliverance

A Simple Theme

Exposition of theme

PSALM 107

Give thanks to the LORD, for he is good; his love endures forever. Let the redeemed of the LORD say this — those he redeemed from the hand of the foe, those he gathered from the lands, from east and west, from north and south. Some wandered in desert wastelands, finding no way to a city where they could settle. They were hungry and thirsty, and their lives ebbed away. Then they cried out to the LORD in their trouble, and he delivered them from their distress. . . . Let them give thanks to the LORD for his unfailing love and his wonderful deeds for men. Let them sacrifice thank offerings and tell of his works with songs of joy (vv. 1–6, 21–22).

Development of theme

In hymn singing, a descant is a soaring counter-melody, usually sung by a few sopranos as a decorative addition to the hymn. The moving theme of this passage is the simple declaration of God's goodness and enduring love. His nature demands that He act on that love and He has done so — in the wilderness, at sea, and in human affairs.

Most likely God's people had been in exile in Babylon. Now back in their native land, they are praising Him again. From this passage, I learn what God is willing to do for me. You might try reading these parts alternately with a friend or spouse or as a family.

Descant:	**He gathers his chosen people from all corners of the earth.**
Theme:	The Lord is good; his love endures forever.
Descant:	**He has redeemed us — paid our ransom, bought us back, covered our debt.**
Theme:	The Lord is good; his love endures forever.
Descant:	**He delivers us from distress.**
Theme:	The Lord is good; his love endures forever.
Descant:	**He leads us on level pathways to his Holy City, where we will settle for eternity.**
Theme:	The Lord is good; his love endures forever.
Descant:	**He satisfies our hunger and thirst with living water and good things.**
Theme:	The Lord is good; his love endures forever.
Descant:	**He brings us out of darkness into his marvelous light.**
Theme:	The Lord is good; his love endures forever.
Descant:	**He heals all our diseases and rescues us from the grave.**
Theme:	The Lord is good; his love endures forever.
Descant:	**He will still every storm of life to a whisper and guide us to our haven of rest.**
Theme:	The Lord is good; his love endures forever!

Personal prayer

Lord, I praise You for Your unfailing love and incomparable deeds of kindness.

286

Descant of Deliverance

A Soaring Descant

Exposition of theme

PSALM 107 *CONTINUED*

He turned rivers into a desert, flowing springs into thirsty ground, and fruitful land into a salt waste, because of the wickedness of those who lived there. He turned the desert into pools of water and parched ground into flowing springs; there he brought the hungry to live, and they founded a city where they could settle. . . . But he lifted the needy out of their affliction and increased their families like flocks. The upright see and rejoice, but all the wicked shut their mouths. Whoever is wise, let him heed these things and consider the great love of the LORD (vv. 33–36, 41–43).

Development of theme

The southeastern region, where I now live, is in its fourth year of drought. Interestingly enough, weather fronts have skirted middle Tennessee many times, bringing storms and showers to neighboring counties, but not a drop to Nashville and Williamson County! There has been a great deal of speculation as to the reasons — our geographical configuration, changes in prevailing winds, even the ozone layer.

Wiser heads, seeking counsel from the Scriptures, have concluded that only God holds the answer, since He alone can "turn the desert into

> **"Since all products come from resources in the earth, all of humanity is dependent upon God's providential care."**

THE LANGUAGE OF MUSIC

Descant

A soaring counter melody, usually sung by several sopranos.

Used as a decorative addition to a hymn, the descant is a very effective musical device which can leave listeners feeling exhilerated.

pools of water and parched ground into flowing springs" (v. 35). The governor of a sister state suffering from the same drought called for a day of prayer for rain. Within twenty-four hours, the whole state was enjoying the first good downpour in weeks!

The Lord gives and withholds blessing according to the faithfulness of His people. Since all products come from resources in the earth, all of humanity is dependent upon God's providential care.

Just as He controls nature, He is also fully capable of ordering human experience. He may choose to humble the arrogant or to exalt the poor and needy. He can silence the wicked and inspire the redeemed to sing His praises. The psalmist suggests, "Whoever is wise, let him heed these things and consider the great love of the Lord" (v. 43).

Personal prayer

As I meditate on Your great love, O Lord, I long for showers of blessing on the barren soil of my life.

287

Toccata of Triumph

Celebrating His Love and Faithfulness

Exposition of theme
PSALM 108

My heart is steadfast, O God; I will sing and make music with all my soul. Awake, harp and lyre! I will awaken the dawn. I will praise you, O LORD, among the nations; I will sing of you among the peoples. For great is your love, higher than the heavens; your faithfulness reaches to the skies. Be exalted, O God, above the heavens, and let your glory be over all the earth (vv. 1–5).

Development of theme

I love to improvise on the piano—to sit down at the keyboard and to freely associate musically, to wing it! The term "toccata" comes from the Italian *toccare*, "to touch" (the keys), and is an early keyboard form designed to showcase the resources of the instrument, the ingenuity of the composer, and the technical virtuosity of the performer.

Part of the extraordinary body of King David's creative work is this toccata of triumph in praise of the Lord's loyal love of Israel. The theme is repeated for emphasis from Psalm 57:7–11.

Being the virtuoso he is, David is not interested in a dull, lifeless recital as he worships, but brings his whole being into the experience. He begins the day with a spontaneous outburst of song, depending not on prepared material, but on the flow of the Spirit to inspire both words and melody.

David's theme is the unsurpassed greatness of God's love which is "higher than the heavens" and His marvelous faithfulness which "reaches to the skies." He exalts his Lord who dwells in the heavens and desires that His glory will per-

288

vade the earth.

King David possessed not only a healthy mindset but the fullness of God in the deep recesses of his being. Because he was in touch with eternity, he was able to interpret reality and to live his life with freedom and authenticity. He beautifully fulfilled and pre-lived Christ's words in John 10:10: "The thief comes only to steal and kill and destroy; I have come that they may have life, and have it to the full."

Personal prayer

O God, I want to sing and make music with all my soul today. I lift up my worship to You because of Your great love and faithfulness.

THE LANGUAGE OF MUSIC
Tocatta
From Italian term, "toccare" to touch (the keys).

Early keyboard form involving improvisation, fugue, and virtuosity desired to show off the resources of the instrument, the ingenuity of the composer, and the virtuosity of the performer.

Toccata of Triumph

Pleading for God's Help

Exposition of theme
PSALM 108 CONTINUED

Save us and help us with your right hand, that those you love may be delivered. God has spoken from his sanctuary: "In triumph I will parcel

out Shechem and measure off the Valley of Succoth. Gilead is mine, Manasseh is mine; Ephraim
is my helmet, Judah my scepter. Moab is my
washbasin, upon Edom I toss my sandal; over
Philistia I shout in triumph." Who will bring me
to the fortified city? Who will lead me to Edom?
(vv. 6–10)

Development of theme

Our do-it-yourself society has developed
another dimension over the past few decades —
professions geared to *helping* us do it ourselves.
All of these professionals — financial advisors,
tax consultants, career counselors, psychologists, family and children's service personnel,
marriage counselors — are in business for the
primary purpose of adding input to our decision-
making. These advisors, especially if they are
Christians, are generally motivated by genuine
concern for people, and we benefit from their
training and expertise.

Solomon, the wisest man who ever lived, said,
"Plans fail for lack of counsel, but with many
advisers they succeed" (Proverbs 15:22). There
are times when tragedies, crises, or life changes
create tension in an individual or a family. Professional Christian counselors who listen with
empathy and a strong commitment to confidenti-
ality can help untangle our knotty problems.
Karen and I have both benefited from this kind of

> *"When tragedies, crises, or life
> changes create tension in an
> individual or a family, profes-
> sional Christian counselors
> who listen with empathy and a
> strong commitment to confi-
> dentiality can help untangle
> our knotty problems."*

godly counsel. (I heartily recommend the counseling model of Dr. Larry Crabb of the Institute of
Biblical Counseling.)

But David sounds a warning note: "Is it not
you, O God? . . . Give us aid against the enemy
[fear, financial reverses, family crises], for the
help of [godless] man is worthless" (v. 12).

The Lord is the source of all personal strength
and confidence and the ultimate answer to every
problem we face in life. Sensitive counselors are
often instruments of help and healing, but "with
God we will gain the victory!" (v. 13)

Personal prayer

*O God, I thank You for Your trained representa-
tive of personal healing and deliverance, but
may I never make the mistake of placing all my
faith in human counsel. Your right hand is my
strength!*

Chant of Curses
Cursing the Wicked

Exposition of theme
PSALM 109

O God, whom I praise, do not remain silent, for wicked and deceitful men have opened their mouths against me; they have spoken against me with lying tongues. . . . Appoint an evil man to oppose him; let an accuser stand at his right hand. When he is tried, let him be found guilty, and may his prayers condemn him. May his days be few; may another take his place of leadership. May his children be fatherless and his wife a widow. May his children be wandering beggars, may they be driven from their ruined homes. . . . May the iniquity of his fathers be remembered before the LORD; may the sin of his mother never be blotted out. May their sins always remain before the LORD, that he may cut off the memory of them from the earth (vv. 1–2, 6–10, 14–15).

Development of theme

David, the man "after God's own heart," is never seen in his true humanity more graphically than in this psalm. On the surface he appears vindictive and cruel. His rhetoric is sharp and his attitude toward his enemies is harsh. David minces no words in letting God know how to dispose of his persecutors. He wants them blotted off the face of the earth! Exterminated! X'd out!

In explosive terms the psalmist describes the scenario as he'd like to see it played out. He asks that these wicked and deceitful men be

> "What we have here is bold, passionate poetry cursing sin and immorality and defending righteousness and morality."

opposed, accused, found guilty, condemned, yanked from positions of leadership, their families made fatherless and husbandless, and their children left to become homeless scavengers of society. As if that isn't punishment enough, David goes on to suggest that their sins be *remembered* while they themselves be *forgotten*, as if they had never existed!

How do we mesh this diatribe with the New Testament imperative to "turn the other cheek"? (Luke 6:29) One must bear in mind that David anticipated a theocracy, an earthly kingdom dedicated to righteousness. He did not have the full biblical revelation we possess today. Heathen peoples, in the ancient world, were corrupt and licentious, and David's righteous stance stood in bold contrast to their debauchery. What we have here is bold, passionate poetry cursing sin and immorality and defending righteousness and morality. In short, David does not deny his angry feelings but freely vents them!

Personal prayer

O God, I learn from David that, if I must let off steam about my circumstances, I can do it safely in Your presence!

Chant of Curses
Praying for Help

Exposition of theme
PSALM 109 CONTINUED

But you, O Sovereign LORD, deal well with me for your name's sake; out of the goodness of your love, deliver me. For I am poor and needy, and my heart is wounded within me. . . . Help me, O

LORD my God; save me in accordance with your love. Let them know that it is your hand, that you, O LORD, have done it. . . . With my mouth I will greatly extol the LORD; in the great throng I will praise him. For he stands at the right hand of the needy one, to save his life from those who condemn him (vv. 21–22, 26–27, 30–31).

Development of theme

The violent enemy David so vividly portrays here spews forth curses until he wears them like a black shroud about himself. I have a hard time condemning David for feeling the way he does

---

> *"I wonder how often my own self-deception, denial, and defensiveness have kept me from a deep work of God in my life."*

---

about this guy! In fact, I admire his honesty.

David is in no condition to avenge or even to protect himself from further insult and injury. He simply doesn't have the resources, physically or emotionally. His body is weakening because of fasting and lack of appetite, and his gaunt appearance serves only to bring on more ridicule.

Realizing his helpless condition, David's prayer is upfront, candid and forthright. He submits to the Lord's sovereignty, appealing to His goodness and love and asking for deliverance.

The key to his prayer resounds like the chord from a great organ echoing in an empty cathedral: "Let them know that it is *your* hand, that *you*, O LORD, have done it" (v. 27). Now David's true motives are clearly seen. By a supernatural work of the Lord, his enemies will know the Source of real power!

I am sometimes guilty of trying to crank up a worship experience without an intense aware-

ness of any supernatural work of God in my life. An honest, vulnerable appraisal provides the rich soil for God to work creatively. I wonder how often my own self-deception, denial, and defensiveness have kept me from a deep work of God in my life. Real need motivates intense prayer. Passionate prayer prompts the Holy Spirit to produce miracles. When I experience a miracle—God's unmistakable touch on my life—I burst out in genuine praise!

Personal prayer

O God, I too extol You. You work daily in my life and continually meet my needs, and I can't help bursting out in praise to Your Name!

Messianic Masterpiece

His Sovereignty

Exposition of theme

PSALM 110

The LORD says to my LORD: "Sit at my right hand until I make your enemies a footstool for your feet." The LORD will extend your mighty scepter from Zion; you will rule in the midst of your enemies. Your troops will be willing on your day of battle. Arrayed in holy majesty, from the womb of the dawn you will receive the dew of your youth. The LORD has sworn and will not change his mind: "You are a priest forever, in the order of Melchizedek" (vv. 1–4).

Development of theme

This important psalm is quoted many times in the New Testament (Matthew 22:44, Mark 12:36, Luke 20:42, Acts 2:34–35, and Hebrews 1:13). From these references we learn that Jesus Himself quoted this psalm often. We also learn that the Holy Spirit inspired it, David wrote

> *"At the end of time the Messiah will wield His holy scepter, ruling all peoples righteously, and His enemies will consequently become His footstool."*

it, and that it is definitely Messianic.

By "listening" carefully, I can "hear" the voice of God speaking to His Son, who would not be born for yet another thousand years! David says: "The LORD (Yahweh) says to *my* LORD (David's Lord, the Messiah): 'Sit at my (the Father's) right hand until I make your (the Son's) enemies a

footstool for your feet.' " (David could have written this amazing prophecy only by divine inspiration!) In this conversation between God the Father and God the Son (Messiah), Messiah is seated at the right hand of God—the place of authority. At the end of time the Messiah will wield His holy scepter, ruling all peoples righteously, and His enemies will consequently become His footstool. Vigorous young warriors, adorned in holiness, will fight in a massive battle against the forces of evil.

Yahweh has proclaimed that the Messiah will be an eternal Priest in the order of Melchizedek. (See Hebrews 5, 6, and 7.) Priest and King will be united in One Person, Israel's true Messiah. As Priest, Christ became His own sacrifice when He died on the cross. As King, He is destined to rule and reign righteously at the end of time—the consummation of the ages.

In a few lines of exquisite Hebrew poetry, the Lord gives us a glimpse into some of the mysteries of His glorious plan of redemption. Old Testament history is full of motifs which will only find their fulfillment at the end of time in Messiah's reign.

Personal prayer

Dear Lord, because of the sacrifice of Your Son, I have eternal life. Because of His predicted rule and sovereign reign, my future is secure!

Messianic Masterpiece

His Conquest

Exposition of theme

PSALM 110 CONTINUED

The LORD is at your right hand; he will crush kings on the day of his wrath. He will judge the nations, heaping up the dead and crushing the rulers of the whole earth. He will drink from a brook beside the way; therefore he will lift up his head (vv. 5–7).

Development of theme

From my perspective there's something wrong with just about everything these days! But these verses assure me that someday soon everything will be set straight, the books will be balanced, and the enemies of God defeated once and for all!

Without the revelation of the New Testament, however, we would be in the dark about this passage. Later witness from God informs us that Christ will come again, accompanied by saints of all ages, to reign on the earth. At that time He will rule from His position of sovereign authority at the right hand of God, the Father. From that vantage point, He will crush kings and judge earthly rulers (v. 5). He will be refreshed (from a lovely, country brook) and exalted (v. 7).

These are lofty thoughts. What do I learn from

all of this? I learn that wickedness will give way to righteousness, that suffering will succumb to good health, that war will be replaced by perennial peace, that unfairness will be supplanted by justice, and that righteousness will reign on the earth.

I derive enormous security from the fact that all conflicts — from international and national to relational and personal — will be finally and ultimately resolved. Only the Lord can do that. Bless His holy Name!

Personal prayer

Dear Lord, I look forward to the dawn of a new day, when You will make all things right. The glorious prospect of the future gives me hope as I face the frustrations of today.

> **"I derive enormous security from the fact that all conflicts will be finally and ultimately resolved. Only the Lord can do that."**

Paean of Praise

Because of Who He Is . . .

Exposition of theme

PSALM 111

Praise the LORD. I will extol the LORD with all my heart in the council of the upright and in the assembly. Great are the works of the LORD; they are pondered by all who delight in them. Glorious and majestic are his deeds, and his righteousness endures forever. He has caused his wonders to be remembered; the LORD is gracious and compassionate (vv. 1–4).

Development of theme

Using an artistically controlled art form — the acrostic — the psalmist celebrates the nature of God. Each line begins with a letter of the Hebrew alphabet, extolling God's glory and majesty, His righteousness, His grace and compassion.

Volumes have been written on knowing about God. We can know all *about* someone, yet never come to know that person intimately. As a kid, I almost worshiped the musical flair and expertise of Ralph Carmichael, noted songwriter, arranger, and composer. I bought his records, corresponded with him, borrowed his scores, and closely followed his brilliant career. But I never got to meet him personally until I was in graduate school. Now I know him as a good friend and colleague. It is that kind of *knowing* that Dr. J. I. Packer intended when he wrote his classic work, *Knowing God.*

We can read about God, study about Him, sing to Him, even pray to Him — without really *knowing* Him. But when we recognize Him for who He is — our Creator and Redeemer — then our spirits cry out, "Abba, Father!"

Personal prayer

I praise You, Lord, not just for the wonderful things You have done in my life, but because of who You are!

A CONTEMPORARY LYRIC

Because of Who You Are

You spoke the word and all the worlds came
  into order,
You waved Your hands and planets filled the
  empty skies,
You placed the woman and the man inside
  the garden
And tho they fell they found compassion in
  your eyes;

One holy night You brought Your promise
  from a virgin,
And Promise grew as He revealed to us Your
  heart;
Enduring love displayed throughout His
  crucifixion,
And in the dark You tore the grave and
  death apart.

Lord, I stand amazed at the wonder of Your
  deeds,
And yet a greater wonder brings me to my
  knees.

Lord, I praise You because of who You are,
Not just for all the mighty things that You
  have done;
And Lord, I worship You because of who
  You are,
You're all the reason that I need to voice my
  praise —
Because of who You are . . . Because of who
  You are!

Words and music by Bob Farrell and Billy Smiley.
© 1982 by Paragon Music Corp.

Paean of Praise

Because of What He Does . . .

Exposition of theme

PSALM 111 CONTINUED

He provides food for those who fear him; he remembers his covenant forever. He has shown his people the power of his works, giving them the lands of other nations. The works of his hands are faithful and just; all his precepts are trustworthy. They are steadfast for ever and ever, done in faithfulness and uprightness. He provided redemption for his people; he ordained his covenant forever—holy and awesome is his name. The fear of the LORD is the beginning of wisdom; all who follow his precepts have good understanding. To him belongs eternal praise (vv. 5–10).

Development of theme

The psalmist develops his theme very specifically here. Our compassionate and gracious Lord has expressed Himself by helping His people — by providing a daily supply of food, by remembering His covenant and keeping His promises to make them victorious in conquest, by bequeathing to them the heathen lands around them, by revealing His power. And wonder of

---

> *"Following His precepts in obedience should be the obvious outcome of my gratitude for all the Lord has done for me!"*

---

wonders, when they continued to grumble and complain against Him, He provided a way back to Him — a plan of redemption and forgiveness!

My Lord is no less active in my life today. He provides for my basic needs — food, shelter, clothing — by allowing me to serve Him through meaningful and fulfilling work. He has blessed me with rich personal relationships with my family and intimate friends. To guide me in facing the hassles of daily living, He has sent His Holy Spirit, and I find myself clinging to Him every day.

The conclusion of this psalm reminds me of Proverbs 1:7: "The fear [awesome respect] of the LORD is the beginning of knowledge." It seems that following His precepts in obedience should be the obvious outcome of my gratitude for all He's done for me!

Personal prayer

I pray that You will fill me with an awesome respect for You, Lord, so that it will be the most natural thing in the world to obey Your rules for right living!

Portrait of a Godly Person

What does a godly person look like?

Exposition of theme

PSALM 112

Praise the LORD. Blessed is the man who fears the LORD, who finds great delight in his commands. His children will be mighty in the land; the generation of the upright will be blessed. Wealth and riches are in his house, and his righteousness endures forever (vv. 1–3).

Development of theme

God has always sought out strong individuals who are willing to commit themselves to courageous leadership. The need has never been more desperate than now! Psalm 112 suggests the prototype for this kind of leader.

What does this person look like?

First, you can usually spot a godly man or woman by his or her *happy* countenance. I don't mean a perpetual ear-to-ear grin or some kind of slaphappy euphoria, but a stillness, a serenity, a relaxing of the facial muscles that is rare in this world of uptight urbanites. Only the indwelling Spirit of God can bring that unearthly peace and joy—a joy that is promised to the one "who finds great delight in [passionate love for] His [the Lord's] commands" (v. 1).

> *"You can usually spot a godly person by his or her countenance. I don't mean a perpetual grin or slaphappy euphoria, but a serenity, a relaxing of the facial muscles that is rare in this world of uptight urbanites."*

C. S. Lewis, internationally celebrated author said, "God cannot give us happiness and peace apart from Himself because it is not there. There is no such thing." Peace is found in a cause or a person greater than oneself. Christ is that quintessential Person.

Second, the godly person is *prosperous* (vv. 2–3). This Old Testament promise for Israel suggests that this godly leader's children will make their mother and father proud, that the family will enjoy agricultural prosperity, and that right living will result in long life.

Our contemporary culture defines prosperity more narrowly in terms of money and financial independence only. I want to be God's man, but I limit the Lord's blessings if I anticipate a financial windfall. I'll take any blessing He chooses to give me—family harmony, spiritual growth, effectiveness in ministry, knowing Him more intimately!

Personal prayer

O Lord, let me be a godly person in a hostile world. Don't let me settle for our cultural definition of prosperity, but open my spiritual eyes to see that Your desires for me are infinitely more satisfying than my limited dreams.

Portrait of a Godly Person

How does a godly person act?

Exposition of theme

PSALM 112 CONTINUED

Even in darkness light dawns for the upright, for the gracious and compassionate and righteous man. Good will come to him who is generous and lends freely, who conducts his affairs with justice. . . . The wicked man will see and be

*vexed, he will gnash his teeth and waste away;
the longings of the wicked will come to nothing
(vv. 4–5, 10).*

Development of theme

Whenever I think of a man of God, I inevitably think of my Dad. A man marked by conviction,

consistency, and energy, he has been my greatest role model.

A man of great strength and generosity, he derives enormous pleasure from being involved with people. He has stood behind my music and has been a real encouragement to me. He is living proof of the paradox in Christianity that, when you give much, it will be multiplied to you (Luke 6:38). His happiness is in direct relation to his active caring for others.

Dad has rock-solid faith. Even when my Mom

"Whenever I think of a man of God, I inevitably think of my Dad. A man marked by conviction, consistency, and energy, he has been my greatest role model."

died, he was unflappable. So deep were his spiritual roots that, when the winds of adversity blew, the branches of that mighty oak swayed, but the taproot held firm. "He will have no fear of bad news" (v. 7). Because his faith is steadfast, his security system could not be taken away. He is acutely aware that the Lord has already conquered the worst possible thing that can happen. His phobias and icy fears melt in the warm sunshine of God's love. Unlike secular man "who will gnash his teeth and waste away" (v. 10), my Dad is part of the unshakable kingdom.

The French have an interesting word, *creneau*. It means "hole" or "opening." To be successful, a businessman has to look for holes or openings in the marketplace. There is a huge *creneau* in the Christian marketplace for godly leaders who have the strength to be role models. The world desperately needs such persons — joyous and prosperous (effective), compassionate and generous, stable and secure. These attributes belong to the kingdom man!

Personal prayer

Lord, I want to be a kingdom man! I'd like to model for others what my father has modeled for me.

SEPTEMBER 17

Anthem of Angels

Call to Worship

Exposition of theme
PSALM 113

Praise the LORD. Praise, O servants of the LORD, praise the name of the LORD. Let the name of the LORD be praised, both now and forevermore. From the rising of the sun to the place where it sets, the name of the LORD is to be praised (vv. 1–3).

Development of theme

Musically inclined or not, have you ever pictured yourself in heaven, singing with the angelic choir? You may not be able to carry a tune now, but if you're a believer, your voice will blend one day with countless millions of others in a glad "Hallelujah!"

The word *hallelujah* comes from two beautiful Hebrew words: *hallel*, "praise," and *jah*, referring to "Yahweh," Jehovah. So, "hallelujah" means "praise the Lord." Taken from the "hallel," a collection of songs sung at the great Jewish festivals — Passover, Pentecost, and Tabernacles — Psalms 113–118 are music for a heavenly choir performance. Our Lord joined in shortly before His death (Mark 14:26).

This psalm begins and ends with an exhilarating call to worship. Praising the Lord is a divine imperative, not an option for the servants of God. You can't plead a case of laryngitis or skip rehearsal. The command is clear. Praise the Lord — "now and forevermore" from "the rising of the sun to its setting" (vv. 2–3).

Only Yahweh — whose name was too sacred even to be uttered aloud by ancient worshipers — is worthy of continual praise. Yet how blithely and flippantly we speak that glorious Name. As we move toward colloquial speech in our prayers, sermons, and lyrics, we need to guard against irreverence and disrespect. We need to speak His sacred Name as if we were breathing a prayer.

Am I praising Him continually — by every

"As we move toward colloquial speech in our prayers, sermons, and lyrics, we need to guard against irreverence and disrespect. We need to speak His sacred Name as if we were breathing a prayer."

action of my life as well as with my vocal chords? Am I praising Him in prayer? Am I praising Him in front of my children as well as in private moments of mediation? It's time for the angelic choir rehearsal to begin! He's coming soon!

Personal prayer

Beginning now, O Lord, keep me accountable for my praise to You. Let it be unending . . . beginning now!

SEPTEMBER 18

Anthem of Angels

Cause for Praise

Exposition of theme

PSALM 113 CONTINUED

The LORD is exalted over all the nations, his glory above the heavens. Who is like the LORD our God, the One who sits enthroned on high, who stoops down to look on the heavens and the earth? He raises the poor from the dust and lifts the needy from the ash heap; he seats them with princes, with the princes of their people He settles the barren woman in her home as a happy mother of children. Praise the LORD (vv. 4–9).

Development of theme

In this descriptive praise psalm, two great themes will echo for eternity through the halls of heaven: God's greatness (vv. 4–5) and His grace (vv. 6–9).

God is great. There is no lord like our Lord. He is unique, over all, above all. He sits enthroned on high (literally: "who makes high with respect to sitting"). In this context, study the magnificent lyric poetry of Isaiah 40:12–41:4. Our view of

> "Who is like the Lord, our God? He is unique—equally at home above the heavens or at the side of the lowliest and loneliest creature."

man tends to be overblown and our view of God, to be disproportionately small. When our vision of God enlarges, our problems will shrink to size.

God is grace (unmerited favor). He manifests grace to us in three ways:

First, from His exalted position in the heavens, He stoops to survey all of creation. The greatest act of divine stooping would come when God the Father "made himself nothing, taking the very nature of a servant, being made in human likeness (Jesus the Son)" (Philippians 2:6–7).

Second, God honors the poor and seats them with the nobility. Our position in the heavenly community will not depend on earthly status or recognition by our peers, but on His grace.

Third, God settles the barren woman in her home "as a happy mother of children." Sarah's miraculous pregnancy was the joy of the ancient world (Genesis 18, 21). Hannah's humiliation was transformed into jubilation (1 Samuel 2). These great ladies were the motifs preparing for the grand theme of Mary, the Jewish peasant girl, who bore the Messiah. This psalm links the song of Hannah (1 Samuel 2:1–10) with the Magnificat of Mary (Luke 1:46–55).

The psalm concludes with a final hallelujah—praise the Lord! God's glory differs sharply from man's glory. Who is like the Lord, our God? He is unique—equally at home above the heavens or at the side of the lowliest and loneliest creature.

Personal prayer

I praise You, Lord, for stooping to lift me up, for seating me at Your banquet table, and for settling me forever in Your home in glory.

Celebration of Deliverance

The earth trembles

Exposition of theme

PSALM 114

Why was it, O sea, that you fled, O Jordan, that you turned back, you mountains, that you skipped like rams, you hills, like lambs? Tremble, O earth, at the presence of the LORD, at the presence of the God of Jacob, who turned the rock into a pool, the hard rock into springs of water (vv. 5–8).

Development of theme

The psalmist doesn't attempt to answer the questions posed in verses 5 and 6. Instead, he commands the earth to tremble in the presence of the Lord, the God of Jacob. Why? Because only He can turn desert rocks into refreshing pools of water. Only He can transform inanimate stones into wells of gushing water. Only He can take my parched, meaningless life and restore it with springs of living water!

The revelation of God's power over nature

> *"If God can control the forces of nature, He can control my seemingly unpredictable life."*

---

was the only thing that encouraged Job when he was hurting. God led him through a painfully revealing process of counseling through such questions as: "Do you know the laws of the heavens? Can you set up God's dominion over the earth? Can you raise your voice to the clouds and cover yourself with a flood of water? Do you send the lightning bolts on their way? . . . Who endowed the heart with wisdom or gave understanding to the mind? Who has the wisdom to count the clouds? Who can tip over the water jars of the heavens when the dust becomes hard and the clods of earth stick together?" (Job 38:33–38).

The Lord has sovereign control over nature. Man can't lift a finger to influence nature. It's unruly, violent, and disobedient; it can only be manipulated and rearranged. But if God can, even on a whim, control the forces of nature, He can exert control over my seemingly unpredicatable life. When I am helpless and lack courage and confidence, I can place unwavering trust in His incomparable power and might.

Personal prayer

O God of Jacob, refresh and renew my life today. Lead me out of the barren desert to an oasis of Your care!

Contrasts

Spirituality Versus Idolatry

Exposition of theme

PSALM 115

Not to us, O LORD, not to us but to your name be the glory, because of your love and faithfulness. Why do the nations say, "Where is their God?" Our God is in heaven; he does whatever pleases him. But their idols are silver and gold, made by the hands of men. They have mouths, but cannot speak, eyes, but they cannot see; they have ears, but cannot hear, noses, but they cannot smell; they have hands, but cannot feel, feet, but they cannot walk; nor can they utter a sound with their throats. Those who make them will be like them, and so will all who trust in them (vv. 1–8).

Development of theme

While heathen nations ask, "Where is their God?" our Lord is going about doing whatever He pleases.

Pagan idols are inanimate—having never possessed life—and obviously impotent. Made by man from the metals of the earth, they are unable to see, to hear, to smell, to feel, to speak, or to move about. God Himself is responsible for the raw materials from which they are molded! Interestingly, the psalmist observes that the artisans who make idols, as well as those who trust in them, will be "like them"—powerless and useless.

> "**We absorb like a sponge the personalities and mannerisms of the people we admire. As mentors and models, they dramatically alter and influence our lives.**"

We tend to become "like" the people we idolize, the environment we live in, even the music we hear! We absorb like a sponge the personalities and mannerisms of the people we admire. As mentors and models, they dramatically alter and influence our lives. It's also true that our minds are somewhat like computers. If we program them with junk, junk comes out! And if any of these people or things become more important to us than God, then we become idolators!

In short, there is only one, authentic, infinite, personal God of the universe. Counterfeit gods are not only disappointing, but dead. What a pathetic waste when a person bestows his allegiance on worthless pieces of junk—whether they be carved images or compact discs! We must focus on the "things that are excellent" (Philippians 4:8).

Personal prayer

O Lord, not to us, but to Your Name be the glory and honor.

Contrasts

Life Versus Death

Exposition of theme

PSALM 115 CONTINUED

May the LORD make you increase, both you and your children. May you be blessed by the LORD, the Maker of heaven and earth. The highest heavens belong to the LORD, but the earth he has given to man. It is not the dead who praise the LORD, those who go down to silence; it is we who extol the LORD, both now and forevermore. Praise the LORD (vv. 14-18).

301

Development of theme

Why don't we sing? The Maker of heaven and earth has given us everything to delight us, but so many people move through the measure of their days like marionettes, with painted smiles and no music in their hearts.

Why don't we sing? There are three primary reasons.

First, the pressures and complexities of modern life can take the song right out of the heart. Contemporary lifestyles often destroy intimacy, the soil in which artistry grows.

Next, we are overexposed to music, especially "elevator music." Second-rate sounds flood the airwaves at home, in the car, in the office, in restaurants. It's like musical wallpaper, so we become spectators rather than participants.

Third, "it is not the dead [persons without the Lord]" who praise Him. The psalmist tells us that they go to a place of *silence* (v. 17). There is no singing there!

Against the backdrop of pagan idolatry, the psalmist pleads with the house of Israel, the house of Aaron, and all who fear the Lord, to place their trust in the Lord and to lift their voices in praise. "Extol the Lord, both now and forevermore" (v. 18).

Personal prayer

O Lord, help me to trust and praise You endlessly. May I personally and with full self-awareness experience Your blessing.

302

A CONTEMPORARY LYRIC

Endless Praise

When I consider all Your heavens,
The works You fashioned with Your hands:
The moon and stars You hung in space —
I wonder at Your mindfulness of man.

I sing the wonder of Your power,
I give the glory due Your name;
I see the splendor of Your holiness,
I marvel that forever You're the same.

I praise You for You alone are worthy,
I bless You for Your love and grace;
My soul finds refuge in Your mercy
And for endless days I'll sing Your
    endless praise!

Words and music by Lynne Brower. © 1986 Singspiration.

Personal Song of Thanksgiving

Deliverance From Death

Exposition of theme

PSALM 116

I love the LORD, for he heard my voice; he heard my cry for mercy. Because he turned his ear to me, I will call on him as long as I live. The cords of death entangled me, the anguish of the grave came upon me; I was overcome by trouble and sorrow. Then I called on the name of the LORD: "O LORD, save me!" For you, O LORD, have delivered my soul from death, my eyes from tears, my feet from stumbling, that I may walk before the LORD in the land of the living (vv. 1–4; 8–9).

Development of theme

I'll never forget the day I discovered that our senior editor at Singspiration Music, Norman Johnson, was terminally ill. I watched him cope with the vicissitudes of suffering for eight years as he battled Lou Gehrig's disease. About a week before he died, he called and asked me to represent the music industry in making some comments at his funeral. He died while listening to Handel's *Messiah.* The "Hallelujah Chorus" was beautifully and victoriously rendered at his memorial service in an arrangement he penned. My dear friend, Norm, went out in a blaze of glory!

Once you've stared Death in the face, he is no longer the fearsome specter that lurks in childhood dreams. In fact, at that moment, God's reality and ultimate victory over death is never more evident.

The bad news of this psalm is that the psalmist, nearing death, was overcome with self-pity and defeat. Briefly, during this episode, life was the pits. The good news is that he didn't rely on human resources to pull him through. Though there is a place for medicine and Christian ministry to the hurting, this psalmist went beyond all such aid and directly into the presence of the Great Physician, the Wonderful Counselor. Furthermore, the Lord heard and answered, choosing to demonstrate His graciousness and compassion (v. 8–9).

A certain responsibility accompanies great deliverance. For the rest of his life this psalmist won't forget God's loving mercy. Adversity has enriched his life. Suffering has purged him of superficiality. Like Job, he can say, "But he knows the way that I take; when he has tested me, I will come forth as gold" (Job 23:10).

> **"Once you've stared Death in the face, he is no longer the fearsome specter that lurks in childhood dreams."**

Personal prayer

O Lord, I don't have to experience serious illness to know Your mercy and grace. You are the Lord of my life . . . and the Victor over death!

Personal Song of Thanksgiving

Promise to Praise

Exposition of theme

PSALM 116 *CONTINUED*

How can I repay the LORD for all his goodness to me? I will lift up the cup of salvation and call on the name of the LORD. I will fulfill my vows to the LORD in the presence of all his people. Precious in the sight of the LORD is the death of his saints. O LORD, truly I am your servant; I am your servant, the son of your maidservant; you have freed me from my chains. I will sacrifice a thank offering to you and call on the name of the LORD. I will fulfill my vows to the LORD in the presence of all his people, in the courts of the house of the LORD — in your midst, O Jerusalem. Praise the LORD (vv. 12–19).

Development of theme

"How can I repay the LORD for all his goodness to me?" This question asked by my ancient colleague rings true for me today. He answers with four "I wills." First, *I will pray.* "I will lift up the cup of salvation and call on the name of the LORD" (v. 13). Second, *I will praise the Lord publicly.* "I will fulfill my vows to the LORD in the presence of all his people" (v. 14). Third, *I will offer sacrifice.* "I will sacrifice a thank offering to you" (v. 17). True worship doesn't come cheap. The psalmist concludes by repeating, "*I will fulfill my vows* to the

LORD in the presence of all his people," adding "in the courts of the house of the LORD — in your midst, O Jerusalem" (v. 19).

He is overwhelmed that the Lord has delivered him from his miserable existence and from death. He is conscious of his servanthood and his sonship. He has become unshackled — freed from the confinement of his chains. He is filled with joy in the awareness that the Lord cares about the death of His saints (v. 15). God's children are safe and secure even at this ultimate moment.

"How can I repay the LORD for all his goodness to me?" I can pray, praise, and offer my life as a living sacrifice. The only fitting conclusion is again, "Hallelujah! Praise the Lord!"

Personal prayer

Thank You, Lord, that I can trust You to be with me and take care of me in life . . . and in death.

> " 'How can I repay the LORD for all his goodness to me?' This question asked by my ancient colleague rings true for me today."

All Glory, Laud, and Honor

Exposition of theme
PSALM 117

Praise the LORD, all you nations; extol him, all you peoples. For great is his love toward us, and the faithfulness of the LORD endures forever. Praise the LORD (vv. 1–2).

Development of theme

I've never been invited to the White House. President Gerald Ford, however, was presented a copy of our musical, "I Love America," and wrote a wonderful letter, extolling that patriotic work.

Psalm 117 is a miniature invitation to people everywhere. The purpose is praise; the place is wherever God's people gather. The reasons for this adulation are given in verse 2. The Lord is to be praised because of His great love and His abiding faithfulness.

The Lord is to be worshiped for who He is — for His character, for His attributes. His covenant love *(hesed)* is loyal and eternal; it is not subject to mood swings and emotional vacillation. His

"Whatever my mood today, I know my Lord is loving and faithful. Whatever adverse circumstances I face today, I know my Lord is loving and faithful."

faithfulness is based on truth *(emet)*. Because the Lord's Word is true or reliable, He is faithful. Loving and faithful. What an apt description of our Lord! The psalmist's response is again, "Hallelujah! — Praise the Lord!"

Whatever my mood today, I know my Lord is *loving and faithful.* Whatever adverse circumstances I face today, I know my Lord is *loving and faithful.* Whatever rejection may come my way today, I know my Lord is *loving and faithful.* Whatever physical ailment I experience today, I know my Lord is *loving and faithful.* Whatever business reverses occur today, I know my Lord is *loving and faithful.* Whatever domestic tension I feel today, I know my Lord is *loving and faithful.* Why worry and fret? He invites me to remember that He is loving and faithful. Praise the Lord!

Personal prayer

Lord, I may be unpredictable and moody, but You can be counted on to be loving and faithful . . . no matter what!

305

Festal Procession

Praising His Loyal Love

Exposition of theme
PSALM 118

Give thanks to the LORD, for he is good; his love endures forever. Let Israel say: "His love endures forever." Let the house of Aaron say: "His love endures forever." Let those who fear the LORD say: "His love endures forever" (vv. 1–4).

Development of theme

The ancient Israelis sang this psalm—the final song in the "Hallel"—as they marched to the sanctuary to worship the Lord. It was used during the Passion Week of our Lord (Matthew 21:9), and it may have been sung in the Upper Room (Matthew 26:30). It was God's loyal love that energized the Israelite army to defeat the surrounding nations.

The wording suggests that these first few verses were either spoken or sung antiphonally. If we read the passage that way, the phrases spring to life:

Congregation:	*"His love endures forever."*
Worship leader:	"Let Israel say . . ."
Congregation:	*"His love endures forever."*
Worship leader:	"Let the house of Aaron say . . ."
Congregation:	*"His love endures forever."*
Worship leader:	"Let those who fear the Lord say . . ."
Congregation:	*"His love endures forever."*

Though I can't understand how this truth meshes with the obvious injustices in the world today, I know that God is loving and good. Though I see only a small slice of history, I know

> **"Though I see only a small slice of history, I know that God's wisdom encompasses all of time and eternity. I'm learning to accept by faith His mysteries."**

that God's wisdom encompasses all of time and eternity. I'm learning to accept by faith His mysteries. "His love endures forever!"

Personal prayer

Lord, this psalm causes me to consider how Your loyal love extends to our nation, to the Wyrtzen household, and to all the community of believers who fear your Name. I praise You for Your enduring love!

Festal Procession

Acknowledging His Deliverance From Distress

Exposition of theme
PSALM 118 CONTINUED

In my anguish I cried to the LORD, and he answered by setting me free. The LORD is with me; I will not be afraid. What can man do to me? The LORD is with me; he is my helper. I will look in triumph on my enemies. It is better to take refuge in the LORD than to trust in man. It is better to take refuge in the LORD than to trust in princes (vv. 5–9).

Development of theme

The stunning thought occurs to me that I've already made most of the major decisions I'll make in this life—choice of spouse, education, profession, Lord and Savior. But some choices present themselves again and again, and I have to de-

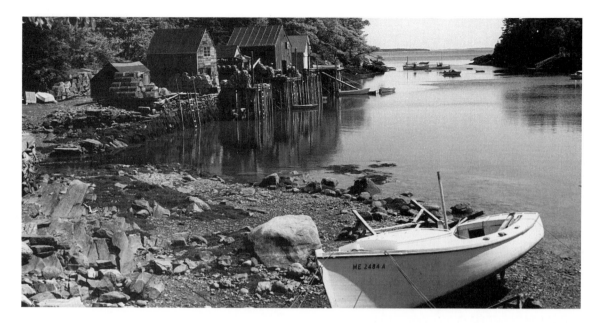

cide what I'm going to do about them.

The psalmist is in the same boat. He can either trust his friends, or he can take refuge in the Lord. He can even consult with "princes" (authorities and experts), or he can cry out to the Lord in his dilemma. Human resources or divine power? Which shall it be?

There is so much room for error. I've made some mistakes through the years; a few have been trivial, others have had more devastating consequences. The choices come again. I can trust in secular philosophy, humanistic psychology, and modern science and technology. I can cast my lot with the scholars and experts of human opinion. Or, I can take the often unpopular stance of placing my faith in the Lord. When I choose the Lord, He erases past error and teaches me to sing again!

Personal prayer

Lord, I'm so prone to human error without Your constant watchcare. Help me always to look to You—not to man-made systems—to define my life and to bring back the music when I falter.

A CONTEMPORARY LYRIC

Teach Me to Sing Again

In my wandering, my heart hardening,
In such little things I made the wrong
   choice;
And for many days, in such little ways,
My life went astray from Your still, small
   voice.

Ever straying, disobeying,
Rarely praying, not judging right from
   wrong!
Needing closeness, not remoteness
I almost lost the joy of Your priceless song.

Teach me to sing again, light up my face
   again,
Help me trust again, dear Lord, today;
Teach me to sing again, lifting my praise
   again,
Free me to love again, dear Lord, I pray.

Words and music by Don Wyrtzen. © 1983 by Singspiration.

Festal Procession

Exulting in Confidence, Triumph, and Joy

Exposition of theme

PSALM 118 CONTINUED

I was pushed back and about to fall, but the LORD helped me. The LORD is my strength and my song; he has become my salvation. Shouts of joy and victory resound in the tents of the righteous: "The LORD's right hand has done mighty things! The LORD's right hand is lifted high; the LORD's right hand has done mighty things!" (vv. 13–16).

> *"A hard-won battle isn't something you can keep to yourself! It's natural to exclaim and exult when a victory is won."*

Development of theme

The psalmist is down for the count! Heathen nations swarm around him like bees, ready to crush and destroy. They have pushed him back until he is ready to fall.

The mighty conjunction *but* signals a dramatic change. "*But* the LORD helped me!" (v. 13) Three times this psalmist has called on the name of the Lord. The Lord's response is to "cut them off." The Hebrew terminology is pretty graphic here. "Cut them off" means to circumcise them" (vv. 10–12). Our Lord is not namby-pamby nor squeamish in dealing with evil. Now the shouts of victory can resound throughout the "tents of the righteous."

A hard-won battle isn't something you can keep to yourself! It's natural to exclaim and exult when a victory is won. This ancient colleague grows eloquent in his praise: "The Lord is my strength and my song; he has become my salvation" (v. 14). I felt much the same say when I wrote "Jesus Is My Music!"

Personal prayer

Lord, help me to go forth in Your Name. You are my strength, my salvation and my song!

A CONTEMPORARY LYRIC

Jesus Is My Music

My life was out of tune and happiness
    eluded me,
My life was dissonant and missing inner
    harmony;
But then I met the Savior and received His
    gift of grace,
And now my heart sings melody.

Jesus is my music, Jesus is my song,
Jesus is my music, I want to sing His praises
    all day long.

Words and music by Don Wyrtzen. © 1977 by Singspiration.

Festal Procession

Anticipating the Coming Kingdom

Exposition of theme

PSALM 118 CONTINUED

Open for me the gates of righteousness; I will enter and give thanks to the LORD. This is the gate of the LORD through which the righteous may enter. I will give you thanks, for you answered me; you have become my salvation. The stone the builders rejected has become the capstone; the LORD has done this, and it is marvelous in our eyes. This is the day the LORD has made; let us rejoice and be glad in it (vv. 19–24).

Development of theme

Karen and I experienced the excitement that is Israel on our trip to the Holy Land. We were deeply moved to see Gethsemane, Golgotha, the Lord's tomb, and so many other biblical settings and scenes. One of the greatest thrills of the trip was entering Jerusalem through one of the many gates in the wall surrounding the ancient city. In fact, we even walked on the walls. While the present wall and buildings were erected in the sixteenth century A.D., the pilgrim feels a sense of expectancy upon seeing those gates!

The topmost stone of each Gothic or Romanesque arch is called the "capstone" — a vital piece of architecture that knits the rest of the stones together. In this psalm the "stone" takes on a symbolic meaning. "The stone the builders

rejected [Jesus Christ, the Messiah] has become the capstone" (v. 22). The builders symbolize the Jewish leaders who not only rejected Him but schemed to have Him put to death (Matthew 26:3–5). Therefore, God would invite others into His kingdom (Matthew 21:43). The psalmist, overjoyed with this new development, bursts into song: "This is the day the LORD has made; let us rejoice and be glad in it" (v. 24).

Most of us try to fill the crowning point of our lives with people or things, but it can only be adequately fulfilled by one Person and that is Jesus Christ. Things, in time, prove to be worthless. Relationships are often broken or grow routine. Achievement may seem meaningless. Only Jesus, our Capstone, can hold our lives together and give them eternal significance.

Personal prayer

Lord, You are the Stone which the builders rejected, but I want You to be the Capstone of my life.

> **"Most of us try to fill the crowning point of our lives with people or things, but it can only be adequately fulfilled by one Person and that is Jesus Christ."**

Praise for the Word of God

Trust and Obey

Exposition of theme

PSALM 119

א **Aleph**

Blessed are they whose ways are blameless, who walk according to the law of the LORD. Blessed are they who keep his statutes and seek him with all their heart. They do nothing wrong; they walk in his ways. You have laid down precepts that are to be fully obeyed. Oh, that my ways were steadfast in obeying your decrees! Then I would not be put to shame when I consider all your commands. I will praise you with an upright heart as I learn your righteous laws. I will obey your decrees; do not utterly forsake me (vv. 1–8).

Development of theme

Psalm 119 is a *magnum opus,* a mighty hymn of praise for the Word of God. The writer of this psalm lived under a lot of pressure — both internal and external. Men of earthly consequence persecuted him and ridiculed his beliefs. The severe test of his faith only strengthened him in his inner man. He became strong and resilient because he placed his faith in the Word of God and meditated on it day and night. The Word became his comfort and his ultimate resource for emotional strength.

> *"Even believers are far more influenced by our materialistic culture than we realize. This psalm stops me short: Am I more deeply affected by the world or by the Word?"*

This work is also an artistic masterpiece. Its structure is simple, elegant, and precise. This is the consummate alphabet psalm in which each line of each paragraph of eight verses starts with the same letter of the Hebrew alphabet. Verses 1–8 begin with the first letter of the Hebrew alphabet; verses 9–16 begin with the second, etc.

As he celebrates the value, worth, and magnificence of the Law, the psalmist almost runs out of words — *commandment, statute, judgment, precept, testimony, way, path.* . . .

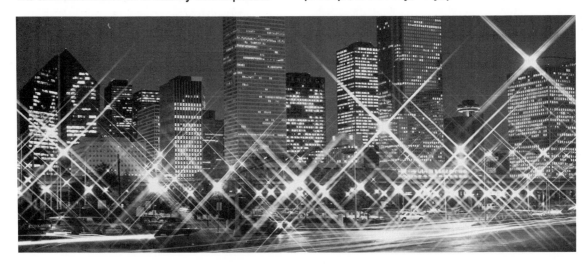

The person who trusts in God's word and obeys it is happy (vv. 1–2). Obedience brings stability and leads to righteousness.

The secular environment or worldly system we live in is diametrically opposed to the Word of God. Its philosophy and value system are poles apart from Christian beliefs, yet even believers are far more influenced by our materialistic culture than they realize. This psalm stops me short: Am I more deeply affected by the world or by the Word?

Personal prayer

Dear Lord, forgive me for not trusting and obeying You. My lack of faith has caused pain and unhappiness for myself and others. As I meditate again on Your Word, fill me with deep joy and peace.

SEPTEMBER 30

Praise for the Word of God
Memorizing the Word

Exposition of theme
PSALM 119 CONTINUED

ב Beth

How can a young man keep his way pure? By living according to your word. I seek you with all my heart; do not let me stray from your commands. I have hidden your word in my heart that I might not sin against you. Praise be to you, O LORD; teach me your decrees. With my lips I recount all the laws that come from your mouth. I rejoice in following your statutes as one re-joices in great riches. I meditate on your precepts and consider your ways. I delight in your decrees; I will not neglect your word (vv. 9–16).

Development of theme

How can a young person in this decadent society hope to lead a pure life? How can one avoid wandering from the truth? How can one be pro-

> *"The way to master the Word is to memorize it—just the way a good symphony conductor memorizes a score."*

tected from committing sin? By mastering God's Word. By allowing it to control his or her life. The way to master the Word is to memorize it—just the way a good symphony conductor memorizes a score. Then, when the spiritual battles come, the Sword of the Spirit can be wielded at a moment's notice, without fumbling for words!

The psalmist asks the Lord's help in learning the divine decrees, then publicly recites God's magnificent Law. He rejoices in following the Lord's statutes as one exults in great riches. At work during the day or in his bed at night, he runs these precepts through his mind. He doesn't intend to neglect them, because God's Law is his delight!

The Word has impacted this psalmist's mindset. He has not programmed his mind with trash and pornographic material which feed lust and lead to unhealthy fantasizing. He doesn't have to live with the pressure and pain caused by an unbalanced, sick mental attitude. His life is pure because his thoughts are pure.

Personal prayer

O Lord, don't let me neglect Your Word. As I hide it away in my heart like nuggets of gold, I am enriched. As I follow its precepts, I'm strengthened for the battle.

Teach me knowledge and good judgment, for I believe in your commands. PSALM 119:65

Praise for the Word of God

"Open mine eyes"

Exposition of theme

PSALM 119 *CONTINUED*

ג Gimel

Do good to your servant, and I will live; I will obey your word. Open my eyes that I may see wonderful things in your law. I am a stranger on earth; do not hide your commands from me. My soul is consumed with longing for your laws at all times. You rebuke the arrogant, who are cursed and who stray from your commands. Remove from me scorn and contempt, for I keep your statutes. Though rulers sit together and slander me, your servant will meditate on your decrees. Your statutes are my delight; they are my counselors (vv. 17–24).

Development of theme

Living is not just a meaningless vacuum for this author-composer. The goal of his life is to keep God's Word. Is this legalism—a slavish adherence to the letter of the Law? No! The psalmist is depending on God's truth for strength and sustenance. This Word is supporting him like a life raft would support a drowning man on a storm-tossed sea. This concept is repeated often in this psalm (vv. 24, 37, 40, 50, 77, 88, etc.).

He prays that his eyes will be opened to behold "wonderful things" out of the Law. He prays for insight and illumination so that God's commandments will not be hidden from him. So intensely involved is he in this quest that his soul "is consumed with longing" for the Law "at all times" (v. 20).

What "wonderful things" do I find for living life in this troubled twentieth century? I love to read the Word aloud; it gets my ear involved as well as my eye. Recently, I read the whole book of Ephesians aloud in one setting. Often, I put outstanding passages on 3 x 5 cards and carry them around with me for ready reference. Second Corinthians 12:9 helps me with feelings of inadequacy and incompetence. Jeremiah 29:11 helps me regarding uncertainty about the future. First Chronicles 28:20 gives me encouragement in my work. Occasionally I make Scripture songs out of these key concepts. Then, the Scripture combined with music, comforts and sustains me.

Personal prayer

O Lord, open my eyes that I may behold "wonderful things" from Your Word today.

> **"Occasionally I make Scripture songs out of key scriptural concepts. Then, the Scripture combined with music, comforts and sustains me."**

Praise for the Word of God

"Song of the soul set free"

Exposition of theme

PSALM 119 *CONTINUED*

ד **Daleth**

I am laid low in the dust; preserve my life according to your word. I recounted my ways and you answered me; teach me your decrees. Let me understand the teaching of your precepts; then I will meditate on your wonders. My soul is weary with sorrow; strengthen me according to your word. Keep me from deceitful ways; be gracious to me through your law. I have chosen the way of truth; I have set my heart on your laws. I hold fast to your statutes, O LORD; do not let me be put to shame. I run in the path of your commands, for you have set my heart free (vv. 25–32).

Development of theme

Rich in contrasts, this passage displays the positive against the negative. First, a mournful tone is heard: "I am laid low"; "My soul is weary"; "Keep me from deceitful ways"; "Do not let me be put to shame" (vv. 25, 28, 29, 31).

Then, on a rising crescendo, the psalmist real-

> *"After receiving my new nature as God's gift of grace, I was inspired to write one of my first songs."*

---

izes the possibilities available to Him through God's Word—renewal, strength, truth, freedom! As he begins to understand these precepts, he is filled with wonder.

Jesus articulated this truth in John 8:31–32: "To the Jews who had believed him, Jesus said, 'If you hold to my teaching, you are really my disciples. Then you will know the truth, and the truth will set you free.' "

This kind of freedom is the definitive answer to bondage, to obsessive-compulsive behavior. After receiving my new nature as God's gift of grace, I was inspired to write one of my first songs—a song that was later recorded by Jerome Hines of the Metropolitan Opera and arranged by noted songwriter, Kurt Kaiser.

Personal prayer

O Lord, set my heart free as I adhere to Your truth and hold fast to Your commands.

A CONTEMPORARY LYRIC

The Day That I Met Jesus

The day that I met Jesus
My life was torn with grief and pain,
My soul had longed for something new in life —
Then I believed, and Jesus came.

The day that I met Jesus
My life was changed — my sins were gone,
The Lord has won Himself a trophy of grace,
For Jesus lives, He lives within my heart.

If I could be the one
To tell you what the Lord has done;
If you would just believe Him
And at this hour receive Him
If you would only let Him conquer you!

Words and music by Don Wyrtzen. © 1964 by Singspiration.

Praise for the Word of God

"Not for selfish gain"

Exposition of theme

PSALM 119 *CONTINUED*

ה **He**

Teach me, O LORD, to follow your decrees; then I will keep them to the end. Give me understanding, and I will keep your law and obey it with all my heart. Direct me in the path of your commands, for there I find delight. Turn my heart toward your statutes and not toward selfish gain. Turn my eyes away from worthless things; preserve my life according to your word. Fulfill your promise to your servant, so that you may be feared. Take away the disgrace I dread, for your laws are good. How I long for your precepts! Preserve my life in your righteousness (vv. 33–40).

Development of theme

What drives me? What hidden desires motivate me to perform? What goals beckon me? Part of being imperfect, human, and fallen is the struggle with mixed motives. I want my life to bring glory to God, but I also want some other things —

> *"Part of being imperfect, human, and fallen is the struggle with mixed motives. I want my life to bring glory to God, but I also want some other things."*

personal fulfillment, meaningful work, the recognition of my peers, financial success, domestic tranquility. O how easy it is to be deceived, to rationalize, to be a self-preservationist! I want to be "in the world but not of it," yet, to be honest, secular culture carries a punch that the Word often doesn't.

This psalmist puts me to shame! He observes the Law wholeheartedly (vv. 33–35), then begs God to purge him of any unworthy motives — "selfish gain," "worthless things" (vv. 36–37). Then he gives us the key to proper motivation for the study of God's Word as well as for all other endeavors undertaken by the believer. "Direct me in the path of your commands" (v. 35). With divine direction, the psalmist knows he can't miss a beat.

If I live to fulfill my own goals and desires or even to satisfy the expectations of others — no matter how worthy — I'll miss the greater blessing of living my life to please God. Obeying His Word is the premiere goal that drives me now!

Personal prayer

O Lord, turn my heart toward Your statutes today. May I not live my life for selfish gain, but to please You!

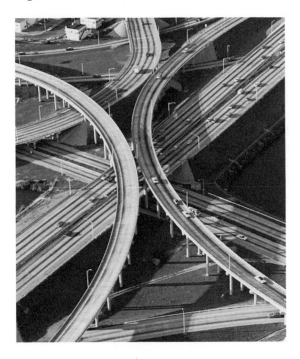

Praise for the Word of God

"I will speak of your statutes."

Exposition of theme

PSALM 119 *CONTINUED*

ו Waw

May your unfailing love come to me, O LORD, your salvation according to your promise; then I will answer the one who taunts me, for I trust in your word. Do not snatch the word of truth from my mouth, for I have put my hope in your laws. I will always obey your law, for ever and ever. I will walk about in freedom, for I have sought out your precepts. I will speak of your statutes before kings and will not be put to shame, for I delight in your commands because I love them. I lift up my hands to your commands, which I love, and I meditate on your decrees (vv. 41-48)

Development of theme

Down through the ages, some have dared to proclaim the Word of God at the risk of endangering their lives or reputations. In 1521 Martin Luther was excommunicated by Pope Leo X. Charles V, emperor of the Holy Roman Empire, ordered him to appear before the Diet (meeting) of princes, nobles, and clergymen at Worms, Germany. They demanded that Luther recant his beliefs, but he refused. "Unless I am convinced by the testimony of the Scriptures or by clear reason (for I do not trust either in the pope or in councils alone, since it is well known that they have often erred and contradicted themselves), I am bound by the Scriptures . . . and my conscience is captive to the Word of God. I cannot and I will not retract anything!"

This psalmist vows to "speak of [the Lord's] statutes before magistrates and kings" (v. 46). In his day that would have been a dangerous thing to do, as it is in some parts of the world today. People like Georgi Vins and my friends, Earl Poysti and Bark and Carleen Fahnestock, boldly proclaim the Word in hostile environments and under adverse circumstances.

Several other bold personal assertions are made in these verses: "I trust in your word" (v. 42). "I have put my hope in your laws" (v. 43). "I will always obey your law" (v. 44). "I delight in your commands because I love them" (v. 47).

Here is a person with a passion for God's Word. He is obsessed with it. He thinks about it constantly. As the Word dominates his thoughts, it changes his life and frees him to face life unafraid.

> **"Here is a person with a passion for God's Word. He is obsessed with it. He thinks about it constantly. As the Word dominates his thoughts, it changes his life and frees him to face life unafraid."**

Personal prayer

O Lord, let me become so immersed in Your Word that I share it freely wherever I go — whether in the company of colleagues or kings!

Praise for the Word of God

Precious Promises

Exposition of theme

PSALM 119 CONTINUED

ז **Zayin**

Remember your word to your servant, for you have given me hope. My comfort in my suffering is this: Your promise preserves my life. The arrogant mock me without restraint, but I do not turn from your law. I remember your ancient laws, O LORD, and I find comfort in them. Indignation grips me because of the wicked, who have forsaken your law. Your decrees are the theme of my song wherever I lodge. In the night I remember your name, O LORD, and I will keep your law. This has been my practice: I obey your precepts (vv. 49–56).

Development of theme

"Your decrees are the theme of my song!" What a mandate for the Christian musician! What a mission statement for a godly artist! As Christopher Smart said in 1763, "Glorious the song,

> **"As I experience the truth of God's Word daily and am convicted by its power, I'm inspired to write meaningful music that will bless and change other lives."**

when God's the theme." The content of our art must be the magnificence of God's truth. Yet it is so easy to water it down, leave it out, or yield to the temptation to explore other areas of thought that are more appealing, more commercial.

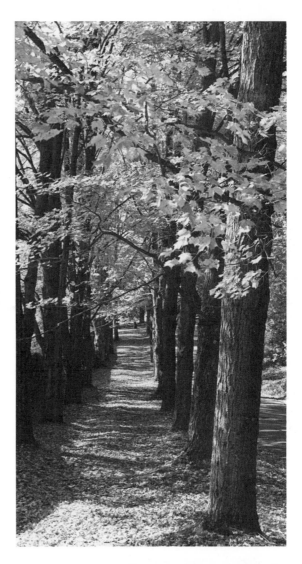

This servant had discovered the rock of God's truth during a particularly painful time of suffering and opposition. The precious promises contained in God's Word had given him hope and comfort. Even in the depths of his dark night, he remembered these promises and recited them. The habits of holiness he had developed sustained him at the time of his greatest need. Therefore, because God's Word has been tried and tested in his life, these precepts now occupy all of his thought. There is no room for lesser interests!

My theme song is that which consumes me because it has been tested and proven. As I experience the truth of God's Word daily and am convicted by its power, my goal or mandate is to set God's truth to music in simple, powerful form.

Personal prayer

O Lord, Your promises preserve my life and comfort me. May Your decrees be the theme of my song for the rest of my days.

OCTOBER 6

Praise for the Word of God

"With all my heart"

Exposition of theme

PSALM 119 *CONTINUED*

ח Heth

You are my portion, O LORD; I have promised to obey your words. I have sought your face with all my heart; be gracious to me according to your promise. I have considered my ways and have turned my steps to your statutes. I will hasten and not delay to obey your commands. Though the wicked bind me with ropes, I will not forget your law. At midnight I rise to give you thanks for your righteous laws. I am a friend to all who fear you, to all who follow your precepts. The earth is filled with your love, O LORD; teach me your decrees (vv. 57–64).

> *"We wake up in the middle of the night, besieged with worries and anxieties. The psalmist wakes up and praises the Lord with all his heart!"*

Development of theme

I remember my high school days, when under pressure to produce and perform, I wanted to be left alone. The result was an unfulfilled inner life, a personal emptiness, and a passionless Christianity. I followed at a distance, because there was little delight and joy in my relationship with the Lord.

This psalmist is committed, dedicated, passionately involved. "I have sought your face *with all my heart*" (v. 58), he declares. Nothing lackadaisical about this man's approach to Bible study! In fact, we'd say that this person is "on fire for the Lord." So strong is his devotion that, even if the wicked were to bind him with ropes, he will not forget the law (v. 61).

Not only does he make all kinds of declarations about what he plans to do in the future, but he has already put feet to his intentions. He takes stock of his actions and chooses to follow God's law (v. 59). He prays, giving thanks for the good guidance of God's Word (v. 62). He befriends fellow believers who share his love and reverence for the Lord (v. 63).

Where is this level of commitment and dedication today? Which of us, living in the midst of a secularistic society, gives this kind of intense devotion and concentration to spiritual matters? We wake up in the middle of the night, besieged with worries and anxieties. The psalmist wakes up and praises the Lord with all his heart!

Personal prayer

O Lord, help me to seek Your face with all my heart!

Praise for the Word of God

"It was good for me to be afflicted."

Exposition of theme

PSALM 119 CONTINUED

ט **Teth**

Do good to your servant according to your word, O Lord. Teach me knowledge and good judgment, for I believe in your commands. Before I was afflicted I went astray, but now I obey your word. You are good, and what you do is good; teach me your decrees. Though the arrogant have smeared me with lies, I keep your precepts with all my heart. Their hearts are callous and unfeeling, but I delight in your law. It was good for me to be afflicted so that I might learn your decrees. The law from your mouth is more precious to me than thousands of pieces of silver and gold (vv. 65–72).

Development of theme

What kind of man is this psalmist? He thanks God for adversity and affliction! He must be sado-masochistic!

Reading on, I understand. "Before I was af-

> *"We contemporary Christians prefer simple answers to very complex issues. We all seem to think there must be an easier way to personal depth and spiritual maturity."*

---

flicted, I went astray, but *now* I obey your word" (v. 67). The painful consequences of sin have driven him to the Word of God and now he considers "the law from [the Lord's] mouth . . . more precious . . . than thousands of pieces of silver and gold" (v. 72)

We contemporary Christians prefer simple answers to very complex issues. We all seem to think there must be an easier way to personal depth and spiritual maturity. But the nature of reality is like a tapestry with knots underneath, a symphony containing dissonance, or a play enhanced by dramatic tension. When I wonder why life with the Lord can't be easier, I am reminded of the song, "No Easier Way," that I wrote with Claire Cloninger.

Personal prayer

O Lord, let me learn to praise You for the hard times that drive me to my knees, and to remember that Your suffering paid the price of my eternal security!

A CONTEMPORARY LYRIC

No Easier Way

Why can't I live my life without losing it?
Why can't I grow without pain?
Why can't I live for You, Lord, without
    dying?
There must be an easier way!

There was no easier way for You,
There was no easier thing You could do;
The cost of my life
Was the cross and the grave,
There was no easier way!

Words by Claire Cloninger and Don Wyrtzen. Music by Don Wyrtzen.
© 1984 Singspiration.

Praise for the Word of God

Living the Law

Exposition of theme

PSALM 119 CONTINUED

’ Yodh

Your hands made me and formed me; give me understanding to learn your commands. May those who fear you rejoice when they see me, for I have put my hope in your word. I know, O LORD, that your laws are righteous, and in faithfulness you have afflicted me. May your unfailing love be my comfort, according to your promise to your servant. Let your compassion come to me that I may live, for your law is my delight. May the arrogant be put to shame for wronging me without cause; but I will meditate on your precepts. May those who fear you turn to me, those who understand your statutes. May my heart be blameless toward your decrees, that I may not be put to shame (vv. 73–80).

Development of theme

This ancient believer-musician places his complete hope in the Word, since the Lord has delivered him from pain and has made of him an example and encouragement to other believers.

> **"Are the pages of my life so marred with my own errors that they are difficult to read? Is the music of my life flat, dull, and boring?"**

He is acutely aware that his very life has come from God. Infinitely powerful hands have made and formed him. He is not a product of chance. Now he requests understanding to learn God's Law so that others will be filled with joy when they observe his life.

The staggering truth dawns that I am the only Bible some people will ever read! Am I living its precepts faithfully so that unbelievers "rejoice when they see me," or are the pages of my life so marred with my own errors that they are difficult to read? Is the music of my life flat, dull, and boring?

I cry out to the Lord for compassion! I need another chance to live out His Word before the world so I will point others to Him.

Personal prayer

Thank You, Lord, for forming me, for forgiving me, and for sending me as Your love letter to the world. May the words and music of my life be consistent with Your truth.

Praise for the Word of God

"A wineskin in the smoke"

Exposition of theme

PSALM 119 CONTINUED

כ Kaph

My soul faints with longing for your salvation, but I have put my hope in your word. My eyes fail, looking for your promise; I say, "When will you comfort me?" Though I am like a wineskin in the smoke, I do not forget your decrees. How long must your servant wait? When will you punish my persecutors? The arrogant dig pitfalls for me, contrary to your law. All your commands are trustworthy; help me, for men persecute me without cause. They almost wiped me from the earth, but I have not forsaken your precepts. Preserve my life according to your love, and I will obey the statutes of your mouth (vv. 81–88).

Development of theme

I've felt like "wineskin in the smoke" — empty and shriveled and useless. I've felt pressure like the thousands of pounds of tension on the strings inside a grand piano. What an encouragement this section is to me!

With dramatic imagery, the psalmist compares himself to "a wineskin in the smoke." In

> *"I can understand this ancient musician's impatience. I have experienced deep hurt, searing anger, and dark despair. I've sometimes wondered where I fit in and where God is when I've needed Him."*

the heat of severe persecution and harassment, his soul is shriveling up like a goatskin, and his eyes, "looking for the promise," grow red and watery.

Then he uses a startlingly modern phrase: "They almost wiped me from the earth" or "wiped me out"! (v. 87) Arrogant persecutors are digging his grave in anticipation of an early death.

Even if all of this is taken figuratively, the metaphors are stunning. In these unbelievably adverse circumstances, the psalmist's faith in God's Word is immovable. He continually voices his hope and trust in God's divine "decrees," His trustworthy "commands," His precepts," and "statutes." The emphasis is on God's Word — not on the wrongs that have been committed.

I can understand this ancient musician's impatience. I have experienced deep hurt, searing anger, and dark despair. I've sometimes wondered where I fit in and where God is when I've needed Him. I've even rebelled and come awfully close to dropping out. Yet, when I allow God to perform on the keys of my life, music comes forth! Like the psalmist, I choose to put my hope in the Word, to honor the Lord, and to wait patiently for Him to work more obviously and directly in my life.

Personal prayer

O Lord, help me, even when under intense pressure and pain, to learn to wait for You to do Your deep work in my life.

OCTOBER 10

Praise for the Word of God

"In all perfection I see a limit."

Exposition of theme

PSALM 119 *CONTINUED*

ל **Lamedh**

Your word, O LORD, is eternal; it stands firm in the heavens. Your faithfulness continues through all generations; you established the earth, and it endures. Your laws endure to this day, for all things serve you. If your law had not been my delight, I would have perished in my affliction. I will never forget your precepts, for by them you have preserved my life. Save me, for I am yours; I have sought out your precepts. The wicked are waiting to destroy me, but I will ponder your statutes. To all perfection I see a limit; but your commands are boundless (vv. 89–96).

Development of theme

I'm a perfectionist by nature. I probably use perfectionism defensively in uncomfortable situations to distance myself from other people. We use all kinds of devices like armor to protect ourselves — humor (being too funny), intellectualization (being too smart), superficiality (being too

"Works of art, clever creations, powerful empires — all are temporal. Only the Word is perfect, boundless, and eternal!"

sweet). Sometimes achievement is an attempt to prove ourselves worthy in the eyes of others and ourselves.

This psalmist has a more realistic view. He promotes the faithfulness of God and His eternal

Word. It's settled in heaven, therefore he can stake his life on its immutable perfection. These qualities of the Word have supported the struggling psalmist in persecution and affliction. Through it all, he's clung to the one sure thing he knows — the Word of God. It has become his delight, his salvation, and his stable reference point.

This section ends with a beautiful, original insight. "To all perfection I see a limit" (v. 96). No matter how high the level of excellence one might attain, the product of human creativity is short-lived at best. Works of art, clever creations, powerful empires — all are temporal. Only the Word is perfect, boundless, and eternal!

Personal prayer

O Lord, I praise You for the absolute reliability of Your Word. Help me to recognize the short-term duration of any work I may accomplish, including songwriting. May I look to Your Word for perfection and not to myself.

Praise for the Word of God

"I have more insight than all my teachers"

Exposition of theme

PSALM 119 *CONTINUED*

מ **Mem**

Oh, how I love your law! I meditate on it all day long. Your commands make me wiser than my enemies, for they are ever with me. I have more insight than all my teachers, for I meditate on your statutes. I have more understanding than the elders, for I obey your precepts. I have kept my feet from every evil path so that I might obey your word. I have not departed from your laws, for you yourself have taught me. How sweet are your words to my taste, sweeter than honey to my mouth! I gain understanding from your precepts; therefore I hate every wrong path (vv. 97–104).

Development of theme

I can recall some teachers and professors who profoundly impacted my life at critical turning points. Mrs. Lillian Gearhart taught me piano; Jay Ciser and Carl Hamilton taught me art; Dr. Charles Horne taught me apologetics; Prof. Howard Hendricks taught me Bible study meth-

> **"I have learned that reading the Word with my own intellect alone is inadequate. I must submit to the Holy Spirit as my teacher. I need His comfort and counsel. Otherwise, the undertow of secular society may pull me down."**

ods; Dean Arlton taught me music history; Dr. Bruce Waltke taught me the Psalms and Hebrew; Dr. Charles Ryrie taught me theology; Dr. Francis Schaeffer taught me about culture. Dr. John F. Walvoord, D. J. DePree, and Bob Steed have been father figures and mentors to me. What a foundation they gave to me!

But this psalmist claims that he has more "insight" than all his teachers, "more understanding than the elders" (v. 100), for "you yourself [the Lord] have taught me" (v. 102)!

I too have learned that reading the Word with my intellect alone is inadequate. I graduated from Dallas Theological Seminary but even though I studied at the feet of the outstanding theologians and Bible scholars I have mentioned, I learned that it is the Holy Spirit who does the real teaching! As R. A. Torrey said, "No amount of mere human teaching, no matter who our teachers may be, will ever give us a correct and exact and full apprehension of the truth. . . . We must be taught directly by the Holy Spirit. The one who is thus taught will understand the truth of God better, even if he does not know one word of Greek or Hebrew, than the one who knows Greek and Hebrew thoroughly . . . but who is not taught of the Spirit.

I also must submit to the Holy Spirit as my teacher. I need His comfort and counsel. Otherwise, the undertow of secular society may pull me down.

Personal prayer

O Lord, Your Word is "sweeter than honey." Feed me by Your Holy Spirit so I may know the truth.

Praise for the Word of God

"Your word is a lamp unto my feet."

Exposition of theme

PSALM 119 *CONTINUED*

נ **Nun**

Your word is a lamp to my feet and a light for my path. I have taken an oath and confirmed it, that I will follow your righteous laws. I have suffered much; preserve my life, O LORD, according to your word. Accept, O LORD, the willing praise of my mouth, and teach me your laws. Though I constantly take my life in my hands, I will not forget your law. The wicked have set a snare for me, but I have not strayed from your precepts. Your statutes are my heritage forever; they are the joy of my heart. My heart is set on keeping your decrees to the very end (vv. 105–112).

Development of theme

How well I remember taking my son, D. J., on a camping trip to northern Michigan. Just the two of us, a small tent, a crackling fire, some fishing poles, and a raft! Wanting to spend quality time with my son, I left my books at home. But just before we went to sleep, D. J. pulled out a flashlight and a book he had brought along! In the pitch dark, the glow of the campfire and the beam from the flash gave us all the light we needed.

Without the searchlight of God's Word, we'd be left to flounder in the dark, looking for the way. But His Law points out the snares of the wicked, and we can avoid stumbling into their traps.

The psalmist continues to take his life in his hands, but he has vowed to follow God's righteous decrees, so there is nothing to fear from visible or invisible foes. While the darkness closes in, he has the enlightenment of the Word and cannot stray from these rock-like precepts

(v. 110).

Not only does this ancient one have light for his present difficulties, but God's statutes are his "heritage forever." He can look forward to life in the light now and throughout eternity. As a result, he offers the "willing praise" of his mouth (v. 108) and obedience to the Word "to the very end" (v. 112).

What the psalmist did not have was an intimate relationship with the Light of the World, who came to banish darkness forever. I walk in the increased illumination of the Messiah—the prophecy fulfilled!

Personal prayer

O Lord, I thank You for sending Christ, the living Word, who walks with me to point out hidden dangers and to shepherd me through the canyons and ravines of my life.

Praise for the Word of God

"I stand in awe."

Exposition of theme

PSALM 119 *CONTINUED*

ס **Samekh**

I hate double-minded men, but I love your law. You are my refuge and my shield; I have put my hope in your word. Away from me, you evildoers, that I may keep the commands of my God! Sustain me according to your promise, and I will live; do not let my hopes be dashed. Uphold me, and I will be delivered; I will always have regard for your decrees. You reject all who stray from your decrees, for their deceitfulness is in vain. All the wicked of the earth you discard like dross;

therefore I love your statutes. My flesh trembles in fear of you; I stand in awe of your laws (vv. 113–120).

Development of theme

Awesome! If I've heard that word once, I've heard it a thousand times. With two teenagers and a steady stream of young friends in and out of the house, I've become convinced that this word is the cornerstone for the vocabulary of young America. They handle greatness with undue familiarity!

Still, *awesome* is a perfectly good word. It's in the dictionary as well as in the Bible itself. Random House defines the word as "characterized by awe—an overwhelming feeling of reverence, admiration, and fear produced by that which is grand, sublime, extremely powerful, or the like." I could use this word to describe Brahm's Fourth Symphony. And the psalmist certainly feels this kind of reverence for God's laws.

Because of the sublime Word of God, the psalmist has a holy hatred for duplicity and doublemindedness. He is opposed by wicked men, the basis of whose argument is falsehood. Being deceived themselves, they use pretense and illogical reasoning to bolster this position. In God's eyes, however, they are "dross"—waste materials that will be removed by His smelting process.

This psalmist isn't gullible enough to believe that he is immune to the seductive wiles of the wicked and prays earnestly for strength to stay true to God's awesome decrees. He actually trembles in God's presence!

I'm wondering if believers in this modern world don't often try to be too cozy, too familiar with God. We sing superficial songs and engage in cliché-ridden, repetitive prayers. Many of us know the *traditions* but have never been moved by the *truth.* We've never felt our flesh quiver in awe—holy respect—as we behold the majesty of God's eternal Word!

Personal prayer

O Lord, when I open Your Word, I'm standing on holy ground. Teach me to tremble in Your presence!

A CONTEMPORARY LYRIC

Holy Ground

As I walked through the door, I sensed His presence;
And I knew this was the place where love abounds.
For this is the temple, Jehovah God abides here;
And we are standing in His presence on holy ground.

In His presence there is joy beyond all measure;
And at His feet, peace of mind can still be found.
If you have the need, I know He has the answer.
Reach out and claim it, you are standing on holy ground.

We are standing on holy ground,
And I know that there are angels all around.
Let us praise Jesus now;
We are standing in His presence on holy ground.

Words and music by Geron Davis. © 1983 Meadowgreen Music Co.

327

Praise for the Word of God

"I am your servant."

Exposition of theme

PSALM 119 CONTINUED

y Ayin

I have done what is righteous and just; do not leave me to my oppressors. Ensure your servant's well-being; let not the arrogant oppress me. My eyes fail, looking for your salvation, looking for your righteous promise. Deal with your servant according to your love and teach me your decrees. I am your servant; give me discernment that I may understand your statutes. It is time for you to act, O LORD; your law is being broken. Because I love your commands more than gold, more than pure gold, and because I consider all your precepts right, I hate every wrong path (vv. 121–128).

Development of theme

Most of us living in affluent America know very little about servanthood. We expect excellent and efficient service from others, and accept it

---

> **"Most of us know very little about servanthood. It is so much more human to desire stardom."**

---

as our due. It is so much more human to desire stardom than servanthood!

Three times in this passage, however, the psalmist — likely a person of honor and prestige in the community — professes his status as a lowly servant before God: "Ensure *your servant's* well-being" (v. 122). "Deal with *your servant*" (v. 124). "I am *your servant*; give me

discernment" (v. 125). He isn't too proud to admit his need to be educated in the royal decrees or to seek divine wisdom for decision-making.

Ancient believers, overcome by the greatness of God and their own worthlessness, often prostrated themselves before the Lord in abject humility (Psalm 5:7). We do well to get on our knees once in awhile, unless the liturgy of our church calls for it!

Yet Jesus, God incarnate, willingly left the glories of heaven to walk the dusty pathways of this earth. He owned no property, sought no public office, accumulated no possessions. "The Son of Man did not come to be served, but to serve, and to give his life as a ransom for many" (Matthew 20:28). He came to serve . . . and to die for my sins!

Such love compels me to fall on my face. "I am your servant; give me discernment that I may understand your statutes" (v. 125).

Personal prayer

Speak, Lord! Your servant is listening!

Praise for the Word of God

"Your word is wonderful!"

Exposition of theme

PSALM 119 CONTINUED

פ Pe

Your statutes are wonderful; therefore I obey them. The unfolding of your words gives light; it gives understanding to the simple. I open my mouth and pant, longing for your commands. Turn to me and have mercy on me, as you always do to those who love your name. Direct my footsteps according to your word; let no sin rule over me. Redeem me from the oppression of men, that I may obey your precepts. Make your face shine upon your servant and teach me your decrees. Streams of tears flow from my eyes, for your law is not obeyed (vv. 129–136).

Development of theme

God's Word is wonderful — marvelous, extraordinary, remarkable! The word *wonderful* literally means "to generate wonder." Even the simple, the unintelligent, the uneducated can grasp its truth when instructed by the Holy Spirit. Its inspiration exceeds that of Shakespeare, Mozart, Milton, Bach, and the greatest poets and composers who have ever lived.

So amazing is the power of these statutes and commands that the psalmist opens his mouth and "pants" for understanding. His deep person-

al longing for the truth is like gasping for breath after running the Boston Marathon.

As I read these verses, I'm reminded of "Wonderful Words of Life," Dad's theme song for the Word of Life Hour. I grew up hearing it.

Personal prayer

O Lord, teach me to love Your truth and see the wonder of Your words!

> *"As I read these verses, I'm reminded of 'Wonderful Words of Life,' Dad's theme song for the Word of Life Hour. I grew up hearing it."*

A WONDERFUL GOSPEL SONG

Wonderful Words of Life

Sing them over again to me,
Wonderful words of life;
Let me more of their beauty see,
Wonderful words of life.
Words of life and beauty,
Teach me faith and duty:
Beautiful words, wonderful words,
Wonderful words of life.

Christ, the blessed One, gives to all
Wonderful words of life;
Sinner, list to the loving call,
Wonderful words of life.
All so freely given,
Wooing us to heaven,
Beautiful words, wonderful words,
Wonderful words of life.

Words and music by Philip P. Bliss.

Praise for the Word of God

"Your word is righteous."

Exposition of theme

PSALM 119 *CONTINUED*

צ Tsadhe

Righteous are you, O LORD, and your laws are right. The statutes you have laid down are righteous; they are fully trustworthy. My zeal wears me out, for my enemies ignore your words. Your promises have been thoroughly tested, and your servant loves them. Though I am lowly and despised, I do not forget your precepts. Your righteousness is everlasting and your law is true. Trouble and distress have come upon me, but your commands are my delight. Your statutes are forever right; give me understanding that I may live (vv. 137–144).

Development of theme

The psalmist is filled with deep love and reverence for the Law. Because the Lord is righteous, His Word is also fully trustworthy. The Lord's promises are fully reliable because they have

---

> **"The Word of God is absolutely trustworthy and reliable! May we not let technological change, moral relativism, scientific advances, or intellectual pride rob us of our confidence in it."**

---

been thoroughly tried, tested, and proven.

But all is not well here. The psalmist is almost worn out with zeal. His enemies ignore the Word of God. He is feeling lowly and despised. Arnold Schoenberg said, "Dissonances are more difficult to comprehend than consonances." Horace labeled it "harmony in discord." The psalmist is alluding to the "discordant harmony" of his existence.

But his depression cannot obliterate his memory of the law. Continual trouble and distress do not snatch away his ingrained delight in the Lord's commands. No matter how lonely or how oppressed he feels, God's Word stands unaffected.

What a comfort to know beyond a shadow of a doubt that the Word of God is absolutely trustworthy and reliable! May we not let technological change, moral relativism, scientific advances, or intellectual pride rob us of our confidence in God's eternal Word!

Personal prayer

O Lord, I praise You and thank You for Your "flawless" Word!

Praise for the Word of God

"Long ago I learned from your statutes."

Exposition of theme

PSALM 119 *CONTINUED*

ק Qoph

I call with all my heart; answer me, O LORD, and I will obey your decrees. I call out to you; save me and I will keep your statutes. I rise before dawn and cry for help; I have put my hope in your word. My eyes stay open through the watches of the night, that I may meditate on your promises. Hear my voice in accordance with your love; preserve my life, O LORD, according to your laws. Those who devise wicked schemes are near, but they are far from your law. Yet you are near, O

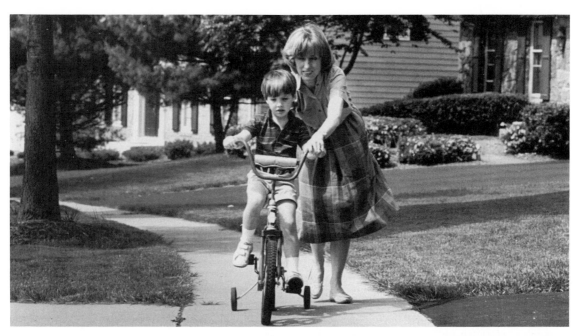

Lord, and all your commands are true. Long ago I learned from your statutes that you established them to last forever (vv. 145–152).

Development of theme

Some of the Scripture songs I learned as a kid have supported me in times of crisis such as those described by this psalmist (i.e. "Thy Word Have I Hid in My Heart," "Thy Word Is a Lamp unto My Feet"). My Mom taught me that music comforts. I remember her singing around the house some of Norman Clayton's lovely songs: "Now I Belong to Jesus" and "We Shall See His Lovely Face."

As trouble sweeps in like a flood, the psalmist gets up before daybreak to pray. Then, at night, restless and sleepless, he meditates on God's promises, likely committed to memory when he was younger. Because he knows the Word, the psalmist can call on it instantly for help in any emergency. He promises to keep the divine statutes (v. 146), to continue to hope (v. 147), and to rest his destiny on the Lord's loyal love and His Law (v. 149). This musician feels close to the Lord because God's Word is lodged firmly in his mind and heart!

Scripture songs are like tapes that play over and over in our minds. Because more of our senses are involved in learning them, they bring God's truth to the forefront of our consciousness. What a glorious wedding when the Word is united with music!

> *"Scripture songs are like tapes that play over and over in our minds. What a glorious wedding when the Word is united with music!"*

Personal prayer

O Lord, thank You for my Mom who taught me hymns and gospel songs when I was young. Now these Scripture songs and biblical promises hold me steady in times of trouble.

331

Praise for the Word of God

"Your compassion is great, O LORD."

Exposition of theme

PSALM 119 *CONTINUED*

ר Resh

Look upon my suffering and deliver me, for I have not forgotten your law. Defend my cause and redeem me; preserve my life according to your promise. Salvation is far from the wicked, for they do not seek out your decrees. Your compassion is great, O LORD; preserve my life according to your laws. Many are the foes who persecute me, but I have not turned from your statutes. I look on the faithless with loathing, for they do not obey your word. See how I love your precepts; preserve my life, O LORD, according to your love. All your words are true; all your righteous laws are eternal (vv. 153–160).

Development of theme

How prone we human beings are to panic when the pressure builds. Our faith shrinks and we're even tempted to avoid unpleasant confrontations at all costs—in other words, to run in the other direction!

The ancient songwriter must have known that trapped feeling. Three times he reminds the Lord of His promise to renew and preserve life: "Preserve my life according to your promise"

"How prone we human beings are to panic when the pressure builds. Our faith shrinks and we're tempted to avoid unpleasant confrontations—to run in the other direction!"

(v. 154). "Preserve my life according to your laws" (v. 156). "Preserve my life, O LORD, according to your love" (v. 159).

Suddenly the theme of this song sounds above the discord of defeat like the clear, sweet note of a lark: "Your compassion is great, O LORD!" (v. 156). The Lord not only knows the feelings of our infirmities and sympathizes with us, but *He desires to alleviate the pain or remove its cause altogether!*

I can't begin to comprehend the love and compassion of the Lord. Under intense emotional pressure, I either abandon it or forget it. Yet He is faithful to supply His mercies in rich abundance if I follow the example of my ancient counterpart and ask for it!

Personal prayer

O Lord, I thank You for Your great love and compassion. Revive my life on the basis of Your truth today!

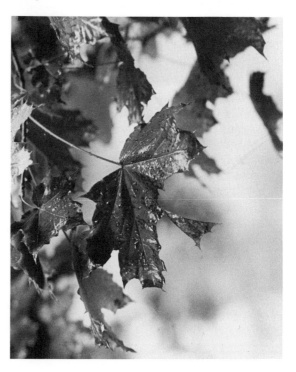

Praise for the Word of God

"I rejoice in your promise!"

Exposition of theme

PSALM 119 CONTINUED

ש Sin and Shin

Rulers persecute me without cause, but my heart trembles at your word. I rejoice in your promise like one who finds great spoil. I hate and abhor falsehood but I love your law. Seven times a day I praise you for your righteous laws. Great peace have they who love your law, and nothing can make them stumble. I wait for your salvation, O LORD, and I follow your commands. I obey your statutes, for I love them greatly. I obey your precepts and your statutes, for all my ways are known to you (vv. 161–168).

Development of theme

What a sunny, bright, and joyful passage! The psalmist has the distinction of having both loved and kept the Law. Now the music in his heart spills across the page in a lilting progression of praise: "I rejoice in your promise" (v. 162). "I wait for your salvation" (v. 166). "I obey your statutes, for I love them greatly" (v. 167). I'm reminded of

> **"This musician isn't experiencing a mid-life crisis. He is exulting in the 'great spoil' he has found in God's Word which has turned his life inside out!"**

the tumbling, dancing counterpoint in a Bach invention or fugue.

This musician has taken his stand for God's Law and has consequently suffered persecu-tion at the hands of heathen rulers. He is not driven by selfish ambition nor is he achievement-oriented. He is not experiencing a mid-life crisis. Rather, he's exulting in the "great spoil" he has found in God's Word. This "find" far surpasses earthly treasures—masterpieces of art and literature, wealth and possessions, even great music! God's Word has turned his life inside out.

I long to be radically changed—to know the psalmist's peace and stability, his patience and personal obedience. I want to love and follow the Word so that I'll be turned inside out!

Personal prayer

O Lord, may my heart rejoice in Your Word! Let me learn to love You with an intensity that is reflected in everything I do or write or sing!

Praise for the Word of God

"My lips overflow with praise!"

Exposition of theme

PSALM 119 CONTINUED

ת Taw

May my cry come before you, O LORD; give me understanding according to your word. May my supplication come before you; deliver me according to your promise. May my lips over-flow with praise, for you teach me your decrees. May my tongue sing of your word, for all your commands are righteous. May your hand be ready to help me, for I have chosen your precepts. I long for your salvation, O LORD, and your law is my delight. Let me live that I may praise you, and may your laws sustain me. I have strayed like a lost sheep. Seek your servant, for I have not for-gotten your commands (vv. 169–176).

Development of theme

This magnificent psalm ends with a very beautiful but humble prayer, encompassing a cluster of pleas for insight and help. Its tone is "the grace of thankfulness."

Five requests rise before the Lord like Berlioz' "Symphonie Fantastique"—each of the five movements more beautiful than the last: "May my cry come before you" (v. 169). "May my lips overflow with praise" (v. 171). "May my tongue sing of your word" (v. 172). "May your hand be ready to help me" (v. 173). "May your laws sustain me" (v. 175).

> *"The psalm concludes at the end of the Hebrew alphabet, but the song plays on . . . in overflowing praise to God for His exquisite, awe-inspiring, magnificent Law!"*

The psalmist, awed by the magnitude and depth of the divine revelation, recognizes his own need for renewal and revival.

In some ways I'm like that other musician. He knows he's not out of danger yet. He's like a sheep that has strayed from the shepherd's side (v. 176). Lost, he longs to be found and restored to the fold. At least he knows his weakness, and that's the beginning of strength.

The psalm concludes at the end of the Hebrew alphabet, but the song plays on . . . in overflowing praise to God for His exquisite, awe-inspiring, magnificent Law!

Personal prayer

O Lord, may my lips overflow with praise today and may my tongue sing of Your Word!

A HYMN OF PRAISE

O Word of God Incarnate

O Word of God incarnate, O wisdom from
   on high,
O Truth unchanged, unchanging, O Light of
   our dark sky;
We praise Thee for the radiance that from
   the hallowed page
A lantern to our footsteps, shines on from
   age to age.

The Church for her dear Master received
   the gift divine,
And still that light she lifteth or'e all the
   earth to shine.
It is the golden casket where gems of truth
   are stored;
It is the heav'n-drawn picture of Christ, the
   living Word.

It floateth like a banner before God's host
   unfurled;
It shineth like a beacon above the darkling
   world.
It is the chart and compass that o'er life's
   surging sea,
'Mid mists and rocks and quick-sands, still
   guides, O Christ, to Thee.

Words by William W. How.
Music—"Neuvermehrtes Gesangbuch" Meiningen Arr. by Felix Mendelssohn.

Imperial March

War

Exposition of theme
PSALM 120

I call on the Lord in my distress, and he answers me. Save me, O Lord, from lying lips and from deceitful tongues. What will he do to you, and what more besides, O deceitful tongue? He will punish you with a warrior's sharp arrows, with burning coals of the broom tree (vv. 1–4).

Development of theme

Why does our Christian pilgrimage seem to be uphill so much of the time? It was the same for the early believers, who faced a tough climb, literally as well as symbolically.

This "pilgrim song" was sung by ancient Israelis as they journeyed up to Jerusalem for their annual feast days. Psalms 120–134 are also identified as "songs of ascent."

The psalmist has been "burned" by lying lips and deceitful tongues. This personal verbal attack made by warlike adversaries is probably only the beginning of more direct assaults. Still, the sting of a slanderous tongue is enough to launch full-scale war.

In verse 3 he addresses his foes with a question: "What will he do to you, O deceitful tongue?" then answers with vibrant imagery. The wicked will be slain with a "warrior's sharp

"The sting of a slanderous tongue is enough to launch full-scale war. God hates slander, lying, deceit, and gossip! They are out of place for the Christian and ought to be replaced by thanksgiving-talk!"

arrows" and "with burning coals" (v. 4). The broom tree is mentioned because its excellent firewood burns bright, long, and hot!

From these verses I learn that God does not deal lightly with untamed tongues. He hates slander, lying, deceit, and gossip! Because individuals are made in the image of God, they are to be treated with dignity and respect, and we are not allowed to speak in an unrestrained manner about them. How typical it is to run rough-shod over God's precious children! Paul speaks against "obscenity, foolish talk, and coarse joking" (Ephesians 5:4). He tells us they are out of place for the Christian and ought to be replaced by thanksgiving-talk!

Personal prayer

Bridle my tongue, Lord, and keep me from speaking irreverently or thoughtlessly. Keep a song on my lips rather than shallow speech.

Imperial March

Peace

Exposition of theme
PSALM 120 CONTINUED

Woe to me that I dwell in Meshech, that I live among the tents of Kedar! Too long have I lived among those who hate peace. I am a man of peace; but when I speak, they are for war (vv. 5–7).

Development of theme

War and peace have long been the topic of lively discussions among political analysts, writers, and thinkers of all generations. But even in these vexing people for too long and ends his song in clashing discord: "I am a man of peace, but when I speak, they are for war" (v. 7).

If we are to be salt and light in a hostile world, we can expect the same kind of opposition. But we have the consolation of a Friend who walks and talks with us and will make us special, distinctive, and unique as we live in our secular culture.

Personal prayer

Lord, as I dwell in "Meshech and among the tents of Kedar," may I keep quiet appointments with You for strength and solace in this foreign land.

A CONTEMPORARY LYRIC

I'll Walk and Talk with Him Today

This world is not my permanent place —
A barren desert land;
But trav'ling this wasteland by His grace,
I'll hold His mighty hand.

This life can be a crowded arcade —
A busy thoroughfare;
Yet quiet appointments can be made
With Jesus anywhere.

I'll walk and talk with Him today
Relating as friend to Friend;
My Lord will lead me thru life's way
As I walk and talk with Him today.

Words and music by Don Wyrtzen. © 1975 Singspiration.

---

peacetime, believers are not at home in this world. Until Jesus comes, there will be, at best, an uneasy truce between the forces of good and evil.

The psalmist laments that he dwells among peoples with whom he has nothing in common. Meshech, located southeast of the Black Sea, was a remote, barbaric tribe (Genesis 10:2). Kedar, south of Damascus in the Syrian desert, was about as far from Meshech as one could get. He was saying, in effect: "I'm surrounded by warlike, nomadic Ismaelites!" He has lived with

Pilgrim Song of Assurance

Thesis: The Lord is My Help

Exposition of theme

PSALM 121

I lift up my eyes to the hills — where does my help come from? My help comes from the LORD, the Maker of heaven and earth (vv. 1–2).

Development of theme

Last summer, while on vacation in New York state, I decided to climb Mt. Colden, one of the steepest peaks in the Adirondacks. Along with several relatives, I started out and, by late afternoon, we had covered approximately ten miles to the top and back! Even though I could barely walk for the next three days, the exhilarating rush of achievement and the view from the top of the mountain were worth a little temporary discomfort!

Mountains were significant in the life of Israel. Not only did they provide natural fortifications

> **"Watching National Geographic documentaries on TV or videotape will never produce the same heady effect as breathing in fresh, clean air and seeing the view from the top!"**

against invading armies, but the mountains were places of comfort and security. Since Jerusalem rested on a cluster of hills, the whole area came to be associated with the Holy City — the dwelling place of Yahweh.

On his way to Jerusalem, this pilgrim observes the surrounding mountains. "Where does my help come from?" (v. 1) he asks, then answers his own question: "My help comes from the LORD, the Maker of heaven and earth" (v. 2). Part of that creation was the thrusting up and heaving of the earth to form the rounded hills and majestic mountains. Noticing His dramatic creation prompts us to remember the Creator.

Vicarious exposure to nature doesn't take the place of being there. Watching National Geographic documentaries on TV or videotape will never produce the same heady effect as breathing in fresh, clean air and seeing the view from the top! We need these reminders of the permanence of God's creative care and His help.

Personal prayer

Precious Lord, remove the cataracts from my eyes. May I be reminded of Your comfort and security when I behold the grandeur of Your mountains!

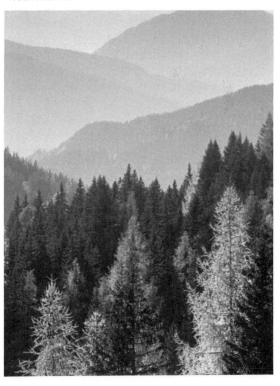

Pilgrim Song of Assurance

Development: Helping in All Eventualities

Exposition of theme

PSALM 121 CONTINUED

He will not let your foot slip — he who watches over you will not slumber; indeed, he who watches over Israel will neither slumber nor sleep. The LORD watches over you — the LORD is your shade at your right hand; the sun will not harm you by day, nor the moon by night. The LORD will keep you from all harm — he will watch over your life; the LORD will watch over your coming and going both now and forevermore (vv. 3–8).

Development of theme

The Divine Watchman! This psalm of assurance gives me a fresh glimpse of God as the One who keeps watch over His children night and day. In the words of the old spiritual, "He never sleeps, He never slumbers."

Perhaps a Levite priest, accompanying the pilgrim on his journey, is speaking here. Note the change in pronouns from *I* and *my* to *you.* He reassures the traveler of the Lord's divine protection as he walks the rugged terrain. We can feel the same sense of protection on crowded superhighways, in high-crime neighborhoods, and on the streets of the inner city. The priest also suggests that God — unlike the Canaanite fertility

> "We can feel the Lord's protection on crowded superhighways, in high-crime neighborhoods, and on the streets of the inner city."

gods — never goes off duty or takes a nap on the job.

The Lord Himself guards us — not some common soldier on night watch! He "watches over" every aspect of our lives — our "comings and goings," our times of rest and recreation. He whose eye is on the sparrow promises to keep an eye on me!

Personal prayer

Precious Lord, thank You for Your watchcare in all circumstances at all times. I can rest, knowing You neither slumber nor sleep.

A SONG OF GOD'S CARE

His Eye Is on the Sparrow

Why should I feel discouraged?
Why should the shadows come?
Why should my heart be lonely
And long for heav'n and home
When Jesus is my portion?
My constant friend is He:
His eye is on the sparrow,
And I know He watches me.

I sing because I'm happy,
I sing because I'm free;
His eye is on the sparrow,
And I know He watches me.

Words by Mrs. C. D. Martin. Music by Charles H. Gabriel.

Pilgrimage to Jerusalem

The Splendor of the Holy City

Exposition of theme

PSALM 122

I rejoiced with those who said to me, "Let us go to the house of the LORD." Our feet are standing in your gates, O Jerusalem. Jerusalem is built like a city that is closely compacted together. That is where the tribes go up, the tribes of the LORD, to praise the name of the LORD according to the statute given to Israel. There the thrones for judgment stand, the thrones of the house of David (vv. 1–5).

Development of theme

Do we drag our heels on Sunday morning or look forward to worship services? Do we expect to meet God there, or do we fail to find Him in our empty ritual and meaningless form?

David has an entirely different attitude as he

> **"Do we drag our heels on Sunday morning or look forward to worship services? Do we expect to meet God there, or do we fail to find Him in our empty ritual and meaningless form?"**

approaches the gates of Jerusalem. His heart is filled with joy and expectancy. "I rejoiced with those who said to me, "Let us go to the house of the LORD" (v. 1). He loves the capital city and looks forward to participating in one of the great festivals of worship there.

Located within the walls are the royal palace, administrative buildings, and sturdy homes of prominent citizens. The entire complex is solidly and compactly constructed. The psalmist also praises it as a civic and spiritual center, where justice is administered and the tribes congregate to praise the name of the Lord.

Jerusalem, teeming with people and activities of all kinds, was an exciting place to visit. One day the New Jerusalem will be the gathering place of peoples of all nations, and the Lord will be glorified forever! For a look at the New Jerusalem, turn to Revelation 21 and read about the Holy City "coming down out of heaven from God as a bride beautifully dressed for her husband."

Personal prayer

Lord, make Your house an exciting place for me to visit. May our worship together become an enriching, exhilarating experience.

Pilgrimage to Jerusalem

Prayer for Peace

Exposition of theme

PSALM 122 *CONTINUED*

Pray for the peace of Jerusalem: "May those who love you be secure. May there be peace within your walls and security within your citadels." For the sake of my brothers and friends, I will say, "Peace be within you." For the sake of the house of the LORD our God, I will seek your prosperity (vv. 6–9).

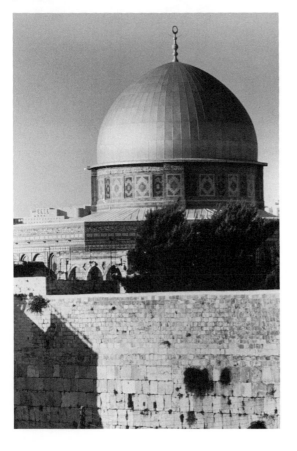

Development of theme

Ancient Israelis were not only to take pride in their capital city, but also to pray for its security. Jerusalem has been a focal point, a hot spot, for centuries. Here David prays for the welfare of his beloved city and for the personal security of others who love her. He prays that there will be peace within the walls and security within the citadels — the two outside limits of the city.

More important than the city or its inhabitants, however, is the house of the Lord. David prays for its prosperity. The King James phrase, "I will seek thy good" (v. 9), is rendered by Luther, "I will seek what is best for you."

We live in a rootless society. Many factors contribute to rootlessness — mobility, industrialization, domestic upheaval, isolation, alienation, etc. The foundations are crumbling. We have

> **"We live in a rootless society. The foundations are crumbling. Our identities are threatened. We feel lost. We have become a society of vagabonds!"**

downplayed community and stressed individualism. Our identities are threatened. We feel lost. We have become a society of vagabonds!

David's roots were in his Lord, his nation, his city, his family. He was not a loner — isolated from culture and tradition, nor was he insulated from regular interaction with people. He was part of a congregation of believers, and his unselfish prayer stretches beyond the bounds of his day to embrace believers of all generations. We are reminded to pray for the peace of Jerusalem!

Personal prayer

Lord, as I pray for the peace of Jerusalem, fill me also with Your serenity and security.

Song of the Slave

Submission to God

Exposition of theme

PSALM 123

I lift up my eyes to you, to you whose throne is in heaven. As the eyes of slaves look to the hand of their master, as the eyes of a maid look to the hand of her mistress, so our eyes look to the LORD our God, till he shows us his mercy (vv. 1–2).

Development of theme

Maclaren, internationally celebrated Scottish pulpiteer, called this psalm "a sigh and an upward gaze and a sigh!"

In this brief passage, a slave lifts his eyes to God and cries out for mercy and deliverance from contempt. He places himself in complete submission to God with the faith that the One who sits enthroned in the heavens can help him. He finds his confidence in the exalted majesty of God. As a slave looks to his master and as a maid looks to her mistress, so also do "our eyes look to the LORD our God, till he shows us his mercy" (v. 2).

Many times I'm unaware that I need help until some crisis or tragedy sharply reminds me that I am very human and needy! Even then, I often go to the wrong sources of help. Experts have their place, but they can never substitute for trust in the Lord who is our ultimate Help.

One of Mom's favorite songs was "There Is No Problem." When I play it, I think of her and of her loving counsel.

Personal prayer

May I lift up my eyes to You, today, O Lord, and lay my burdens at Your throne.

"Many times I'm unaware that I need help until some crisis or tragedy sharply reminds me that I am very human and needy!"

A CONTEMPORARY LYRIC

There Is No Problem

There is no problem
that Jesus cannot solve,
And not a need
He cannot satisfy;

There is no heartache
He cannot understand,
He is omniscient
and knows the reasons why.

CHORUS
So I can trust Him
when I'm hurting deep inside —
And I can pray to Him
in whom I may confide;
There is no pain
my Lord has never known
Because He's Lord,
I lay my burdens at His throne.

There is no valley
where Jesus has not been,
And not a test
that He has ever failed;

There is no conflict
He cannot comprehend —
He is the Savior
Who on a cross was nailed.

Words and music by Don Wyrtzen. © 1981 by Singspiration.

Song of the Slave

Release From Contempt

Exposition of theme

PSALM 123 CONTINUED

Have mercy on us, O LORD, have mercy on us, for we have endured much contempt. We have endured much ridicule from the proud, much contempt from the arrogant (vv. 3–4).

Development of theme

This is an earnest plea for deliverance from contempt and ridicule. Wounded and hurting, the author cries out, "LORD, have mercy on us!" (v. 3).

At times, an agonized cry for mercy is the only recourse we can take. Christians, in all walks and circumstances of life, have had to take it on the chin for their faith.

The Apostle Paul had more than his share: "Five times I received from the Jews the forty

> *"The Lord must laugh at our complaints. We're soft! We need to toughen up and learn how to take anything the Enemy can dish out!"*

lashes minus one. Three times I was beaten with rods, once I was stoned, three times I was shipwrecked, I spent a night and a day in the open sea, I have been constantly on the move. I have been in danger from rivers, in danger from bandits, in danger from my own countrymen, in danger from Gentiles; in danger in the city, in danger in the country, in danger at sea. . . . I have labored and toiled and have often gone without sleep; I have known hunger and thirst and have often gone without food; I have been cold and naked" (2 Corinthians 11:24–27).

This missionary martyr suffered for *doing* God's will; he didn't suffer for *not doing* God's will. Under abnormal stress and pressure, he reached unscaled heights of achievement, exploits, and excellence — not the least of which was writing almost half of the New Testament!

For it was Paul who also said, "I consider that our present sufferings are not worth comparing with the glory that will be revealed in us" (Romans 8:18).

The Lord must laugh at our complaints. We're soft! We need to toughen up and learn how to take anything the Enemy can dish out because "the one who is in you is greater than the one who is in the world (1 John 4:4)."

Personal prayer

O Lord, I'm ashamed when I read the recital of injustices and wrongs committed against the great saints of the ages. Help me to shape up as Your man in my own hostile environment.

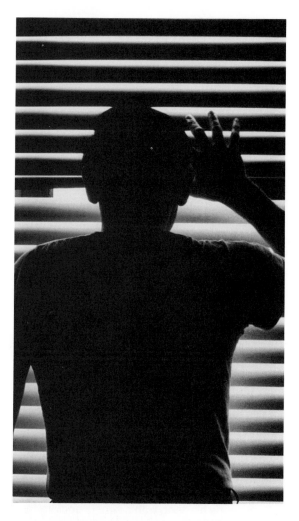

Deliverance in the Dorian Mode

First Motif: Protection

Exposition of theme

PSALM 124

If the Lord had not been on our side—let Israel say—if the Lord had not been on our side when men attacked us, when their anger flared against us, they would have swallowed us alive; the flood would have engulfed us, the torrent would have swept over us, the raging waters would have swept us away (vv. 1–5).

Development of theme

The dorian mode is a musical scale which sounds somewhat like minor. Melodies written in this mode have a somber feeling. David has narrowly escaped grave danger, and his song gives the impression that he is still gasping for breath!

> **"I haven't yet been asked to put my life on the line for my faith, but I have felt the flood waters of emotional pressure engulfing me."**

THE LANGUAGE OF MUSIC

Dorian Mode

The church modes were a medieval system of scales.

The first authentic mode (scale) is called dorian (the white keys on the piano from D to D). The mood is dark, melancholy, and somber. It is the basis for much folk music.

If the Lord had not delivered him, the surrounding nations would have "swallowed [him] alive" (v. 3).

Not only is David's life in jeopardy, but the entire nation of Israel is at risk. Enraged heathen nations pursue God's precious jewel like a flash flood that can swiftly destroy everything in its path.

These verses comprise more than a footnote in ancient history. This is a crisis of major proportions—a situation in which an entire nation can

343

be obliterated from the earth! But God intervened and protected them.

I haven't yet been asked to put my life on the line for my faith, but I have felt the flood waters of emotional pressure engulfing me. I know what it's like to feel pain from crisis in close personal relationships and from trauma related to upheaval in the circumstances of life. These verses are a reminder to me that God is always with me to sustain and uphold me. Since the Lord is on my side, I will never be swallowed up or destroyed. Nothing and no one can harm me. I'm safe!

Personal prayer

I praise You for being on my side and for Your protection in all kinds of danger — internal and external.

world can give me hope and help?

David's metaphor of the bird in the fowler's net is so appropriate. Israel was that "bird" enmeshed in the strands of the net, ripe to be torn by the teeth of wild animals (v.6). The Lord broke the framework and allowed the bird to fly free, suggesting the utter helplessness of the trapped

> *"He is the Creator of heaven and earth. He is also quite competent to sustain His creation and to hear the helpless cries of His creatures."*

one and the need for radical intervention from the outside.

No wonder David bursts forth with thanksgiving and praise! "Praise be to the LORD" (v. 6) who has marvelously revealed His power to come to the aid of the weak. Because he is the great Creator of heaven and earth, He is also quite competent to sustain His creation and to hear the helpless cries of His creatures.

David ends his song with a simple declaration of faith. I return to my own original question: "What in the world can give me hope and help?" Maybe that's just it! True intervention and help don't exist "in the world"! David's overwhelmingly satisfying answer is good enough for me: "My help is in the name of the LORD, the Maker of heaven and earth" (v. 8). I claim that promise!

Personal prayer

May I place complete confidence in Your ability to help me today, O Lord, whatever I may be facing.

OCTOBER 30

Deliverance in the Dorian Mode

Second Motif: Help

Exposition of theme

PSALM 124 CONTINUED

Praise be to the LORD, who has not let us be torn by their teeth. We have escaped like a bird out of the fowler's snare; the snare has been broken, and we have escaped. Our help is in the name of the LORD, the Maker of heaven and earth (vv. 6–8).

Development of theme

I probably don't realize just how spiritually destitute I am! To add more stress, I sometimes ponder the uncertainty of the future. What in the

Hymn of Trust

Security

Exposition of theme

PSALM 125

Those who trust in the LORD are like Mount Zion, which cannot be shaken but endures forever. As the mountains surround Jerusalem, so the LORD surrounds his people both now and forevermore. The scepter of the wicked will not remain over the land allotted to the righteous, for then the righteous might use their hands to do evil (vv. 1–3).

Development of theme

This is a beautiful hymn about the inner security of believers—both in the time of David and for today.

The nation Israel was in grave danger of being dominated by foreign powers, but the Lord promises His people that He will not allow this scepter of wickedness to remain over them as long as they place their trust in Him (v. 3). A New Testament quotation comes to mind: "God is faithful; he will not let you be tempted beyond what you can bear. But when you are tempted, he will also provide a way out so that you can stand up under it" (1 Corinthians 10:13).

If Israel will just trust in the Lord, they will be blessed with a deep sense of inner security and unshakability. They will be like Mount Zion which

is solid and immovable. They will be like a mountain rooted deeply in the bed-rock of the earth. The Lord's protective care will encircle them at all times like the mountains surrounding Jerusalem. He will be for them an impregnable wall of defense.

My sense of security cannot be based on quality in human relationships or the relative stability of life's circumstances. It must rest squarely on the Lord Himself who is immutable and unchanging. He is my mountain! I must believe that, apart from the irrationality of my feelings. Then I will be secure . . . whether I feel like it or not!

Personal prayer

I thank You, Lord, that my security is like Mount Zion, unshakable and deeply embedded in Your attributes.

> **"My sense of security cannot be based on quality in human relationships or the relative stability of life's circumstances. It must rest squarely on the Lord Himself who is immutable and unchanging. He is my mountain!"**

Blessed are all who fear the LORD, who walk in His ways. PSALM 128:1

PANORAMA PHOTO BY GARY IRVING

Hymn of Trust

Prayer for Personal Integrity

Exposition of theme

PSALM 125 CONTINUED

Do good, O Lord, to those who are good, to those who are upright in heart. But those who turn to crooked ways the Lord will banish with the evildoers. Peace be upon Israel (vv. 4–5).

Development of theme

The term *falsetto* refers to "an unnaturally or artificially high-pitched voice or register, especially in a man." In early music, prior to 1600, singers especially trained in falsetto sang the high parts of masses and motets. These tones, tending to

short-lived. On the other hand, God's reward for arrow-straight, true-pitch living is eternal life in His presence and His "Well done!"

Personal prayer

Give me a vision of You, Lord — unshakable, unchangeable, and secure. Keep me true and straight!

> **"I struggle to remain perfectly true to my calling as a Christian musician in a world that loves artificiality and pretense."**

be nasal and weak, are mostly used today for comic effect.

Here the psalmist contrasts the "upright" (straight-as-an-arrow, honest, unswerving in principle) with the "crooked" (bent, devious, dishonest, untrue). God calls me to "be real" in my relationship with Him. He expects me to stay true and not to deviate from the course He has assigned me. Genuine godliness will be blessed, while those who "bend" His rules or adopt a "falsetto" approach to life will be "banished with the evildoers" (v. 5).

I struggle to remain perfectly true to my calling as a Christian musician in a world that loves artificiality and pretense — "a good show." But the applause of the crowd, while sweet to the ear, is

---

A MEANINGFUL LYRIC

To Be What You Want Me To Be

To be what You want me to be, dear Lord,
   I'll live for eternity;
To be more like Your Son, dear Lord —
   I've only just begun.

To be what You want me to be, dear Lord,
   I'll live for eternity;
To be more like Your Son, dear Lord,
   Until the race is won.

To be what You want me to be, dear Lord,
   I'll live so the world can see
The image of Your Son, dear Lord —
   Unite our hearts as one.

Words and music by Don Wyrtzen © 1972 Singspiration

A Brief Jubilate

Joy and Restoration

Exposition of theme

PSALM 126

When the LORD brought back the captives to Zion, we were like men who dreamed. Our mouths were filled with laughter, our tongues with songs of joy. Then it was said among the nations, "The LORD has done great things for them." The LORD has done great things for us, and we are filled with joy (vv. 1–3).

Development of theme

Anyone who has ever experienced the loss of a loved one, financial reverses, serious illness, or imprisonment of any kind will treasure this psalm! The first few verses vibrate with the sheer joy of deliverance after long years of burden-bearing and captivity!

Most likely, the psalmist is referring to the time immediately after the return of the nation Israel from its exile in Babylon (537 B.C.). Happiness and exuberance reign supreme. God's people probably have to pinch themselves to believe they are really free! Laughter comes easily. Jubilant shouting is heard often. The Israelites, in typical Oriental abandonment, release their pent-up feelings in a flood of healing, restorative praise.

The Gentile outsiders looking on say in amazement, "The LORD has done great things for them!" (v. 2). No nation has ever been restored after deportation! It is as incomprehensible to these ancient people as it would be if the Soviet Union suddenly decided to release all their political prisoners!

It is this euphoric sensation of delight and joy that should seize me every time I meditate on all the great things the Lord has done for me. If I spent more time dwelling on God's major triads — "the great things" — there would be less time for the minor irritations and frustrations of life!

Personal prayer

Remind me, O Lord, of the major triumphs You have accomplished in my behalf — my salvation, my eternal security, my constant protection — and don't let my song lapse into a minor mode!

> **"If I spent more time dwelling on God's major triads — my salvation, my eternal security, my constant protection — there would be less time for the minor irritations and frustrations of life."**

NOVEMBER 3

A Brief Jubilate

Hope and Full Deliverance

Exposition of theme

PSALM 126 CONTINUED

Restore our fortunes, O LORD, like streams in the Negev. Those who sow in tears will reap with songs of joy. He who goes out weeping, carrying seed to sow, will return with songs of joy, carrying sheaves with him (vv. 4–6).

Development of theme

Unless you know something of the topography of Israel, you can't fully understand the faith demonstrated by the psalmist in this prayer.

The Negev—the desert south of Judah—con-tains many "wadis" that are bone-dry eleven months of the year. But in the twelfth month, during the rainy season, these dry stream beds quickly fill with water and become raging torrents. This psalm cries out for that kind of dramatic change in the history of Israel as the captives flow back to their native land.

The second metaphor is equally graphic. Before irrigation, sowing and reaping in this barren part of the world were extremely difficult. Seed was often sown with little prospect of harvest. Yet the ancient musician believes that God will send life-giving rains and, even after long neglect, that the desert will bloom once more. The weeping sowers will return "with songs of joy" to greet the returning captives.

What a comfort to know that the Lord can take my dried-up, unproductive life and drench it with His showers of blessing! All the self-improvement courses and how-to books in the world combined with herculean human effort cannot begin to match the incomparable grace and mercy of God!

Personal prayer

Lord, change the dry, barren riverbeds of my life into raging streams in the desert.

"What a comfort to know that the Lord can take my dried-up, unproductive life and drench it with His showers of blessing!"

A GOSPEL SONG

There Shall Be Showers of Blessing

There shall be showers of blessing:
This is the promise of love;
There shall be seasons refreshing,
Sent from the Savior above.

Showers of blessing,
Showers of blessing we need:
Mercydrops around us are falling,
But for the showers we plead.

Words by Daniel W. Whittle (Based on Ezekiel 34:26).
Music by James McGranahan.

350

Solomon's Pilgrim Psalm

Futility of Work Apart from God

Exposition of theme

PSALM 127

Unless the LORD builds the house, its builders labor in vain. Unless the LORD watches over the city, the watchmen stand guard in vain. In vain you rise early and stay up late, toiling for food to eat — for he grants sleep to those he loves (vv. 1–2).

Development of theme

Solomon, the wisest man who ever lived and one of the greatest kings of Israel, teaches us that it is useless to attempt anything without God's approval and blessing whether it be building a house, making a home, guarding a city, earning a living, or even trying to get a decent night's sleep!

There is a simple interdependence in all of life — a basic theme that underlies the complex movements of our daily existence. That theme is the sovereignty of God — the fact that as Number One in the universe, He has everything under His control.

A building contractor can erect a house, but, whether he acknowledges it or not, he's dependent upon the Lord for the right weather conditions, raw materials for building supplies, and the strength to build. A couple can get married and start a family, but unless they practice faith in the Lord, there is less than a 50 percent chance that their marriage will survive. An army can be mustered to defend cities and countries, but true peace comes only from God. Inspiration for

> *"To attempt anything without God's help is like trying to get my sailboat to tack by blowing into the sail. I have to wait for the breath of God!"*

worthwhile artistic achievement is God's gift. The ability to earn a living — both talent and drive as well as health and stamina — are His gifts. And even relief from one's labors — refreshing sleep — comes from the hand of a loving Father.

Diligence without divine blessing is an exercise in futility. For me to attempt anything without God's help is like trying to get my sailboat to tack by blowing into the sail. I have to wait for the breath of God!

Personal prayer

Lord, I confess my utter dependence on You. Teach me to wait on inspiration from You in all my endeavors.

A FOOTNOTE ON SOLOMON

Solomon's name in Hebrew is "shalmōh," "peaceable." He was the third and last king of a united Israel. He built the kingdom to its greatest strength in terms of material prosperity, geographic extension, and military might. Though very wise and intelligent, Solomon in his later years lost his spiritual discernment. His life style became political, amoral, voluptuous, and apostate. This formerly wise king brought the nation to the brink of dissolution.

Solomon's Pilgrim Psalm

Reward of Children Sent from God

Exposition of theme

PSALM 127 *CONTINUED*

Sons are a heritage from the LORD, children a reward from him. Like arrows in the hands of a warrior are sons born in one's youth. Blessed is the man whose quiver is full of them. They will not be put to shame when they contend with their enemies in the gate (vv. 3–5).

Development of theme

Many young couples in our society seem to be content to remain childless. Their two-paycheck incomes buy a lot of convenience and a lot of "stuff." But few of them realize how children can enrich life by forcing us outside our self-centered routines. Few of them understand that children stretch our horizons and prompt us to higher goals. Few of them ever consider how lonely they'll be in old age. And almost nobody ever mentions the importance of bringing up godly children to build a dynamic Christian community that can impact our culture and civilization!

Part of the current erosion of the family is simply that children are undervalued. They are often viewed as excess baggage, an inconvenience. They seem to get in the way of career aspirations, create pressure on the woman, robbing her of youth and beauty and sapping her energy.

> *"From the Oriental point of view, children were seen as 'a heritage from the LORD,' a reward, and tokens of His grace."*

352

They are considered, by some, as more of a liability than an asset.

How different from the Oriental point of view! Children were seen as "a heritage from the LORD" (v. 3), a reward, and tokens of His grace. Furthermore, the possibility of becoming the mother of the Messiah was the coveted goal of young Hebrew women.

To the Hebrew man, adult children were regarded as a means of defense—"arrows in the hands of a warrior" (v. 4) and support—"when they contend with their enemies in the gate" (v. 5). Cases were tried and business was transacted at the gates of the city, and if a man were to encounter difficulty, he could count on his grown sons to lend strength to his argument.

Biblical couples considered children a special gift from God. Those who were childless or who had lost a child expressed their grief openly (Genesis 30:1; 1 Samuel 1:3–17). Infertile couples now have some medical options to improve the chances of pregnancy, or, failing that, might consider adoption. Still, God sets aside very special people who will neither get married nor have children because of their unique calling. God has not placed us on an assembly line. He loves to handcraft Rolls Royces!

A few years ago I expressed my dreams for my own family in a prayer song entitled, *Bless Our Home.*

Personal prayer

Dear Lord, I thank You for D. J. and Kathy and for the love and support they give me.

NOVEMBER 6

Count Your Many Blessings

Present Blessings

Exposition of theme

PSALM 128

Blessed are all who fear the LORD, who walk in his ways. You will eat the fruit of your labor; blessings and prosperity will be yours. Your wife will be like a fruitful vine within your house; your sons will be like olive shoots around your table. Thus is the man blessed who fears the LORD (vv. 1–4).

Development of theme

"Blessed (supremely happy) is the person who has meaningful work and a fruitful family." This paraphrase of Psalm 128 reduces the abundant life to its simplest terms. Yet many in our contemporary society, including Christians, take such humble gifts for granted and expect more!

Solomon, in all of his brilliance and wisdom, takes us back to the basics. Fearing God (reverencing and obeying Him) will bring blessing, he

> *"Many in contemporary society, including Christians, take for granted the blessed gifts of meaningful work and a fruitful family—and expect more!"*

states. Then he enumerates the gifts of grace that follow: food to sustain life, productive work, and family. The wife and mother is depicted as a "fruitful vine"; the children, little "olive shoots" (v. 3). This metaphor of a bountiful table is God's true picture of prosperity and happiness, not material wealth.

Personal prayer

Lord, help me to fear You and walk in Your way today. Give my wife and children a special touch of Your grace so they may bask in the happiness of Your presence with them.

Count Your Blessings

Count your blessings — name them one by
one;
Count your blessings — see what God hath
done;
Count your blessings — name them one by
one;
Count your many blessings — see what God
hath done.

When you look at others with their lands
and gold,
Think that Christ has promised you His
wealth untold;
Count your many blessings — money cannot
buy
Your reward in heaven nor your home on
high.

Words by Johnson Oatman, Jr.   Music by Edwin O. Excell.

NOVEMBER 7

Count Your Many Blessings

Future Blessings

Exposition of theme

PSALM 128 CONTINUED

*May the LORD bless you from Zion all the days of
your life; may you see the prosperity of Jerusalem, and may you live to see your children's children. Peace by upon Israel (vv. 5–8).*

Development of theme

The psalmist moves now from individual happiness in the context of a single family to national
prosperity within the context of the nation of Israel. He longs to see Jerusalem, the City of Zion,

> *"We make much of the sins of the
> fathers being visited on future
> generations, but fail to speak of
> the blessings of the righteous fil-
> tering down through the
> generations."*

prospering and flourishing all the days of his life.
From her, blessings will flow out to all nations on
earth.

The young father pictured earlier in the psalm
is now a grandfather, observing the blessings of
the Lord falling on many generations. We make
much of the sins of the fathers being visited on
future generations, but fail to speak of the blessings of the righteous filtering down through the
generations (vv. 3, 4, 6).

I remember well my paternal grandparents.
They both died when I was seven years old.
However, since they lived in our home during
their latter years, they left an indelible impression of security and godliness.

The psalmist concludes with a lovely benediction: "Peace be upon Israel!" Thus, he expresses for all of us the deepest longing of our
hearts — peace. Deep personal peace doesn't
come from things. It flows from warm, intimate
relationships and from a close walk with God.

Personal prayer

*Dear Lord, as we learn to walk more consistently
by Your side, give us the peace that passes
human understanding. If You don't come soon,
may I live to hear my grandchildren singing
Your praises!*

Opus of Oppression

Deliverance

Exposition of theme

PSALM 129

They have greatly oppressed me from my youth — let Israel say they have greatly oppressed me from my youth, but they have not gained the victory over me. Plowmen have plowed my back and made their furrows long. But the LORD is righteous; he has cut me free from the cords of the wicked (vv. 1–4).

Development of theme

We desperately need to grapple with a theology of suffering. Many Christians are surprised and even shocked when they're called upon to experience any degree of pain. This leads to a feeling of displacement, dislocation, even disinheritance. We may be confused and feel a profound sense of injustice. We may feel that more was promised than was delivered. Our doubt, anger, and resentment may even shake the foundations of our faith.

This psalmist laments, in a kind of summary, all of the national disasters that have befallen his people and prays for the overthrow of their enemies. Israel has suffered indignity, ignominy, and hostility for generations. She has been besieged continuously by the Canaanites, the Aramaeans, the Ammonites, the Edomites, the Philistines, the Assyrians, and the Chaldeans. He remembers many such attacks from his youth, but he also recalls that the enemy has never prevailed against him for long.

The literary figure is gripping! Israel is pictured as a poor wretch lying face down on the ground as plowmen cut deep furrows in the tender flesh. This gives us some ideas of the extreme suffering and severe pain that was commonplace for that nation.

But the psalmist does not dwell on these inhumane acts. He praises the righteous Lord who has delivered his people. He has "cut them free from the cords of the wicked" (v. 4).

Perhaps we need to learn about adversity from ancient Israel. Perhaps we need to remember that suffering is part of being human in a fallen world, that ungodly people suffer too. And perhaps we need to remind ourselves that our God is a righteous God. Justice will ultimately prevail. He has promised victory and deliverance — if not immediately — then in the world to come!

Personal prayer

I thank You, Lord, for Your righteousness. I pray that You will execute justice in my life and by Your mercy cut me free from the cords of wickedness.

Opus of Oppression
Vindication

Exposition of theme

PSALM 129 CONTINUED

May all who hate Zion be turned back in shame. May they be like grass on the roof, which withers before it can grow; with it the reaper cannot fill his hands, nor the one who gathers fill his arms. May those who pass by not say, "The blessing of the Lord be upon you; we bless you in the name of the Lord" (vv. 5–8).

Development of theme

Why does it seem as if the nonbelievers in this world get all the breaks and have all the fun? They live fast, hard, and, it appears, free!

But we can take great comfort in the promise of this psalm. No matter how it may seem, the wicked are doomed to failure. (See Psalm 37:1–2.) This psalmist has the big picture, and

---

> **"Why do nonbelievers get all the breaks and have all the fun? They live fast, hard, and, it appears, free!"**

---

our confusion stems from our limited and cloudy vision.

Still, my ancient colleague covers all his bases and prays for the vindication of his people. He pictures the Israel-haters as tufts of grass on a Palestinian roof. They wither even before the owner has a chance to pluck them. They're not worth the time it takes to weed them out! He'll leave them to the blazing sun of God's wrath.

The psalm ends with a strong suggestion to fellow Israelites to withhold blessing from pass-

ersby on the street. It has always been customary in Israel to greet people by invoking God's blessing on their lives. In this case, the passionate musician/poet holds out for silence: "Don't say, 'The blessing of the Lord be upon you' " (v. 8).

When Karen and I visited Israel, the people often greeted us with a friendly "Shalom" — "Peace be unto you." They're still looking for the fulfillment of prophecy. Justice will prevail in the end, and Israel will be utterly and finally vindicated. It also follows that, if I am suffering unjustly, I can expect satisfaction from a just God. In the meantime, I need to concentrate on my Savior, whose suffering I will never be able to imagine or comprehend in this life (Romans 8:18)!

Personal prayer

I thank You, Lord, that You are the answer to all injustice and inhumanity in this world and that You are still in control. Help me to trust in the fulfillment of that prophecy just as my Israeli neighbors do.

THE LANGUAGE OF MUSIC

Opus
A Latin term meaning "work."

An opus is a musical composition or set of compositions.

Motet of Mercy

Forgiveness

Exposition of theme
PSALM 130

Out of the depths I cry to you, O Lord; O Lord, hear my voice. Let your ears be attentive to my cry for mercy. If you, O Lord, kept a record of sins, O Lord, who could stand? But with you there is forgiveness; therefore you are feared (vv. 1–4).

Development of theme

When I think of God's accounting ability, I cringe, much like the author of this psalm. Suppose every unkind word I had ever spoken, every lie I had ever told, every shortcut I had ever taken, every word of gossip that ever passed my lips, ever lustful thought I had ever entertained, every sin I've ever committed were recorded on audio and videotape to be played back at will?

My fellow musician sums it up succinctly: "Who could stand?" (v. 3).

Though I am saved by grace, I am constantly engaged in a wrestling match between the old sin nature and the new man. As the Apostle Paul complained: "I know that nothing good lives in me, that is, in my sinful nature. For I have the desire to do what is good, but I cannot carry it out. For what I do is not the good I want to do; no, the evil I do not want to do—this I keep on doing" (Romans 7:18–19).

There is a way out, however. It's a one-word

> **"God chooses to pardon the penitent sinner. If He did not, we would all be destroyed by His judgment."**

answer. Forgiveness. In His infinite mercy, God chooses to pardon the penitent sinner (Isaiah 55:6–7). If He did not, we would all be destroyed by His judgment. Because we have been forgiven much, we are able to respond in grateful praise. We will be moved to revere and respect Him, to worship and adore Him, to follow and obey Him!

Personal prayer

I cry out of the depths to You for mercy, O Lord! I need Your forgiveness again and again.

Motet of Mercy

Hope

Exposition of theme
PSALM 130 CONTINUED

I wait for the Lord, my soul waits, and in his word I put my hope. My soul waits for the Lord more than watchmen wait for the morning. . . . O Israel, put your hope in the Lord, for with the Lord is unfailing love and with him is full redemption. He himself will redeem Israel from all their sins (vv. 5–8).

Development of theme

There are several musical terms for "pause" or "rest." Pauses in music, the cessation of sound,

357

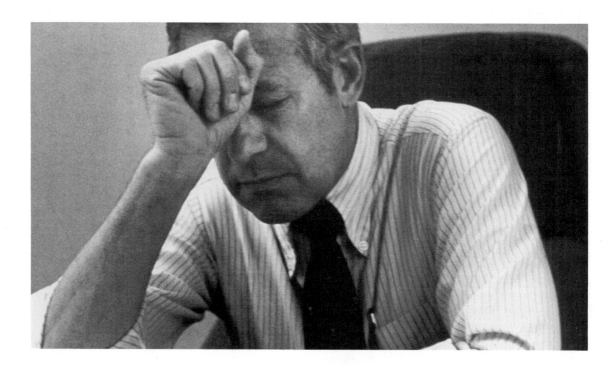

"As I wait in the darkness of uncertainty and human inadequacy, I rest in the fact of His sunrise that is surely coming . . . tomorrow!"

affect the flow of a piece and create variety and diversity. Delay, anticipation, build-up are all crucial in musical dynamics.

This pilgrim psalmist understands the value of patient waiting. Thoroughly familiar with the holy writings of the Old Testament prophets, he trusts the Lord for ultimate fulfillment of His promises — God's unfailing love and His full redemption. Lawrence Richards, in his work, *Expository Dictionary of Bible Words,* says, "It is striking to note that in all the Old Testament's exploration of the meaning of *padah* ("redeem or ransom"), only in Psalm 130:7–8 is this concept associated with redemption from sin." His sovereign hand is not forced by human entreaties unless the time is right. He hears prayer, then acts according to His own schedule.

In ancient times watchmen were posted atop the broad gates of Jerusalem to sound the alert if signs of imminent danger were observed. The night watches were long and arduous. If the watchmen could make it until the first rays of the rising sun, they could rejoice in their security for yet another night. Waiting in darkness merely emphasized the glory of the sunrise!

As I wait in the darkness of uncertainty and human inadequacy, I rest in the fact of His sunrise that is surely coming . . . tomorrow!

Personal prayer

Lord, I'm waiting as patiently as I know how. And in the process of waiting, I find a blessing, for I am looking forward to Your glorious coming and to an eternity spent in Your presence!

Harmony of Humility

Exposition of theme
PSALM 131

My heart is not proud, O LORD, my eyes are not haughty; I do not concern myself with great matters or things too wonderful for me. But I have stilled and quieted my soul; like a weaned child with its mother, like a weaned child is my soul within me. O Israel, put your hope in the LORD both now and forevermore (vv. 1–3).

Development of theme

David's reign as Israel's greatest king was matched by his contributions to art and literature, including the most profound psalm lyrics ever written. While he extended Israel's borders to their limit, made Jerusalem the capital city, and founded an eternal dynasty of which our Lord, the Messiah, descended, he was also a virtuoso harpist and led a sweeping renaissance of Israeli culture. He accomplished this through building

> *"The Lord hates arrogance and pride, which result in overwhelming self-confidence and insensitivity to others."*

THE LANGUAGE OF MUSIC

Harmony
Tones sounded simultaneously as opposed to melody which is a succession of tones.

Harmony can be either consonant (pleasant-sounding) or dissonant (unpleasant-sounding). "How good and pleasant it is when brothers live together in unity" (harmony) Psalm 133:1.

---

instruments, teaching music, and composing the temple liturgy.

With all his worldly "success," David was a humble man with a childlike faith in God. His soul was still and quiet (v. 2) because he was not neurotically driven by selfish ambition. He wrote: "He makes me lie down in green pastures, he leads me beside quiet waters" (Psalm 23:2). As a weaned child no longer needs its mother's milk, he learned to receive his nurture from the Lord: "You prepare a table before me" (Psalm 23:5). His value system was founded on God's eternal principles, not on ego-driven materialism.

The Bible stresses humilty. To the humble, God gives salvation (Psalm 18:27), sustenance (147:6), and grace (Proverbs 3:34). The Lord hates arrogance and pride, which result in overwhelming self-confidence and insensitivity to others. This attitude is self-destructive. David is the consummate model of a creative artist and successful entrepreneur who didn't let his notoriety and fame go to his head. Trusting in the Lord is the opposite of pride and the only route to deeply satisfying human fulfillment.

Personal prayer

O Lord, "lead me beside quiet waters" and give me rest from my obsessive behavior. I'm tired of the pressure I impose on myself. Help me to trust in You today for everything I need.

359

Recitative of Remembrance

Remembering David

Exposition of theme

PSALM 132

O Lord, remember David and all the hardships he endured. He swore an oath to the Lord and made a vow to the Mighty One of Jacob: "I will not enter my house or go to my bed—I will allow no sleep to my eyes, no slumber to my eyelids, till I find a place for the Lord, a dwelling for the Mighty One of Jacob" (vv. 1–5).

Development of theme

It is impossible to overestimate the contribution made by Bill and Gloria Gaither to the gospel music field. Bill's down-to-earth wisdom, combined with Gloria's reflective lyricism, has produced some of our best contemporary songs and hymns—"Because He Lives," "Something Beautiful," "There's Something About That Name," "The Family of God," "Let's Just Praise the Lord," and hundreds more. I love the reality

---

THE LANGUAGE OF MUSIC

Recitative

A rhythmically free declamatory vocal style for delivering a narrative text or a passage in this style.

Examples would be Bach's incomparable recitatives in his *St. Matthew Passion.*

---

of their lives and the passion they bring to their work. Bill has been a friend, advisor, and encourager to me. Both Bill and Gloria have written so many of the praise songs that speak to

people's hearts and enhance our worship experience.

David was such a leader, and this psalm celebrates his devotion to the nation he served and the Lord he worshiped. The nation had been restored from exile in Babylon, and its people were keenly aware of David's legacy.

He evidenced his commitment by swearing an oath that he would not rest until he found a place of worship in which the Lord could dwell. This oath most likely referred to David's intense desire to build the temple (2 Samuel 7). So fervent was this desire that he vowed neither to enter his house nor to sleep until his mission was accomplished (vv. 3–5). Because of this single-minded devotion, God made a covenant (contract) with David. This covenant, with future implications, was extremely significant, particularly during the leadership of Ezra and Nehemiah.

What a mentor David is to me! His commitment to the Lord resulted in concrete action. David was much more than a sentimental, romantic leader; he was serious and committed, and God dealt with him accordingly. What a crying need there is for leaders like this today!

Personal prayer

O Lord, deepen my commitment and conviction. I want to be deadly serious about Your business and my relationship with You.

"These early saints were serious about their faith. Prayer and praise were not perfunctory, for worship was a priority in their lives."

NOVEMBER 14

Recitative of Remembrance

Resolving to worship

Exposition of theme
PSALM 132 CONTINUED

We heard it in Ephrathah, we came upon it in the fields of Jaar: "Let us go to his dwelling place; let us worship at his footstool—arise, O LORD, and come to your resting place, you and the ark of your might. May your priests be clothed with righteousness; may your saints sing for joy." For the sake of David your servant, do not reject your anointed one (vv. 6–10).

Development of theme

Ephrathah? Jaar? What are these places with the strange-sounding names? They were towns where the ark (covenant box) rested in limbo until David moved it to Zion (2 Samuel 6). Ephrathah was an old name for Bethlehem, where our Lord was born. Jaar was also known as Kiriath Jearim—the "city of forests," one of the four leading cities of the Gibeonites (Joshua 9:17).

The ark was God's earthly dwelling—His footstool, in the sense that it was His earthly throne. Because it symbolized the awesome presence of God, the ark often went ahead of the Israeli army in battle.

The people are praying that God will reveal Himself again to them, that their priests will be "clothed with salvation," and that their saints will "sing for joy" (v. 16). The prayer concludes with a petition that David, the "anointed one," will not be rejected. The word *anointed* in Hebrew is *masiah* which is transliterated "Messiah, anointed one." Appearing only thirty-nine times in the Old Testament, this word is often a synonym for "royal office." It is used especially to identify the royal line of David (Psalms 2:2; 18:50; 24:9; 29:10, 132:10, 17).

These early saints were serious about their faith. Prayer and praise were not perfunctory, for worship was a priority in their lives. How human it is to take God for granted! Praise the Lord for the passionate leadership of King David!

Personal prayer

Clothe me with righteousness today, O Lord, that I may sing for joy!

361

Recitative of Righteousness

Reiterating the Lord's Oath

Exposition of theme

PSALM 132 CONTINUED

The LORD swore an oath to David, a sure oath that he will not revoke: "One of your own descendants I will place on your throne—If your sons keep my covenant and the statutes I teach them, then their sons will sit on your throne for ever and ever." For the LORD has chosen Zion, he has desired it for his dwelling: "this is my resting place for ever and ever; here I will sit enthroned, for I have desired it—I will bless her with abundant provisions; her poor will I satisfy with food. I will clothe her priests with salvation, and her saints will ever sing for joy. "Here I will make a horn grow for David and set up a lamp for my anointed one. I will clothe his enemies with shame, but the crown on his head will be resplendent" (vv. 11–18).

Development of theme

This psalm confirms that God's promises will be fulfilled no matter what the circumstances. God had made specific promises to King David about his dynasty—promises regarding the sanctuary and Mount Zion which would be blessed with food for the poor, salvation for the priests, and joy for the saints (vv. 15–16). Under David's reign the tiny land expanded ten times over, became a powerful nation, and occupied almost all the land God had promised to Abraham.

The "burning lamp" is a word picture borrowed from the furnishings of the tabernacle and symbolizing the continuation of David's dynasty which would come to a glorious culmination in David's Greatest Son, the Messiah. The metaphor for the Messiah is the animal horn, an ancient symbol of strength and vigor. This horn, or

powerful ruler, would sprout and flourish. In moving poetry the Lord reiterates His oath to David: From his line would come the Messiah, David's Descendant and the Coming One, the ultimate Priest and King of Israel! The Jewish people living in Jesus' time believed that the Messiah would be a Davidic ruler who would establish the long-promised kingdom. David was God's prototype of the Messiah, His Son.

Whatever my circumstances right now, I can rest in the fact that God fulfills His promises. His covenant is solid and sure. His program is moving along right on schedule. Just as He blessed David, He is about to touch my life in a unique way.

Personal prayer

May I rest in the surety and certainty of Your promises today, O Lord.

The Beauty of Unity

Exposition of theme

PSALM 133

How good and pleasant it is when brothers live together in unity! It is like precious oil poured on the head, running down on the beard, running down on Aaron's beard, down upon the collar of his robes. It is as if the dew of Hermon were falling on Mount Zion. For there the LORD bestows his blessing, even life forevermore (vv. 1–3).

Development of theme

When Israel celebrated her great religious festivals, families came together to worship the Lord. These "homecomings" were accompanied by colorful pageantry and moving music.

Left to right, top row: Joel Wyrtzen, Kathy Wyrtzen, Jonathan Wyrtzen, D.J. Wyrtzen, Tim Oris, Steve Cox, Tami Oris, Kim Cox. **Left to right, middle row:** Karen and Don Wyrtzen, Dave and Mary Wyrtzen, Betsy Oris, Jack and Joan Wyrtzen, Mary-Ann and Dave Cox, Sr., Christine and Ron Wyrtzen. **Left to right, bottom row:** Dave and Carol-Sue Cox-Merkh, holding Shellie Merkh, Jamie Sue Wyrtzen, Jenae Wyrtzen, Dave Merkh, Jr., Ryan Wyrtzen, Joshua Wyrtzen, Cindy and Dave Cox, Jr., holding Timothy Cox.

Last June we had a Wyrtzen family reunion. How I love my own immediate family, but this gave me a chance to see members of my extended family too! My sister Mary-Ann and her husband, Dave Cox, are the founders and directors of the Word of Life Seminary in Brazil. My sister, Betsy, teaches at Mountainside Christian Academy in Schroon Lake, N.Y. My brother, David, with his wife Mary, pastors the Midlothian Bible Church in Texas. My brother, Ron, is a Christian businessman, who sells precision ski boats. His wife, Christine, is a prominent recording artist. My Mom went to be with the Lord a few years ago, but He provided a wonderful new wife for Dad. He and Joan are busy serving the Lord as the founder and first lady of Word of Life International. Each one unique, yet with a common bond of love and unity.

In this passage David agrees that it is "good and pleasant" when believers live in unity, and uses two striking word pictures to illustrate this idea—the "oil" that anointed Aaron and the "dew" from Mount Hermon. The oil of anointing ran down Aaron's beard and onto his breastplate containing the names of the twelve tribes of Israel. So also, the unity of worshipers in Jerusalem will consecrate the nation. Heavy mountain dew from the north fell on Zion, invigorating and nourishing the vegetation. So also, meaningful worship blesses the nation.

I need this reminder of the importance of family and community. In the press of publishing deadlines and concert commitments, I have a tendency to lose touch with family members and even with the local church support group of believers. Strong, creative leaders need to feel part of a caring fellowship and not live and work solo—independently of others.

Personal prayer

O Lord, someday we will all come together for a great Family Reunion. Teach me that I belong to the greater family of God, and make me accountable for keeping up family ties!

Benediction to the Pilgrim Psalms

Exposition of theme
PSALM 134

Praise the LORD, all you servants of the LORD who minister by night in the house of the LORD. Lift up your hands in the sanctuary and praise the LORD. May the LORD, the Maker of heaven and earth, bless you from Zion (vv. 1–3).

Development of theme

I'm intrigued by the relationship between the act of leading people in worship and the boon of personal blessing spelled out in this psalm. This unusual benediction, given by the congregation to their leaders, exhorts the priests and Levites to keep up the good work!

These ministers are encouraged to continue their personal times of devotion in order to undergird their public ministry. Leaders who have to bear heavy burdens for others day and night (v. 1) are especially vulnerable to attacks from the Enemy. When they are physically and emotionally exhausted, their spiritual guard is down. It is imperative, then, that they be lifted up in prayer by members of their congregation, just as Aaron and Hur lifted up Moses' hands during the long hours of the battle with the Amalekites (Exodus 17:8–16).

The final words of this psalm flow like a sooth-

> **Benediction**   The invocation of a blessing to conclude public worship.

ing balm across troubled and tired spirits: "May the LORD, the Maker of heaven and earth, bless you from Zion" (v. 3). Our Lord, not the lifeless pagan gods of the ancient world—such as the Canaanite god, Baal—created the universe and can certainly strengthen His faithful representatives.

I am deeply touched by the significance of this psalm for my own life and work. First, I'm reminded that the effectiveness of my public ministry is dependent, to a great degree, upon keeping a vital and dynamic personal relationship with the Lord. I also have a number of close friends who regularly and faithfully pray for me (Nelson, Bill, Mrs. Meurlin), and a corps of choir members and church musicians who remember to pray for me when they see my name on a piece of music. I have no way of knowing what my life would be without this consistent, loving care and support!

Personal prayer

O Lord, thank You for the intercessory prayer of Christian friends. I am blessed, both by serving You and by the encouragement and concern of those who act as a link for refueling my tired spirit.

> *"I have close friends who faithfully pray for me, and a corps of choir members and church musicians who remember to pray for me when they see my name on a piece of music."*

A Musical Mosaic

A Litany of Praise

Exposition of theme

PSALM 135

*Praise the L*ord*. Praise the name of the L*ord*;*
*Praise him, you servants of the L*ord*, you who*
*minister in the house of the L*ord*, in the courts of*
*the house of our God. Praise the L*ord*, for the*
*L*ord *is good; sing praise to his name, for that is*
*pleasant . . . O house of Israel, praise the L*ord*;*
*O house of Aaron, praise the L*ord*; O house of*
*Levi, praise the L*ord*; you who fear him, praise*
*the L*ord*. Praise be to the L*ord *from Zion, to him*
*who dwells in Jerusalem. Praise the L*ord
(vv. 1–3, 19–21).

Development of theme

Because this psalm is a compilation of quotations from other Old Testament sources, the form is a musical mosaic of praise based on the Law, the Prophets, and the Psalms.

The theme — praise — should be the theme of my life, but how does a busy musician, husband, and father find time for praise? I am not always physically present in the "house of the Lord," but somewhere in transit — torn between the roles I'm called to play in the world in which I live. But I can make praise a priority, then spend those precious moments or hours meditating on God's goodness, greatness, and faithfulness — wherever I am.

Having a daily quiet time with the Lord is vital. I've used many different approaches over the years — reading the Bible through in one year; incorporating five Psalms a day plus one chapter from Proverbs, studying a book of the Bible in depth, with the aid of an excellent commentary; reading the Word aloud; etc. A special blessing comes when I read the Bible and pray with Karen. How easy it is to neglect that precious time!

> **Mosaic**   A decorative piece of art in which small pieces of multicolored material (i.e. tiles) are inlayed to form a picture or pattern.
>
> **Litany**   A prayer consisting of invocations and supplications by the worship leaders with alternate responses by the congregation.

What a missed opportunity!

No one is exempt from the roll call of the faithful. The houses of Israel, Aaron, and Levi (vv. 19–20) include all who fear and reverence the Lord. We are called to praise Him in the house where He dwells — Jerusalem (Zion), for the ancient worshiper; our individual local churches, for the contemporary saint. The psalm ends as it begins, with a mighty "Hallelujah!" ("Praise the Lord!")

Praise is easy for a musician, you say, but what about the person who's tone-deaf or can't carry a tune? I would suggest that you try singing along with one of our major Christian artists on cassette tape. If you're an instrumentalist, play the melody of some hymn or contemporary Christian song. Write down your thoughts about the Lord — whether they rhyme or not — then share them with a friend.

A faithful heart, an earnest desire to please the Lord, a life dedicated to His glory — *these* are the most eloquent songs of praise!

Personal prayer

I join with my ancient Levite brothers, Lord, in praising Your name for Your goodness and faithfulness.

Our God Is In Control

Our God is in control,
Though pressures burden the soul;
He allows both major and minor
In His perfect harmony.

Yes, our God is in control,
Though pressures burden the soul;
His sovereign plan is a symphony
Which will sing for eternity.

As we place our faith in the Lord,
Our worry will decrease;
And when we delight ourselves with His Word,
We sense His perfect peace.

Words and music by Don Wyrtzen. © 1976 by Singspiration.

NOVEMBER 19

A Musical Mosaic

Longing to Praise

Exposition of theme
PSALM 135 CONTINUED

For the LORD has chosen Jacob to be his own, Israel to be his treasured possession. I know that the LORD is great, that our LORD is greater than all gods. The LORD does whatever pleases him, in the heavens and on the earth, in the seas and all their depths. He makes clouds rise from the ends of the earth; he sends lightning with the rain and brings out the wind from his storehouses. . . . Your name, O LORD, endures forever, your renown, O LORD, through all generations. For the LORD will vindicate his people and have compassion on his servants (vv. 4–7, 13–14).

366

> "*I always wanted to please my Dad—to be the best I could be, to perform well in recital, to speak and teach effectively, to achieve so that he would be proud of me.*"

Development of theme

My dad, Jack Wyrtzen, has had an aura of authority about him for as long as I can remember. A man of unusual strength and energy, he founded Word of Life International from scratch. He now ministers in camps, Bible institutes, clubs, concerts, rallies, and through media all over the world.

As you might imagine, his presence has been strongly felt in our home. I always wanted to please him—to be the best I could be, to perform well in recital, to speak and teach effectively, to achieve so that he would be proud of me. His image, in my concept of reality, has profoundly affected my view of God, the transcendent Sovereign of the universe!

The motive behind the praise in this psalm is the sovereignty of God, who chose Israel as His "treasured possession" (v. 4), demonstrated His superiority over pagan deities (v. 5), and still orchestrates all the events of Israel's history — past, present, and future (vv. 8–13).

Knowing that God never changes and that He is as concerned with the daily agenda of Don Wyrtzen as with the affairs of mankind, I am moved to write a song of praise.

Personal prayer

Lord, I acknowledge You as Sovereign — my Complete and Ultimate Authority. I long to please You in everything I think or do.

NOVEMBER 20

A Musical Mosaic

Legacy of Praise

Exposition of theme
PSALM 135 CONTINUED

He struck down the firstborn of Egypt, the firstborn of men and animals. He sent his signs and wonders into your midst, O Egypt, against Pharaoh and all his servants. He struck down many nations and killed mighty kings — Sihon king of the Amorites, Og king of Bashan and all the kings of Canaan — and he gave their land as an inheritance, an inheritance to his people Israel (vv. 8–12).

Development of theme

Two Hebrew words are linked to the concept of inheritance — y*aras,* which means "to become an heir" or "to take possession," and *nahal,* which indicates "giving or receiving property." The Lord promised an unbelievable inheritance

> *"I've known the joy of walking in green pastures with my Lord. I've sensed His breath on my soul and have been inspired to compose songs and musicals to His glory."*

to Israel, and modern Israel's expansion is motivated by a strong belief in this ancient right. So far, Karen and I haven't lived long enough to inherit property, possessions, or money from parents or other relatives, so we have to use our imagination to grasp this.

But a forty-acre farm or $100,000 in bonds could never be compared to the inheritance of Israel. God's people inherited "many nations" (v. 10)! And the legacy lives on, to be fulfilled only when the Lord returns to reign in the New Jerusalem!

Again, the historical events surrounding Israel's inheritance are catalogued — the "signs and wonders" God sent against the Egyptians, culminating in the killing of their firstborn (v. 8); God's leadership in the occupation of Canaan, including His divine intervention in the overthrow of heathen kings (vv. 11–12).

I share in this legacy of love and praise. I've been delivered from sin and have received God's gift of grace. I've felt His work in my life as He overthrows bastions of fear, insecurity, and depression. I've known the joy of walking in green pastures with my Lord. I've sensed His breath on my soul and have been inspired to compose songs and musicals to His glory. And someday I'll enter into the promised rest of Israel to enjoy Him forever!

Personal prayer

Lord, as You performed signs and wonders in Israel, please work supernaturally in my life and bless me with Your inheritance of peace.

Testament, this psalm is often called "The Great Hallel."

In the first few verses the psalmist commands his listeners to praise the Lord by giving thanks. Basic to this thanksgiving is the awareness and conviction of the Lord's goodness. Because He is good, His loyal love continues forever. He is eternally bound to His people by virtue of His solemn covenant (contract) with them. And who is behind this covenant, the very nature of which is loyal love? "The God of gods" (v. 2). "The LORD of lords" (v. 3).

NOVEMBER 21

Antiphonal Psalm of Love

Introit: Calling the Congregation to Praise

Exposition of theme

PSALM 136

Give thanks to the LORD, for he is good. His love endures forever. Give thanks to the God of gods. His love endures forever. Give thanks to the LORD of lords: His love endures forever. . . . Give thanks to the God of heaven. His love endures forever (vv. 1–3, 26).

Development of theme

In this marvelous antiphonal psalm, which was used liturgically in worship by ancient Israelis, one part of the congregation sang the theme and the other responded with the refrain. Twenty-six times the refrain — "His love endures forever" — is repeated. Today we would call this a "hook," the big idea, the major thesis, the central concept.

Because this was a favorite festival song and because its theme was predominant in the Old

368

Antiphonal   Relating to a responsive alteration between two groups of singers (i.e. like two choirs echoing each other). Andrea and Giovanni Gabrieli are known for brilliant antiphonal brass writing.

Introit   A short musical composition played or sung at the beginning of a worship service.

Antiphonal Psalm of Love

Service of Praise:
Praising the Lord for Creation

Exposition of theme

PSALM 136 *CONTINUED*

To him who alone does great wonders, His love endures forever. Who by his understanding made the heavens, His love endures forever. Who spread out the earth upon the waters, His love endures forever. Who made the great lights — His love endures forever. The sun to govern the day, His love endures forever. The moon and stars to govern the night; His love endures forever (vv. 4–9).

Development of theme

Preoccupied with business as usual, I have the tendency to sleepwalk through life, ignoring the beauties of creation around me. Television and films can dim our sight to a real visual experience, just as Muzak can jade our hearing so we don't really hear good music. Or I concentrate on biblical truth, while failing to observe God's testimony in nature. I believe it's possible to be too serious, too scholarly, too cognitive. Perhaps that's why so few people produce great art!

The psalmist is strongly motivated to give

"When I'm tempted to revel in self-revulsion, self-pity, feelings of worthlessness and despair, I need to remember that God loves me with a loyal love that will endure forever!"

The original summons is restated in verse 26. "Give thanks to the God of heaven. His love endures forever." This is the only time in the Psalms where God is referred to as the "God of heaven," though Ezra and Nehemiah pick up the phrase in later writings. (See Ezra 1:2 and Nehemiah 1:4.)

When I'm tempted to revel in self-revulsion, self-pity, feelings of worthlessness and despair, I need to remember that God loves me with a loyal love that will endure forever! This is the only strong, adequate basis for any positive feelings about oneself.

Personal prayer

O Lord, I give thanks for Your goodness and for Your loyal love which stands forever firm, no matter how weak and indecisive I may be.

"In poetic form the psalmist enumerates the splendors of nature — the land, the waters, the dazzling stars and planets — spread out like a diamond necklace against a black velvet curtain."

> *"God's loyal, enduring love extends to this century and to you and me on this special day. What greater cause for giving thanks?"*

thanks because of his keen observation of God's magnificent creation. He alone "does great wonders" (v. 4). Mere man cannot even begin to fathom the genius and power necessary to fashion the heavens.

In poetic form the psalmist enumerates the splendors of nature — the land, the waters, the dazzling stars and planets — spread out like a diamond necklace against a black velvet curtain. All of these represent gifts of grace that contribute to our equanimity and well-being. Each one gives unique testimony to the eternally enduring love of God. We live in an ultimately benign cosmos, not a hostile universe, and behind it all is the unfathomable love of God.

Surprised by the full circle of a rainbow or the breathtaking sight of the aurora borealis, the great "northern lights," I am moved to praise. "His love endures forever!"

Personal prayer

Lord, I thank You for the astonishing beauty of Your creation. Make me more aware of my surroundings as I brush against Your brilliant designs and help me to hear this silent song of Your love!

Antiphonal Psalm of Love

Service of Praise:
Thanking the Lord for His Acts in History

Exposition of theme
PSALM 136 CONTINUED

To him who struck down the firstborn of Egypt
> *His love endures forever.*
and brought Israel out from among them
> *His love endures forever.*
with a mighty hand and outstretched arm;
> *His love endures forever.*
to him who divided the Red Sea asunder
> *His love endures forever.*
and brought Israel through the midst of it,
> *His love endures forever.*
but swept Pharaoh and his army into the Red Sea;
> *His love endures forever.*
to him who led his people through the desert,
> *His love endures forever.*
who struck down great kings,
> *His love endures forever.*
and killed mighty kings —
> *His love endures forever.*
and gave their land as an inheritance,
> *His love endures forever.*
an inheritance to his servant Israel;
> *His love endures forever.*
to the One who remembered us in our low estate
> *His love endures forever.*
and freed us from our enemies,
> *His love endures forever.*
and who gives food to every creature.
> *His love endures forever.*
Give thanks to the God of heaven.
> *His love endures forever.*

(vv. 10–18, 21–26)

Development of theme

God's loyal, enduring love extends to this century and to you and me on this special day. What greater cause for giving thanks?

Personal prayer

O Lord, thank You for the thread of Your love in the tapestry of human history. Along with my ancient Israeli brother, I praise You today!

NOVEMBER 24

Songs of Zion In a Strange Land

Weeping over Jerusalem

Exposition of theme

PSALM 137

By the rivers of Babylon we sat and wept when we remembered Zion. There on the poplars we hung our harps, for there our captors asked us for songs, our tormentors demanded songs of joy; they said, "Sing us one of the songs of Zion!" How can we sing the songs of the LORD while in a foreign land? If I forget you, O Jerusalem, may my right hand forget its skill. May my tongue cling to the roof of my mouth if I do not remember you, if I do not consider Jerusalem my highest joy (vv. 1–6).

Development of theme

Sometimes crying is more appropriate than singing! I find myself at times feeling homesick for the past. I've looked back with longing to the days when I was growing up on Word of Life Island, Schroon Lake, New York, where we spent won-

"I find myself at times feeling homesick for the past. But we can never go back—except in our memories."

derful summers. Or the days when I was in public school in Maplewood, New Jersey. Or the beautiful high school campus of Hampden DuBose Academy in Zellwood, Florida. But we can never go back—except in our memories. I can identify with these homesick Israelites.

The people of God are homesick for their beloved homeland. Captive in Babylon, hundreds of miles from Jerusalem, they lament the loss of their freedom. Even the tough Israeli spirit—known for its fervor and fire—is quenched, and all they can do is weep. They have been deeply hurt by slavery and oppression.

When their captors demand entertainment—"one of the songs of Zion"—they refuse and hang their harps on the poplar trees "by the rivers of Babylon" (vv. 1–3). The motivation for music making had been hammered out of their lives!

Instead, the psalmist reminisces about Jerusalem, where tribes and families once gathered

371

to praise the Lord. He will remember those days at all costs and vows to consider Jerusalem his "highest joy" (v. 6). Remembering will keep his zeal fresh.

This psalmist, like other musicians who despair over lost opportunities, is open to a deep work of God in his life. When the Lord restores His glory to Zion, there will be singing and dancing! But that will come later. Because God is good, the future will be good if we walk with Him!

Personal prayer

O Lord, do an exciting and colorful work in my life also, and may I burst out in creative worship of Your mighty name and awesome power!

Songs of Zion In a Strange Land

Judging Israel's Captors

Exposition of theme

PSALM 137 CONTINUED

Remember, O LORD, what the Edomites did on the day Jerusalem fell. "Tear it down," they cried, "tear it down to its foundations!" O Daughter of Babylon, doomed to destruction, happy is he who repays you for what you have done to us— he who seizes your infants and dashes them against the rocks (vv. 7–9).

Development of theme

The Jews have never been reticent about expressing anger. These verses reflect their deep mourning while in exile as they cry out to the God of justice to repay their enemies for cruel and barbaric treatment.

The Edomites are singled out first. These pagan people celebrated while Jerusalem was de-

> *"Pouring out bitterness and hurt can be the beginning of healing; pretending the hurt doesn't exist leads only to mental and physical illness."*

stroyed. (See Ezekiel 25:12–14 and Joel 3.) The Babylonians, guilty of a brutality that almost defies description, are next. Deep sadness and bitterness are poured out against these heathen oppressors who had smashed the Israelite children "against the rocks" (v. 9)! The victimized Israelites are demanding that God do the same to their enemies' children!

What do we have here? Certainly not the "turn the other cheek" ethic of the New Testament.

There is an honest facing up to the cold reality of violence and raw evil in the world. Apart from God's grace and His redemptive power in the human heart, people are capable of exacting terrible atrocities against their neighbors! Yet this psalm is, no doubt, a poetic catharsis. Pouring out bitterness and hurt can be the beginning of healing; pretending the hurt doesn't exist leads only to mental and physical illness.

I'm grateful for the honesty and candor of this ancient psalmist, but even more grateful for the New Testament revelation that there is forgiveness for me as well as for those who have wronged me!

Personal prayer

Lord, help me to acknowledge the deep, inner pain in my life. I claim Your forgiveness and grace for my life today.

David's Vow of Praise

Praise for Boldness

Exposition of theme

PSALM 138

I will praise you, O LORD, with all my heart; before the "gods" I will sing your praise. I will bow down toward your holy temple and will praise your name for your love and your faithfulness, for you have exalted above all things your name and your word. When I called, you answered me; you made me bold and stouthearted. May all the kings of the earth praise you, O LORD, when they hear the words of your mouth. May they sing of the ways of the LORD, for the glory of the LORD is great (vv. 1–5).

Development of theme

King David has a full-hearted faith which he expressed uniquely and creatively. In these deeply satisfying verses, David praises the Lord *before the gods of the pagans!*

> **"Like David, we need to take our stand boldly 'before the gods,' declaring our faith and singing praise to the Lord!"**

Dr. Elton Trueblood, in his book, *Alternative to Futility,* says, "The basic defect of the Protestant churches lies not in their divided condition but in their insipidity. They show so little imagination. The same kind of dull and lifeless service is repeated endlessly, whatever the occasion. We are in a time of crisis when we need a dynamic fellowship to turn the world upside down. What we are offered is a stereotype. A man, having

become convinced that we are in a race with catastrophe, may seek the very bread of life, but in practice he is forced to sing sentimental songs with words he does not mean, listen to some comforting platitudes, and finally shake the minister's hand at the door, because there is no other way to escape! In short, this kind of church illustrates Professor Whitehead's dictum perfectly. 'It is in full decay because it lacks the element of adventure.' "

We need "adventurous fellowship." Like David, we need to take our stand boldly "before the gods," declaring our faith and singing praise to the Lord! ·

Personal prayer

I long to praise You, Lord, wholeheartedly, courageously, and creatively. As I bow before You, inspire me with songs of praise and worship.

Vow   A solemn promise or assertion by which a person binds himself to an act, service, or condition.

David's Vow of Praise
Prayer for Fulfillment

Exposition of theme
PSALM 138 CONTINUED

Though the LORD is on high, he looks upon the lowly, but the proud he knows from afar. Though I walk in the midst of trouble, you preserve my life; you stretch out your hand against the anger of my foes, with your right hand you save me. The LORD will fulfill his purpose for me; your love, O LORD, endures forever — do not abandon the works of your hands (vv. 6–8).

Development of theme

I have long been intrigued with the idea of knowing God's will and have opened myself to His loving guidance and direction. He has led me specifically by His Word and His Spirit, and it is comforting to know that He cares more about my character than about my performance. He is gradually teaching me about reality and values as well. Because I believe He desires intimacy with me, I pray about every detail of my life. Sometimes He uses friends, circumstances, even books to point me in the right direction. Dr. James I. Packer's writings on guidance have been extremely helpful. And because I have a passion for music and communication, He allows me to be involved in creative projects for His glory and honor.

> *"God has led me specifically by His Word and His Spirit, and it is comforting to know that He cares more about my character than about my performance."*

I understand David's plea for fulfillment in this psalm. Though I am not comparing myself with Israel's greatest king, I know something about the course of his career as a musician. From the description of his boyhood, it is obvious that David had talent and quickly became proficient. He was a skillful harpist. (The Hebrew roots for *skill* and *wisdom* are the same!) He was a passionate lyricist, responsible for at least half of the Psalter, a collection of poetry embodying intricate form. He was a man favored by God who "preserved" his life and gave it "purpose."

As one who is prone to melancholy, the last part of this passage comforts and encourages me: "The LORD will fulfill his purpose for me!" (v. 8). He designed me. He brought me into being. He is with me. He hasn't forgotten me. He hasn't overlooked me in the grand scheme of things. My life has a divine purpose and goal. I can stand with the Apostle Paul and say, "Being confident of this, that he who began a good work in you will carry it on to completion until the day of Christ Jesus" (Philippians 1:6). What a promise!

Personal prayer

Thank You, Lord, for promising to fulfill Your purpose for my life! I believe it and claim it!

Symphony of God's Attributes

First Movement:
He Knows Everything (Omniscience)

Exposition of theme

PSALM 139

O Lord, you have searched me and you know me. You know when I sit and when I rise; you perceive my thoughts from afar. You discern my going out and my lying down; you are familiar with all my ways. Before a word is on my tongue you know it completely, O Lord. You hem me in — behind and before; you have laid your hand upon me. Such knowledge is too wonderful for me, too lofty for me to attain (vv. 1–6).

Development of theme

This magnificent psalm opens with a frightening assertion of God's omniscience. Omniscience is a lofty theological term which means that God knows everything — everything actual and everything possible. In fact, His knowledge covers both the realms of reality and the imagination.

God knew David inside out (v. 1). He knew

> **"Gloria Gaither's profound phrase sums it up so well: 'For the one who knows me best, loves me most.' "**

what time he got up in the morning and what time he went to bed at night (vv. 2–3). He even knew David's thoughts before he framed them into words (v. 4).

The New Testament confirms this attribute of God. "He [Jesus] did not need man's testimony about man, for he know what was in a man" (John 2:25). This is terrifying news to the one whose mind is riddled with sinful thoughts and who acts on those impulses.

But to the person who understands God's unconditional love and acceptance, His omniscience is good news! Gloria Gaither's profound phrase sums it up so well: "For the one who knows me best, loves me most." This maximum exposure of my personality, combined with my Lord's total acceptance of me, boggles my mind. It is also what makes the gospel so unbelievably thrilling!

Personal prayer

Lord, you know everything about me, yet You love me anyway!

Symphony of God's Attributes

Second Movement:
He is Everywhere (Omnipresence)

Exposition of theme

PSALM 139 CONTINUED

Where can I go from your Spirit? Where can I flee from your presence? If I go up to the heavens, you are there; if I make my bed in the depths, you are there. If I rise on the wings of the dawn, if I settle on the far side of the sea, even there your hand will guide me, your right hand will hold me fast. If I say, "Surely the darkness will hide me and the light become night around me," even the darkness will not be dark to you; the night will shine like the day, for darkness is as light to you (vv. 7–12).

Development of theme

Upon learning that God knows the worst about him, David's first impulse is to run! Fallen, sinful humanity always attempts to flee from the presence of the absolute holiness of God. But there is no place to hide, for God is everywhere! He's omnipresent!

God is everywhere, but He is not *in* everything. That's pantheism. He is infinite and personal, but He is self-contained and separate from His creation. Nothing escapes His notice.

The comforting thought is that, if He is everywhere, He is also immediately accessible! I can make contact with Him immediately and instantly. He is right here! Distance between God and me is created, not on His initiative, but by my sin and guilt. Where God is, there can be no evil. Light and darkness do not coexist at the same place at the same time.

Martin Luther once said, "Music is one of the greatest gifts that God has given us: it is divine and, therefore, Satan is its enemy. For with its aid many dire temptations are overcome; the devil does not stay where music is."

I am newly encouraged to make music. For where God is, there can be no evil. Where God is, there is music!

Personal prayer

O Lord, I'm happy that I can't flee from Your presence. I'm comforted by the fact that You are everywhere and that music is praise to Your name!

THE LANGUAGE OF MUSIC

Symphony

A Greek term for "sounding together."

For all intents and purposes it is a sonata for orchestra. The most important form of orchestral music, it developed in the mid 18th century in a rather pure form and reached its highest development in Beethoven (who pulled, stretched, and expanded the form). Prime examples would be Beethoven's nine symphonies or Brahm's four symphonies.

Symphony of God's Attributes

Third Movement:
He is all-powerful (Omnipotence)

Exposition of theme

PSALM 139 CONTINUED

For you created my inmost being; you knit me together in my mother's womb. I praise you because I am fearfully and wonderfully made; your works are wonderful, I know that full well.

> *"These verses describing reproduction are among the most touching and tender in all the Bible."*

My frame was not hidden from you when I was made in the secret place. When I was woven together in the depths of the earth, your eyes saw my unformed body. All the days ordained for me were written in your book before one of them came to be. How precious to me are your thoughts, O God! How vast is the sum of them! Were I to count them, they would outnumber the grains of sand. When I awake, I am still with you (vv. 13–18).

Development of theme

God is all-knowing, ever-present, and *all-powerful!*

Aware that the darkness could not hide him from God (vv. 12–13), David was moved to meditate on God's supernatural superintendence, even in the most private depths of his mother's womb!

These verses describing reproduction are among the most touching and tender in all the Bible. Realizing that he has been "fearfully and wonderfully made," David considers God's orchestration of his own conception and development: "You knit me together in my mother's womb. . . . My frame (skeleton) was not hidden from you when I was made in the secret place. . . . your eyes saw my unformed body" (vv. 13, 15–16).

God is fully cognizant of the union of sperm and egg, the attachment of the embryo to the uterine lining, and the development of that tiny life according to His timetable.

This passage gives every human being a remarkable basis for self-worth. From the moment of conception, God is present, and through every phase of development thereafter. How can peo-

A CONTEMPORARY SONG

Fearfully and Wonderfully Made

Fearfully and wonderfully made,
I'm unique, one of a kind,
Fearfully and wonderfully made,
My beginning was God's design.

He was with me before my birth
And formed my being with care,
I'm a person of infinite worth—
A masterpiece beyond compare!

Fearfully and wonderfully made,
I'm woven as His tapestry;
Fearfully and wonderfully made,
I'm created for eternity.

His imprint is seen everywhere,
And He has plans for me;
In secret He knew I was there—
A mystery of God's decree!

Fearfully and wonderfully made,
I'm woven as His tapestry;
Fearfully and wonderfully made,
I'm created for eternity.

Words and music by Don Wyrtzen. © 1984 Singspiration Music.

ple decide to abort what God deems so precious and valuable? The human embryo is not the result of a biological accident, no matter what the circumstances. Rather, it embraces the image of God and is not to be equated with junk or trash to be discarded! God presides over the mysteries of human reproduction and because He does, all life has meaning and eternal significance.

Personal prayer

O Lord, I praise You for creating my inmost being. I praise You because I am fearfully and wonderfully made.

377

December *PSALMS 139–150*

PANORAMA PHOTO BY GARY IRVING

Symphony of God's Attributes

Finale: David's Response

Exposition of theme

PSALM 139 CONTINUED

If only you would slay the wicked, O God! Away from me, you bloodthirsty men! They speak of you with evil intent; your adversaries misuse your name. Do I not hate those who hate you, O LORD, and abhor those who rise up against you? I have nothing but hatred for them; I count them my enemies. Search me, O God, and know my heart; test me and know my anxious thoughts. See if there is any offensive way in me, and lead me in the way everlasting (vv. 19–24).

Development of theme

Piano tuning is a fine art. A piano has three strings for each tone. If the instrument is flat, the strings must be tightened; if it is sharp, the strings must be loosened. The piano tuner always has a point of reference — "A-440" — using either a tuning fork or an electronic device called a strobetuner. But he also depends on his

---

"The Master Tuner may have to tighten the strings, but the final result will be a beautifully voiced instrument of praise."

---

ear — perfect pitch or good relative pitch — and a thorough acquaintance with harmonic intervals.

After cataloging the sins of God's enemies, who are consequently his as well, David focuses on himself. Unlike those who "misuse" the name of the Lord, David prays, voluntarily submitting himself to God's tuning fork: "Search me"; "Test me"; "See if there is any offensive way in me"

(vv. 23–24). In effect, he is saying: "LORD, let me know if my life is out of tune!"

As is true so many times in the Psalms, David meets trouble with an expression of faith in the nature of God. He is both infinite and personal, transcendent and immanent — far above to watch over us, yet within to guide us. He knows how it feels to be human, because He came in the flesh and walked where we walk (John 1:1, 14).

David finds a deep wellspring of comfort and serenity in these harmonious attributes.

As the tuning fork is applied to my life, I can "hear" the flat keys. The Master Tuner may have to tighten the strings, thus producing temporary pain and stress. But the final result will be a beautifully voiced instrument of praise, fit for a heavenly concerto!

Personal prayer

O Lord, let me know if my life is out of tune! Search me, test me and check me out. I long to sing and play in perfect harmony with Your plan!

Imprecatory Impromptu

David Prays for Justice

Exposition of theme

PSALM 140

Rescue me, O LORD, from evil men; protect me from men of violence, who devise evil plans in their hearts and stir up war every day. They make their tongues as sharp as a serpent's; the poison of vipers is on their lips. Keep me, O LORD, from the hands of the wicked; protect me from men of violence who plan to trip my feet. Proud men have hidden a snare for me; they have spread out the cords of their net and have set traps for me along my path. O LORD, I say to you, "You are my God." Hear, O LORD, my cry for mercy. O Sovereign LORD, my strong deliverer, who shields my head in the day of battle — do not grant the wicked their desires, O LORD; do not let their plans succeed, or they will become proud (vv. 1–8).

Development of theme

Again David vents his emotions, hence the title for this psalm. An "imprecation" is a curse on the wicked. An "impromptu" is a musical piece played extemporaneously. David is spontaneously engaging in an emotional outburst in song. The tone is harsh, strident, and dissonant.

In his opening prayer, David prays for justice and protection from the wicked. He then proceeds to curse them for their vicious character. Their tongues are poisonous; their hands do evil things; their minds devise all kinds of cunning

> **"David is spontaneously engaging in an emotional outburst in song. The tone is harsh, strident, and dissonant."**

plots to trap David and take him off the scene.

In verses 6–8, he praises God's sovereignty, using military imagery to affirm His protective power. David then concludes this section by praying for the divine restraint of the wicked.

David's prayer life is marked by honesty and openness. He never denies the reality of internal pressure. He is obviously fearful and his emotions are churning, but he feels perfectly free to dump all of this junk on God. God is certainly big enough to take it!

The great psalmist was very objective about his suffering, but because he acknowledged it and worked through it, he was able to cope, with God's help. I can do the same!

Personal prayer

O Strong Deliverer, I pray that You will protect me from the cunning schemes of ungodly persons. I pray also that You will protect me from myself and deliver me from unnecessary guilt and fear.

Imprecatory Impromptu

David's Response to His Enemies

Exposition of theme

PSALM 140 CONTINUED

Let the heads of those who surround me be covered with the trouble their lips have caused. Let burning coals fall upon them; may they be thrown into the fire, into miry pits, never to rise. Let slanderers not be established in the land; may disaster hunt down men of violence. I know that the LORD secures justice for the poor and upholds the cause of the needy. Surely the righteous will praise your name and the upright will live before you (vv. 9–13).

Development of theme

This psalm is best grasped against the backdrop of the Judeo-Christian ethic. God is holy, righteous, and pure. Man is evil, unfair, and deceit-

> **"We need to learn to hate evil as much as God does, but we are more addicted to happiness than commited to holiness."**

ful. The morality is clear-cut and unrelenting. Because I desperately want to give people the benefit of the doubt, I sometimes tend to be "marshmellowy" about ethics.

David's intimate walk with God produced an objectivity that enabled him to see things monochromatically (in black and white). Artistic thinking in grays doesn't work in the areas of personal morality. This kind of reasoning results in a naive and shallow view of sin. We need to learn how to hate evil as much as God does, but we are more

addicted to happiness than committed to holiness.

While David's prayer may seem a little shocking to those of us living in a society tainted by secular humanism, we must bear in mind that his enemies were malicious men. They were as annoying as insects, as repulsive as reptiles, and as lethal as sharks. They were cunning and predatory—out to kill!

He responds with equal passion. He prays that the poisonous words of the wicked will boomerang. He prays that "burning coals" will fall on their heads like volcanic residue from Sodom and Gomorrah (Genesis 19). He prays that their slander will be self-defeating and that disaster will pursue them and bring them down.

Like the clash of cymbals, a stunning thought strikes my consciousness; *David's righteous wrath was not directed against his enemies, but poured out to God in a prayer song!* When I am most troubled by injustice and unkindness, I can "talk it out" with God through music rather than "taking it out" on others!

Personal prayer

O Lord, I'm glad David was a passionate person too! And I've learned today that I don't have to act on my negative impulses, but can pour them out before You in healing, restorative prayer and praise!

THE LANGUAGE OF MUSIC

Impromptu

An improvisation or composition suggestive of improvisation.

A piece that has a somewhat casual, spur-of-the-moment, feeling. The "pneumatic odes" of Ephesians 5:19 were somewhat like impromptus.

Evensong

Song of Protection

Exposition of theme

PSALM 141

O LORD, I call to you; come quickly to me. Hear my voice when I call to you. May my prayer be set before you like incense; may the lifting up of my hands be like the evening sacrifice. . . . But my eyes are fixed on you, O Sovereign LORD; in you I take refuge — do not give me over to death. Keep me from the snares they have laid for me, from the traps set by evildoers. Let the wicked fall into their own nets, while I pass by in safety (vv. 1–2, 8–10).

Development of theme

For many people prayer is a one-liner beginning with "Gimme." For others, it's a hasty "thank you" mumbled over meals, or a bedtime blessing left over from childhood. For David, prayer was a way of life.

Here David bows before the Lord during the evening sacrifices. We're allowed to peer over his shoulder as he observes this meaningful ritual. First, he calls on the name of the Lord — a name that, in its very use, promises power. His words rise like sweet perfume because they flow from a sincere heart. He lifts his hands in a posture of praise and commitment and prays, with open eyes fixed on his Lord.

The prayer itself is spelled out in specific terms — for the presence of the Lord (v. 1), for

> *"Here David bows before the Lord during the evening sacrifices. His words rise like sweet perfume because they flow from a sincere heart."*

preservation of life (v. 8), for supernatural discernment of snares set by the wicked (v. 9), for vindication (v. 10).

I am reminded of the life of Queen Esther

---

en rapport *If a persons' heart is "en rapport" with God, prayer can be free, personal, and can assume many forms:*

Kneeling	**Alone**	**In the temple**
1 Kings 8:54	*Mark 1:38*	*2 Kings 19:14*
Standing	**Together**	**At the riverside**
Jeremiah 18:20	*Psalm 55:18*	*Acts 16:13*
Sitting	**At fixed times**	**On the seashore**
2 Samuel 7:18	*Psalm 55:17*	*Acts 21:5*
Lying prostrate	**At any time**	**The battlefield**
Matthew 26:39	*Luke 18:1*	*1 Samuel 7:5*
With hands uplifted	**Everywhere**	**Spontaneously**
1 Kings 8:22	*1 Timothy 2:2*	*Matthew 6:7*
Silently	**In bed**	**Liturgically**
1 Samuel 1:13	*Psalm 63*	*Psalm 120–126*
Out loud	**In the open field**	**Literally for everything!**
Ezekiel 11:13	*Genesis 34:11, 13*	*Philippians 4:6*

(Esther 1–10). Haman, the highest noble under King Xerxes, had a vendetta against the Jews, especially Mordecai, Esther's guardian. He even erected a gallows, seventy-five feet high, on which to hang Mordecai. Instead, Esther acted responsibly, God acted sovereignly, and the tables were turned!

What comfort there is in the knowledge that God has a plan for us that will not be thwarted by the worst the wicked can do!

Personal prayer

O Lord, I know You hear my prayers just as You heard King David's. Don't let me fall into the traps set by the world, but let this humanistic society hang itself by its own rope while "I pass by in safety."

DECEMBER 5

Evensong

Song of Sanctification

Exposition of theme

PSALM 141 CONTINUED

Set a guard over my mouth, O LORD; keep watch over the door of my lips. Let not my heart be drawn to what is evil, to take part in wicked deeds with men who are evildoers; let me not eat of their delicacies. Let a righteous man strike me — it is a kindness; let him rebuke me — it is oil on my head. My head will not refuse it. Yet my prayer is ever against the deeds of evildoers; their rulers will be thrown down from the cliffs, and the wicked will learn that my words were well spoken (vv. 3–6).

Development of theme

David had the right idea. His aspirations were lofty; he was just too human to attain them! Still, he longed to be pure, blameless, and sanctified (set apart).

"God has set me apart for His ministry, but He has also blessed me with godly friends who pray for me and point out possible dangers I am too blind to see."

In this passage he submits three parts of his body to the Lord for cleansing — his lips and mouth, lest he speak evil (v. 3); his heart, lest he become involved in sensual pleasures (v. 4); his head, lest his mind toy with the evil schemes of the wicked (v. 4). In fact, he asks for corrective support from godly friends.

God never intended for us to face life alone. If we isolate ourselves from real, down-to-earth relationships, the Enemy will subtly distract us, seduce us, and then devour us. My close friends — Nelson Bennett, Bill Rigg, and Bob Steed — regularly pray for me, communicate with me, and generally hold me accountable. Karen and I also attend a small group Bible study, where we experience rich Christian fellowship in a private setting. Without this support, we would be depriving ourselves of one of the greatest blessings the Lord gives us — intercessory prayer.

In unity there is strength to endure temptation, to make a frontal attack on societal sins, and to stand firm against the Enemy. God has set me apart for His ministry, but He has also blessed me with godly friends who pray for me and point out possible dangers I am too blind to see.

Personal prayer

O Lord, I thank You again for such prayer warriors as my dad and his wife, Joan; Karen's mom, Ruth Parr, and a few others who faithfully hold me up in prayer. I know You have brought these people into my life to help me fight the battle . . . and win!

Longing and Lament

"I cry aloud to the Lord!"

Exposition of theme

PSALM 142

I cry aloud to the LORD; I lift up my voice to the LORD for mercy. I pour out my complaint before him; before him I tell my trouble. When my spirit grows faint within me, it is you who know my way. In the path where I walk men have hidden a snare for me. Look to my right and see; no one is concerned for me. I have no refuge; no one cares for my life (vv. 1–4).

Development of theme

David's circumstances couldn't be worse! He is hiding out in a cave with the murderous King Saul in hot pursuit. David is utterly helpless and alone.

His prayer is more of a demand than a polite request. He is crying "aloud," literally shouting at God!

Every trail and road is mined and booby-trapped, and David is spooked. He's afraid to make a single move! Not only is he in a position of grave physical danger, but he's psychologically bankrupt as well. Isolated, he feels that "no one cares" (v. 4).

I understand this feeling. As long as I can remember, I've been quiet, introverted, high-strung, and overly sensitive. You probably wouldn't be able to tell from observing me, but deep inside is a very fragile persona. There are times when I feel that I might as well drop out because no one cares. It's the price one pays for having the volume turned up too high on life!

David has "no refuge" (v. 4) — no place and no one but God. Actually, that's exactly where the Lord wants us. The best place to be is in a posi-tion of absolute dependence upon God. Most of us still believe we can make it in our own strength, that we make life work on our own. The real truth is that *He* gives us the power to do everything we do. "You may say to yourself, 'My power and the strength of my hands have produced this wealth for me.' But remember the LORD your God, for it is he who gives you the ability to produce wealth, and so confirms his covenant" (Deuteronomy 8:17–18). Some people aren't blessed because they're depending too much on their own talent.

Personal prayer

O Lord, I'm only too conscious of my weakness and vulnerability. Please show me Your strength at the point of my deepest need!

AN APPROPRIATE GOSPEL SONG

No One Ever Cared for Me Like Jesus

No one ever cared for me like Jesus
There's no other friend so kind as He;
No one else could take the sin and darkness from me,
O how much He cared for me!

I would love to tell you what I think of Jesus
Since I found in Him a friend so strong and true.
I would tell you how He changed my life completely;
He did something that no other friend could do.

All my life was full of sin when Jesus found me,
All my heart was full of misery and woe;
Jesus placed His strong and loving arms around me,
And He led me in the way I ought to go.

starve herself to death? How could this skinny person look at herself in the mirror and think, "I'm too fat!"? Why did she try to control her life through diet and exercise instead of turning to the Lord for answers to her problems? Depth psychology may provide some insights regarding the dynamics of this disease, but God's Word penetrates the mysteries of human existence and provides final resolution in Jesus Christ.

David did have the good sense to turn to the Lord. His consuming desire was to be able to

> *"How is it that a beautiful and gifted young woman like Karen Carpenter could literally starve herself to death?"*

praise the Lord and thus present a strong witness to other believers.

We don't have to fear the strength of our "enemies" — pride, out-of-control ambition, destructive use of sexuality, craving for status and things. The Lord has given us every resource needed to grow healthy, to build up our sin-immune system. We need to move from milk to meat! "Anyone who lives on milk, being still an infant, is not acquainted with the teaching about righteousness. But solid food is for the mature, who by constant use have trained themselves to distinguish good from evil" (Hebrews 5:13–14).

As we continue to eat heartily from God's Word, we'll be filled with His goodness and Spirit. Seeing the change, the righteous will "gather about" in open-mouthed wonder and praise to God!

DECEMBER 7

Longing and Lament

"They are too strong for me."

Exposition of theme

PSALM 142 CONTINUED

I cry to you, O Lord; I say, "You are my refuge, my portion in the land of the living." Listen to my cry, for I am in desperate need; rescue me from those who pursue me, for they are too strong for me. Set me free from my prison, that I may praise your name. Then the righteous will gather about me because of your goodness to me (vv. 5–7).

Development of theme

Contemporary Christians are suffering from spiritual anorexia. Ignoring the Lord's bountiful feast spread out in His Word, we're literally starving ourselves to death! And instead of being strong and robust in the faith, we're weaklings, cowering in the face of real conflict and adversity. Like David, we look at the opposition and say, "They are too strong for me!" (v. 6).

How is it that a beautiful and gifted young woman like Karen Carpenter could literally

Personal prayer

O Lord, when there is so much rich food available for our spirits, why do we starve ourselves? Lead me to the banquet table and let me feast on Your Word so my brothers and sisters in Christ may be fed and encouraged.

Pathetique Sonata

First Movement
"My spirit grows faint within me."

Exposition of theme

PSALM 143

O LORD, hear my prayer, listen to my cry for mercy; in your faithfulness and righteousness come to my relief. Do not bring your servant into judgment, for no one living is righteous before you. The enemy pursues me, he crushes me to the ground; he makes me dwell in darkness like those long dead. So my spirit grows faint within me; my heart within me is dismayed (vv. 1–4).

Development of theme

In this age of focus on physical fitness, I wonder if we give nearly as much thought to the condition of our spirits. The body can look pretty good on the outside, while spiritual rigor mortis is in the process of setting in! Too many of us are "faint." We're spiritual wimps!

I'm impressed all over again with David's brutal honesty about himself. He doesn't attempt to project positive images or to numb himself into relief through positive mental attitudes. He's forthright and objective. His lament is real and

---

THE LANGUAGE OF MUSIC

Pathétique

A French word meaning "emotional" and "full of pathos" (not necessarily sad).

Beethoven's Sonata op. 13 in C minor is called, "Sonate Pathétique." Tchaikovsky's Symphony No. 6 in B minor is called "Patétique Symphony." The Bible is full of emotional sensitivity, personal sympathy, and compassion. (See John 11 or Matthew 26:36–39.)

---

rich in its intensity. Emotionally, he has pulled the blanket of dark despair over his head. Because he's spiritually impoverished, he's ready for a mighty work of God in his life.

And he desperately needs one. In verses 3 and 4, he tells us that his enemies are still pursuing him relentlessly and that he is being forced to entomb himself in desert caves for protection.

In this psalm, I don't hear the mighty warrior king of Israel. Instead, I hear the pathetic plea of one who recognizes that power comes, not from physical strength or military strategy, but in trusting the faithfulness and righteousness of God.

Personal prayer

O God, hear my prayer today. The macho image is not for me. I confess my inability to work out the details of my life or even to protect myself! Be merciful to me.

Pathetique Sonata

Second Movement
"My spirit faints with longing."

Exposition of theme

PSALM 143 *CONTINUED*

I remember the days of long ago; I meditate on all your works and consider what your hands have done. I spread out my hands to you; my soul thirsts for you like a parched land. Answer me quickly, O LORD; my spirit faints with longing. Do not hide your face from me or I will be like those who go down to the pit (vv. 5–7).

Development of theme

David was no stranger to suffering. It became the foundation upon which the Lord erected a rich, intimate relationship with him.

The psalmist is now rescued through reminiscence. He considers God's mighty acts in history. He meditates on His supernatural works. These thoughts begin to restore and renew him.

Before, David's personality resembled a dry, parched land. Now, he recognizes his inner thirst and longing for God and reaches out to his heavenly Father. His request is of the utmost urgency. He feels as if he is about to die, to "go down to the pit" (v. 7). Perhaps his most horrifying thought is that the Lord will overlook him!

Spiritual pain is often the catalyst for change and growth. As I reach the end of my own limited resources, I grope toward God in desperation. He closes that great gap with His own presence and lets me know that He has not overlooked my need!

He Looked Beyond My Fault

Amazing grace shall always be my song of
   praise —
For it was grace that bought my liberty —
I do not know just why He came to love me
so —
He looked beyond my fault and saw my
need.

I shall forever lift mine eyes to Calvary
To view the cross where Jesus died for
me —
How marvelous — the grace that caught my
falling   soul
He looked beyond my fault and saw my
need.

Words by Dottie Rambo. Music adapted from Londonderry Aire.
© 1967 by Heart-Warming Music.

Personal prayer

*O Lord, please look beyond my fault to see my
need. My soul thirsts for You like a parched land.
Refresh me with the rains of Your love.*

Pathetique Sonata

Third Movement
"May your good Spirit lead me on level ground."

Exposition of theme

PSALM 143 CONTINUED

Let the morning bring me word of your unfailing love, for I have put my trust in you. Show me the way I should go, for to you I lift up my soul. Rescue me from my enemies, O LORD, for I hide myself in you. Teach me to do your will, for you are my God; may your good Spirit lead me on level ground. For your name's sake, O LORD, preserve my life; in your righteousness, bring me out of trouble. In your unfailing love, silence my enemies; destroy all my foes, for I am your servant (vv. 8–12).

Development of theme

At the moment of rebirth, when the human spirit is "yielded and still," the Holy Spirit moves in to make His home and to provide assistance for our pilgrimage with God.

Even David anticipated something of this divine exchange, I think. His despairing prayer, filled with strong, virile verbs, is the night sky against which the dazzling stars of God's grace through His Spirit are displayed.

Guide — David prays, "Show me the way" (v. 8), sensing that God's guiding Spirit will not leave him stranded, nor remove him from the unfailing love that is everlasting.

Enabler — "Rescue me from my enemies" (v. 9), he continues. It is the Spirit of God who enables and empowers. David's many military coups were a result of divine intervention by the Enabler.

Teacher — "Teach me to do your will . . . may your good Spirit lead me on level ground" (v. 10). The Holy spirit is our Teacher/Interpreter. It is He

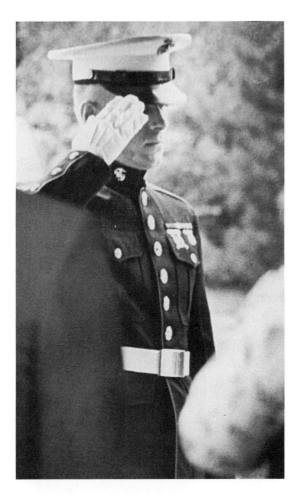

Imperial March

David in Combat: Celebrating the Past

Exposition of theme

PSALM 144

Praise be to the LORD, my Rock, who trains my hands for war, my fingers for battle. He is my loving God and my fortress, my stronghold and my deliverer, my shield, in whom I take refuge, who subdues peoples under me. O LORD, what is man that you care for him, the son of man that you think of him? Man is like a breath; his days are like a fleeting shadow (vv. 1–4).

Development of theme

David was the General MacArthur of his day — a conquering hero. He begins this stirring psalm by remembering past victories and enemies who have been subdued under him. But who forged David's career? Who gave him genius for military strategy? Who trained his hands for war and his fingers for battle? The Lord!

David had a personal relationship with God, who is strong, solid, and immovable, yet warm,

---

> *"David went forth in God's strength to crush his enemies in battle. We are to do the same!"*

---

who explains spiritual mysteries and levels the ground of our understanding.

Comforter-"For your name's sake, O LORD, preserve my life . . . bring me out of my trouble" (v. 11). God's Spirit whispers words of encouragement and calls to our minds His mighty works in our behalf. He banishes discouragement and puts a song in our hearts!

Personal prayer

O Lord, fill me with Your Spirit today. Guide me, enable me, teach me, comfort me. I need help as I continue my pilgrimage.

loving, and intimate. He was David's Fortress, Stronghold, Deliverer, and Shield (v. 2). David went forth in God's strength to crush his enemies in battle. We are to do the same! (See Ephesians 6.) God's character — His nature and attributes — sustained David and made him bold and courageous — a winner!

What is almost incomprehensible to me is that this mighty God of war invites me — weak and wandering though I be — into His presence to receive the same kind of strength that He gave David. He promises to be my Shield and Deliverer in the spiritual battles I must fight. Like David, I can be a conquering hero . . . in Him!

Personal prayer

O Lord, be my Rock, my Fortress, My Deliverer, and my Shield today. My battles are not as obvious as David's, but they are just as deadly!

THE LANGUAGE OF MUSIC

March

Music for soldiers, usually involving strongly accented beats in groups of four.

Marches are usually dignified, ceremonial, and military. A good example is Arthur Sullivan's stirring hymn, "Onward Christian Soldiers."

DECEMBER 12

Imperial March

David in Combat: Pleading for Help in the Present

Exposition of theme

PSALM 144 CONTINUED

Part your heavens, O LORD, and come down; touch the mountains, so that they smoke. Send forth lightning and scatter the enemies; shoot your arrows and rout them. Reach down your hand from on high; deliver me and rescue me from the mighty waters, from the hands of foreigners whose mouths are full of lies, whose right hands are deceitful. I will sing a new song to you, O God; on the ten-stringed lyre I will make music to you, to the One who gives victory to kings, who delivers his servant David from the deadly sword. Deliver me and rescue me from the

390

hands of foreigners whose mouths are full of lies, whose right hands are deceitful (vv. 5–11).

Development of theme

David set his faith firmly in divine intervention rather than in human strategy. He longed for a dazzling supernatural display of God's power! He wanted to see the heavens illuminated by holy fireworks, to see God's own Fourth of July celebration (v. 5)! He knew that when God sent

---

> *"We often do it all backwards today — cranking up a praise experience while nothing is happening in our lives!"*

---

forth lightning, enemies were scattered (v. 6), and when God sprung His bow and shot His arrows, villains were put to rout (v. 6).

David was praying for deliverance *now!* His enemies were foreigners with lying tongues, impure motives, and corrupt actions. He desperately needed a divine rescue action.

What inspiration for music! In ancient Israel the creative process worked like this:

Genuine need — God's people were backed against the wall.

Imminent danger — They faced the possibility of being wiped out.

Honest lament — They groaned and cried out to the Lord for salvation and deliverance. Whole families clothed themselves in sackcloth and ashes, fasted, and prayed.

Divine intervention — The Lord heard their cry and supernaturally delivered them.

Genuine praise — They worshiped God for His mighty works!

We often do it all backwards today — cranking up a praise experience while nothing is happening in our lives! Yet David was so confident of success that he wrote this psalm of victory *before the fact!* Considering the unchanging nature of God and His faithfulness, I can begin *now* to compose music in gratitude *for who He is and what He is going to do for me!*

Personal prayer

O Lord, even before You do Your next exciting work in my life, may I burst forth in creative worship of Your mighty name and power!

DECEMBER 13

Imperial March

David in Combat: Anticipating Peace and Prosperity

Exposition of theme

PSALM 144 CONTINUED

Deliver me and rescue me from the hands of foreigners whose mouths are full of lies, whose right hands are deceitful. Then our sons in their youth will be like well-nurtured plants, and our daughters will be like pillars carved to adorn a palace. Our barns will be filled with every kind of provision. Our sheep will increase by thousands, by tens of thousands in our fields; our oxen will draw heavy loads. There will be no breaching of walls, no going into captivity, no cry of distress in our streets. Blessed are the people of whom this is true; blessed are the people whose God is the LORD (vv. 11–15).

Development of theme

Only a survivor or a veteran of war in some strife-ridden part of the world, can really appreciate the absence of conflict. Harry Bollback, Dad's colleague, is an ex-Marine who fought in World War II. But some of the guys — including Ike

Eickleberger and Pete Monfore, who saw duty in the Korean conflict — never made it back. They died on Heartbreak Ridge. Whenever I return to the U.S.A. after being out of the country, I'm

---

"I don't spend much time wondering if I'll be captured and exiled by foreign invaders. For His own reasons, God has blessed America . . . for now!"

---

overwhelmed by our freedom. We owe it to men like these!

In this psalm David is projecting into a future when world-wide peace will reign once more. In order to understand his point of view, I have to do just the opposite.

I have to think about the hot spots of the world — Nicaragua, Panama, Libya, Israel! Insulated from most physical violence as we are in America, I don't have to be concerned that my son, D. J., or my beautiful Kathy will be harmed by a flying bullet or will step on a landmine (v. 12). I don't have to fear that bombs will destroy the farms of our country so that there will be no food in the supermarket (v. 13). I don't spend too much time wondering if I'll be captured and exiled by foreign invaders (v. 14). For His own reasons, God has blessed America . . . for now!

But David reminds us of the divine condition for peace and prosperity: "Blessed are the people whose God is the LORD" (v. 15). There are definite signs of disintegration in our society: Families are in crisis, our economy is shaky, and our military strength is questionable. Could it be that we've forsaken the Lord?

Personal prayer

O Lord, I long for Your blessing of world peace. Take control of our economy, our national security, and international affairs, so that all nations will know that You are our God!

Praise to the King

His Attributes and Acts

Exposition of theme

PSALM 145

I will exalt you, my God the King; I will praise your name for ever and ever. Every day I will praise you and extol your name for ever and ever. Great is the LORD and most worthy of praise; his greatness no one can fathom. One generation will commend your works to another; they will tell of your mighty acts. They will speak of the glorious splendor of your majesty, and I will meditate on your wonderful works. They will tell of the power of your awesome works, and I will proclaim your great deeds. They will celebrate your abundant goodness and joyfully sing of your righteousness (vv. 1–7).

Development of theme

This noble praise psalm begins the grand doxology (Psalms 145–150) of the entire Psalter, bringing this anthology of ancient worship songs to a mighty crescendo. Excitement builds, erupting in a fulfilling climax of praise in Psalm 150 — the Old Testament Hallelujah Chorus!

David begins by extolling God the King. He covenants with the Lord to praise His name on a daily basis. He vows to keep the relationship fresh, not taking anything for granted.

The psalmist praises the Lord for both His attributes and His acts. Only God is worthy of

> **"The Lord's attributes and actions are the concepts I must meditate on. What poems, songs, and holy literature should spring forth from these exalted thoughts!**

praise because of His divine personality and unprecedented acts in history. God is not an absentee landlord of His universe! Future generations will tell the stories revealing His glorious splendor and majesty.

What a model for my own praise experience! I need to daily celebrate the Lord's attributes and actions in my life. How does His character affect me personally? Can He ever act toward me in an unloving way? Is He capable of upholding and sustaining me?

These are the concepts I must meditate on. These are the things I must pray about. These are the images and pictures of God I must write down to preserve for future generations of believers. What poems, songs, and holy literature should spring forth from these exalted thoughts!

Personal prayer

My God and King, You alone are worthy of daily and forever praise! I exalt and declare Your goodness to all generations.

Praise to the King

His Love

Exposition of theme

PSALM 145 CONTINUED

The LORD is gracious and compassionate, slow to anger and rich in love. The LORD is good to all; he has compassion on all he has made. . . . The LORD is faithful to all his promises and loving toward all he has made. The LORD upholds all those who fall and lifts up all who are bowed down. The eyes of all look to you, and you give them their food at the proper time. You open your hand and satisfy the desires of every living thing (vv. 8–9, 13b–16).

Development of theme

When I think of God's Fatherlove, I see His grace and compassion (v. 8), His goodness and mercy (v. 9), His faithful promises (v. 13), and *his open hand* (v. 16).

Our God is not stingy, but lavish in His gift-giving. He is a God of extravagance. He delights in caring for His children. Over and over again in His Word we are reminded of His gracious provi-

sion, both physically and spiritually: "They feast on the abundance of your house; you give them drink from your river of delights" (36:8). "You crown the year with your bounty, and your carts overflow with abundance" (65:11). "The Lᴏʀᴅ is my shepherd, I shall not be in want" (23:1). The refrain is echoed in the New Testament: "I have come that they may have life, and have it to the full' (John 10:10).

That greatest Gift was God Himself in human flesh!

> **"Our God is not stingy, but lavish in His gift-giving. He delights in caring for His children.**

Personal prayer

My Father God, I thank You for Your open hands which have satisfied the deepest desires of my heart through Jesus Christ . . . and keep on giving every day of my life!

393

Praise to the King

His Glory

Exposition of theme

PSALM 145 *CONTINUED*

All you have made will praise you, O LORD; your saints will extol you. They will tell of the glory of your kingdom and speak of your might, so that all men may know of your mighty acts and the glorious splendor of your kingdom. Your kingdom is an everlasting kingdom, and your dominion endures through all generations (vv. 10–13).

Development of theme

I read the words of this passage and try to envision the kingdom described here — its glory, its splendor, its everlastingness!

God's kingdom — not made with hands — is

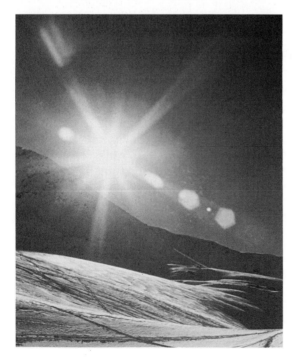

> *"At the center — radiant and brighter than the sun — is the King Himself. His dominion is not transitory; it is an everlasting kingdom, enduring through all generations."*

filled with His glory and reflects His power and might. At the center — radiant and brighter than the sun — is the King Himself. His dominion is not transitory; it is an everlasting kingdom, enduring through all generations (v. 13).

So moved am I that I break forth into a song of praise:

Praise to the King

You are my God and King,
Of Your greatness I will sing;
I will thank You all my days
And thru eternity give Your praise.

I sing of Your wondrous fame
And bow before your name;
For You rule in sovereignty
And reign in glorious majesty.

I give thanks for Your goodness
And celebrate Your kindness.
I bow in humility
Before all You've done for me.

Then someday when You come for me
I'll be caught up to glory,
And I'll join the angelic train
To sing of Your sovereign reign.

Words and music by Don Wyrtzen. © 1980 Singspiration.

Personal prayer

King of kings, I praise You for Your mighty deeds in my life and look forward to joining that "angelic train" in glory!

Praise to the King

His Listening Ear

Exposition of theme

PSALM 145 CONTINUED

The LORD is righteous in all his ways and loving toward all he has made. The LORD is near to all who call on him, to all who call on him in truth. He fulfills the desires of those who fear him; he hears their cry and saves them. The LORD watches over all who love him, but all the wicked he will destroy. My mouth will speak in praise of the LORD. Let every creature praise his holy name for ever and ever (vv. 17–21).

Development of theme

Picture the Lord. What image do you see? He's a perfect King — infinitely powerful and totally just. But He is also a loving Father — intimately near, warm, and personal. He is just exactly what each of us needs. How sad that many of us try to keep Him at arm's length most of the time!

King and Father. It may be easier to accept the image of God as King than as Father. Some, whose childhood memories are scarred by thoughts of unloving, insensitive parents, need to learn the definition of *father* by studying this psalm. This Father is never inattentive, neglectful, or too busy.

Even to those of us who were blessed with godly fathers, this concept may seem foreign to

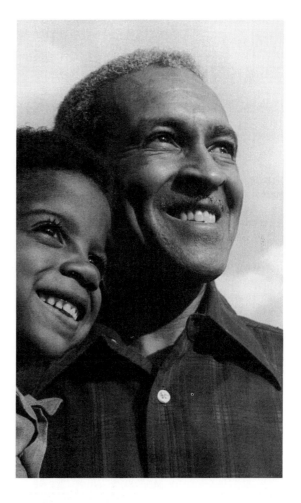

us. We're so busy declaring our independence, toughing it out alone, and proving ourselves that we lose sight of the truth that self-sufficiency never results in lasting satisfaction. We need to learn that we are most satisfied and safest in the arms of our heavenly Father. He is "near to all who call on him" (v. 18). How amazing!

Personal prayer

My God and King, I'm so glad You showed me something of Your heart through my dad and that I have only to turn to your Word to be further reminded of Your active love and care.

> **"We're so busy declaring our independence, toughing it out alone, and proving ourselves that we lose sight of the truth that self-sufficiency never results in lasting satisfaction."**

The Ultimate Priority

Praising His Greatness in Creation

Exposition of theme
PSALM 146

Praise the LORD. Praise the LORD, O my soul. I will praise the LORD all my life; I will sing praise to my God as long as I live. Do not put your trust in princes, in mortal men, who cannot save. When their spirit departs, they return to the ground; on that very day their plans come to nothing. Blessed is he whose help is the God of Jacob, whose hope is in the LORD his God, the Maker of heaven and earth, the sea, and everything in them — the LORD, who remains faithful forever (vv. 1–6).

Development of theme

Music has always been as necessary to me as breathing. Melodies tend to stick to me like glue, playing over and over in my "inner ear" tape deck. A moving praise song such as "His Name Is Wonderful" evokes a whole emotional gestalt of feelings, memories, and associations. Certain songs, such as "In the Sweet By and By," "O That Will Be Glory for Me," and "When We All Get to Heaven" remind me of friends and loved ones who are waiting for us there — my mom, Karen's dad, the Barclays, Tim Walvoord, Louis Paul Lehman, and others. For me, music is a big part of the rhythm and meaning in life and, like David, I want praise to be the top priority of my life.

It's easy to praise the Lord when I see Him at every turn — at the seaside, in the mountains, in the snow frosting the trees outside the window of my study.

But God's unshakability is appreciated even more when seen against the backdrop of human weakness and transience. As David pointed out,

> *"Have I let the plastic things made by humans blind me to authentic masterpieces created by God?"*

"Mortal men . . . cannot save" (v. 3). Their final destiny is the grave; on the day of death their well-strategized plans come to nothing.

As the year draws to a close, I need to reevaluate my commitment to the Lord. Have I kept my priorities in order? Have I praised the Lord every day through meditating on His Word, through prayer, through music? Have I let the plastic things made by humans blind me to authentic masterpieces created by God? Have I cultivated a sense of His presence, so that I can know Him whom I've never seen? Am I worshiping Him with my whole person or with my head? Objective knowledge is a poor substitute for subjective intimacy and involvement!

Personal prayer

Dear Lord, I want to praise You as long as I live. Make me sensitive to Your beauty in creation and may I move from an awareness of Your power and might to a warm, personal relationship with You.

The Ultimate Priority

Praising His Grace in Provision

Exposition of theme

PSALM 146 CONTINUED

He upholds the cause of the oppressed and gives food to the hungry. The LORD sets prisoners free, the LORD gives sight to the blind, the LORD lifts up those who are bowed down, the LORD loves the righteous. The LORD watches over the alien and sustains the fatherless and the widow, but he frustrates the ways of the wicked. The LORD reigns forever; your God, O Zion, for all generations. Praise the LORD (vv. 7–10).

Development of theme

The Lord is to be praised, not only for His greatness in creation, but also for His provision on behalf of His people. He shows His loving favor in many ways. He helps the oppressed, feeds the hungry, sets prisoners free, makes the blind see, lifts up the fallen, loves the righteous, watches over aliens, sustains the homeless, and frustrates the wicked.

There are many prophetic allusions to the marvelous gifts of God's grace. (See Isaiah

> *"The whole purpose of God's redemptive plan in history was "to the praise of his glorious grace"*

42:6–8.) The New Testament records the fulfillment of this prophecy: "The Spirit of the LORD is upon me, because he hath anointed me to preach the gospel to the poor; he hath sent me to heal the broken-hearted, to preach deliverance to the captives, and recovering the sight to the blind, to set at liberty them that are bruised" (Luke 4:18 KJV). Indeed, the whole purpose of God's redemptive plan in history was "to the praise of his glorious grace" (Ephesians 1:6).

God's grace was personified through His Son, the Lord Jesus Christ. It is through Him and Him alone that we can be saved (Ephesians 2:8–9). He is the only, true hope for fallen man.

The psalmist concludes by reminding us that the Lord reigns forever. He ends as he began — with a paroxysm of praise, "Hallelujah!"

Personal prayer

Dear Lord, I thank You for Your "glorious grace" and what it has done in my life. I thank You for the Lord Jesus Christ who personifies Your grace — Your undeserved favor.

A CONTEMPORARY PRAISE SONG

To the Praise of His Glorious Grace

Let us praise the One who chose us,
Let us thank the One who knows us;
Set apart, blameless in His sight;
Through the Son we have faith, we have
    life —
To the praise of His glorious grace.

May the God of our Lord, the Almighty
    Father,
Give you wisdom and peace, His comforting
    Spirit;
That you may know His love,
And you may know His riches, and you may
    know His mighty strength —
To the praise of His glorious grace.

Words and music by Michael W. Smith and Deborah D. Smith.
© 1983 Meadowgreen Music Co.

DECEMBER 20

A Very Personal Doxology

He heals me . . .

Exposition of theme
PSALM 147

Praise the LORD. How good it is to sing praises to our God, how pleasant and fitting to praise him!

The LORD builds up Jerusalem; he gathers the exiles of Israel. He heals the brokenhearted and binds up their wounds. He determines the number of stars and calls them each by name. Great is our LORD and mighty in power; his understanding has no limit. The LORD sustains the humble but casts the wicked to the ground (vv. 1–6).

Development of theme

I've both experienced and observed "brokenheartedness," and it's a devastating blow either way. The holidays, when families come together to make memories, are especially poignant and difficult for some of us who are still grieving. It's so hard to accept the fact that I will never again see Mom or Karen's dad on this earth.

That's why this passage from Psalm 147 is so timely. David is referring, of course, to the exiled

---

> **"God loves to restore and rebuild. Just as He rebuilt Jerusalem after the Babylonian Exile, He accepts any penitent sinner for remodeling."**

---

captives of Israel when he says, "He [the Lord] heals the brokenhearted and binds up their wounds" (v. 3), but he might be speaking of any broken heart anywhere.

Sometimes the "wounds" are caused by some significant "other" in one's life; sometimes they are self-inflicted through sin. But God loves to restore and rebuild. Just as He rebuilt Jerusalem after the Babylonian Exile, He accepts any penitent sinner for remodeling. The only prerequisites are honesty, humility, and homage. The believer (or unbeliever) who truly repents and returns from sin is fully forgiven, restored, and radically rebuilt!

When we honestly face our grief or our sin and submit it to the Lord, He responds in grace by forgiving and healing. This profound, personal work then becomes the basis for authentic praise. I face an extravagant future with the Lord in glory, when I will see Mom and Karen's dad again. We'll have a lot of catching up to do!

Personal prayer

Praise the Lord! I join in praising Your holy, precious name. I praise You for healing the brokenhearted and for setting us free to sing praise!

A Very Personal Doxology

He delights in me . . .

Exposition of theme

PSALM 147 CONTINUED

Sing to the LORD with thanksgiving; make music to our God on the harp. He covers the sky with clouds; he supplies the earth with rain and makes grass grow on the hills. He provides food for the cattle and for the young ravens when they call. His pleasure is not in the strength of the horse, nor his delight in the legs of a man; the LORD delights in those who fear him, who put their hope in his unfailing love (vv. 7–11).

Development of theme

There are some things a father never forgets — his child's first steps, the first words, the first Christmas. I'll always remember the rush of pride I felt when our son, D. J., got the music award as a senior at Brentwood Academy. I felt the same deep emotion when his sister, Kathy, became the spelling champion of her class in Grand Rapids. My kids have delighted me on many occasions. Last Christmas, I was especially proud of D. J. when he visited the Heaston family every day to see their daughter, Heather, who was recovering from the auto accident that took the life of her sister, Leesha.

Though it blows my mind, I know how the Lord must feel when His children do well! "He delights in those who fear him" (v. 11). God is unimpressed by brute strength, but He "takes great pleasure and enjoyment in" the reverence of His children. We are created to praise, and when we learn to do that well, we know we're pleasing Him.

As we become aware of God's delight, we'll experience the gift of His glorious grace. We, in turn, will delight in Him—a wondrous, intimate interplay between God, the Father, and His children.

Personal prayer

Praise the Lord! I thank You and praise You for delighting in me. I place my confidence in Your glorious grace and unfailing love today.

DECEMBER 22

A Very Personal Doxology

He gives me peace . . .

Exposition of theme

PSALM 147 CONTINUED

Extol the LORD, O Jerusalem; praise your God, O Zion, for he strengthens the bars of your gates and blesses your people within you. He grants peace to your borders and satisfies you with the finest of wheat. He sends his command to the earth; his word runs swiftly (vv. 12–15).

Development of theme

David and the other psalmists had long been buried with their fathers when the angels sang the first Christmas carol: "Glory to God in the highest, and on earth peace to men on whom his favor rests" (Luke 2:14). How those ancient songwriters would have rejoiced at the coming of the Messiah—the "Prince of Peace" whom Isaiah foretold (Isaiah 9:6)!

Here the psalmist exhorts the inhabitants of the Holy City to praise the Lord. I can hear the harmony of soprano, alto, tenor, and bass as the "voices" blend in a choral anthem of peace.

Soprano—The high notes soar: "He strengthens the bars of your gates" (v. 13). These people need not fear invasion or attack. The Lord Himself stands at the gate to turn back any who should not enter.

Alto—Providing mellow, rich support is another voice: "And blesses the people within you" (v. 13). Blessing comes from His presence within. "Be born in me tonight," I echo.

Tenor—A strong male voice takes the lead and the song continues on a rising note of joy: "He grants peace to your borders" (v. 14). Peace! Peace! Where is peace in this chaotic world?

Bass — Deep and vibrant comes the reassuring word: "[He] satisfies you with the finest of wheat. . . . He sends his command to the earth. His word runs swiftly" (vv. 14–15). The Lord provides. Not only does He satisfy our hunger for food, but He sends His Word — the written Word and the living Word! Jesus Christ is born! He lives to bring peace!

Personal prayer

Praise the Lord! I thank You for the gift of Your Word which sustains me. But I thank You even more for the gift of Your Son, Immanuel — God with us!

DECEMBER 23

A Very Personal Doxology

He sustains His Word . . .

Exposition of theme

PSALM 147 CONTINUED

He spreads the snow like wool and scatters the frost like ashes. He hurls down his hail like pebbles. Who can withstand his icy blast? He sends his word and melts them; he stirs up his breezes, and the waters flow. He has revealed his word to Jacob, his laws and decrees to Israel. He has done this for no other nation; they do not know his laws. Praise the LORD (vv. 16–20).

Development of theme

What a wondrous wintertime scene is painted in this passage! The greatness of the Lord is perceived by the effect of His Word. He speaks, and the elements of nature obey. When He commands winter, blizzards occur. "He spreads the

---

> *"At His command, the spring thaw sets in, rivers run, like the melting of an icy heart in the warmth of His love."*

---

snow" and "scatters the frost" (v. 16). "He hurls down his hail like pebbles" (v. 17). The icy blast is almost felt as well as seen in this graphic word picture.

Similarly, at His command, the spring thaw sets in, rivers run, like the melting of an icy heart in the warmth of His love. His Word is inviolable, authoritative, and sure.

The most powerful display of His grace was the gift of His written Word. The magnificence of the Mosaic Law and the earth-shattering ethical insights of His decrees were His special gift to Israel. No other nation then possessed the glory of His commandments.

Through Israel His Word comes down thorugh the generations. It was the Word of God that sustained King David throughout his turbulent life. It is His Word that sustains us. Through His precious Word we receive His gifts of grace. Praise the Lord!

Personal prayer

O Lord, I praise You for the gift of Your written Word which sustains and quickens my spirit.

DECEMBER 24

Canticle of Praise

All Creation Sings Praise

Exposition of theme

PSALM 148

Praise the LORD. Praise the LORD from the heavens, praise him in the heights above. Praise him, all his angels, praise him all his heavenly hosts. Praise him, sun and moon, praise him, all you shining stars. Praise him, you highest heavens and you waters above the skies. Let them praise the name of the LORD, for he commanded and they were created. He set them in place for ever and ever; he gave a decree that will never pass away (vv. 1–6).

Development of theme

On this night of nights, all creation erupts in a cosmic explosion of joy: "Hallelujah!" The psalmist's poetic expression is intensified by the

---

THE LANGUAGE OF MUSIC

Canticle

In liturgy a Scripture text similar to a psalm but occuring outside of the Psalter.

Examples would be: "My soul doth magnify the Lord" (Luke 1:46), and "Lord, now lettest thou thy servant depart in peace" (Luke 2:29).

---

use of personification. The luminaries in the heavens praise the Lord (v. 1). The angels — heavenly hosts — praise the Lord (v. 2). All the elements of nature praise the Lord (vv. 3–4).

What motivates all of creation to praise the Lord? The fact that its very existence is based on the Word and decree of the Lord. On this night, hundreds of years after this psalm was written, the Word became flesh and dwelt among us — like a candle igniting a forest fire that would banish the darkness forever! (Luke 2)

But what if Jesus had not come?

Personal prayer

Jesus, I'm so glad You came! I join with all creation in singing Your praises!

A CHRISTMAS PRAISE SONG

Alleluia, Our Redeemer Came

What if Jesus had not come to earth
    that first Christmas long ago?
His tender mercy and His sweet forgiveness
    would be joys our souls would never
    know.
Darkness ruled the hearts of all mankind
    on that night Jesus came;
But heaven's light was shining
    in that wondrous Baby's smile,
And a grateful world would never be the
    same!

Alleluia, our Redeemer came!
Alleluia, praise His holy name!
Jesus came to Bethlehem, and His glory
    filled the skies with song!
Alleluia, let our voices sing
"Alleluias" for the joys He brings
    to our hearts at Christmastime
    and each day throughout the year.

Words and music by Greg Nelson, Don Wyrtzen, and Phill McHugh.
© 1987 by Don Wyrtzen Music and Singspiration, New Wings Music, Greg Nelson Music, and River Oaks Music co.

Canticle of Praise

Earthly hosts sing praise

Exposition of theme

PSALM 148 CONTINUED

Praise the LORD from the earth, you great sea creatures and all ocean depths, lightning and hail, snow and clouds, stormy winds that do his bidding, you mountains and all hills, fruit trees and all cedars, wild animals and all cattle, small creatures and flying birds, kings of the earth and all nations, you princes and all rulers on earth, young men and maidens, old men and children. Let them praise the name of the Lord, for his name alone is exalted; his splendor is above the earth and the heavens. He has raised up for his people a horn, the praise of all his saints, of Israel, the people close to his heart. Praise the LORD (vv. 7–14).

Development of theme

All nature sings praise to the Lord! The list of members in the great universal choir is a kaleidoscope of animate and inanimate creatures — sea creatures, lightning and hail, snow and clouds, small creatures and flying birds, kings and princes, rulers and nations, young men and maidens, old men and children — all crying out with joy, all praising the Lord together!

Why do they praise Him? First, they are responding to the glory of His name (v. 13). Sec-

ond, they realize that His glory transcends His creation (v. 13). Third, they are praising Him in gratitude for the king He has given Israel (v. 14) — a prelude to the coming of Christ!

Why do I, who now know the Messiah, often neglect praise? Why is my heart sometimes unresponsive? Could I be guilty of worshiping the creation rather than the Creator (Romans 1:25)? How do I alter this condition? By bowing again before His cradle throne, by cherishing this Gift from the Father, by adoring Him!

Personal prayer

O Lord, I adore You! I cherish the gift of Your salvation and commit myself again to You with full fervor and joy!

"I often neglect praise? Why is my heart sometimes unresponsive? How do I alter this condition? By bowing again before His cradle throne, by cherishing this Gift from the Father, by adoring Him!"

A CHRISTMAS CAROL

O Come, All Ye Faithful

O come, all ye faithful, joyful and
    triumphant;
Come ye, O come ye to Bethlehem;
Come and behold Him, born the King of
    angels:
O come let us adore Him,
O come, let us adore Him,
O come, let us adore Him, Christ the
    Lord!

Yea, Lord, we greet Thee, born this happy
    morning;
Jesus, to Thee be all glory giv'n;
Word of the Father, now in flesh
    appearing:
O come, let us adore Him,
O come, let us adore Him,
O come, let us adore Him, Christ the Lord!

Words — Latin hymn, 18th C. Trans. by Frederick Oakeley, Music — Wade's *Cantus Diversi*

Motet for the Meek

Motivation for Praise

Exposition of theme

PSALM 149

Praise the LORD. Sing to the LORD a new song, his praise in the assembly of the saints. Let Israel rejoice in their Maker; let the people of Zion be glad in their King. Let them praise his name with dancing and make music to him with tambourine and harp. For the LORD takes delight in his people; he crowns the humble with salvation. Let the saints rejoice in this honor and sing for joy on their beds (vv. 1–5).

Development of theme

How quickly we forget! Once the gift is unwrapped and we exclaim over it, we lay it aside for a bigger and shinier one! What have I done with the gift of God's Son and the salvation that cost Him so dearly?

The psalmist prods my conscience when he calls on the people of Israel to "sing a new song" even while they are resting (v. 5)! I shouldn't have to be reminded. My joy in the Lord should be so full that it spills over in spontaneous praise!

Then I read on and am convicted all over again. Israel is commanded to express her joy with dancing and instrumental performance (v. 3). Not only are we to use our voices and musical instruments, but also our bodies in complete, free, and uninhibited rejoicing. Yet danc-

> *"Not only are we to use our voices and musical instruments, but also our bodies in complete, free, and uninhibited rejoicing."*

ing is an art form virtually unheard of in today's worship services! It is foreign to our culture, by and large, yet when we are too proper, too controlled, we may miss some of the blessings God has in store for us.

Consistent and creative praise keeps faith alive and growing. I must envision God as loving, caring, and delighting in me. Then I will be inspired to use all the gifts He has given me in exuberant praise!

Personal prayer

Teach me a new song, Lord, and may I learn to express my joy with unrestrained enthusiasm!

THE LANGUAGE OF MUSIC

Motet

A polyphonic (many voices) choral composition on a sacred text usually without instrumental accompaniment.

There are two different types of motet: Medieval and Renaissance.

DECEMBER 27

Motet for the Meek

Summation of Praise

Exposition of theme

PSALM 149 CONTINUED

May the praise of God be in their mouths and a double-edged sword in their hands, to inflict vengeance on the nations and punishment on the peoples, to bind their kings with fetters, their nobles with shackles of iron, to carry out the sentence written against them. This is the glory of all his saints. Praise the LORD (vv. 6–9).

Development of theme

God calls on Israel not only to praise His name but also to execute vengeance on the nations. The Israelites were to worship Him, yes, but they were also to stand for God's justice and to put down evil in the world. They would be praising with their mouths while brandishing a double-edged sword in their hands!

The psalmist gives us no romanticized view of God. He calls for the annihilation of heathen nations, for wicked kings to be fettered, and for His

---

"The Lord needs some young Vance Havners who have the conviction to write and speak out against hypocrisy and evil."

---

absolutely just sentence to be carried out. As His saints obey the Lord, they experience His glory.

What a study in contrasts — worship and vengeance, praise and power! If this seems strange, it may be because we are comfortable with doublemindedness. We want to be intimate with God while "cozying up" to evil on the side. The Lord wants us to be "wise about what is good, and innocent about what is evil" (Romans 16:19). We're open to praising God, but we're not as interested in balancing our worship with a holy hatred of sin. He calls us to praise and to prophesy. He needs some young Vance Havners who have the conviction to write and speak out against hypocrisy and evil. He needs worship leaders — "praise spokesmen" — but He also summons contemporary prophets — "praise motivators" — who will cry out against injustice and sin in our world.

Personal prayer

May I have the inner strength not only to praise You, Lord, but to take a stand for righteousness in the circles where I live and work.

The Hallelujah Chorus

The "Where" of Praise

Exposition of theme
PSALM 150

Praise the LORD. Praise God in his sanctuary; praise him in his mighty heavens (v. 1).

Development of theme

This psalm is an orchestra of praise — every instrument imaginable poised and lifted up in worship, celebrating God's incomparable excellence.

Wherever His creatures live, God should be praised, the psalmist says. First, he encourages believers to praise the Lord in the sanctuary. Second, he urges the angels to praise the Lord in the sky, the vault of heaven. Since God's glory fills the universe, His praise must do no less!

Many of us organize our lives into neat, convenient categories — business, domestic, spiritual. We find it hard to think about praising the Lord at work, or while swimming or playing tennis, or at home with the family. Worship is slotted in on Sundays and Wednesday nights. Many of us have fallen into the sacred versus secular dichotomy, which robs us of spontaneity and vitality in our relationship with the Lord. Such a narrow concept of praise leads to a life of truth without beauty which, in turn, can result in legalism, disillusionment, or even rebellion.

We need to learn to praise the Lord wherever we are. We ought to try standing around the dinner table, holding hands with our loved ones, and singing the "Doxology" together. We ought to dare humming the tune to a hymn at break in the office. We ought to join some major community choir in the Easter or Christmas season and sing the "Hallelujah Chorus," and allow ourselves to lose control of our emotions, letting the tears flow down our cheeks and the chills run up our spines. That will be a preview of heaven when we join the angelic choir of millions upon millions! Hallelujah!

Personal prayer

Dear Lord, may I be bold enough to praise You wherever I am today — at home, in the office, in the midst of recreation, or at church. You inhabit praise, so my joyful heart is Your "sanctuary."

Hallelujah Chorus

G. F. Handel
Arr. by John W. Schaum

Hallelujah Chorus

Hallelujah! Hallelujah! Hallelujah!
Hallelujah!
Hallelujah! Hallelujah! Hallelujah!
Hallelujah!
For the Lord God omnipotent reigneth.
Hallelujah! Hallelujah! Hallelujah!
Hallelujah!

The kingdom of this world is become
the kingdom of our Lord, and of His
Christ;
And He shall reign forever and ever,
King of kings! and Lord of lords!

And He shall reign forever and ever,
King of kings! and Lord of lords!
Hallelujah! Hallelujah! Hallelujah!
Hallelujah!
Hallelujah!

Words — Rev. 19:6. Music — George Frederick Handel

the Messiah

Handel

The Hallelujah Chorus

The "Why" of Praise

Exposition of theme

PSALM 150 *CONTINUED*

Praise him for his acts of power; praise him for his surpassing greatness (v. 2).

Development of theme

Why should believers praise the Lord? The answer is simple: Because He deserves it!

He spoke the world into being, established the first couple in their garden home, then provided redemption for all mankind when they sinned. The Redeemer paid for your sins and mine on a Roman cross thousands of years later. We honor and extol Him for these mighty deeds and saving acts. That's reason enough to praise Him.

But there is more. If He did nothing at all, there would still be necessity for praise. We are created for communion with God. We are His admiring audience, His fans, who applaud Him for the glory of His attributes and the beauty of His character.

THE LANGUAGE OF MUSIC

Hallelujah Chorus

Perhaps the most famous of choral compositions.

Composed by George F. Handel for his oratorio, "Messiah," the Hallelujah Chorus is a definitive exclamation of praise to God. "Hallelujah" comes from Hebrew ("Hallelujah"—"Praise the Lord"). "Alleluia" is the Latinized spelling.

We must move on from knowing the facts about Him to knowing *Him*. We must move from distance to intimacy. Then we can truly join the heavenly band in singing:

Gloria in excelsis Deo!

Angels we have heard on high,
Sweetly singing o'er the plains,
And the mountains in reply,
Echoing their joyous strains.

Gloria in excelsis Deo!
Old French Carol.

Personal prayer

Gloria in excelsis Deo! I'm eager to praise You in celestial language, Lord. Teach me to sing like the angels!

DECEMBER 30

The Hallelujah Chorus

The "Who" of Praise

Exposition of theme

PSALM 150 CONTINUED

Let everything that has breath praise the LORD. Praise the LORD (v. 6).

Development of theme

Who should praise the Lord? The psalmist answers in verse 6. "Everything that has breath" should praise the Lord. All of creation should be involved (Psalm 148:7–12). Infants and children are included (8:2). Even animals are not left out (Job 38–41). Worship is not the exclusive prov-

ince of pastors, Christian celebrities, or worship leaders. All believers should join the creation in exalting and honoring the Lord. It's a privilege and joy!

In fact, when we sing, our Lord sings with us! When we worship, He worships with us (Psalm 22:22; Hebrews 2:12). The believer has no higher calling!

Personal prayer

Dear Lord, may I praise You with every breath I take! And may I so inspire others with the music You give me that all creation will join in the chorus!

A CONTEMPORARY PRAISE SONG

Our Sacrifice of Praise

We bow and worship Him, our Lord and
    King—
  Forever and ever His praise we'll sing;
To Him all honor, love, and thanks we
    bring—
  And to His attributes we cling.

We'll tell the world the glory of His name—
  And tell how for sinners the Savior came;
We'll spread thru all the earth His wondrous
    fame—
  Unchanging, always He's the same!

Jesus our Saviour lives forevermore—
  He rose from the grave to die no more;
His mercy, grace and glory we explore—
  And, winged by faith, our spirits soar.

He is deserving of all thanks and praise—
  With joy overflowing our hearts we raise;
We'll sing and sing of Him for endless
    days—
  This is our sacrifice of praise!

Words and music by Don Wyrtzen. Based on Hebrews 13:15.
© 1973 Singspiration.

The Hallelujah Chorus

The "How" of Praise

Exposition of theme

PSALM 150 CONTINUED

Praise him with the sounding of the trumpet, praise him with the harp and lyre, praise him with tambourine and dancing, praise him with the strings and flute, praise him with the clash of cymbals, praise him with resounding cymbals (vv. 3–5).

Development of theme

We are to praise Yahweh with every kind of musical form and instrument available!

In ancient times, great national feasts and sacred occasions were ushered in by the fanfare of the trumpet (2 Chronicles 5:1–14). These trumpets were most likely rams' horns, primitive versions of modern valve trumpets and fluegelhorns (Psalm 150:3). The shophar or trumpet was also used at the battle of Jericho. David's harp was also a simple instrument, which he played sensitively and gloriously, but was not a modern-day pedal harp.

Timbrels (tambourines), strings, and flutes are mentioned as vehicles of praise in verse 4. Joyous celebrations of victory were marked by the use of these instruments accompanied with dancing (149:3). Dancing was an integral part of Hebrew worship. Miriam danced to the tambourine (Exodus 15:20–21). So also did the women who greeted Saul and David in their moments of victorious celebration (1 Samuel 18:6–7). King David was so elated by the return of the ark of the covenant to Jerusalem that he broke into dancing (2 Samuel 6:14–16). Because of the influence of asceticism, many today feel that any movement of the body to music is evil. However, liturgical dance is certainly biblical, and the body is to be a reflector of His grace.

In verse 5, clashing cymbals are mentioned. In fact, Asaph, one of the premiere musicians in ancient Israel, was a cymbal player (1 Chronicles 15:19). So we see that every kind of instrument, form, and sound is called upon to praise God — solemn and festive, percussive and melodic, gentle and strident, dissonant and consonant,

> *"We are to take the old-fashioned message of the gospel and translate it into the language of today. Luther did. Sankey did. Rodeheaver did. Let us follow in their footsteps and in the steps of David, that greatest musician of the ancient world!"*

fast and slow, stirring and meditative.

The church is just beginning to take advantage of the technological revolution — synthesizers, multi-track recording techniques, etc. Our challenge is to praise the Lord with our whole being and with every instrument at our disposal. We are to take the old-fashioned message of the gospel and translate it into the language of today. Luther did it in the sixteenth century. Sankey did it in the nineteenth century. Rodeheaver did it in the early twentieth century. Let us follow in their footsteps and in the steps of David, that greatest musician of the ancient world!

Personal prayer

Dear Lord, help me to praise you with my whole being — heart, soul, mind, and body — and with all the instrumental forms, sounds, and inventions available to me.
SOLI DEO GLORIA!

Worthy Is The Lamb

Arr. by Don Wyrtsen

Wor- thy is the lamb,

Wor- thy is the lamb,

Worthy is the Lamb that was slain,
Worthy is the Lamb that was slain,
Worthy is the Lamb that was slain, to receive:
Power, and riches, and wisdom, and strength,
Honor, and glory, and blessing!

Worthy is the Lamb,
Worthy is the Lamb,
Worthy is the Lamb that was slain,
Worthy is the Lamb!

Revelation 5:12

411

POSTLUDE *What I've learned from the Psalms*

A Musician Looks at the Psalms revels in three-part form. Each day of the journal has been divided into an exposition of the theme, a development of the theme, and a prayer (or recapitulation). The book itself also follows a three-part structure: prelude, body of work, and postlude.

A postlude is a closing piece of music, often an organ voluntary at the end of a worship service. I would like to use this postlude to share with you what I have learned from the Psalms. I can synthesize it into one big idea:

Only the Lord gives us a clear, accurate picture of reality. Without His divine revelation we don't have an adequate basis for our identity, our values, or our morality.

To elaborate I will state seven basic principles I have learned from my study of the Psalter, the ancient hymnbook of Israel. They give beautiful, sensitive answers to the meaning of life and form the architecture of a Judeo-Christian philosophy of life.

First, my being and existence have eternal value because I am made in God's image. I have learned that God "created my inmost being" and that "I am fearfully and wonderfully made" (Psalm 139:13–14). I am a person of infinite worth and dignity–"a little lower than the angels" and "crowned with glory and honor" (8:4–5). In Genesis 1:27 the Word explicitly says that God created me "in His own image." I am never to believe the Enemy's incessant message that I am valueless and worthless. Indeed, rather I am crowned with meaning and majesty!

Second, my deepest longings to be loved and to be special are met in the Lord. I've learned that His loyal love endures forever (Psalm 136). Nothing I could ever imagine or experience can keep me from God's love (Romans 8:38–39). Based on this love, I am safe and secure in Him (Psalm 16). But not only do I possess inner security in the Lord, I am also adequate and special because of Him. I am to rule over God's glorious creation (8:6). Only the Lord defines the universe and brings meaning to the particulars of life. Only He has it all together. Therefore, when I experience deep longings—hunger and thirst—they are met in the Lord. "As the deer pants for streams of water, so my soul pants for you, O God" (Psalm 42:1, see Isaiah 55:1–2). Therefore, I don't need to distort reality or distract myself from pain because my Lord ultimately gives me all I need. My inner core is only satisfied in Him!

Psalm to Jesus

As a stream to the desert sand,
   As a rain to the vine;
As a shade to the barren land,
   So Your heart is to mine.

As a beam to the darkest night,
   As a calm to the sea;
As a kiss to the frightened child,
   So Your love is to me.

Yet, my heart longs for more,
   Lord, my soul thirsts for more—
My spirit hungers for more of You.

As a rose in the summer sun,
   So my heart longs for more of You!

Words by Nan Allen, Music by Don Wyrtzen. © 1988 by Singspiration.

Third, my mind can be renewed and refreshed by meditating on the Word. My study of the Psalms has taught me that the real battles of life are fought in the mind. One's perception of reality determines his response to life. The Jewish nation was distinctive among the heathen peoples of the ancient world because their minds were filled with the magnificence of the law. I have the capability of running video-tapes in my brain that either tear me down or lift me up. I can think negatively or positively. You see, our lives can only be "transformed by the renewing of our minds" (Romans 12:1–2).

Joy comes from a refreshed and renewed mind. This is a major theme in the Psalter. "The law of the LORD is perfect, reviving the soul. The statutes of the LORD are trustworthy, making wise the simple. The precepts of the LORD are right, giving joy to the heart. The commands of the LORD are radiant giving light to the eyes" (Psalm 19:7–8). Our thoughts, our cognitions govern our lives. They affect our choices and our choices predetermine our feelings. We all bear scars from the fall of man. One of our major wounds is to think inaccurately about moral truth. This is why we desperately need daily exposure to and immersion in God's Word.

Fourth, my life can have direction and purpose through obedience to God's truth. The whole subject of the will of man and how it relates to the sovereignty of God is very complex. But we can all grasp the fact that our choices are based on our thoughts. We will not choose to go God's way until we begin to think His thoughts. Our minds function on a cybernetic principle: we are goal-oriented. We will passionately pursue goals that we believe will give our lives meaning. The psalms teach us that the only ultimate meaning and deep personal fulfillment come from obedience to God's Word. The old hymn says it so simply, yet profoundly: "Trust and obey, for there's no other way to be happy in Jesus but to trust and obey." (John Sammis) David, the chief musician says, "But from everlasting to everlasting the LORD's love is with those who fear him, and his righteousness with their children's children—with those who keep his covenant and remember to obey his precepts" (103:17–18, 20). We can choose to praise, adore, and worship the Lord, whatever our circumstances.

Fifth, my feelings can be experienced and expressed without fear or guilt. The Psalter really expresses two major motifs that are repeated again and again: *Life is tough but God is good.* These psalmists, ancient songwriters, lived in a

413

period of severe adversity and upheaval. They knew what is was like to suffer, to groan and to cry out, but they worshiped a God who was big enough to handle their problems. Therefore, they poured out their souls to Him. Their prayers were moments of catharsis: "Out of the depths I cry to you, O LORD; O LORD, hear my voice. Let your ears be attentive to my cry for mercy" (130:1–2). They knew that "weeping may remain for a night, but rejoicing comes in the morning" (30:5). We are called to be holy, not happy. But many of us are addicted to happiness rather than committed to holiness. We gladly trade ultimate joy for short-term relief. The psalmists teach us to face life squarely—to look life right in the eye! In the nature of reality we will experience suffering and joy, pain and peace, adversity and felicity. Right now, we're pilgrims—"just a passin' through." This world is *not* our home. It's abrasive. We're not comfortable here. We're not totally at home yet, not fully satisfied. We're restless until we find God because we were made for eternity! We can allow ourselves to lament individually and nationally.

Sixth, reality can only be grasped when I intimately embrace Jesus Christ as my Lord and Savior. Because the Apostle Paul had further revelation from God, he knew more about the Gospel than did King David. Yet, even in the Psalms, we see the Gospel taking shape in seedling form. Here are the key ideas. I would encourage you to think about them, apply them to your own life, and then make some concrete decisions about them.

• *I'm a precious person made in God's image.* God "created my inmost being." "I am fearfully and wonderfully made" (Psalm 139:13– 14; see Genesis 1:27).

• *I will live forever.* David said that he would "dwell in the house of the LORD forever" (Psalm 23:6).

• *I have sinned.*

But David himself was flawed and sinful. He says, "Have mercy on me, O God, according to your unfailing love; according to your great compassion blot out my transgressions. Wash away all my iniquity and cleanse me from my sin" (Psalm 51:1–2).

• *I need a Savior.* I believe that Jesus Christ is the Messiah of the Psalms. Listen to the mournful music of these moving words: "My God, my God, why have you forsaken me?" That's a *direct quote* from Psalm 22:1. Those exact words were spoken by Christ as He bore the sins of the world on a Roman cross (Matthew 27:46)!

• *I must choose to accept Him or reject Him.* Why must I choose? Why must I personally decide? Because "the LORD watches over the way of the righteous, but the way of the wicked will perish" (Psalm 1:6). I must accept Christ as my Savior and must simply ask Him to come into my life. "Yet to all who received him, to those who believe in his name he gave the right to become children of God" (John 1:12). What gave Him the authority? He rose from the dead! (See Psalm 16:9–10 and Acts 2:31.) Why don't you choose to accept Him right now as your Lord and Savior? He is the supreme Answer to the question of life.

Seventh, my being and personality will live forever, either with the Lord or apart from Him. David talks about being led "in the way everlasting" (Psalm 139:24). He says that he will be pursued by goodness and love all the days of his life. And he concludes the most sublime lyric ever written by saying, "I will dwell in the house of the LORD forever."

J.S. Bach signed his works in a unique way. It is an apt closing, a perfect signature, to this journal.

Soli Deo Gloria!
"To God be the glory!"
Don Wyrtzen

SUBJECT INDEX

SONGS INDEX

* Singspiration Music/ASCAP. All rights reserved. Used by permission of the Benson Company, Inc., Nashville, TN.